The Mental
as Physical

*International Library of Philosophy
and Scientific Method*

Editor: Ted Honderich

A Catalogue of books already published in the
International Library of Philosophy and Scientific Method
will be found at the end of this volume

The Mental
as Physical

Edgar Wilson

ROUTLEDGE & KEGAN PAUL

London, Boston and Henley

First published in 1979
by Routledge & Kegan Paul Ltd
39 Store Street, London WC1E 7DD,
Broadway House, Newtown Road, Henley-on-Thames, Oxon RG9 1EN and
9 Park Street,
Boston, Mass. 02108, USA

Set in 10/11 Times by
Computacomp (UK) Ltd, Fort William, Scotland
and printed in Great Britain by
Redwood Burn Ltd Trowbridge and Esher

British Library Cataloguing in Publication Data

Wilson, Edgar
The mental as physical. – (International
library of philosophy and scientific method).
1. Mind and body
I. Title II. Series
128'.2   BF161   79–40703

ISBN 0 7100 0316 1

To Jen, Nicki and Jessica

CONTENTS

Contents

Contents

ACKNOWLEDGMENTS

The very considerable extent of my debt to the published work of others will, I hope, be as obvious as I have tried to make it.

I am personally indebted in a variety of ways to Geoff Midgeley, Rom Harré, Jane Heal, Mike and Susan Singleton, John and Sarah Anderson and Sonia Greger.

I am especially indebted to Ted Honderich, Colin Strang, Karl Britton and to the trustees of the Samuel Taylor Coleridge Research Studentship in the University of Newcastle upon Tyne, for the financial support for two years from 1972 to 1974. Mike Bavidge has been my treasured adversary in philosophy. Above all I am indebted to my wife, Jennifer.

I am pleased to acknowledge specifically permission to reproduce Figures 12, 14 and 20 from *Cybernetics*, by F. H. George (1971), courteously granted by the publisher, Hodder & Stoughton.

INTRODUCTION

1 BACKGROUND

This book is an extended essay on the basic idea that the mental and the physical are identical, and on some of the consequences that seem to follow from it. These matters are particularly interesting and important at the present time, for two main reasons. First, during the last few decades there has been such a remarkable advance in the scientific understanding of ostensibly mind-directed behaviour in terms of its physical determinants that physical monism promises more than ever to provide the basis of a coherent account of all human behaviour. Second, the traditional institutions of morality and criminal law continue to be based on conceptions of personal identity, autonomy and responsibility, which are at odds with the aforementioned advances in the scientific understanding of human behaviour. In short, some of the most intractable of all philosophical problems are raised again in their contemporary form.

The present revival of these perennial issues must be seen against a historical background of 'aggression' by physical determinism that has progressively accounted for more and more of the phenomena that once were widely held to be outside the sphere of the physical–causal categories. Human mentality, rationality and purposefulness now stand among the phenomena that come within the compass of scientifically based explanations along lines already indicated by Leucippus and Democritus. The central question raised in the book is whether the hypothesis of mind–brain identity provides the key for a final foreclosure of physicalism on the domain of human mentality, rationality and purposefulness.

It is true that the recently influential exponents of linguistically oriented analytical philosophy counted among their greatest successes the dissolution of such perennial and vexatious problems as the relation between mind and body, and putative conflicts between determinism and free-will and moral responsibility. Two generations of philosophers have tackled these problems with the methodological metaphors of language games and logical geography and so have been deluded into the belief that 'the Science game' can be 'logically' disconnected from philosophy and ordinary life. But the history of ideas and culture testifies against this. What would significant change be like if it were not exemplified by what happened to common belief and practice in both philosophy and ordinary life after Galileo and Darwin? Analytical solutions to supposedly pseudo-problems have for the most part turned out to be pseudo-solutions to problems that, if not demonstrably bona fide problems, at any rate are presently back again as large as life and at the centre of philosophical interest.

Mind–brain identity theory is among the most discussed topics on the current philosophical scene. It links up in a more or less systematic way with a cluster of other current problems including the controversy about reasons and causes as explanations of human behaviour, controversies concerning the analysis of causality, the view taken of the nature and scope of scientific explanations and the views taken of the interplay or isolation of scientific theoretical concepts and ordinary concepts of actions, reasons and desires.[1] Less often considered in this connection, but no less cogent, are the implications these controversies have for other perennial problems of free-will and determinism, moral responsibility, penal philosophy, and their potential practical consequences for ethics and criminal law.

2   RATIONALE

It is clear that the mind–body problem has ramifications in most of the main areas of philosophical inquiry, which is why Schopenhauer called it the world-knot. It is a rash fellow indeed therefore who addresses himself to all of these questions at once without good reason or good excuse. I should have preferred to be able to offer genius as sufficient excuse. Since I cannot, I submit as good reason the claim that it is not possible adequately to deal with the practical problems raised in a new and urgent form by recent developments in science without also dealing in some way with the cluster of interconnected questions mentioned above.

This large claim is based not only on the negative view that the

2

celebrated analytical revolution in philosophy in this century has failed to yield adequate results using a piecemeal approach exclusively, though it is true that these methods have failed to provide a basis for solving even those problems their principal exponents were most confident of having solved. The main basis of the claim that such a wide range of issues should be considered together is the thesis that intractable philosophical disagreement of the sort evident in the perennial debates about mind–body and free-will versus determinism are due mainly to deep-rooted differences in world view. Root metaphysical models, not mundane muddles, are likely to be at the root of intractable disagreement; and such disagreements are not so much solved or dissolved by analysis as rendered otiose through one of the conflicting models becoming redundant.

What I refer to here as root metaphysical models, other philosophers have called fundamental metaphors,[2] ultimate presuppositions,[3] root metaphors,[4] co-ordinating analogies,[5] and primary metaphysical directives.[6] A root model is a basic idea initially drawn from some area of experience which structures and co-ordinates different kinds of experience by extension of the key ideas embodied in the root model. The significance of the concept of metaphysical root models for the scope and rationale of the present thesis lies in the suggestion that such models structure entire world views, and so reflect themselves not only in belief but also in decision and action. Support for a root model therefore is not confined to some immediate area of disagreement such as mind–body, reasons–causes, phenomenalism–mechanism, free-will–determinism, or crime–disease taken individually, but extends much further to embrace other areas also. Conversely, the ramifications of the overthrow or redundancy of a root model in one area extend far beyond the area itself. For these reasons it is both desirable and necessary to pursue disagreement about the mind–brain relation into the other areas related to it.

If further justification than this were required for the imprudent scope of this book, then there is the growing acceptance among philosophers that philosophical inquiry should resume the role it neglected in this century, of aiding investigations into practical human problems, in this case morals and jurisprudence. Also, in spite of this growing trend, insufficient attention has been paid to the need to provide an overview of the relations between the more recent developments in philosophy of mind and action, ethics and penal philosophy, as these reflect the import of recent developments in science and medicine. For I believe that we are undeniably in a period where the exponential growth of scientific knowledge and technique seems likely to bring about significant and far-reaching change in man's traditional self-image.

Finally, I endorse the view that there is very little evidence that philosophers, merely by analysing common-sense knowledge and ordinary language can produce anything worth-while by way of solutions to the perennial philosophical problems that bedevil the practical affairs of men.[7] Therefore, I have felt it encumbent upon me to appeal to and to emphasise, more emphatically than is usually considered necessary or appropriate for an essentially philosophical essay, the kind of contemporary scientific theory, techniques and evidence I hold to be significant. In this spirit I hope to do a little underlabouring for the exponents of neuropsychology, cybernetics, and systems and information science and at the same time show that philosophers have not been talking nonsense all these millenia either.

So much then by way of explanation for the unfashionable scope of the ambitions of this book. It now remains to indicate the strategic development of the argument to follow.

3 SYNOPSIS

In its barest outline the argument takes the form of six related propositions.

1 Interpretation of the relation between the mental and the physical depends upon the root metaphysical model within which the relation is conceived.

2 There is currently a general shift from a traditional, orthodox root model of persons to a physicalist model influenced by developments in the mental and related sciences which suggest that the mental is identical with the physical.

3 If the mental is identical with the physical then mind-directed human behaviour (action) is subject to the same categories of causal determination as other physical processes.

4 If human action is completely determined by physical causation then the traditional supposition of free-will in attributing moral responsibility is misconceived because it requires what is physically impossible.

5 If the supposition of free-will is misconceived then the consequence seems to be that the traditional, orthodox, concepts of moral responsibility and blame are otiose.

6 If the concepts of moral responsibility and blame are otiose, then one significant consequence seems to be that there is no specially moral justification for punishment in criminal law, based on deserts.

The argument can be conveniently divided into five parts. Part One deals with general questions of conceptual thinking, metaphysical

4

models and two rival models of man in particular. Part Two is devoted to mind–brain identity theory including the scientific basis for it, various formulations of it and the outstanding objections to it. Part Three concerns causality, causal necessity and human action. In Part Four the traditional questions of free-will and moral responsibility are considered in the light of the preceding discussion of identity theory. Finally, in Part Five some of the consequences of physical determinism for law are discussed.

A summary of the argument developed in more detail is as follows.

In Chapter I the view is advanced that the roots of philosophical disagreement are in the nature of conceptual thinking itself. In general, conceptual thinking essentially involves pattern recognition, symbolic representation and modelling processes, including the metaphorical and analogical extension of existing schemata in the assimilation of new experience. It is argued that some schemata or patterns (so-called 'root models') permeate, and predominate in an individual's perception, interpretation and understanding of his experience. The predominance of any given model is subject to change, but the shift from one root model to another involves redundancy, or the erosion of commitment, rather than systematic disproof.

In Chapter II the thesis is then advanced that there are currently two main competing root models of the world, and of human personality in particular, that structure belief about and action towards human individuals. These root models are dubbed here the orthodox–animistic (OA) model and the physicalist–objective (PO) model. Disputes about the mental and the physical are rooted in a conflict between these two root models, and the implications of such disputes therefore extend beyond the area of philosophy of mind. It is argued that recent developments in science promise (or threaten) to render the explanatory power of the PO model sufficient to account for phenomena previously held to be explicable only in terms of the concept of mind within the OA model. The provisional conclusion drawn from this discussion is that the PO model is increasingly perspicuous and that it has significant implications for ethics and jurisprudence.

In Chapter III it is shown how the prevailing, essentially Cartesian, orthodoxy gives rise to the central problem of the relation between two (putatively) categorially distinct domains, the mental and the physical. The history of unsatisfactory attempts to resolve this problem is outlined, and general criteria for a satisfactory solution proposed. The thesis that the mental is in some sense identical with the physical is then introduced as a possible solution to the perennial problem of the mental–physical relation, and the reasons for considering it as a possible solution are examined including a survey of the evidence from neuropsychology and related developments in such fields as cybernetics and general system theory.

In Chapter IV, on the supposition that mind–brain identity theory (IT) promises to satisfy the criteria for a solution to the main mental–physical problem, several different formulations of the theory are examined and some of their main shortcomings shown. Then, a reconstituted ('bi-perspectivist') version is proposed as a basis for examining the various objections to IT.

In Chapter V the main outstanding objections to IT from considerations of logic, empirical science and epistemology are each considered in turn. The main (provisional) conclusion drawn is that, given the thesis that a root-model shift is involved from the OA to the PO model of persons, IT is, on the basis of the empirical evidence, a perspicuous and logically coherent hypothesis. None of the objections considered is decisive against it.

In Chapter VI the main issue raised is whether, if behaviour can be explained in terms of physical causal states and processes, it is therefore completely physically determined. This raises prior questions about the general status of the principle of causality and the causal relation. Specifically the question is raised whether causation is (1) phenomenal succession only or (2) productive connexity. It is argued that the traditional Humean view of causation as regular phenomenal succession is inadequate. A physical realist view is advanced which corresponds to common-sense intuitions that causes produce their effects with natural necessity. Causality, the principle that every event has a cause, is presented as a synthetic *a priori* principle.

In Chapter VII the thesis is advanced that the orthodox account of mind-directed behaviour is incoherent mainly because it asserts a categorial difference between reasons and causes, while at the same time supposing reasons and motives to make a difference to the bodily movements involved in actions without offering a satisfactory explanation of how the difference is brought about. It is suggested that these incoherencies are compensated for by corresponding incoherencies in the phenomenalist account of causation, especially the supposition that anything can cause anything. In this way the orthodoxy achieves a spurious coherence. If, however, the phenomenalist account of causation were undermined, that is superseded by the pro-ductive-connection view, then the incoherencies in the OA account of action are irreconcilable within the OA model. The possibility is then examined that these incoherencies can be reconciled within the PO model given the postulate of IT so that human action can be adequately accounted for in terms of productive causal connections. The main conclusion of this chapter is that IT, together with the shift to the PO root model, provides the basis of a coherent account of human action in physical–causal terms.

In Chapter VIII the traditional question of free-will versus determinism is examined from the viewpoint of specifically *physical* determinism introduced by the shift to the PO root model and the postulate of IT. The central conflict is between (1) the prevailing orthodox view that physical determinism does not affect the concept of free-will if there is some significant sense in which an act was avoidable, i.e. the agent could have done (was able, had the capacity to do) other than he did, and (2) the physical determinist view that behaviour is determined not only by abilities or capacities but also by instantaneous states. The implication drawn from the thesis of physical determinism is that free volition in the sense traditionally presupposed for specifically moral responsibility requires logical and physical impossibilities of the first order.

In Chapter IX the main consequences of physical determinism for the traditional concept of moral responsibility and moral institutions are then considered. Contrary to what many determinists have suggested, that it is wrong to blame offenders because offences that are causally determined are inevitable and so invariably excusable, it is argued that the aspects of moral responsibility related to guilt and blame are otiose within the emerging physicalist model. The main (supposed) implications of this result for personal relations and social institutions are considered. The conclusion reached is that, although the emergence of the PO model renders otiose the traditional concept of free-will and the peculiarly vituperative aspects of moral responsibility, this does not entail the dire consequences for human life, personal relations and social institutions that some philosophers have supposed.

In Chapter X some of the fundamental consequences of IT and the emerging PO, model for criminal law and the assumptions of jurisprudence are considered. Three features of the previous argument are shown to be relevant to current legal problems: the idea of root models of man and conflict between them; the notion of an analytical isolation of participant and observer perspectives on action; and the idea of 'eidescopic shifts' between root metaphysical models. Two current legal issues are taken as a focus of discussion:
1 the reasonable man criterion of criminal responsibility in provocation law;
2 the thesis that crime is disease.

In Chapter XI the principles used in law for determining criminal culpability are considered, with special reference to the reasonable man criterion of provocation law and the objective test that applies it. It is suggested that the shift to a PO model undermines the main assumption underlying the principles for determining criminal guilt, namely that there is some relevant sense in which an offender could have done other than he did. The principles embodied in the reasonable man criterion may stand however as a criterion of accountability within a framework of strict liability for offences. The main practical consequence of this conclusion is that the role of the courts should be to establish only the accountability of an offender for a technical offence. Sentencing should be primarily a matter for experts, based on an assessment of the causal determinants of the offence.

In Chapter XII the thesis that crime is disease is examined, together with various objections to it. It is argued that the deterministic thrust of the 'disease' thesis is more appropriately rendered in terms of the more general category of disorder with which it is usually conflated. It is suggested that in the taxonomy of disorder crime is appropriately regarded as maladjustment between the individual and his environment. It is argued that, if this distinction is made between disease and maladjustment, the deterministic thrust of the crime-as-disease thesis might be sustained against the main objections to it, particularly the implication that a treatment or social hygiene approach to crime is more apt than punishment.

4 PRECEDENTS AND TRENDS

Although the general thesis is one that I have nurtured for some time, it highlights a discernible trend in recent philosophical thought. I would make special mention of some of the most important recent contributions along the same lines of the present thesis. The root-model hypothesis of metaphysical systems has been most clearly articulated by Stephen C. Pepper.[8] The notion of root-model shifts is related to Thomas Kuhn's central thesis about paradigm changes in scientific revolutions[9] and has also been proposed in more generalised form by Donald Schon.[10] The idea of conceptual relativity and the role of fundamental world views has in fact come to enjoy something of a vogue.[11]

The history of something like mind–brain identity theory is an ancient one. So much so that one is tempted to say that examination of the antecedents of the current debate only goes to show that there is nothing really new under the sun. But in truth the current debate does owe much that is new to the seminal works of Herbert Feigl,[12] the United Front of Sophisticated Australasian Materialists,[13] and the American Eliminationists.[14] The definitive formulations of the problem however will probably turn out to be influenced by those thinkers such as von Bertalanffy,[15] Rapoport[16] and Laszlo[17], who have written within the framework of cybernetic and system-theoretic ideas, which have not as yet influenced the philosophical mainstream in any far-reaching way.[18]

English-speaking philosophy continues to be dominated by Hume's view of causation as a regular succession of phenomena. The physical realist views advanced here however are fairly well-known heresies which have their antecedents in Spinoza and Peirce among philosophers. The same ideas have recently been articulated again from the perspectives of modern biology and psychology by Lorenz[19] and Piaget[20]. Among philosophers who have recently nailed their colours to the same mast of real, productive, causal connections, Bunge,[21] Harré[22] and Madden[23] are among the most prominent.

The field of human action theory is still largely dominated by the metaphors of 'language games' and 'logical geography', according to which reasons and causes are categorially different concepts. Nevertheless the recent trend has been increasingly to challenge this particular aspect of the orthodoxy, and Davidson[24] and Honderich[25] have made important contributions in this connection.

Hard determinism has never lacked prominent advocacies even during the heyday of 'dissolutionist' analysis, but these have been based almost without exception on either general metaphysical or psycho-analytical considerations. *Physical* determinism has had fewer spokesmen than might be expected, although Honderich has made out a case for the coherence of this position, with an eye to neuropsychology. It is perhaps indicative of the trend outlined in the present book however that at least one formerly prominent advocate of the 'two-domainist' explanation of human behaviour, Charles Taylor, has come to acknowledge and argue for the coherence and explanatory power of a teleological determinism based on the circular causal control processes of central nervous mechanisms.[26]

Recent philosophical discussion of criminal law has taken place for the most part within the framework of the recent analytical orthodoxy. This explains why the still prevalent view among philosophers is that developments in science which support traditional deterministic views of human behaviour have few, if any, implications for legal institutions based on free-will, guilt and blame. Nevertheless, there is clear evidence in the literature of penology[27] and forensic behavioural science[28] that developments in human science make it increasingly difficult to sustain the traditional legal view of offenders and to justify current approaches to dealing with crime. Notably, members of the British Psychological Society have recently expressed the view that even the present state of psychological knowledge would seem to make nonsense of the current legal concepts of responsibility and guilt.[29]

PART ONE

Ingrained hypotheses do feel obvious no matter how redundant they may be.

Gilbert Ryle (1950, p. 76)

I

CONCEPTUAL THINKING AND PHILOSOPHICAL DISAGREEMENT

An examination of any philosophical argument will presuppose, either explicitly or implicitly, some general view of the nature of human understanding and conceptual thinking and some corresponding view of the nature of philosophical disagreement. A proper examination of these matters is the subject of quite other books than the present one.[1] However, a brief consideration of the nature of understanding and disagreement provides, I believe, an indispensable background to the perennial arguments about the mind–body problem, free-will and moral and legal responsibility, which are my main concern.

This chapter begins, therefore, with a brief account of the assumptions about understanding and conceptual thinking underlying the following discussion. Consideration will then be given to some general questions concerning conceptual systems and their adequacy as world views.

1 UNDERSTANDING AND THE SEARCH FOR PATTERN

First of all, I shall assume that the search for understanding is in general a 'search for pattern',[2] 'pattern' being any distinguishable interrelation of phenomena and/or concepts. At the perceptual level this involves the discernment of phenomenal *gestalten*.[3] Abstract conceptual thinking as in, for example, mathematics and science involves the further dimension of symbolic representation, but none the less here the process of pattern recognition is significantly similar.[4]

The positive or active process of pattern discernment in science through imaginative construction and reconstruction of models (both

13

mechanical and mathematical) has been extensively explored in recent philosophy of science.[5]

It has become increasingly apparent that this characteristic human activity is not confined to sensory perception, abstract symbolic representation and imaginative model-building in science. It is arguable that there is nothing peculiarly scientific about scientific theorising.[6] Recent writers have drawn attention to the central importance of models, metaphors and analogies in science and the creative arts alike.[7] Moreover, it is increasingly widely recognised that the potent cognitive force of analogy and metaphor goes beyond merely drawing attention to suggestive similarities; it brings about entirely new insights and understanding.[8] Things are not just seen to be *like* something else, they are seen *as* something else.

1.1 *Conceptual Systems*

The product of the processes of pattern recognition and/or modelling described may be characterised as a conceptual schema or *system*. In general terms a conceptual system will consist of basic conceptual elements such as object, attribute, quantity, relation, mode, etc., each with its various types and tropes, the elements being interrelated by ostensively and operationally based connections or associations of a more or less stable nature, which when formalised (hypostatised) assume the status of rules. The system of rules represents the logic of the system and delineates its 'logical space(s)'. It is important to mark at this stage that the logical relations of the system have an ostensive or operational basis which bears the ultimate burden of conviction attached to logical relations as formally represented.[9] In the last resort the phenomenological and intentional are prior to the extensional logic of formal relations, and in practice understanding and explanation ultimately rest on the intuitive recognition of an 'authentic' pattern of relationships (i.e. one carrying intuitive conviction and corroborated in the language community), not only in the domain of ordinary discourse but also in the formal domain of science.

2 CONCEPTUAL STRUCTURES AND UNDERSTANDING

We might say in a general way that understanding experience will minimally in some way involve classification within a conceptual system, i.e. the structure of categories, types and relations established by 'intuitive induction' out of the individual's experience. Classification of

14

phenomenal pattern is the basis of the individuation of objects and behaviour. Classification of concepts within a conceptual system establishes patterns of categorial relations or 'addresses' within a conceptual system. Understanding involves interpretation in terms of existing concepts. New experience, in so far as it is understood, will either modify or extend them. So, for example, the Hollywood Indian 'fire-water' marks a transition from a pre-distillation conceptual structure to the understanding of rye whiskey which is compresent with the acquisition of the concept 'rye whiskey'.

The investigations of Bruner and Postman into the relationships between perception, understanding and interpretation provide a neat demonstration of these rudimentary principles at the level of visual perception. They exploit the existence of a genetically prior type structure associated with playing cards ('red-heart', 'red-diamond', 'black-spade', 'black-club') by introducing ambiguous types ('black-heart', 'red-spade', etc.) to be identified. What is demonstrated is that identification of new ambiguous types is initially made confidently but erroneously in terms of the existing types (i.e. '5 black-heart' as '5-heart' (unambiguous) or '5-spade'). Repeated exposure leads to a period of uncertainty. It might with some justification be said that up to this point the subject is not 'seeing' what he is looking at, and this, because what he sees is in some sense predelineated by what he expects to see. Once the ambiguity is recognised or intuited, that is to say once the new types have been established, then usually no further problem is experienced in correctly identifying cards that are then 'ambiguous' only in relation to the previously established and expected types. (Interestingly, however, some subjects persistently had considerable difficulty in assimilating the new types and expressed great confusion in the identifying process.)[10]

This evidence from visual perception suggests a basic schema for other more complex and abstract processes of understanding and interpretation. That is to say, understanding involves classification under concepts. The individual's conceptual system continuously undergoes modification and extension. At any given time it will be co-extensive with his understanding of the world; indeed, in a sense indicated by the early Wittgenstein, will constitute his world.[11] In short, an individual's conceptual system constitutes his view of the world, and sets limits to what for him is possible or conceivable.

3   ROOT MODELS

On this account, understanding is identical with the categorising or typing process, that is to say it largely involves interpretation in terms of an existing conceptual system. In this way conceptual systems will always at least *tend* to be homogeneous with the systems genetically prior to them.[12]

The sense of homogeneity intended here is suggested by Stephen C. Pepper in a work on evidence (*World Hypotheses*). According to this view, any adequate conceptual system must be derived from a *single* categorially primitive structure or 'root metaphor' embodying the individual's predominant experience.[13] Such primitive structures will hereafter be called 'root models'. Pepper originally suggested that there are four comprehensive homogeneous conceptual systems or 'world views' in the occidental tradition, each of which is derived from a different root model and each equally capable of providing an independent conceptual framework for a more or less consistent and complete understanding of all experience. (The notion of complete understanding or 'adequacy' requires some elaboration which will be undertaken later.)

The relationship suggested here between root models (e.g. A and B) and developing conceptual systems (e.g. a; a'; a"; and b; b'; b";) might be schematically represented as in Figure 1.1. Adequate world views must be homogeneous, Pepper suggests, because any synthesis of different 'root' concepts or categories either is sterile or leads to confusion. In a similar connection Dorothy Emmett has suggested also that the demand for systematic unity is a check on the vagaries of 'mere subjectivism'.[14]

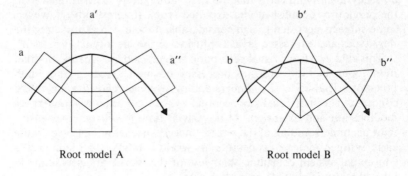

Root model A   Root model B

Figure 1.1

Against these arguments we should bear in mind that in fact thought processes are typically heterogeneous. Without entering into tendentious discussion at this stage, it is surely a non-controversial fact that in general we commonly proceed on the basis of different metaphysical presuppositions depending on the purpose at hand. To take as examples three of Pepper's autonomous root metaphors: in dealing with artefacts we adopt a mechanistic model; in dealing with biological or social systems we adopt organic models; and for general pragmatic purposes we adopt a 'contextualist' model, i.e. derive our terms of reference from contextually given factors. The descriptions we render of these dealings will accordingly reflect the model categories through which they are understood. It is perhaps extravagant therefore to refer to such heterogeneous assortments of categories as a system.

The problems raised in attempting to present anything so comprehensive as a metaphysical world view are of a different order altogether from the practical problems of life, but even for this purpose comprehensiveness does not necessarily entail the logical coherence associated with homogeneous conceptual systems developed from a single 'root model'. At this level, non-contradiction is secondary to the force of conviction attached to the individual's fundamental categories.[15] Some philosophers would go so far as to argue that it is inconceivable that an individual's conceptual schemata could be perfectly comprehensive and homogeneous.[16]

4 CONCEPTUAL RELATIVITY

Leaving aside the question of homogeneity, it seems clear that an individual's (peculiar) conceptual schemata will determine the interpretation he consciously places on a given experience. It may seem that this claim is pedestrian enough to avoid controversy, but since it has not gone unchallenged some elaboration is perhaps necessary. If we presuppose that a given pattern of sensory stimuli is common to different observers, then we might borrow Chomsky's terminology, and say that this together with the sensory receptor systems constitutes the physical basis of the pre-conscious 'deep-structure' underlying the individual's perception of the observed phenomena. The corresponding concept given rise to in consciousness and expressed in the 'surface' structure of the natural language will be determined by the mediating and transformative operation of the individual's system of beliefs or conceptual structure.[17] Thus for example, similar pathological behaviour as observed by medieval and twentieth-century observers with similar sensory receptors is (presumably) perceived, described and understood differently as 'demonic possession' and 'schizophrenia', as a direct function of the observer's different concepts or belief systems. For minimum purposes of illustration let us suppose that the vocabulary of demonism includes 'teleological', 'pernicious' and 'transmigratory'. So

17

when a demonist finds a person exhibiting violent behaviour and crying hysterically he will formulate some explanatory hypothesis such as that the body of this person has been possessed by a transmigratory agency of diabolical malevolence (the conceptual process presumably involving some sort of imagery akin to the proverbial wolf in sheep's clothing). By contrast the psycho-physiologist has a category system that includes bodies and law-like relations but not supernatural agencies; so he will explain the phenomenon in such terms as 'cell', 'neurone', 'genetic', 'behavioural'.

Moreover, an individual's conceptual schemata will determine not only how he sees things in the world but equally how he reacts to them. Thus the demonologist might attempt to dispossess the demonic power by sympathetic magic or by invocation of some counter-mandatory demon, and the psycho-physiologist will seek to modify the conjunction of clinical factors that he regards as causally necessary and sufficient for the occurrence of the observed phenomena.

Conceptual relativity, and so by extension relativity of understanding and description based upon some thesis akin to Pepper's root metaphor theory, is an issue that has not engaged the interest of philosophers in this century to the extent that it might, until comparatively recently.[18] The mainstream of recent philosophy in the analytical tradition has tended to stop short of or bypass differences in presuppositions even while acknowledging the philosophical interest such differences hold; otherwise something like an ontology of common sense has been assumed. One consequence of neglecting the theory of presuppositions is that the metaphysical aspect of perennial philosophical disputes has remained in an unsatisfactory condition.[19]

It is true that in the past philosophers addressed themselves to the problem of conceptual relativity. Francis Bacon recognised that individual perception and understanding is significantly influenced by such factors as sex, religion, class and personal experience.[20] Others have indeed been concerned with similar problems,[21] and reference has already been made to a notable and more recent contribution, in Stephen Pepper's work. The main exploration of the problem, however, has undoubtedly been carried out in the fields of the sociology[22] and psychology[23] of knowledge, where the general thesis maintained is not essentially different from Bacon's at the beginning of the seventeenth century. This is echoed in Marx's celebrated dictum that it is social existence that determines men's consciousness not consciousness that determines men's existence.[24] It would also be widely accepted now that motivational and valuational factors are equally potent in determining perception, conception and world view.[25]

Theories of conceptual relativity have been criticised for a variety of reasons, but this is not the proper place to discuss them.[26] As I shall show presently, I agree with those who argue that profound issues cannot be settled by facile appeals to relativity, but for the present purposes there is much to be said for the view that the notion of conceptual and linguistic relativity is, quite simply, *pedestrian*, and that serious doubts about the sociology and psychology of the matter are entertained only by those who, in Russell's telling phrase, have been hopelessly infected with philosophy. Accordingly, we may take it that perception, understanding, description, interpretation, explanation, accommodation, attitude and action depend on conceptual or categorial schemata, and are variable.

5   ADEQUACY AND EXPLANATION

An adequate conceptual system may be defined as one that has the scope and precision to render possible a complete account of the individual's experience[27] to his own satisfaction. As already said, Pepper maintains that any adequate conceptual system must also be homogeneous, being derived from a single root model. Its cognitive strength is derived from its comprehensiveness and the mutual corroboration (coherence) of its elements, since it will not be exposed to contradiction and refutation by facts from outside the system. (I have argued, however, that a comprehensive conceptual system or world view need not necessarily be homogeneous to be adequate in the sense defined above; cf. Section 3 above.) Following Pepper further, therefore, experience that cannot be accounted for in terms of the system will eventually lead either to the system's rejection, or to its extension towards a greater comprehensiveness as a homogeneous system, or, as I have suggested, to a heterogeneous system. Examples of inadequate systems requiring such change, i.e. systems lacking in scope and/or precision, are provided by mechanism and anthropomorphism.

5.1   *Scope*

A rudimentary mechanistic conceptual structure, with basic categories 'substance', 'location', 'time' and 'relating laws', does not have the scope necessary to account for such fundamental elements of experience as conscious states and the bilateral interaction between conscious states and physical states. It therefore leads to either a dogmatic denial of cognitive significance to such concepts, as in the epiphenomenalism of Thomas Huxley, or otherwise to their reduction to (or construction from) mechanistic concepts as in the radical behaviourism of Watson and the earlier Skinner.

5.2   Precision

A primitive anthropomorphic conceptual system, which attributes the identifiable events in the world that are not clearly due to ordinary human agency to the doings of a menagerie of supernatural agencies or spirits, lacks the precision necessary to account adequately for the prolific variety of distinguishable objects and events. A spirit may be alternatively angry or pleased, invariant or capricious, embodied or disembodied (or even transient), intractable or amenable, etc., and with no discernible principle determining the variance. In short, the concept of 'spirit' is so imprecise as to be both epistemologically and pragmatically valueless.

It must be evident, however, that the significance of the concept of adequacy so defined, and its criteria of scope and precision, depend upon an appeal to some extra-systemic evidence and criteria. We must presume that neither the consistent mechanist nor the consistent anthropomorphist regard their categories as (internally) inadequate, and so the question of adequacy arises only in terms of some other conceptual system. The Cartesian dualist or the Berkeleyan idealist for example interpret their phenomenal experience in such a way as to deem the corresponding mechanist's account inadequate, but these are external judgments. The same may be said *mutatis mutandis* of anthropomorphism or indeed of any other conceptual system. The impropriety of appeals to external evidence and criteria as a basis of claims about purely conceptual inadequacy becomes clearer if we recall the principle that, for experience to be meaningful, that is to say to be understood at *all*, then it must be interpreted through some conceptual system. It follows that inadequacy claims about a system can be formulated only in terms of another co-extensive and mutually exclusive system. A corollary of the principle is that *any* conceptual system will have the merit of internal adequacy. This is so simply because the limit of my conceptual system, and of the language giving it expression, is the limit of my world.

Consider again the previous example comparing the categories and understanding of the demonologist and the psycho-physiologist. The same pathological behaviour is understood and described with equal (internal) consistency and serviceability, but in two co-extensive and mutually exclusive conceptual systems, as either 'demonic possession' or 'schizophrenia'. The demonologist's system is adequate, as demonology, but his world does not contain such things as 'noradrenaline' or 'psychosis'. Similarly, the psycho-physiologist's conceptual system is adequate as psycho-physiology but his world does not contain such things as 'demoniacal spirits'. Each system renders an adequate account of experience by structuring the world experienced, in the manner of the Kantian categories of the Analytic of Reason, but with the crucial difference that the categorial elements are variables. The primitive categories of Western culture, which our descriptive metaphysicians have sought to show are universal, seem not to be essential to the construction of an adequate world picture. Other cultures have adequate cosmologies based on quite different primitive categories derived from other kinds of experience.[28]

We can now return to our point of departure, recognising that a major source of philosophical problems lies in co-extensive and mutually exclusive perception and interpretations of the same 'given' phenomena in terms of different conceptual schemata or systems. This principle is true not only of external (interpersonal) disagreement, but also, by virtue of the heterogeneity of individual conceptual systems, of problems posed by and of the individual himself, the adequacy of one schema or sub-system being queried in terms of another schema or sub-system.

6   INCOMPATIBILITY

In characterising the adequacy of a conceptual system as being co-extensive with the understanding it affords, and inadequacy as being therefore *necessarily* an extra-systemic or external relation, we raise the very large and fundamental question of the comparison and evaluation of different conceptual systems. If we do not share Austin's satisfaction with the observation that there is a difference in classifications when faced with indissoluble disagreement,[29] and seek some basis for comparison between different systems of equal (internal) adequacy, then we must look for some criterion other than adequacy. We can proceed by recognising that what is seen to be significant is substantially determined by the user's purposes. Therefore if two systems can be said to be related to or derived from a common purpose, then this *purpose* would provide the common ground for a comparison between two systems of equal internal adequacy.

When there is a difference in purpose it will be difficult or more likely pointless to consider the comparative merits of different schemata. Gilbert Ryle has developed this point with some labour and force for the case of logically distinct categories,[30] showing how for example the accountant's categories provide an account of 'university' which is adequate for the particular purpose of double entry bookkeeping but that this purpose is only one of many that may serve.

That A should choose to use concept X where B uses concept Y is a matter of comparatively slight philosophical interest however if the

21

purposes of A and B differ significantly. If A is an accountant using X economic concepts and B is a *littérateur* using Y critical concepts, then the difference in their equally adequate accounts of say the contents of the university library are unlikely to cause even a philosophical uproar and Austin's sanguinity is fully justified. This much is obvious. Given a shared purpose, however, then pragmatic considerations may assert themselves. The point here is best illustrated by a consideration of cases; so consider the cases of numerals and number.

Both Roman and Arabic numerals serve the same purpose of symbolically representing numbers, with similar adequacy in the sense defined, each having the required scope and precision. The Arabic system, however, offers the pragmatic advantages of greater conciseness and simplicity, which account for its almost universal adoption. An interesting and illuminating exception is in the case of marking livestock, where the Roman system is still used for the good pragmatic reason that its simpler articulation makes it more easily written upon frisky beasts. That the Arabic system generally prevails over the Roman is because it generally serves a common purpose more conveniently. Similarly, the modern history of number and mensuration is dominated by denary sets and these remain the most common number-concept system. The choice of the denary set as basic is of course arbitrary and is doubtless due to some functional relationship between the number ten and the most commonly encountered groups of objects in the operational experience of the community (ten fingers?) making its use convenient. However, with the growth of interest in automatic computing machines, the enormous technical convenience of a basic two-state ('bi-stable') system has resulted in the universal adoption of the binary system for the particular purpose of automatic digital computation.[31]

In general, among the systems understood (if there is more than one) that system will be adopted which most conveniently fulfils the user's purpose.

7   REDUNDANCY

Our next consideration is to establish how and according to which principles, if any, one conceptual system may prevail over another that is co-extensive with it and serves the same purpose, but less conveniently or aptly. It will be useful to consider these questions with special reference to developments in scientific knowledge because these issues are more clearly delineated and have been extensively discussed in recent philosophy of science.

The conspicuous failure of philosophers to reach consensus on fundamental issues after centuries of debate has often been contrasted unfavourably with the consensus among scientists which is still commonly supposed to be reflected in scientific progress.[32] We might, therefore, expect that a study of scientific methodology will cast some light on the causes of the apparent failure of philosophers to achieve consensus. Until the recent past it had been widely supposed by students and admirers of scientific achievement that this success derives from a substantial logical and methodological basis which endows science with a special way of establishing the truth and eliminating falsehood. The recent history of the philosophy of science however has shown that this conception of the scientific enterprise is, to say the least, misleading. It now seems evident that, while science undoubtedly chooses its evidence in a particularly irrefutable way and presents it with an unusually formal rigour, it nevertheless does not differ essentially from other domains of intellectual endeavour in deriving in the final analysis from some basic, spontaneous ordering insight or intuition − Kuhn's 'paradigm', Pepper's 'root metaphor', etc. Highly developed models or high-level hypotheses derived from them cannot easily be refuted or disproved by straightforward logical contradiction. Moreover, whatever is to count as evidence or fact, as well as any interpretation placed upon it, already depends on the metaphysic implicit in the paradigm or 'root model'. The problem of incompatible but co-extensive models and high-level theories derived from them is not therefore entirely a question of formal proof or disproof because much of what goes on is better represented by the aphorism, 'old paradigms never die, they only fade away'.[33] If the same purpose is to be served by two competing hypotheses that render accounts of equal (internal) adequacy and one is significantly more convenient than the other, then, on the principle of least resistance, the least convenient hypothesis will simply fall into desuetude, and the model from which it is derived will be weakened. Continuous failure to develop satisfactory non-metaphysical theories that conform to a particular root metaphysical model will generally wear down loyalty to it.[34]

The celebrated dispute between Galileo and the Roman Church exemplifies several of the points made here.

1 The dispute was ostensibly between co-extensive and mutually exclusive theories (heliocentric and geocentric representations of observed motions in the solar system).
2 In so far as Galileo and his critics shared the same purpose of rendering the most convenient representation of the movements of the heavenly bodies, then it seems clear that this, i.e. (1), was not the real bone of contention at all.
3 The real bone of contention arose from Galileo's ostentatious

insistence that the new paradigm not only rendered the old one astronomically redundant but contradicted portions of the Scriptures, since this involved his critics' higher purpose of maintaining the authority of the Church.

4 Finally, the Copernican revolution was not effected through any proof by Galileo or by anyone else, but quite simply because the heliocentric model is the simplest, the most perspicuous and the most *convenient* for the working astronomers' purposes. That this is so is evident from the fact that, although at least since Einstein there has been no conceptual obstacle to employing the geocentric model, it is nevertheless not used.

7.1   *Redundancy*

It was David Hume who pointed to the philosophical significance of the important preliminary part of Galileo's argument in the *Dialogues on Two World Systems*. The argument is directed not against the Aristotelian astronomy, but against the categorial metaphysical distinction between celestial and elementary (terrestrial) substance, assumed by Galileo's scholastic critics.[35] This (paradigmatic) distinction presumably provided the rationale for the scholastic professor Cremonini's apocryphal refusal to peep through Galileo's telescope, the point being of course that, given this categorial distinction, there could not be, in principle, any relevance for bodies celestial in principles derived from observations of bodies elementary.[36] So, while the conceptual shift from geocentric to heliocentric world systems entailed the redundancy of the Ptolemaic system as a live scientific hypothesis within the fabric of human purposes it served, a more fundamental and far-reaching consequence of the shift was the weakening or undermining of the underlying scholastic celestial/elementary metaphysic or paradigm that sustained an essentially anthropocentric cosmology. The ultimate consequences of this shift were the disappearance of an entire conceptual system, along with its terminology, from the ordinary language community.

7.2   *Gestalt Switch*

Conceptual shifts of the kind described have often been likened to the phenomenon of Gestalt switch[37] where, typically, the same visual datum can be organised or interpreted in significantly different ways, as exemplified by the reversal of figure and ground in a line drawing (Figure 1.2). In this example, it may be said that the two *gestalten* (A) and (B) are each in turn 'redundant' as the other becomes dominant. The

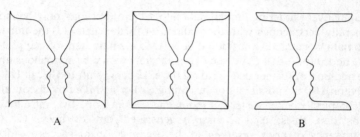

A　　　　　　　　　　　　　　　　B

Figure 1.2

Gestalt-switch model of conceptual shifts is undoubtedly suggestive for cases where substantially the same data are significantly reorganised, as in the case of the Ptolemaic–Copernican systems. It is arguable, however, that this shift phenomenon is possible only in relation to some other framework (the page-plane in the example given) and for this reason Gestalt-switch does not adequately characterise a shift in world view or root model, since in such cases no meta-view exists in relation to which the root model switch can take place.[38]

7.3 *Eidescopic Shift*

A more suggestive model, and one more representative of a situation in which new data are progressively added to the organising Gestalt, is provided by what might be called 'eidescopic' shift − derived from a kaleidoscopic model.[39] In this model the organisation given to the data represented by points (its meaning) changes significantly with the addition of further data, as illustrated schematically by the sequence in Figure 1.3.

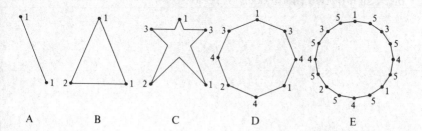

A　　　　　B　　　　　C　　　　　D　　　　　E

Figure 1.3

Noteworthy features of this model include (1) the possibility of inclusion of prior data in successive *gestalten*; (2) the possibility of

25

imaginatively ordering limited data into a form that may only be more generally perspicuous with the addition of further data; (3) the initially anomalous status of transitional data (e.g., a single item of (say) 'D-4' data added to Gestalt C (i.e. the five-point star) would be anomalous until the addition of further data induced the eidescopic shift to Gestalt D (the polygon); (4) the possibility of sustaining earlier *gestalten* by discounting eidescopically inconsistent (anomalous) data or by introducing translation rules, e.g. a triangle generated out of lines; (5) the redundancy of prior *gestalten* in the organisation of successive data, given the purpose of both maximising and optimising the systematic interrelation of data. Also, (6) the emergence of different *gestalten* does not necessarily occur through systematic scrutiny and interpretation. It is more apt to regard it as the spontaneous presentation of a perspicuous order among the data; in this schematic case, now a line, now a triangle, now a star, a polygon, a circle.[40] The concept of eidescopic shift is thus capable of modelling several important characteristics of philosophical disagreement arising from different conceptual models, namely:

1 the supersession of lower-order models or theories by higher-order models or theories with greater empirical content;
2 the anticipation of ultimately well supported theories on limited data;
3 the problematical status of new discoveries in relation to established models and theories;
4 an important psychological fact characterising orthodoxy in the face of significant model shifts, namely the adherence to former ordering patterns after other, more perspicuous patterns emerge; and finally,
5 the supersession of *gestalten* (models or paradigms) involves *redundancy* rather than disproof.

I shall take up these issues again in Chapter III in connection with physicalist accounts of mentality. Meanwhile it is time to turn to a discussion of two root models of persons.

II

TWO INCOMPATIBLE
MODELS OF PERSONS

Thus far we have assumed that the basis of perception and conceptualising processes lies in the patterning or modelling of experience; that certain (variable) root models determine the interpretative conceptual system derived from phenomenal data and that conceptual systems and their underlying root models may become redundant when similar purposes are served more effectively by alternative models or systems.

We may now come directly to the point of the present book and consider the important case of two root models providing co-extensive and incompatible accounts of human experience, namely, what I shall call the orthodox-animistic model (hereafter the OA model) and the physical-objective model (hereafter the PO model).[1] Finally some of the implications of the conflict between the two models are suggested.

1 THE ORTHODOX MODEL: THE ONTOLOGY OF COMMON SENSE

The model of the world with the widest currency in our own culture has been assiduously described in recent times by philosophers in the analytical tradition beginning with G. E. Moore, who have established that, so far as is known (to common sense), there are basically two sorts of things in the world, namely material objects and acts of consciousness.[2] This of course is essentially the Cartesian dualist metaphysic with material objects characterised by their extension (occupancy of space), location, mass, persistence in time, resistance to touch etc., and acts of consciousness by the illumination of self-awareness and other-awareness, non-location in space, etc.

In keeping with this model, the OA concept of the human individual or person is a body endowed with or possessed of consciousness (or mind). The 'person' is typically conceived of as greater than the sum of his material and conscious parts, since a person may be either unconscious or even (at least as a logical possibility) disembodied.[3] Within the structure of the OA model human bodies are conceived of as not essentially dissimilar to other material objects.[4] The distinctive characteristics of a person are still those enumerated by Descartes, that it 'doubts, understands (conceives), affirms, denies, wills, refuses and also imagines and senses' (Second Meditation): in short, sentience, sapience and volition.

It is characteristic of this view that in virtue of their mental attributes human persons are in some important sense or other set apart from the natural processes of cause and effect that determine the course of natural events, including those in the bodies of persons themselves. Whereas the behaviour of bodies is invariably determined by the pushes and pulls of natural causation, the actions of persons are consciously and freely chosen, with the exercise of some judgment, and perhaps some ingenuity; after some deliberation, from some desire, in the light of some belief; according to some value, with some purpose in mind, to do with some inexistent goal, perhaps related to some personal commitment, to some socially constituted practice, embedded in some communal form of life, (possibly dedicated to the exaltation of Man and even to the greater glory of some God). 'Animism', therefore, is an appropriate term for this view in so far as it denotes the view that all or some manifestations of human life and mind are due to the operation of something that is of a nature different to that of the body.[5]

The most recent manifestations of animism appear in the guise of conceptual and linguistic animism. Instead of an insistence on some irreducible animating thing or principle, there is instead an insistence on irreducible animistic explanations, concepts and language. But in so far as the same root model is involved, this is merely a reflection of local philosophical fashions. The OA model of human persons is the one most manifest to common sense.[6] It is both the culmination and the residue of a tradition that presumably originated in the prescientific ages when man's intentional world contained a wide variety of person-types or animistic agencies, that is to say agencies whose acts were seen as causally indeterminate and ostensibly freely chosen.

Originally not only living things were personified but also elemental forces, the sun, the wind, the rain, etc., and even inanimate objects. Man's understanding and assimilation of these phenomena was an extension of his understanding and assimilation of the existence of other human persons as sentient, sapient, willing beings. Thus, for example,

Lucretius cites the legend of Agamemnon who sacrificed his daughter to appease the goddess Diana, who he believed was angry with him and was therefore delaying his fleet with contrary winds, and Plutarch reports solemn sittings in judgment on offending inanimate things in Draco. The notorious *Malleus Maleficarum* is a systematic and comprehensive handbook on medieval animism.[7] Even much later, in the seventeenth century, the literal currency and credence attached to supra-human but animistic demon-types and demonic possession is testified to by the notorious witch hunts of Loudon and Salem. The survival of concepts of other-than-human persons or animistic agencies in recent times is extensively documented in the literature of social anthropology, which demonstrates also, interestingly enough, that such concepts are not necessarily altogether more naive than those of some contemporary philosophers. In fact, it seems that even where such material objects as rocks and trees are believed to be endowed with personal attributes, a distinction may still be made between their status as other-than-human persons – i.e. as they affect human affairs – and their otherwise inanimate status.[8]

2   THE PHYSICALIST MODEL: THE ONTOLOGY OF PHYSICALISM

2.1   *The OA View of Science*

The development of Western culture out of its Hellenic scientific root might be seen as substantially an endeavour to eliminate the egocentric perspective from man's view of the world and his place in it. To de-animise inanimate objects, elemental forces and eventually even 'animate' objects, short only of man himself, it has proved enough to direct systematic attention to the phenomena themselves, so recognising their natural causal mechanisms and patterns of regularity in their occurrence.[9] For it is a commonplace that once the productive causal mechanisms of an event have been revealed,[10] or when the event has been identified as an instance of or is related to a familiar pattern of events[11] (i.e. has been interpreted through a system of beliefs about natural law), then the event is usually treated as understood (explained, accounted for).

The process of de-animising man's view of the world has been achieved largely through an exercise of scientific inquiry within the OA world view, and so Wilfred Sellars has rightly stressed that the OA or 'manifest image' of man is not a pre-scientific one. It is a model, however, within which 'doing science' is regarded as simply one among many activities that the OA person can choose to perform. The scientist's analysings, doubtings, understandings, affirmings, denyings, willings, refusings, imaginings and sensings are considered to be no more than on a par with those of the accountant, the theologian, the historian, the poet or the man in the street, and his model of the world does not offer a rival or alternative view to the basic OA model.[12] According to this view it is a profound mistake to suppose that scientists could render explanations of all human experience in terms of causal–deterministic categories. A particularly interesting case in point is the mechanistic root model which has been held by some prominent scientific materialists, such as Hobbes, La Mettrie and Huxley, to render an alternative account of human experience and behaviour to that of the orthodox dualism. On this model, with its basic categories of mass, force, location and time, the universe has typically been modelled after clockwork, and human activity on merely more complex machines, mind being conceived of as no more than an epiphenomenon of their working and, in Huxley's well-known words; 'as completely without power of modifying that working as the steam whistle which accompanies the work of the locomotive engine is without influence on the machinery'.[13] With human artefacts as root models, however, it is clear that classical mechanistic materialism is simply second-order animism, the OA model at one metaphorical remove, and so does not transcend the categories of the OA model.[14] Nevertheless, it is precisely the orthodox thesis, namely that science does not offer or support an alternative model of the world and of persons, that is now in doubt and which is the focus of our present concern.

2.2   The PO View of Science

The account of the material world rendered by science is that it is composed of sub-atomic and atomic particles or energy quanta in incalculable permutations and hierarchically ordered combinations throughout a universal mass–energy continuum. No one now seriously claims that science offers a rival account to the material world of common sense with its tables and chairs so well worn and well loved by philosophers.[15] It has been commonly acknowledged that the physicist, the chemist, the engineer and the joiner deal with essentially the same physical stuff, only under different descriptions related to the differing perspectives inherent in different orders of aggregation or organisation. But in the domain of the life sciences such as biology, biochemistry, neurology and behavioural psychology, the elements of a PO model of persons and their activity is developed which is purported to be the basis of an adequate radical alternative to the OA model.

Wilfred Sellars has suggested[16] that OA science is characterised by its pre-hypothetical status; that is, it is science that has not developed to the stage of postulating explanatory entities or relations that are inferred from observational data but are not themselves observed. Specifically, the emergence of the PO model of persons and their behaviour, it is suggested, is a development of a hypothetico-deductive science of postulated entities or illata. The burden of this thesis is born by appeal to developments in analytical behavioural psychology and the neurology of the central nervous system, particularly of the brain, in constructing a physicalist model. Briefly, according to this thesis, the postulates of the behavioural psychologist, that is the hypothetical events inside the human organism considered as a 'black-box', serve to mediate between observable input–stimulus and output–response phenomena. They also coincide with the entities investigated by the neurologist in the central nervous system and, again, with the reference of first-person introspective reports of conscious experience. By identifying the central nervous processes with the reference of first-person reports, the egocentric perspective of conscious experience is triangulated out and the behaviourist's model telescopes into the neurologist's model, which is therefore capable of modelling all human activities, including the existence of the OA model itself, in terms of the same inter-subjective observation language of physics. The essential PO model so described will be discussed later and is not here in question, but the rationale offered in its support is. For it overlooks the simple historical fact that scientists since pre-Socratic times have postulated explanatory hypotheses and entities, and we need look no further than the case of the micro-structure of matter to realise that the postulates of twentieth-century atomic physics are not essentially different, *qua postulates* or illata, from those of the earlier Atomists. Indeed, even the most crass forms of animism postulate explanatory entities and relations, animistic ones.

This does not mean however that there is no radical distinction between the OA model of man, along with its conception of the scientific enterprise, and the PO model suggested by the contemporary life sciences, or that the PO model is not capable of providing an alternative to the OA model. But we must recall that there is certainly nothing novel in the hypothetico-deductive study of human character and behaviour; nor is even the systematic study of the central nervous system of recent development.[17] We must therefore look elsewhere than to hypothetical entities and processes to account for any more recent and radical development of the possibility of a PO model for human experience.

2.3   The Systemic Paradigm

It seems likely that the possibility of a shift between OA and PO models of persons turns on the shift from an analytical to a systemic conception of the objectives of science, especially biology and the human sciences. The magnitude and scope of this shift suggests an eidescopic shift in perspective which is consistent with what we might expect of a shift in root model, and is illustrated by the following statements. The first is from a well-known work by a highly regarded historian of science, who in 1939 asserted that: 'Its [science's] means are mainly the finer and finer analysis of a plant or organ into simpler elements (preferably those of physics and chemistry) not its perception as a whole. *Divide et impera* in knowledge as in politics'.[18] In contrast, two years later in 1941 an eminent psychologist was claiming that: 'In the course of the past two decades it has been almost generally recognised by biologists and psychologists that the clarification of the problem of wholes is essential for the programme of study of the organism'.[19]

Although biology and Gestalt psychology provided a conceptual origin for recent general thinking on wholes, Angyal correctly anticipated the importance of developments in systems-cybernetic studies for this programme.[20] In the event, the publication in 1943 of seminal papers in neuropsychology[21] and cybernetics[22] marked the emergence of a formal theoretical basis for a specifically PO model of human persons and their purposeful behaviour, based on the principles of self-regulation through 'circular' causal processes of feed forward and negative feedback. As Norbert Wiener later observed,[23]

> It will be noted that our point of view considerably transcends that current among neurophysiologists. The central nervous system no longer appears as a self contained organ, receiving inputs from the senses and discharging into the muscles. On the contrary, some of its most characteristic activities are explicable only as circular processes emerging from the nervous system into the muscles and re-entering the nervous system through the sense organs whether they be proprioceptors or organs of the special senses. This seemed to us to make a new step in the study of that part of neurophysiology which concerns not solely the elementary processes of nerves and synapses but the nervous system as an integrated whole.

Although the emphasis on wholes has emerged only comparatively recently as a central concern of modern life sciences, it is anything but novel. In fact, it is as old as philosophical materialism itself. Democritus accounted for rationality in terms of mathematical *relations*, and Lucretius recognised the crucial importance of organisation or system to the emergence of life and mind from inanimate atoms. He argued that:[24]

> It is of the greatest consequence in what order all the primary ele-
> ments are placed, in what way they are combined and what motions
> they reciprocally impart and receive. ... I am not suggesting that every
> substance capable of producing sensible things produces sensations as
> a matter of course but that the supremely important factors are first
> the size and shape of the particles that produce the sensible, and
> secondly *their motion order and position*.

It is evident that from the earliest times metaphysical materialists have
operated with a root model essentially similar to the one that has begun
to receive wider recognition only recently with the development of
systemic theories and the accumulation of 'hard' evidence from science.
In particular, it cannot be emphasised enough that the concepts of
relation and order have featured in materialist and physicalist accounts
of mentality and purpose since ancient times. Too often materialism and
physicalism are regarded as limiting explanations to what can be said
about the tangible properties of 'stuff'. Consequently, such phenomena
as consciousness and purpose are categorially set apart from 'body'. But
clearly this has been no part of the physicalist tradition. Organisation is
as much a part of the perennial physicalist picture as mass–energy is.
Recent developments in information theory and cybernetics therefore
must be seen as bringing systematic order into our understanding of the
realm of organisation, just as physics has brought order into the realm of
matter and energy.

2.4 *The PO Model of Persons*

The conceptual significance of this step or shift for our view of persons
lies in the new possibility of rendering a purely physical account of
important elements of human conscious (mental) experience and mind-
directed behaviour hitherto regarded as categorially distinct from the
physical domain. Such concepts as purpose, intention, motivation,
memory and choice are now amenable to interpretation in terms of the
states of open physical systems capable of self-organisation and self-
regulation, both internal (homeostasis) and external (metastable
equilibrium).[25] The situation that now exists, therefore, is that typical
and defining person categories such as purpose, intention, etc., can be
replaced by co-extensive categories or terms in the PO language of
cybernetics, with no loss in explanatory force; or rather, following our
model of conceptual redundancy, it becomes not only increasingly
difficult but otiose to deny the explanatory force of system and
cybernetic concepts in the study of human behaviour.[26] The PO model of

the human person is that of a biophysical system endowed with an exceptionally high degree of systemic integration and organisation and within which such relational concepts as 'system', 'equilibrium' and 'self-regulation' are co-extensive with the conceptual and explanatory role of the substantive 'mind' in the OA model.

Furthermore, the new ideas provide a key to the problem of systematically relating neurophysiological factors to social and cultural ones. For as Northrop pointed out, cultural factors are related to biological factors in social institutions by the biologically defined purposeful behaviour of human neurological systems. The behaviour of men can be, and is, causally determined by embodiments of ideas as well as by particular environmental facts.[27] Thus the physicalist categories have been elaborated so that they do not reject or omit, procrustean fashion, socially rooted purposes, norms and ideals, because on this view embodied ideas defining purposes or ideals really matter. So much, for the present, for the PO model of persons, except to say that the development of something like an appropriate systems philosophy is a possibility that is only just beginning to be explored.[28]

It is evident from this brief outline of the elaborated physicalist model of persons that it is in conflict with some central features of the orthodox model. The conflict turns on whether or not human persons are set apart in some way from natural processes of cause and effect in virtue of their mentality and purposefulness, or whether those attributes which the orthodoxy takes to be definitive of human persons can be adequately accounted for in a physicalist model.

3   THE VIABILITY OF THE PHYSICALIST MODEL

Having suggested that there are two root models of human experience and behaviour underlying the perennial mind–body dispute and that they are opposed in fundamental ways, we should now briefly consider whether or not the existence of these opposed models and the possibility of OA redundancy is a matter for serious consideration and not pointless or idle conjecture as some philosophers have suggested.[29]

3.1   A priori *Objections*

A resolution of the essential questions of the scope and precision of the PO model clearly turns in part on the outstanding issues arising from the physicalist account of sentience, sapience and volition to be discussed later. But on the basis of the previous discussion of conceptual systems, their adequacy and explanatory force, there can be no *a priori* obstacle to the transition to a PO model. Indeed, the issue would seem to turn largely upon a spontaneous shift to a new paradigmatic root model with the accumulation of evidence from the life sciences. (This is not of course the same as saying that an empirical demonstration of complete one-to-one correspondence between mental and physical phenomena would '*prove*' mind–brain identity or '*disprove*' dualism in any formal sense.)

In considering philosophical objections to this view it is useful to mark a peculiar paradox: that conceptual processes and the language giving them expression require a considerable degree of hypostatisation of the objects or events rendered; whereas the objects and events themselves, also including the processes of conceptualising and symbolic expression, are subject to endless change. In a word, dynamic processes (including cognition) can be conceived and represented only through substantially static forms. This fact means that in situations involving significant change there is inevitably a tendency for prior established concepts and language to be maintained on pain of unintelligibility. The maintenance of orthodoxy becomes a purpose in itself (as the regular letters-to-the-editor of our newspapers daily testify when they express disapproval of language 'abuse', as though the writer's own particular world-view, language and preferred usage had sprung spontaneously and full-grown out of the primaeval slime, instead of being, as it is, the immediate end product of an ongoing process).[30]

In the case of the particular disagreement arising out of conflict between OA and PO models, it is evident that, although the central concepts of the OA model are co-extensive with, and are formulated towards, similar descriptive and explanatory ends, many of the arguments directed by the orthodoxy against the physicalist account ignore the scientific evidence and seem to be designed specifically to maintain the OA model for its own sake, or to limit significant philosophical inquiry to analysis within this model, quite independently of its descriptive and explanatory powers or its coherence.[31]

Again, paradoxically, it is orthodox philosophers who most often argue against a PO model, rather than the members of the ordinary language community whose corporate authority is obliquely appealed to in such matters. In practice, the ordinary language community continues to absorb diachronic meaning shifts, that is meaning change over time, with neither premeditation nor qualm, as indeed it has always done where this has served a desired purpose.[32] To express a platitude in what is perhaps a dark saying: in general, where innovative usage has served to express a newly conceived intention, then there has been a semantic osmosis through the analytic–synthetic conceptual membrane. For example, a First Elizabethan speaker's use of 'see' would presumably not include any reference to (say) retinas, so that no analytical relationship between 'see' and 'retina' exists for such a person; for him the relationship would be synthetic. For a Second Elizabethan subject, however, given the orthodox education and discourse of his time, 'see' can perhaps literally mean only 'see with eyes, i.e. retinas, etc.'. The notion of vision *without* retinal stimulus becomes incomprehensible for such persons, which is to say the relation between 'see' and 'retina' is an analytic one. This slide or transformation of a synthetic into an analytic relation is the result of the dissemination of the findings of empirical neuropsychology into the appropriate eidos of the language community.[33]

What is essentially involved here is that, so far as the possibility of a PO model is concerned, the purpose of the OA philosopher differs from that of the PO philosopher. The maintenance of orthodoxy (the final epistemological authority of the subject; the orthodox view of the moral responsibility of persons etc.) is opposed to physicalist attempts at understanding human behaviour by investigating what 'makes it go' and how this is related to our ordinary understanding of the same behaviour. It is, I am sure, a measure of the poverty of much modern philosophy that this latter task is not considered a proper subject of philosophical interest.

3.2   The Physicalist's Purposes

Perhaps more must be said about the physicalist's purposes. Three of these seem to be of particular importance.

3.2.1   The physical as common denominator
First, material or physical entities have a fundamental categorial status in most adequate categorical systems,[34] though of course there is considerable debate as to the ontological character of such physical entities (i.e. entities for which the evidence is space–time–causal and essentially publicly observable). Realists therefore do best to follow Herbert Feigl in philosophical prudence by assuming a physicalist as opposed to a materialist ontology, since the question of the ultimate nature of the mass–energy substrate is thereby left open.[35] One physicalist purpose can therefore be regarded as an attempt to render a coherent account of experience in terms of basic physical concepts which everyone already understands and accepts.

3.2.2   The physical as regulator of speculation
The distinctive feature of science, as we have already observed, is not its use of such devices as explanatory hypotheses, models and regulative

36

principles, since these are general characteristics of thought present in other fields such as theology and literature. The distinguishing feature of science is the systematic rigour with which its unobserved or unobservable elements, spontaneously, imaginatively and essentially intuitively formulated as they are, are tested against the publicly observable. The process of rendering a scientific or PO account of experience is an ongoing one of repeated or recursive comparison of the PO conceptual model with intersubjectively confirmable experience (i.e. iteration of model and physical world).

So saying, it is now clear that the neo-Kantian metaphysic and theory of knowledge outlined earlier has gone too far in allowing the same validity to co-extensive conceptual systems with equal internal adequacy, but which have mutually exclusive categories. What has been described is rather a pluralistic subjective-psychology of knowledge which leaves out of account how the structure built up by empirical inquiries checks the proliferation of merely fanciful metaphysical interpretations.[36] For example, as hypotheses, Thor and macro-electrostatics serve ostensibly similar descriptive and explanatory functions, but electrostatics represents a model emerging out of the influence of a closer attention to and more extensive interaction with the observable phenomena of thunder. Similarly weight gain on combustion is explicable either by means of phlogiston or an atmospheric oxidation hypothesis. Again, the dominance of oxidation theory is the result of closer and more extensive interaction with the observable phenomena of combustion. Disease and sickness are ostensibly accounted for with equal (internal) adequacy by demonic possession, spontaneous generation or germ theory. The prevalence in our own culture of the regulative principle implicit in germ theory (namely, to identify microphysical causal agencies) is also the result of closer and more extensive interaction between the perceiving subject-system and the observable phenomena of disease. It is important to mark here that the predictive power that characterises scientific hypotheses is not entirely an end in itself as has sometimes been supposed, but is an important validating-constitutive criterion for the acceptability of the scientist's descriptions and explanations. A second physicalist purpose can therefore be seen as an attempt to provide a coherent account of experience without recourse to entities and concepts which cannot be validated by being incorporated into a completely objective schema.

In general, therefore, the purpose of those philosophers who advocate a PO model of persons and mind is to reconstitute the metaphysics of the mental and the physical, taking as basic the physical categories as these have been elaborated by science.

37

3.2.3   *Perspicuity of the physical account*

Related to the two physicalist purposes just given is a third factor in the development of physicalism which is not, properly speaking, a purpose at all. This has to do with the fact that, when a physicalist account of events is established, it has frequently proved otiose to sustain alternative competing accounts. Thus scientists have sought to discover what makes things 'go', and very likely without any conscious and deliberate purpose of elaborating a physicalist metaphysic. Indeed, they frequently undertake their inquiries in the belief that their work has, or need have, no implications outside of science. Newton and more recently John Eccles are typical figures who have elaborated key aspects of a basically physicalist picture, but who have not thought that their work supported a physicalist world-view more than another. And yet, once the 'mechanisms' of events have been revealed, it has frequently proven otiose to insist on alternative and competing descriptions and explanations.

Philosophical and lay physicalism therefore is as much a matter of the *perspicuity* of the physicalist model as it is a deliberate attempt to build on a common denominator, or to provide a coherent objective account of human experience. Indeed, we might say that its perspicuity stems from its coherence and objective truth, and its increasing pervasiveness or 'aggression' is due to the fact that we all recognise the physical categories and so most of us are open to explanations that elaborate on them. Needless to say, however, physicalism will not be perspicuous to those who, like the scholastic professors of Galileo's time, ignore or discount the relevant scientific facts.

3.3   *The Prospect for Physicalism*

Brief reference has been made to the way in which conceptual models emerge initially from a close and extensive interaction with given phenomena, and the ways in which concepts and models formulated in this way by innovators subsequently become common currency when they effectively serve a common purpose; also, reference has been made to how the limits imposed by the physical data source exert, in the last resort, a unique regulative influence – since to misinterpret a cliff edge is to fall over it. It is in this way that astronomy has developed the heliocentric model that rendered the Ptolemaic geocentric model redundant; geology and biology have generated an evolutionary model to replace the spontaneous generation of Genesis, and psychology and medicine have generated a disease model to replace the demonology of the *Malleus Maleficarum*. The question before us now is whether or not the exponentially increasing activity of individuals engaged in such sciences as physiology, biochemistry and cybernetics is generating a 'heliocentric' PO model of man to replace the 'geocentric' OA root model of the homuncular person. Enough has been said so far, I believe, to establish that this may well be the case. In any event, no constructive purpose is served by dismissing the matter on *a priori* grounds as some writers have done. The issues raised by this possibility are of the most far-reaching kind, and not without irony. Gilbert Ryle's gibe against the mechanistic materialists, that we may yet even venture the hazardous leap to the hypothesis that man is after all man,[37] turns out to have the post-neurocybernetic catch that perhaps, after all after alls, even a de-homunculised (OA) man is a bad metaphor for (PO) man.

I take it therefore that the prospect of a dominant PO model of man is more than a mere speculative daydream for philosophers of the fatalist–determinist–materialist monist school. On the contrary, apart from the merely parochial controversies of academic philosophers, the more public stir caused from time to time by writers such as the behavioural psychologist B. F. Skinner[38] and the biologist Jacques Monod[39] is evidence enough that the re-modelling process, initiated by Leucippus and Hippocrates and developed through the models of Hobbes, La Mettrie, Huxley, Watson, Hebb and other contemporary psycho-physiologists, is already going on. This process is unquestionabiy a matter of philosophic concern and is of the very first importance for any study of human behaviour. For as Piaget has said:[40]

> The modern child moves in an atmosphere of mechanism and scientific explanation. It is not that adults bring any pressure to bear upon the childrens' minds, but simply that nowadays to walk down a street imposes a whole conception of the world.

4 CONSEQUENCES OF PHYSICALISM

Here we should pause to consider an important challenge to the physicalist's programme of rendering explanations of human behaviour in terms of the PO model. It is argued that the physicalist enterprise is pointless, a side issue, even if it should turn out that a mind–brain IT were a valid and substantiated hypothesis.[41] The crux of this argument is that what is important is to formulate *fruitful* explanations of behaviour. Human affairs involve not only bodily movements, which can be adequately explained in physical–causal terms, but also things like institutions, mores, values, reasons, rules, imperatives and motives. The problem of providing fruitful explanations of behaviour involving concepts of these kinds is quite separate from the problem of whether or not physical accounts can ultimately be rendered of such behaviour. The suggestion is that there is no reason to suppose that the PO model will prove the most fruitful with respect to the common explanatory purposes served by different accounts: that indeed a robust sense of proportion would suggest quite the opposite.

This argument strikes us most forcefully when we consider the field of aesthetics. Clearly we would not begin to learn to explain a ballet's choreography by embarking on a study of physiology. This much is uncontroversial. The issue becomes interesting, however, when we consider the fields of ethics and jurisprudence. As has already been said, the prevailing conventional wisdom is that when we talk science and when we talk morality not only do we talk in logically different ways, but moreover these different ways cannot be in conflict. A fuller discussion of this widely received view is deferred until Chapter VII (Section 4). At this stage it is sufficient to point out that there is no sanction for it.[42] Certainly different sorts of account *need* not be in conflict. But proof that they *cannot* be in conflict is a very different matter, and has not to my knowledge been offered by those who hold the view. Conversely, the improbability of such a proof ever being given is suggested by a consideration of cases where different language manifestly generates conflicting descriptions and explanations. Consider, for example, the once common explanation for a soldier's not going over the top in terms of cowardice, which conflicts with an alternative (objective) physicalist account of his not going over the top in terms of dysfunction. As a matter of fact, the moral value judgment has proven likely to be rendered otiose when the dysfunction is established. In this case sensory motor dysfunction is caused by exposure to artillery barrages, i.e. 'shellshock'.

When the physicalist extends deterministic explanation to *all* behaviour, including normal, mind-directed behaviour, objectors usually construe it as an affront to common sense, logic, human dignity or all three. It is typically objected that the causal determinist thinks that delinquents are unwell because their behaviour is caused, and since he thinks that commonplace acts are caused then presumably he thinks that all people are unwell.[43] Whereas it is readily conceded that there may be persuasive causal explanations of behaviour that is recognised to be abnormal, it is (rightly) held to be logically absurd to infer from this that all behaviour is abnormal or unwell, and to conclude that all moral discourse is therefore otiose. For it is to *normal* behaviour, that is the behaviour of normal individuals, that value appraisal and moral condemnation is addressed.[44] On this construal, the determinist's argument is simply fallacious, and if determinists really do think in this way they are surely confused and mistaken. The question is whether they do think in this way, and if so whether they must do so.

It may be that there are some determinists who reason that, since all unwell behaviour is caused, and since also all commonplace behaviour is caused, then all commonplace behaviour is unwell. This reasoning clearly commits the elementary fallacy of undistributed middle term, since clearly behaviour may be caused without being unwell. But this is the determinist's whole point, is it not? The determinist does not, or at any rate need not, think that commonplace behaviour is unwell. His point is simply that behaviour is none the less causally determined for being non-pathological.

The force of this point against normative moral evaluation in an OA framework is this: when moral judgments of behaviour are in fact rendered otiose (as in such cases as certifiable madmen and imbeciles), they are not rendered otiose because they are about behaviour that is pathological or deviant or antisocial (quite the opposite), but because they are either explicitly or implicitly understood to be about behaviour, the causes of which are necessitating.[45] The fact that 'immoral' behaviour is held to be committed by individuals supposed *not* to be pathological is therefore irrelevant to the conflict between causal and other accounts. The point is that the acts in question are *caused*, no matter what other *descriptions* are offered of them and their effects and no matter how hidden from ordinary view the causes are. In manifestly pathological cases descriptions and explanations in the logic of causes conflict with the descriptions and explanations of the logic of morality. The OA moral conception of the state of affairs as it 'ought' to be succumbs, by something like psychological attrition, to the PO model of the state of affairs as it *is*. The same conflict arises in other less manifest cases and with potentially the same result, depending upon the perspicuity of the operating causes, namely that the OA moral account is rendered otiose. In this way I take it that the old conflicts between morality and judicial sanctions, and scientific determinism are resurrected if the domain of mind (of motives, reasons, etc.) is explicitly linked to the domain of physical causation by a PO mind–brain identity hypothesis.

The conclusion I draw from this brief preliminary discussion of the *prima facie* problems surrounding moral responsibility and the scientific determinism implied by physicalism is that, contrary to the prevailing conventional wisdom, the existence of different descriptions and explanatory logics does not *itself* establish that there is no conflict between them. A PO mind–brain identity hypothesis can therefore not be dismissed as a side-issue where explanations of human behaviour rendered in the logic of physical causality conflict with other OA

41

accounts and where similar purposes of understanding, prediction and control are served. Stated plainly, a shift from an OA to a PO model of human persons and their behaviour has significant implications for ethics and jurisprudence.

PART TWO

Let us not proceed like a man who should try to discover the melodies that an organ can play in the individual pipes.

F. H. Lange (1925, p.161)

III

THE MENTAL AND THE
PHYSICAL

1   CARTESIAN DUALISM

It is not to the present purpose to rehearse comprehensively the histories of the two root models of persons described in the last chapter. In any case it has been abundantly documented elsewhere.[1] It is sufficient for the present purpose to note that the perennial themes of scientific materialism and physicalism (i.e. the essentials of the PO model) have been atomistic monism, the presupposition of universal and invariant natural law (and determinism in morality), nominalism and mathematical empiricism. The immaterial character of mind is typically conceived not substantially (as psyche, soul or spirit), but in the immaterial domain of *relations* (form or organisation or system) and dynamics (motion and change).

The perennial themes of dualist orthodoxy (i.e. the essentials of the OA model) have been human divinity, extra-mundaneity, the existence of an immaterial psyche or soul or mind and the primacy of reason in determining acts of will. Therefore, although Descartes is conventionally taken as the point of departure for modern philosophy, his philosophy of mind largely amounts to a concise rationalist formulation of ideas already explicit in the Greek–Hebrew–Christian tradition. That is, as Descartes says:

> I have on the one hand a clear and distinct idea of myself as a *thinking non-extended thing* and on the other hand, a distinct idea of my body as an *extended, non-thinking thing;* it is therefore certain that I am truly distinct from my body and can exist without it.[2]
> What is a thinking thing? A thing that doubts, understands, affirms, denies, wills, refuses, and also imagines and senses.[3]

The ideas I have of [material things] which are distinct. ... First I have a distinct image of that quantity which philosophers commonly call continuous, or of the *extension* in length, breadth and depth which is in that quantity, or rather in the things to which it is attributed. Further, I can distinguish several parts in it and attribute various sizes, shapes, locations and movements to each one of them. And finally I can attribute certain durations to each of these movements.[4]

The Cartesian formulation of psycho-physical dualism remains essentially unchanged to the present. Certainly its religious strand has faded, shrunk with the development of post-scientific metaphysics and epistemology, but it remains as large as life in the fields of ethics and jurisprudence (both philosophical and practical). To the extent therefore that 'reasons are cogent for us only when our inarticulate feelings of reality have been impressed in favour of the same conclusion',[5] the Cartesian dualist model of persons and their behaviour can be taken *in toto* as the root metaphysical model of the prevailing orthodoxy. In recent times the dualism has been construed as a linguistic, conceptual, logical or phenomenological one, rather than a substantial one, but the distinctions drawn are still along the same lines as those drawn by Descartes.

2 THE CENTRAL MIND–BRAIN PUZZLE

2.1 *The Problem*

The Cartesian dichotomy between mind and body as immaterial and material *substances* poses the problem of their relation or interaction. If the stuff of mind is so different from the stuff of body that it can at least logically exist apart from it, then how do they influence one another? The central issue arising from the dichotomy (its very point) is that it is a commonplace of experience that human behaviour is determined by individual acts of will, following on rational deliberation based on memory, perception, imaginative anticipation and motivated choice. But if 'will', 'reason', 'memory', 'perception', 'imagination', 'motive' and 'choice' have their being in the domain of mind, without extension, and are 'truly distinct from body', then *what* is the nature of their relationship, and specifically how do acts of volition produce bodily movements? The problem remains essentially the same if we substitute the up-to-date rubric of 'dimensions' for the Cartesian substances.[6] An approach such as Descartes' own pineal gland hypothesis is notoriously inept and inadequate, although the hunt for the pineal grail is still on.[7] Unless we are to neglect philosophy altogether and (prematurely) beg the

46

question by proclaiming that interaction occurs in some ineffable domain of brute phenomenal–causal fact, then here we have the central problem in the philosophy of mind.

Certainly there are many purposes for which the need for a solution is not pressing, simply because for these purposes there is no *problem*; for many purposes no practical consequence follows from a conceptual mind–body dichotomy. Concern with the metaphysics of mind is not a primary requisite for artistic expression, for example, and even most life science can be conducted quite effectively under any number of different metaphysical presuppositions about the nature of mind and body and their relation. Still, there can be no doubt that the mind–body dichotomy is a philosophical problem that requires a solution,[8] even though some philosophers seem prepared to leave the question open in the interests of preserving man's traditional self-image.[9] Similarly, there is no doubt that traditional ethical questions of free-will and determinism, and jurisprudential questions of responsibility and punishment, which are bound up with the mind–body problem, are serious philosophical questions which require solutions.

2.2   *Post-Cartesian Proposals*

The philosophy of mind after Descartes is largely the history of attempts to abolish or dismiss, solve, resolve or dissolve the mind–body problem. The history of such attempts is a hoary one which has been summarised and documented almost *ad nauseam*, so it is not necessary to give more than the briefest outline of some of them.[10]

1 *Abolition* Some philosophers have sought to dismiss or abolish the problem by denying one or other of the elements in the dichotomy. Extreme subjective idealists such as Berkeley and Fichte (in their different ways) have denied the material reality of the external world, but only on pain of adopting highly problematical alternative hypotheses. Extreme materialists such as Hobbes, La Mettrie and Thomas Huxley stop short of denying sense and reason to human bodies altogether, but have maintained an almost equally radical epiphenominalist thesis which denies the influence of mind on body.

2 *Solution* Solutions have been offered which retain both mental and physical elements and account for their spatio-temporal relation both non-causally and causally. *Non-causal* solutions include continuous miraculous intervention (Malebranche's occasionalism); synchrony, on the model of clocks (Leibnitzian monadology); and psycho-physical parallelism (e.g. Clifford). *Causal* solutions include outright claims to a mind–body interaction mechanism (Descartes, Eccles) and appeals to the physical principle of action at a distance, by analogy with

47

electromagnetic and gravitational force-fields (Sherrington).

3 *Dissolution* Some philosophers have sought to dissolve the problem by deeming it to be in some way misconceived.

Metaphysical dissolution takes the form of a double-aspect theory whereby some sort of transcendental reality is perceived by the subject in two distinct aspects as the mental and the physical. Examples of solutions of this type are Spinoza's infinite substance, Kant's noumenal thing-in-itself and Russell's neutral locus of phenomenal causation, which is neutral with respect to both the mental and the physical.

Analytical dissolution has usually been claimed by philosophers of a positivist or quasi-behaviourist persuasion in this century. The whole problem is declared to be misconceived in the first place, owing to conceptual confusions arising from the misuse of language, specifically the reification of concepts denoted by nouns in the material mode. The dissolution of mind–body interaction as a pseudo-problem in this way has commonly been accompanied by a Procrustean denial of some of the most commonplace experiences, such as privacy, that is the subject's privileged access to or acquaintance with the contents of his own 'mind' (as in dreams, reveries, pretence and unexpressed thoughts and feelings), or by the denial of meaning to the language in which we talk about them.

2.3 *Criteria for a Solution*

None of the solutions proposed to date has found universal or even general acceptance. The failures are instructive, however, because they indicate criteria that must be satisfied by any model that is to accommodate or resolve the ostensible mind–body antinomies into platitudes. Two such broad criteria are that any solution should be:
1 metaphysically conservative;
2 true to experience.

Metaphysical conservatism This is essentially the parsimonious principle of Occam's Razor, which has been variously formulated either as (1) 'entities' or (2) that 'plurality' should not be posited without necessity, or that (3) nothing that can be explained by a few things should be explained by more.[11] The 'razor' is commonly regarded as a regulative principle in the formulation of scientific hypotheses. It seems itself to embody an important principle of the logic of metaphysical presuppositions, viz. that when an individual's primary metaphysical directives repeatedly either fail to produce or are superfluous to the production of satisfactory working hypotheses at the ostensive–pragmatic level, then his loyalty to them is weakened. It is worth repeating at this point the principle that, in the matter of metaphysical presuppositions, the establishment of alternative systems is largely non-programmatic, that is to say it is not so much a matter of doctrinaire advocacy or systematic demonstration as what is perspicuous within the system of purposes already determined by the belief systems of the language community. Accordingly, metaphysical–dissolutionist theories of the neutral monist type as well as extravagant speculative idealism of the Berkeleyan variety, which gratuitously invoke metaphysical entities, supernatural agencies or general epistemological factota, are as a matter of fact unlikely to achieve general acceptance if more economical ontologies serve the same explanatory purpose.

Truth to experience Any conceptual shift that resolves the ostensible puzzles will be true to experience. As Butler observed, theory has to allow us, not deny us, the observations from which we start.[12] Butler's reference to observation rather than 'fact' is significant, in view of the growing realisation in recent times that 'facts' can only be regarded as highly interpreted observations. The problem becomes even more complex when we recognise that the level of observation itself is far from being uncontaminated by the observer's system of beliefs.[13]

Nevertheless, a useful distinction can still be made between the observational level of the external senses, at which there may be a common ground of agreement between individuals holding conflicting beliefs, and the higher levels of interpreted fact. By the truth-to-experience criterion, extreme idealism and extreme materialism both fail, through each denying the ostensible dichotomy involving the other. The various non-causal parallellist accounts fail, by failing adequately to account for ostensible interaction; and causal accounts based on Hume's thesis that 'anything can cause anything' are highly problematical and stand or fall with the phenomenalist model of causation which will be discussed in Chapter VI (Section 3.3). Analytical dissolutionist theories fail by denying 'privileged access'. The truth-to-experience criterion does not of course entail that prevailing orthodox metaphysics and interpretations are inviolate – on the contrary, we have already argued that the process of re-interpretation is of the very essence of the philosophical enterprise. What it *does* entail is that reinterpretation should be observation-based rather than speculative, or dogmatic, or doctrinaire conservative. Specifically it means that highly interpretative concepts such as 'divinity', 'moral being' and so forth – in so far as they are rational (rather than revelational), are logically secondary to the eidos that emerges from the observational level. The observational basis of such higher-order concepts as human intelligence, purposiveness, personal identity, intentionality, conscience, the 'ought' and resentment is always subject to reinterpretation through the process of interaction between root models and their basis in observation.

3   THE MIND–BRAIN IDENTITY THEORY

A dissolutionist account of the mind–body relation which we have not considered thus far has been recently advanced by latter-day sophisticated materialists. In its baldest (and therefore its most misleading) formulation the thesis advanced is that 'Mind is simply the brain'.[14] That is to say, a relationship of strict identity is said to hold between mental events and certain physical states of the brain that are *ostensibly* in some correspondence relation with them. In this way the problems surrounding 'interaction' do not arise. The *ontological* dualism implicit in the orthodoxy is construed as a linguistic duality describing two sides of the same coin: the coin being a unique physical object, namely the human brain. Unlike previous physicalist accounts, therefore, the conventional manifestations of 'mind' are not explained *away* by this hypothesis in the reductionist manner of 'nothing-but' accounts. The hypothesis thus purports or promises to satisfy both of the criteria for a solution to the mental–physical puzzle, because it is both metaphysically conservative and true to experience in so far as it is non-reductionist with respect to phenomena.

4   EVIDENCE FOR IDENTITY THEORY

Before proceeding to elaborate and discuss the hypothesis in some detail it is perhaps necessary to offer some further preliminary justification for attaching special importance to what might be regarded as nothing more than yet another mistaken or misguided attempt to resolve this perennial problem. Four general considerations together lend special force to this hypothesis:
1 the generally acknowledged success of physical science in describing inanimate nature;
2 the breakdown in the distinction between inanimate and animate nature;
3 the *prima facie* evidence relating mind and body;
4 the scientific evidence relating mind and brain.

4.1   *The Success of Physical Science*

Any thesis derived from physical science carries special force in our own culture. Since Galileo first distinguished between objective and subjective qualities of experience and stressed the need for a quantitative measure of qualitative phenomena as a prerequisite for a proper understanding of the natural world, the progress of physical science has been exceedingly impressive. By extruding the egocentric perspective from his account of the world, the scientist has undoubtedly made clear advances towards a recognition of the way things are, rather than the way individuals might merely imagine, or desire, or presuppose them to be. It is scarcely necessary to mention again (though I shall) the momentous shift in perspective entailed by Galileo's successful advocacy of the Copernican hypothesis.

At issue was not only the interpretation of astronomical data, but a whole human egocentric purview.[15] As the heliocentric hypothesis prevailed, so the (anthropocentric) geocentric astronomy along with Aristotle's whole corpus of teleological physics was rendered otiose.

Subsequent developments through Newtonian mechanics, the chemistry of Lavoisier, the electromagnetic theories of Faraday and Maxwell to modern atomic theories have extended, reinforced and persuasively demonstrated the claims of physical objective science to render a veridical account of the inanimate natural world on the metaphysical monistic model of Democritus. (This is not the place to discuss the epistemological basis of theoretical physics. I take it however that quantum uncertainty is not opposed to the Democritean principles, though this question continues to be debated by philosophers.[16]) What this account entails is a critical–objective, but above all a realistic, account of the world and of man's place within it. The considerable labours of Plato and Kant notwithstanding, the dictum that 'man is the measure of all things' is to be construed as a mere truism: *of course* human knowledge is *human* knowledge. The important thing is that it is knowledge *that* – knowledge *about* something, namely the pre-existing, external and inter-subjective world revealed (however obliquely) by sense.

4.2 The Breakdown of the Animate–Inanimate Dichotomy

A central tenet of the present orthodox doctrine is that there is a categorial distinction between 'animate' and 'inanimate' things. Modern science has, on the contrary, conclusively demonstrated what was already accepted in ancient times, that is that organic life is possible only through its embodiment in natural cycles linking organisms to plant life and inanimate matter. At an early stage Wöhler's synthesis of urea showed that compounds, up till then considered the exclusive product of organisms animated by some extra-mundane vital force, were the synthesisable product of indisputably inorganic compounds (potassium cyanate and ammonium sulphate). At the organic level, the ambiguous status of viruses demonstrates how problematical the categorial distinction is: outside the body they manifest inanimate characteristics (e.g. crystallise); inside the body they behave animately (e.g. propagate). Already in the nineteenth century it was realised that conventionally animate processes were subject to the same energy conservation laws as inanimate processes. The distinction has become increasingly blurred during this century. Such phenomena as morphogenesis, ontogenesis and the thermodynamic equilibrium of organisms, for example, had previously been taken as evidence of the operation of some extra-mundane factor (entelechy, elan-vital).[17] In recent times each of these phenomena has (typically) been shown to have, on the contrary, an entirely mundane biophysical explanation. Thus it has been demonstrated that chemical concentrations are the only necessary and sufficient determinants of the geometrical symmetry of cell division or meiosis.[18] Similarly the systematic development of the individual, with characteristics drawn equally from each parent, is accounted for by the genetic function of DNA.[19]

The physicist's universal and invariant Second Law of Thermo-dynamics for physical systems, in its classical formulations by Kelvin and Clausius, maintains that physical systems tend to degenerate from states of high energy, high order (organisation) and low entropy, to states of low energy, greater disorder and high entropy, thus tending towards a universal norm. The capacity of living organisms to apparently defy the classical formulation (by surviving, in the case of man, for threescore years and ten) was taken as evidence that life was set apart from merely physical processes. However, the capacity of living things to defy the Second Law of Thermodynamics has been shown to be due to the fact that the classical formulations are only a special case of the more general laws applying to open systems (i.e. the case of no energy, transactions across the system boundaries).[20] That is to say, quasi-stable *open*-system processes, whether they are turbo-jet engines or human individuals, are not determined by the laws regulating *closed* systems, for the very good reason that they are *open* systems; they sustain states of quasi-stable equilibrium determined by laws regulating open systems which involve importing energy across the system boundaries. This is possible through participation in higher-order (more comprehensive) systems, which, in so far as *they* are closed, *are* subject to the classical Second Law.

In short, criteria that have been employed to characterise animate objects and processes, as against inanimate ones, have repeatedly been satisfied by objects and processes that are unequivocally within the domain of *inanimate* physical science. (The important problems of purpose and teleology have already been mentioned and will be discussed in greater detail in Chapter VII (Section 7.3).)

4.3   Commonplace Evidence Relating the Mental and the Physical

The most obvious indication of the relation between mind and body is in the case of mental states associated with the appetites: we are alert and animated (up to a critical point) when hungry, and soporific and quiescent when sated. The effect of injuries such as head blows and severe bodily wounds was already emphasised by Lucretius as bringing about alterations in the states of mind ranging from mild faintness and dizziness to severe dementia. The effects of illness are similar (and were responsible for the celebrated materialist revelation of La Mettrie). Mental depression accompanies the common cold and influenza, delirium and hallucinations accompany fever, and almost insane optimism accompanies terminal tuberculosis. The gross influence of drugs on states of mind and behaviour was known and catalogued by the Chinese in the third millenium. Alcohol is a notorious suppressor of the self-critical 'faculties', and hallucinogens (hashish, peyote), euphoriants (cocaine), and the opiates are all well-known sources of extra-mundane states of mind. Even the humble tea-leaf holds promise of transcendental raptures, as the poet Lotung records.[21]

The *prima facie* evidence relating mind to body, and particularly to the brain, is ancient, commonplace and well established. So much so that, while many will deny that the relationship is one of identity rather than some form of correspondence, no one will deny that it exists. This is clearly reflected in the idioms of ordinary usage in which 'mind' and 'brain' are in fact used with an equivocation indicative of synonymity. Thus locutions of the sort 'the brains of the family' are commonly used to indicate qualities of mind. Conversely, the newspaper headline announcing the 'German Measles Link with Mind Damage'[22] indicates a widely understood equivocal reference to brain damage. Against a formalised I-hypothesis, however, it is objected that in concentrating on mere symptoms (brain processes and behaviour) we lose the thing in itself (the mind); at its most banal, the ghost[23] and the switchboard operator.[24] To this objection Lange has pointedly replied, 'Yes, if anyone could show us that after the elimination of all of the symptoms, there is anything left' (i.e. that they are symptomatic of).[25]

5   SCIENTIFIC EVIDENCE RELATING THE MENTAL AND THE PHYSICAL

In considering the scientific study of mind, it is necessary to recall the (somewhat artificial) distinction between the observational level of natural philosophy and the more abstract and universal levels involving quantification and general explanatory schemata. At the present time the accumulation of clinical and experimental evidence is considerable. There has also been considerable progress in the development of hypothetical conceptual models which serve as powerful and persuasive synthesising and heuristic devices. Even so, the development of detailed and mathematically rigorous representations of phenomena conventionally associated with mind, and of the putatively 'psychic' determinants of human behaviour, is still in its infancy.

One consequence is that in the present state of the art it is impossible to predict with precision normal human behaviour. It might even be said that predictability will *never* be achieved. This is by no means fatal to the physicalist case however as I propose to show in Chapter VIII (Section 6.2.5).

5.1 *Behaviourism*

It is appropriate to begin this discussion of the scientific basis of physicalist accounts of mentality by saying something briefly about behaviourism, because this constitutes the first attempt to apply the rigorously objective and quantitative methods of science to the study of human behaviour, and also because behaviourism, which was largely instrumental in discrediting introspective procedures in psychology, has also been the scientific paradigm for a recent and influential generation of philosophers whose concerns have ostensibly been conceptual and linguistic.[26] More specifically, some proponents of an identity hypothesis have accepted a behaviourist account of mental phenomena other than sensations.[27]

Although behaviourism shares certain features with physicalism, it differs from it in the crucial respect that it ignores or discounts precisely those central nervous states and processes that in the emerging physicalist model, constitute the physical basis of mentality and mind-directed action.[28] Largely for this reason behaviourism loses the power to render adequate accounts of mentality and mind-directed behaviour. Thus, for example, whereas behaviourists are committed to accounts of consciousness and 'verbal behaviour' based upon slight movements of the speech apparatus,[29] there is conclusive clinical evidence that it is nothing of the sort, but involves rather the activity of central nervous and brain systems.[30] As Karl Pribram has wittily put it, the behaviourists' arguments ring hollow once it is recognised that the head is not.[31] This, of course, is a purely empirical point and many objections are raised to behaviourism and physicalism alike on conceptual grounds. Much more needs to be said, therefore, particularly with regard to what are called 'institutional facts' and the social and cultural aspects of mentality, before a physicalist account is made adequate. This can, I believe, be done (see Chapter IV, Section 4.1, and Chapter V, Section 4).

For the present purpose it is sufficient to say that the many criticisms that have been directed against behaviouristic–scientific accounts[32] of mind-directed action do not tell against physicalism. This is because the PO model is capable of accounting for mind and mind-directed action without Procrustean reduction of the phenomena. In fact, it is the evidence from neuropsychology and biophysics that represents the real challenge to the OA model of persons.

5.2 *The Neurophysiological Basis of Mind*

Charles Sherrington once said that, whereas there is no demonstrable scientific account of the relation between the physical and the mental, 'busy common sense' goes forward treating the two together as one,[33] without taking much care of the innumerable philosophical discussions that the question has raised in the past. This is in keeping with the general thesis advanced here, that the status of the concept of mind is dependent on the model that emerges perspicuously out of experience. For this reason, that is to draw attention to the perspicuity of a physicalist account of mind, it would be desirable to present a more extensive account of the 'experience of those who work in the nervous system' than would normally be appropriate or necessary in a philosophical essay.

Other good reasons for undertaking such an account would be to avoid the error, too often committed by philosophers, of proceeding as though scientists were attempting to investigate 'the hurly burly of criss-crossing contingencies'[34] involved in human behaviour with the technological and conceptual equivalents of a knife and fork; and also to confound the view that no amount of scientific evidence is relevant to a conceptual paradox,[35] by suggesting some of the prodigious sophistication and problem-solving power of the PO model. However, though desirable, it is not convenient to present here even an adequate summary of the vast body of relevant scientific evidence now available. Fortunately this may not be necessary because of the increasing number of up-to-date and readily accessible synoptic works on the subject.[36] What I am certain about is that developments in mind–brain science over the last few decades have been so remarkable that they constitute the basis for a radical shift from the prevailing OA model of persons to the PO model. There is no once-and-for-all divide separating con-ceptual–analytic relations and empirical–synthetic ones, certainly not in the case of the mind–body problem. It therefore behoves philosophers to acquaint themselves with the range and cogency of these facts before they presume to make pronouncements about what is and what is not 'logically possible' for physical systems, and whether or not coherent scientific explanations can be framed of mind-directed behaviour.

Even though a fully adequate account is inconvenient and perhaps unnecessary here, there is nevertheless still something to be had from at least mentioning the sort of scientific developments that seem to have such far-reaching implications for man's prevailing self-image. It is convenient to consider the scientific evidence relating mind to brain under three rather arbitrary heads: technology, empirical data and theory. Each is of fundamental importance and relates to each of the others.

5.2.1 *Technology*

Just as developments in astronomy in Galileo's time and the metaphysical consequences that followed from them were bound up with the development of a technology of optics, so developments in neuropsychology are bound up with the development of an adequate technology. It is therefore a matter of some philosophical moment that in the last few decades there have been substantial and unprecedented advances in surgical techniques, psychological testing, electro-technology, psychopharmacology and biophysics which provide new data which bear heavily and perhaps decisively on an understanding of the mind–brain relation.[37]

5.2.2 *Empirical data*

The vast accumulation of empirical data[38] is of three main types.

First, there is considerable circumstantial evidence from comparative anatomy and psychology correlating both phylogenetic and ontogenetic development of brain size and complexity with corresponding developments in manifest intelligence. This strongly suggests that brain structure is a necessary condition and possibly, taken in its dynamic aspect (temporal structure), also a *sufficient* condition for mind.[39]

Second, there is well-established evidence for the localisation of the physical basis of mental functions in the brain, such as sense, emotion, memory and motor control, so that, as Sperry has reported, it is a common observation that destruction of a brain part through trauma, anoxemia, etc., commonly leads to an irreversible permanent loss of the corresponding facet of mental awareness with consequent loss and crippling of the cognitive self.[40]

Third, it has come to be recognised that the functional interrelation of brain systems is crucial to consciousness and mental function.[41] It is not that in some vague or mystical way the sum is greater than the parts, but that it is the *relation* between the various multiple activities that is of importance.[42]

Among the most remarkable and illuminating clinical results made possible by technological advances are those reported of split-brain surgery. In such cases, individuals who have undergone surgery to separate the brain's cerebral hemispheres at the commisure (bridge) of the corpus collosum not only acquire dual (independent) memories but also manifest dual 'mind' and dual personality.[43] This evidence strongly suggests that mind and personality may be based only in the functional integration of brain sub-systems so that anatomical duality entails functional duality, dual decision systems, dual memory and dual minds. It is interesting to compare these results with clinical cases of multiple personality.[44]

Functional integration of brain–mind activity is controlled mainly through two physical systems; the endocrine system[45] and the frontal lobes of the brain.[46] The endocrine system exercises a potent and often spectacular influence on mentality and behaviour.[47] There is evidence, however, that the frontal lobes may exercise a decisive influence on choice and action.[48] Among the most remarkable evidence indicating the role of the frontal lobes in controlling mental activity and behaviour is the behavioural disinhibition associated with damage to the medio-basal zones.[49] In the celebrated case of Phineas Gage, the medio-basal zones were destroyed by a tamping bar which penetrated the skull in a blasting accident. Whereas Gage's memory, skills and intellectual capacities were unimpaired, his previously sober and considerate demeanour was dramatically transformed so that he became irascible, inconsiderate and given to profanity.[50] Evidence of this sort strongly suggests that proper or appropriate functioning of cerebral systems is not only a necessary, but also a sufficient, condition for socially tolerable behaviour.

5.2.3 Theory

Scientific studies of the physical basis of mind require the development of a theoretical corpus with a scope and precision equal to the task. It is possible to identify four major areas of related developments in recents decades which show every evidence of meeting these requirements.

1 Conceptual models and hypothetical constructs of brain–mind mechanisms have been proposed that have great power and generality. Among the most notable of these are Craik's and Hebb's. Craik's hypothesis is that the physical basis of mind lies in the formation of neural analogues or models of the external world as the basis of perception, memory, reasoning and planning.[51] Hebb's more specific 'cell-assembly' hypothesis is able to account for such phenomena as abstraction, association and serial thought processes.[52] The models of

brain self-scanning and pattern-discerning mechanisms investigated by Grey-Walter seem capable of explaining other important aspects of mind such as self-consciousness, learning, personality and psycho-pathology.[53] Finally, information flow models of behaviour such as MacKay's have proved fruitful in accounting for not only perception and memory but also invention and imagination in terms of hierarchies of statistically self-organising systems.[54]

It is evident that the physical basis of mind is not to be formulated in the framework of Newtonian mechanics presumed by many philosophers, but in the global distribution of electrodynamic patterns of brain events whose significance lies in their (statistical) distribution in frequency, phase and space.

2 Closely related to the development of conceptual models such as those just mentioned has been the application of mathematical logic to the development of a more general theory of neuronal nets.[55] This is based on the well-founded assumption that the neurone is a discrete binary (on/off) decision unit. If so, there is no reason to suppose that the responses and interrelations of the nervous system are so complex that they cannot be represented as the operation of mechanisms.[56]

3 Other important general theoretical developments have been cybernetics[57] and information theory.[58] The central technical concept of cybernetics, feedback, is appropriate to the representation of self-regulated purposive behaviour, because it takes the behaviour-controlling variable to be the *difference* between a pre-existing goal state and an instantaneously given state. Thus 'circular causation' replaces the linear causation of stimulus response mechanisms. Although these ideas were initially developed in automatic-control theory for guided weapons systems, they have proven equally applicable to the human nervous system.[59]

Similarly, the mathematical theory of communication was first developed to deal with the engineering problems of preserving signals without distortion in transmission and was not concerned with meaning as intention (message). However, many investigators have pointed out that information theory based on the statistical, probablistic, sequential and recurrent characteristics of a language may be interpreted as an account of meaning (as association or intention) also.[60]

The importance of the development of formal theories of control and communication lies, therefore, in the possibility of rendering rigorous and possibly quantitative representations of central nervous processes which can be interpreted as representations of purpose and meaning in the conventional senses of the words in ordinary usage.

4 General system theory is more comprehensive than cybernetics and communications theory, concerned as it is with all of the transactions

involved in system behaviour, that is to say with energy as well as information.[61] The central thesis is that the behaviour of superordinate systems (sets of elements in interrelation) differs from that of the subordinate and related elements in isolation, but is amenable to representation and quantification in terms of such concepts as whole, organisation, directiveness, dynamic interaction, equilibrium, equifinality, homeostases, etc. In this way it is suggested that the phenomena of life and mind that have given rise to animism may be accounted for in a generalised theory of systems: the proper basis of a unified science.[62]

5.2.4 *Experiment*

Many of the conceptual models of the physical processes involved in mind-directed behaviour have been incorporated and tested in experimental hardware.[63] Whatever criticisms might be advanced against extrapolation, from the behaviour of artefacts to human behaviour, it must be acknowledged that configurations of electromechanical or chemical components have manifested behaviour that, if exhibited by organisms, would normally be taken as unmistakable evidence of the functioning of mind.[64] There is, in fact, good reason to believe that the concepts and principles of cybernetics, communication and general system theory are just what is needed for representing the physical processes that underlie not only homeostasis,[65] perception[66] and motor action,[67] but the highest manifestations of mind also.[68]

5.2.5 *Summary*

In the comparatively recent past the scientific understanding of the physical basis of mind has experienced something like a 'quantum jump' in extent and complexity. New experimental techniques have provided a wide variety of empirical evidence extending the physical accounts of phenomena conventionally attributed to mind. The empirical findings are structured within a theoretical corpus which provides concepts appropriate to the peculiar and complex nature of the phenomena concerned. In principle, the hypotheses also provide a basis for applying quantitative methods; without (radical behaviourist fashion) at the same time subjecting the phenomena to an *a priori* Procrustean bed, where significance and scope is arbitrarily subject to the constraints of theory and technique. There is some reason to believe that the phenomena of life and mind previously attributed to the 'mind' in some categorial sense may be, in principle, adequately explained in terms of deterministic scientific concepts and intersubjectively confirmable observation.

However, the main point to be made still turns on the argument presented earlier concerning eidescopic shifts, that with the progressive elimination of all the physical 'symptoms' of mind we are liable to go beyond the elucidation of *correlative* physical mechanisms to discover that we have nothing left to call mind at all. For I want to suggest that the real force of the scientific evidence lies in the progressive erosion of the orthodox concept of mind as something independent of physical objects and forces and their complex dynamic relations.

6   EIDESCOPIC SHIFTS AND PHYSICALISM

It is now opportune to consider the accumulating evidence for a physicalist account of the mental in the light of the earlier discussion about root model shifts to sketch some flesh on to the bones of the eidescopic shift schema that was outlined in Chapter I (Section 7).

First, the schema represents the progressive elaboration of the materialist–physicalist model towards more precise and empirically well-founded articulations of the basic categories adequately to explain more and more phenomena.

Thus the rudimentary speculative atomism of Leucippus and Democritus is based on slim evidence and provides a generally acceptable account of, if anything, only inanimate objects and events (cf. Figure 1.3A). The emphasis on relations and order evident in Lucretius articulates vital features of the atomist account but without significantly increased empirical content (cf. Figure 1.3B). Much later developments, such as Wöhler's synthesis of urea, which break down the orthodox distinction between inanimate and animate substance, involve a substantial shift in empirical scope and precision, and thus in the general plausibility of the PO model (cf. Figure 1.3C). The developments in cybernetics elaborate the basic physical–causal categories into the domain of purposive and teleological behaviour and so largely realise, conceptually at least, the precise articulation of physicalism to account for mind-directed *behaviour* (cf. Figure 1.3D).

The outstanding deficiencies in the model as elaborated thus far are to account for the relations between the phenomenology of consciousness (belief, desire, etc.), the formulation of plans and intentions, and the initiation of action to realise them. Although this final eidescopic shift is precisely the main one under discussion in the book, the development of information-processing models and neural-net theory promises to be just what is needed in the way of scientific theory for elaborating the PO categories to account adequately for all 'mental' phenomena (cf. Figure 1.3E).

Second, implicit in this necessarily sketchy exposition is the supposition that scientific theory may converge, as near as needs be, to an approximation of the way things really 'go'.[69] But as the schema suggests, a final picture may be anticipated by speculative thinking of genius on much scantier data than would be required for the general acceptance of a more fully articulated picture. This would be the case with early materialists and physicalists such as Lucretius, who, it might reasonably be said, anticipated with their conjectures much later developments.

Third, the problematical status of developing physicalist accounts in relation to well-established, animistic models is evident throughout the history of philosophy beginning with Socrates' objections to Anaxagoras' materialism. Indeed, many philosophers have rejected altogether the possibility that empirical science could ever decide metaphysical issues. This explains why, for example, some 'animistic' scientists such as MacKay and Eccles who are fully aware of the patently physicalist data emerging from the human sciences construe them within a theistic world-picture.[70]

Fourth, as the last reference to contemporary animistic or 'irrationalist' scientists shows, there is a tendency for holders of a prior orthodoxy, be it philosophical, religious or some other, to resist the alternative more perspicuous 'eidos' as it emerges.

Finally, it is abundantly clear, for the reasons just given, that, as the eidescopic shift from the orthodox–animistic to the physicalist model of human action takes place, this is not due to the logical refutation of the prior position through the results of 'crucial' experiments, but involves the growing acceptance of and eventually overwhelming plausibility of competing physicalist accounts of the same phenomena.

7 RECAPITULATION AND ORIENTATION

It has been suggested that there are two perennial root models involved in mind–body disputes. The difficulties in the orthodox account have been highlighted. A brief review has been made of attempts at resolving these difficulties and the conclusion reached that no attempted resolution has hitherto been adequate. Two general criteria for a satisfactory solution have been adduced from the failure of previous attempts. Reasons for considering a mind–brain identity theory have been offered, based primarily upon developments in the life sciences which support the physicalist alternative to the orthodox model.

The thesis that mind is identical with brain has therefore recommended itself to philosophers for four main kinds of reason.

1 *It resolves problems inherent in the orthodoxy*, namely:

(i) why mind and body (brain) should be related at all;
(ii) why a particular mind (personality) should be related and confined to a particular body (brain);
(iii) why (putatively) categorially distinct substances (or 'domains') should interact;
(iv) how (putatively) categorically distinct substances (or 'domains') do interact.

2 *It fulfils the general requirements for an adequate resolution of problems inherent in the orthodoxy*:
  (i) the condition of metaphysical conservatism is satisfied because an identity theory is monistic;
(ii) it is true to experience because nothing is introduced and the phenomena of common experience are not reduced.

3 *It is consistent with a mature scientific psychology.* Taking a mature scientific psychology to be concerned with inner states accessible to introspection and expressed in the language of first-person reports, as well as with overt behaviour, an IT affirms not only the cognitive status but also the causal efficacy of inner 'mental' states, because these are held to be identical with those states of the central nervous system with which they are ostensibly correlated.

4 *It promises to resolve the outstanding conceptual problem* facing physicalist accounts of mentality to do with the relation between the phenomenology of consciousness and human action – behaviour.

IV

MIND-BRAIN IDENTITY
THEORY

1 PRECEDENTS

It has already been suggested that the PO model is a perennial one which is gaining wider acceptance as a result of developments in the human sciences. Mind–brain identity theory is central to the physicalist view in its contemporary form. However, views very like IT have been espoused at least since Descartes.

Spinoza's double-aspect view of the mind–body relation is ostensibly neutral monist, but once the pantheistic–panpsychist symmetry is replaced by the asymmetry of a system–cybernetic-based realism, it offers cogent arguments for those who would go further and substitute a bedrock of fundamental particles for the transcendental infinite substance.[1] In the same way the redundancy of the Kantian noumenon leaves something very like an identity model of the mind–brain relation, for Kant suggested that the extended objects of external sense might very well possess thoughts presented consciously to their own internal sense.[2]

Kant was also anticipated by the French materialists; Robinet for example maintained that perception and desire are the conditional actions of brain mechanisms and that willing is the 'inner subjective side' of the natural mechanical processes of enactment.[3] We also find the basic model in evidence in eighteenth-century Britain. Sensation and thought were regarded as functions of the brain (by Joseph Priestley); as accompaniments of the material movements of the nervous system (by John Toland) and as being due to vibrations of the brain (according to David Hartley).[4]

The development of neuro-science during the nineteenth century against a background of the spectacular successes of physics, chemistry and evolutionary biology contributed to a wider acceptance of what is essentially an identity view. Fechner expressed it in terms of a vivid and influential (but also misleading) container analogy, according to which the mental is the physical 'from the inside'.[5] The model underlying Wündt's account of the relation between the causal and teleological conceptions of human behaviour is essentially similar. He holds that the difference between teleological and causal conceptions is not an objectively valid difference that divides the context of experience into two unlike provinces, but that the two ways of conceiving things are formally different only, so that to every purposive relation there belongs a causal connection.[6]

The advent of relativity and indeterminism in physics, the radical behaviourist psychology of the post-Victorian era and the analytical revolution in philosophy rendered the mind–body problem less fashionable, although it never became a completely redundant issue even among professional philosophers. Nevertheless, there is no doubt that the metaphysics of body–mind ceased to exercise philosophers in the analytical mainstream until its comparatively recent revival.

2   RECENT FORMULATIONS

2.1   *Leibnitz's Law*

The thesis that the mental is *identical* with certain brain processes, rather than being related in some other way to the brain, has already been briefly mentioned. It is open to quick refutation if Leibnitz's criterion of the identity of indiscernibles is adopted together with its converse that identicals are indiscernible.[7] It follows from this criterion that a putative identity can be refuted by establishing even a single difference between the elements identified, whereas on the other hand proof of identity requires that there is *no* difference that would render the elements non-identical.

Now discernibility of the mental and the physical by the Cartesian criteria of thought and extension is clear phenomenologically and is reflected in ordinary language. It is apparently sufficient to refute the I-hypothesis. Such a refutation is too facile, however, and recent advocates of the theory have explicitly and unrepentantly adopted Leibnitz's criterion. Surprisingly, however, this has rarely been directly quoted in the debate, so it is useful to begin the present discussion by doing so here. The passage that exercises mind–brain protagonists is presumably the following:[8]

> Two terms are the same if one can be substituted for the other without altering the truth of any statement. If we have A and B, and A

enters into some true proposition, and the substitution of B for A wherever it appears results in a new proposition which is likewise true, and this can be done for every such proposition then A and B are the same, they can be substituted for one another as I have said.

2.2   Three Distinctions

I-theorists have sought to fulfil this requirement on the basis of three important distinctions.

1   The distinction between sense and reference[9]

The essence of this distinction is that different terms or expressions may have a common reference and the reference of a proposition is its truth value. Substitution of terms with a common reference (in non-intentional contexts) leaves the reference and therefore the truth value of the proposition unchanged even when the *sense* of the proposition is significantly altered. Frege's by now celebrated example is that of the morning star and the evening star which happen to be the same thing, namely the planet Venus. Propositions about the morning star are true in virtue of factual truths about the planet Venus. Their truth value remains unchanged when 'evening star' is substituted for 'morning star' although the *sense* is altered considerably (may even be in-comprehensible).

2   The distinction between evidence and the evidenced

I-theorists are realists of various stripes. The realist position with regard to the ontological status of postulates of scientific theories is that to have a good reason to accept a theory is to have good reason to accept the entities that it postulates.[10] The phenomena or 'raw data' of immediate experience therefore constitute only the observational *evidence* for scientific theories, including their postulated entities, and should on no account be identified with the postulates (an error liable to be committed within for example phenomenalist or instrumentalist ontologies). The relationship between the evidence of direct observations, cloud chambers, oscilloscopes etc. and the objects of science is only through a more or less elaborate theoretical corpus. An analogy (no more) from everyday experience is how the phenomenal data of audio, visual and tactile sense is evidence for the existence of an object which is taken to be a substantial object in space–time and the causal epicentre of the phenomenal data.

3   The distinction between direct and indirect modes of confirmation

The above distinction between (direct) evidence and the (indirectly) evidenced holds in all cases except that in which the evidenced is precisely the perceiving subject's perceivings. In this unique case the datum is not evidenced; it is *evident*.[11] In this unique case therefore there are available two modes of confirmation that an occurrence has taken place: the direct for the individual in whom (which?) the occurrence occurs, and the indirect, open to all individuals through the mediation of the (immediate) evidence of their own external senses.

2.3   *Summary Statement of IT*

The various versions of IT all employ these distinctions more or less explicitly to fulfil Leibnitz's criterion of identity, so that the theory may be summarily represented as follows. In ordinary usage, and in behavioural psychology, certain terms that function as mediators in descriptions of stimulus–response relationships (evidenced) happen, as a matter of fact, to have a reference. This reference coincides with the reference of certain terms used by the neuropsychologist to describe the activity of the central nervous system, particularly the brain (also evidenced), in mediating the same stimulus–response relations. Furthermore, as perceiving subjects we are *directly* acquainted, let us say through introspection, with the same mediating processes: they are *evident* to us. The references of behavioural, neurophysiological and introspective terms each serve the same function, the mediation of stimulus–response relations.

By a process of triangulation based on inferences drawn from neuropsychology, the scientific terms used to describe the causes of behaviour are taken to have the same reference as the terms used to describe (report or express) immediate experience. That is to say, the objects of neurology (brain processes) are taken to be identical with the objects of immediate experience (mental states). The inferences are considered to be straightforward, as follows.[12] As a (scientifically informed) observer I know about the brains of others and the role they play in mediating stimulus–response relations; by analogy, and from the fact of my membership of a common biological species (based on the sobering evidence of mirrors, bleeding, procreativity etc.), I believe myself to have a similar brain. In my role as observer I count the reports of immediate experience of others as reports of mediating processes in them, and it is apparent that these are compresent with brain processes of a particular sort. By analogy I take the mediating processes directly evident to myself to be compresent with processes in my own brain. The Penfieldian observer–introspector can even become aware, without resort to analogy, that to be undergoing a brain process of a certain sort is to have an experience of a certain sort.[13]

However, there is a difference in the way that the evidence is presented: directly in the case of immediate experience, indirectly in the case of observation (whether behavioural or neurophysiological), and there are corresponding differences in the modes of confirmation of the evidenced. Both of these differences are reflected in different modes of expression: roughly speaking, the mental and the physical respectively. Introspective or immediate terms and expressions (the mental) and scientific observation terms (the physical) therefore have different *senses*. But Leibnitz's criterion of truth-value preserving substitutivity is satisfied by the *common reference* of mental and physical terms. Any unintelligibility generated by substituting mental terms for physical terms in physical contexts and vice versa is admitted, but is regarded as being due simply to contingent ignorance about, or unfamiliarity with, the factual truths about the common reference of these terms. As Smart says, 'sensations do in fact have all sorts of neurophysiological properties. For they are neurophysiological processes'.[14] Finally, it is suggested that human behaviour, like all physical processes, is causally determined and can be fully and adequately explained in terms of the space–time–causal laws of science, once the introspective or mental terms entering into non-causal accounts have been shown to have physical references.

2.4   Three Variants of IT

Although the foregoing summary outlines the essentials of an IT, it has become something of a convention to distinguish three significant variants. These might be called 'Raw-Feelist', 'Critical Realist' and 'Eliminationist' views. Each will now be briefly discussed and an examination made of some main shortcomings in each. A reconstituted version will be outlined before some of the main objections to an IT are considered. The reconstituted version I shall dub 'biperspectivist' because the term has been used by Rosenbleuth and Laszlo in a similar way, though they do not attach it to precisely the thesis proposed here. The distinctions drawn between different 'isms' are instructive but should not be taken to indicate any fundamental disagreement about the basic PO model; rather there is a difference in emphasis only.

2.4.1   The Raw Feelist version

This version is associated with Russell,[15] Feigl[16] and Pepper.[17] It is characterised by the sophisticated quasi-idealist view that the 'physical' with which the mental is identified is ultimately constructed out of the immediate data of consciousness or 'raw feels' of direct acquaintance:[18]

> Speaking ontologically ... the Identity Theory regards sentience (qualities experienced and in human beings knowable by acquaintance) and other qualities (unexperienced and knowable only by description) *the basic reality*. It shares with certain forms of idealistic metaphysics ... a conception of reality and combines with it the tenable components of materialism, viz. the conviction that the basic laws of the universe are physical. [i.e., explanatory premises do not contain irreducibly teleological concepts.]

Shortcomings

Idealism What is most dubious about this view is the idealism. It is open to all of the stock arguments against the view that the world is asymmetrically ideal – above all the sheer *implausibility* of supposing that the physical world as intersubjectively confirmed does not have existence prior to intelligent life which is the product of its evolution. Physical realist considerations suggest an asymmetrically *physical* rather than an asymmetrically 'ideal' reality. In any case, if alternative views do the same job without involving controversial idealist aspects they seem more likely to prevail.

The 'raw-feel' versus 'physical-real' distinction By taking immediate raw feels to be merely the evidential basis of our knowledge of the physical world, this view over-emphasises the distinction between the 'given' and the products of inference. Russell states the problem laconically as follows: 'Naive realism leads to physics, and physics, if true, shows that naive realism is false. Therefore naive realism if true, is false; therefore it is false'.[19] However, the primitive sensations or 'raw feels' presupposed by this view are in fact rarely encountered. They are merely an analytical abstraction from ordinary adult experience. Ordinarily we perceive *objects*, because we interpret what we feel as we feel it. We see objects, not light reflected from edges and angles.[20] Recent developments in the physiology of vision support the realist view, notably the postulation of invariancing mechanisms in the eye's line-scanning processes, which entails that perceived visual form is objective visual form because the influence of the system itself in differential sensory information-processing is self-cancelling (rather as a balance does not weigh itself, and in effect as a televisual image does not include cameras, cables, transistors, etc.).[21] There is in fact reason to suppose that at least in the case of the location and form of material objects our perceptions are normally veridical: 'What you see (physical objects) is what you get (reality)!'

2.4.2   *The Critical Realist version*
This version (perhaps best known as central state materialism) is associated with what has been called 'the United Front of Sophisticated Australasian Materialists', notably Place,[22] Smart[23] and Armstrong.[24] The distinguishing characteristic of this view is that the true nature of the mental is really a particular (i.e. sentient and sapient) sort of physical process, namely that of the central nervous system, the physical process being ontologically, though not epistemologically, primary. The mental is thus held to be continuous with the inanimate world described by physics.

Earlier formulations of the view (Place and Smart) were mainly concerned to give a physicalist account of those residual 'mental' phenomena that resisted behaviourist analysis. Later formulations have followed Armstrong in extending the 'central-state' account to the whole range of mental phenomena. Armstrong's *magnum opus* in fact is concerned with the secondary task of the identity theorist (the primary task being to establish the logical coherence and nature of the identity), that of demonstrating that a materialist theory is consistent with our ordinary concepts of mind by working through the consequences of the main thesis that mental states are *inner* states apt for causing behaviour, behaviour being the ostensible foundation of and therefore the link with the concepts embodied in ordinary language.

Shortcomings
Behaviourism and the meaning of mental terms The critical realists have been unable to shed the thrall of scientific behaviourism and the behaviouristically oriented philosophy of ordinary language usage. Where immediate inner experience is acknowledged it has been regarded as of trivial consequence for the meaning of even phenomenal terms,[25] whereas, as others have rightly recognised, it is precisely the illumination of direct experience that is epistemologically crucial[26] (not to say paramount for obvious aesthetic and humane reasons). It is the same residual commitment to behaviourism that is a major shortcoming of Armstrong's particular materialistic analysis of mind. He simply shifts the focus of attention from the behavioural stimulus to the response.[27] By committing himself to a formula for mental states as states 'apt for bringing about certain behaviour',[28] he leaves out precisely that feature of 'the mind' that is found to be least amenable to a materialistic interpretation.[29] As a result he is repeatedly involved in modifications or contradictions of the basic formula.

The first modification, that perception is a mental state *apt for being brought about by* certain sorts of sensory stimuli, is accountable on the same behaviourist lines, simply by reverting to the stimulus. However, other cases are not. Only shortly after defining mind behaviourally,[30] Armstrong is already explaining that 'it is possible to be aware of one's mental states without saying anything. *Nor does such awareness seem to be a mere disposition* or capacity to make a statement',[31] that is to say capacity to emit 'verbal behaviour'. By failing to modify his formula accordingly, after-images,[32] intentions,[33] idle wants[34] and transitive sensings,[35] for example, are subsequently given 'epicyclic' behavioural definitions in terms of 'normal' behavioural responses, even though these states may be perfectly normal, independent and commonplace in themselves. And it is precisely the *non*-behavioural character of such states that has convinced many philosophers that a behaviouristic brand of physical realism is unacceptable.

This objection tells against the critical realist version, but is not decisive against all versions of IT. For having proposed a causal theory of mental dispositions it is not then necessary to define dispositions operationally. To illustrate: a non-causal theory of brittleness regards it as nothing more than the disposition of an object to break when (say) dropped on hard ground. The character of an object is thus defined directly in terms of possible (i.e. inexistent) relations with other objects. In contrast a causal theory regards brittleness as denoting a certain type of crystalline material-structure defined within the nomological net of physics without reference to any particular set of possible circumstances (impact, sheer, bending etc.) related to other objects. The various particular possibilities are predictable given the properties and states of the object itself. It is these properties and states that are definitive, causally efficacious and central to the causal account of dispositions, not just a particular set of probability inferences concerning end conditions (circumstances) that may contingently obtain. Brittleness inheres in things as structure, and is a causal factor in breaking (a formal cause in Aristotle's terminology).

Accordingly there is hardly more reason to define mental states generally in terms of their aptitude for bringing about behaviour than there is to define brittleness in terms of particular stress conditions instead of inherent structure, or lobsters in terms of their aptness for being boiled and eaten in a restaurant instead of zoological criteria. Once the evidence of neuropsychology is admitted, it is more coherent to define conscious mental states generally in terms of certain sorts of introspectible or immediately (self) evident central nervous states, sub-classes of which as a matter of fact are crucially involved with behaviour and perception. With this shift in emphasis there is no behaviourist problem about after-images, idle wants, transitive sensings and so on; they are other sub-classes of the general class of mental states. Also, other important cases such as dreams and hallucinatory states become intelligible as the 're-programming' of the central nervous system, or even just 'noise', having nothing whatever to do with behaviour.[36]

2.4.3 *The Eliminationist version*

This version of the thesis was anticipated by Farrel,[37] but is associated primarily with Rorty,[38] Feyerabend[39] and Cornman.[40] It is characterised by the thesis that the 'mental' that is identified with the physical is nothing more than a verbal fiction (like demons and phlogiston). It is therefore not even, strictly speaking, proper to speak of identity at all if this implies the existence of the mental side of the equation; for, strictly speaking, the point of the theory is to interpret it out of existence. Feyerabend, for example, has argued that other versions of IT[41]

> try to combine two tendencies in an empirical statement of the form:
> X is a mental process of kind $A \equiv X$ is a physical process of kind α.
> But this hypothesis backfires. It only implies that mental events have physical features; it also seems to imply (if read from right to left) that some physical events, viz. central processes have non-physical features. The monist by the very content of his thesis of monism acknowledges the correctness of a dualist point of view. ... The proper procedure for him to adopt is to develop his theory without any recourse to existent terminology.

Shortcomings

Duality of properties or features denied It seems quite inescapable that the mental and the physical are *phenomenologically* different, that is to say are distinguished by immediately apprehended and confirmable properties. Indeed, this datum is at the very root of the Cartesian dichotomy and, however it is reinterpreted along tough-minded lines, seems bound to be acknowledged.

The concern about phenomenal properties is liable to turn out to be something of a red herring when the important issue is the ontological and cognitive status of the mental and the physical. If it is established on other grounds that this phenomenological dichotomy involves neither an ontological nor an explanatory one, then the identity theorist's essential points have been made and phenomenal properties might be accounted for within the new model.

Adverbial elimination of phenomenal properties Following on the proposal to deny the duality of properties (which in itself may be unimportant), it is sometimes suggested in effect that phenomenal properties can be eliminated *altogether* along with 'sensations', which would be of the utmost importance. It is, for instance, a dubious consequence of Cornman's formulation of an 'adverbial-theory' of objectless sensings (which nevertheless is otherwise an important contribution to the physicalist model of the mental). Briefly it suggests that reporting expressions of the form 'I am having a red sensation' are more appropriately rendered as 'I am sensing redly', that is to say, the object of sense (the red-sensation) is eliminated and what remains is a sen*sing* (process), which may happen to be identical with, and so reducible to, a physical process.[42] The result is actually inconsistent with Cornman's own analysis of manifestly reductivist identity theories, which he rejects on the grounds that sensations have properties that cannot be ascribed to the physical.[43] That is to say, according to Cornman some properties that prohibit a mental–physical reduction supposedly do not prohibit an elimination.

Yet the proposed elimination of sensations and the reduction of sensings to physical processes clearly present the same reductionist problem with regard to phenomenal properties as a straightforward reductionist thesis does. In fact, Cornman thinks he has overcome the problem by arguing that after elimination and reduction there is nothing left for 'mental' properties to be properties of, so that the phenomenal properties of sensations just disappear![44] Another argument he offers is that adverbial 'properties' are not really properties of physical processes or events at all, but merely describe them more precisely.[45] But both of these arguments might equally be advanced in support of the direct reductionist thesis that he has found reason to reject precisely because of irreducible phenomenal properties.

This establishes the requirement for a more adequate account of the phenomenal properties of 'mental' events than has been offered by physicalists so far. Merely to conjure them away by whisking the reference of their grammatical subject out from under their newly acquired adverbial feet, or else by means of cunning verbal disguises such as calling them descriptions instead of properties,[46] is surely unsatisfactory.

Having briefly outlined the essentials of the principal variants of an identity hypothesis and discussed what I take to be some outstanding shortcomings, it is now possible to formulate a re-constituted IT that more adequately represents the explanatory power of the PO model.

3   BIPERSPECTIVISM

3.1   *Three Key Concepts*

Throughout the previous discussion emphasis has been repeatedly placed upon the fundamental importance of root models in providing an adequate conceptual framework for questions as a prerequisite for developing adequate solutions. What I want to suggest is that there are certain general concepts within the emerging PO model, as fleshed out by relatively recent developments in science, which are particularly appropriate for a resolution of the old mind–brain puzzles. Methodologically, this means that we follow Quine and begin 'where we are at', with the information and fruitful hypotheses already available, rather than attempting an impossible regression to a given unstructured epistemological fundament or engaging in untrammelled speculative metaphysics. The concepts I take to be most important are 'organisation', 'relation' and 'channel of communication' (or access). Each of these concepts may be given more or less rigorous mathematical definitions. It is unlikely that such definitions are yet applicable to the biological and psychological domains, however[47] (and if they were, a formal treatment is much beyond this writer's competence). For the present purpose it is sufficient to have a qualitative grasp of the concepts concerned to be able to appreciate their relevance to a physicalist account of mind.

3.1.1 *Organisation*
The importance of the pervasive principle of the association of discrete elements into organised wholes, or systems whose peculiarity lies precisely in their *organisation*, was suggested by Lucretius. It has been stressed with increasing effect in recent times by systems theorists. Initially we can define a system broadly as sets of elements in interrelation.[48] A thing is called a system to identify the unique mode by means of which it is seen. We call a thing a system when we wish to express the fact that the thing is perceived/conceived as consisting of a set of elements or parts, that are connected to each other by at least one discernible distinguishing principle.[49] For example, eleven discrete individual football players constitute a football team, an organised system of footballers. Similarly, a molecule is an organisation of discrete atoms, a watch an organisation of discrete parts, a state an organisation of discrete institutions, and institutions in turn organisations of discrete individuals. And so forth and so on. Organisations or systems affect the character of their constituent sub-systems, which accordingly change their character, or set of relations, when they are outside of the organisation. This is in contrast to aggregates (e.g. piles of wood, heaps of sand, rabbles), whose constituent elements behave in the same way whether they are included in aggregates or not.

3.1.2 *Relation*
Implicit in the concept of organisation or system is the concept of

relation, that is to say the principle through which discrete discernible elements are conjoined together to form an organised whole, whose essence is its organisation.[50] Such a relation holds for example between the discrete numbers 1, 3, 5, 7, when organised in that serial order (and only in that serial order) to form the simple organisation termed arithmetic progression. The relevant relation of the discrete values in the serial organisation is characterised by the general expression for the value of the nth term in the series as '$2n - 1$'.

Relations such as those obtaining in numerical series or between elements of structures (e.g. bridges, and crystals) are essentially static. These contrast with dynamic relations. In dynamic relations the relation between elements is through some change in a functional relationship in time. They are exemplified by vector quantities such as velocity in mechanics, related predator–prey populations in ecology, and market investment indices in economics. Thus, given as elements two discrete bodies, the earth and a motorcar in motion, they are conveniently represented as a simple system in which the two elements are organised through a dynamic relationship represented by the velocity of the motorcar relative to the earth. In both static and dynamic organisations the system and the organised elements are numerically, though not functionally, identical.

3.1.3 *Channel of communication (or mode of access)*

This is the mechanism that governs the transmission of a signal between input and output and is therefore directional. In the human case, sensory receptor cells act as input and motor end-organs as output. The familiar distinction between 'observed' and 'introspected' experience which forms the basis of the concepts of 'physical' and 'mental' domains of conscious awareness can be more definitely characterised in terms of the channels of communication or modes of access through which information is processed. It will be recalled that the PO model of consciousness has already been elucidated in terms of 'experienced integration' of the brain's functional subsystems (Section 5.2.2 of Chapter III).

The distinction now to be drawn is suggested by considering, first, that the quality of our experience of objects in the 'external world' is radically dependent upon the sense modality through which causal links between the brain and the outside world are completed. The world we ordinarily perceive is structured by a combination of the inputs to sight, hearing, smell, taste and touch in conjunction with the kinaesthetic sense. The peculiar quality of experience associated with a channel of communication through a given sense modality is, quite simply, not available to an individual in whom the necessary sensory system is absent or otherwise inoperative. The blind man has no conception of the quality of visual experience. This is evident from, for instance, the fact that people who have had vision endowed in later life are unable to discriminate shape visually (as they are able to do colour) though the capacity for shape discrimination through touch is well established.[51] That is to say, the visual quality of shape is radically different from the tactile quality, though the two sets of information (those mediated through vision and touch) have a common origin and are combined in the normal perception of the shaped object. In short: *the quality of experience of the external world is determined by the sense through which it is mediated.*

Also, it is well established that the peculiar quality of experience mediated through a given sensory channel is independent of the ultimate origin of the information signal. This is demonstrated by the clinical evidence of cases where the nerves from different sensory channels in the afferent systems have become cross-connected, so that, for example, inputs to a tactual nerve that has been connected to an audial channel to the brain are experienced as sound. Similarly, cross-connection in the efferent system can, for example, 'railroad' an intention to smile into a wink. The same conclusion can be drawn from the evidence of 'phantom limbs', where amputees continue to report feeling the limb. Such cases are attributed to the spontaneous or extraneously induced activity of the residual sensory channels. In short: *the quality of experience determined by the activity of a neural net forming a sense channel is invariant with respect to the origin of the activating stimulus.*

To generalise: different channels of communication within the range of external sense determine different qualities of immediate experience. Similar differences hold for intradermal sense (i.e. proprioception and positional sense). This suggests that the phenomenal basis for the conceptual distinction intradermal or internal versus external is the qualitative difference in experience determined only by different sense modalities. By normal extension, brain processes not specifically associated with sense uniquely determine the quality of experience Kant called inner sense, i.e. memory, imagination, emotion, etc. This is born out by the evidence from brain pathology and electrode stimulation of the brains of conscious and articulate subjects. For example, what goes on in the occipital lobes is experienced as vision; what goes on in the amygdala is experienced as rage. The difference between vision and rage is the difference between occipital lobe-centred processes and amygdalan-centred processes (i.e. processes centred in different areas of the physical brain), not a difference between the physical and the non-physical.

3.2   *Mind as Organisation, as Relations and as Mode of Access to the Brain*

Having characterised the PO system's concepts of 'organisation', 'relation' and 'access', we are now in a position to reconsider more fully the puzzles of mind and brain and the nature of their interaction. To do this it is convenient to proceed by degrees, by reconsidering two theories of mind that attempt to solve the puzzles by laying the (ontological) ghost of the orthodox Cartesian thinking thing. Although, as I believe, each attempt makes an important conceptual gain over the problematic OA account, it is also evident that each leaves unsatisfied some essential requirement of a completely adequate account.

3.2.1   *Mind as organisation*

According to a quasi-behaviourist analysis, we begin to understand the nature of the concept of mind if we grasp the character of the relationship between different logical categories of discourse. Ryle's[52] well-known rendering of this argument appeals to analogies in the relations between a university and its constituent colleges, museums, libraries and so on, and similarly between an army and its constituent divisions, regiments, companies and so on. Rehearsing the argument, in such cases it is an ontological mistake to suppose that the university or the army are something numerically additional to their constituent elements. What we have essentially are not two sorts of *things*, but *two ways of talking* about the same thing(s), two logically distinct descriptive and explanatory categories. The next move is by appeal to zeugma: to show that logical absurdity results from conjoining concepts from different categories as in 'she came home in tears and a sedan chair' (because in this expression 'in' functions equivocally between the different categories appropriate to 'tears' and 'sedan chair'). From these considerations it is argued that mind is not a ghostly substantial thinking-thing as is supposed. To use Brian Farrell's expression, it is not the sort of thing that is a 'sort of thing' at all. 'Mind' functions conceptually and in discourse in much the same way that 'university' and 'army' do. The confusion in the orthodox view of mind has remained undetected because the grammatical correctness of expressions employing substantive 'mental' terms disguises their categorial irregularity. Once this is revealed, it becomes clear that, just as when we talk about a university we are referring to (an organisation of) discrete colleges and so on, likewise when we talk about mind we are talking in a particular way about discrete behavioural acts (or dispositions to act), and nothing else. Ergo, the orthodox concept of mind as a substance is a specious, para-mechanical hypothesis, a verbal mirage.

This ingenious approach to a solution to the old body–mind puzzle makes a very important gain by demonstrating that mind is not a substantial sort of thing (be it ever so ghostly). The anti-Cartesian criticism goes too far, however, in supposing that because the mind is not numerically additional to observable (macro-) bodily objects and events then it is nothing at all. For, *pace* Ryle and the whole behaviourist tenor, to be consciously aware is not merely to be behaving or to be apt to behave in a certain way. To suppose that it is, as Ogden and Richards first pointed out, is to feign anaesthesia.[53] And it is also to ignore everything that has been learned about the central nervous system and its relation to behaviour during more than a century of investigation. Indeed, the behaviourist's arguments ring hollow once it is recognised that the head is not.[54]

Mental states such as reverie or dreaming for example are not characterised by their aptness for bringing about even verbal–descriptive behaviour about reveries and dreams (as Ryle and Malcolm would have it) any more than a lobster (as already remarked) is characterised by its familiar but inessential aptness to be potted and *haute cuisine*d. The 'whatever it is' that distinguishes 'mind' from the aggregate of behavioural elements is the basis of the category difference and so of the category mistakes. Ryle stresses the logical distinction, but does not elucidate its basis, beyond asserting that it is perfectly proper to say in one logical tone of voice that there exist minds and in another logical tone of voice that there exist bodies. The basis of the logical distinction is the organisation inherent both in intelligent patterns of discriminative behaviour and in the physiological processes necessary to it. Accordingly, while mind is not a substantial something, neither is it a nothing; it has to do with the *organisation* of the behaving system and its observable behaviour.

3.2.2 *Mind as relations*

A relational theory of mind which presumes the central importance of organisation has recently been advanced by John Taylor, among others.[55] This reformulates the traditional materialist account more specifically in terms of the physiology and logic of neural networks and by analogies with electronic data-processing systems. As in other central-state theories, the evidence for mental events is taken to be problem-solving behaviour at the macroscopic level. The basis of such behaviour – the basis of 'mind' – is taken to lie in the covert micro-processes in the neural nets comprising the decision elements of the central nervous system. The novel feature of this account of mind is the suggestion that, like mathematical relations, the dynamic relationships between the states of the physical organisation of neural nets embodying memory in the brain and the changes in state brought about by internal and external processes are not additional to the discrete neural elements related (i.e., they are not 'something'), but they are the non-physical basis of mind. Mind is based in the ongoing processes of comparison of data, or the continuous changes in system state in the limbic and reticular formations of the brain. As Taylor says: 'I am suggesting that mental sensations have non-physical characters in that they are composed of relationships with other ongoing sensations'.[56]

The indifference to philosophical niceties suggested by Taylor's formulation does not detract from the real advance made. The advance is the recognition that, while 'mind' is not *something* in the same way that the brain is a thing, it is not merely a verbal mirage either. Positively, it suggests that mind is in the ongoing comparison *relations* within an organisation of neural nets.

By saying nothing more than that mind is in the changing relations among physical states, however, we are still left with the residual phenomenal puzzle of the difference in quality between the mental and the physical. This difficulty is apparent in the question-begging locution that Taylor is driven to in order to formulate the relational theory. The 'non-physical character' of mental sensations is accounted for by its being composed of relationships with 'other ongoing sensations'. Clearly this is question-begging, and does nothing to elucidate the conceptual transition from 'system states' and 'relations' to 'sensations' and 'mind'.

3.2.3 *Mind as channel of communication or access (biperspectivism)*
The notion of mind can be further clarified, beyond the advances made by the organisational and relational insights, by returning to the notion of access previously outlined.

Since the notion of *access* is central to an adequate PO account of the mind–brain puzzle, further elaboration is in order. Intelligent life involves making significant discriminations in the individual's (i.e. subject-system's) interaction with the world. The discriminatory *behaviour* that I manifest is not different from another's, and is known to me through my external sense channels. The discriminations that I observe myself make are therefore not essentially different from the discriminations I observe others making.[57] In my own case, however, I am a privileged observer; in the case of others I am not. What is different is that I have direct or non-inferential access to my internal processes. Indeed, in an important sense I *am* my internal processes. I do not (normally) have access to the internal processes of others because (normally) there is no channel of communication open to me. Quite simply, the channels normally end at the other's epidermis. Of course, as many modern materialists have argued, I do *in principle* have access to the intradermal processes of another (his 'covert behaviour') by using instruments that act as prostheses to my senses for this purposes, such as the stethoscope, the fibre optic intrascope or the electro-encephalograph. Such devices are, however, nothing more than sensory prostheses which extend the range which I normally have access to *with my external senses*. The various information channels open to the perceiving subject can be represented diagrammatically as in Figure 4.1.

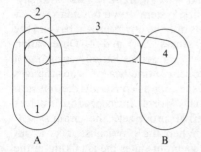

A Self

B Other

1 Self–information path – internal

2 Self–information path – external

3 (Normal) other information path – external

4 (Prosthetic) other information path – internal

Figure 4.1

The important feature of this open system representation of the information flow-paths characteristic of observation and introspection is that it establishes the basis of the physical–mental distinction in the channels of information flow in relation to boundaries. Para-normal possibilities aside, this representation is essentially ontologically neutral, though it is not insignificant that the system boundaries are physically determined by the epidermis and the extremities of the external sense organs. Here also, incidentally, is a representation of the old subjective idealist puzzle that all experience is 'mental' since both 'inner' and 'outer' channels are integrated in the same brain. This account is similar in essentials to that offered by Bertrand Russell, who suggested that[58]

> when, on a common sense basis, people talk of the gulf between mind and matter – what they really have in mind is the gulf between a visual or tactile percept and a 'thought' – e.g. a memory, a pleasure or a volition. But this as we have seen is a division within the mental world.

What is suggested here, however, is not an essentially idealist account of a division within the mental world, but a realist account; namely that the nature of the division is determined by the physical channels of access through which information is communicated.

The 'luminous' quality of consciousness that the observing system has of its own processes of discrimination is associated with the direct *access* of self-information, what Kant called inner sense and D. M. Armstrong has recently called self-scanning.

On an organisational—relational theory of mind, then, a given brain process can be integrated with and brought within the brain 'scanning' processes sustaining consciousness, by different channels of communication represented by 1, 2, 3 and 4 in Figure 4.1. That is to say, either *directly*, from within the cognating system's own boundaries 1, or *indirectly*, via communication channels into the environment beyond the system boundaries via the external senses 2, 3 and 4. Observation involves loops into the environment via the senses (strictly speaking, a subject—object supra-system); and so discontinuities or state-changes (data) within the internal sections of such loops constitute the physical domain within the privileged observer's world. Introspection involves channels restricted entirely to internal processes, the brain's self-scannings constituting inner sense. When the physicalist talks about 'comparison relations among successive brain states' he is talking in the *observer* mode related to channels of communication giving access via the external senses; that is to say, he is referring (essentially) to the physical processes of *another* (though he may have access to his own processes, *as if* they were those of another, through external sense). When the relations are between states within his own epidermis, the processes of his own central nervous system unmediated through external sense, they have the phenomenal quality that constitutes the mental world of the (privileged) observer. The privilege is with respect to the intradermal processes of the central nervous system of his own body.

It is interesting and instructive to note that previous talk in a similar vein about 'inner' and 'outer' modes of access to a unique process relied on a misleading 'container' metaphor or model. Thus:[59]

> When anyone stands inside a sphere its convex side is for him quite hidden by the concave surface; conversely, when he stands outside, the concave surface is hidden by the convex. Both sides belong together as inseparably as the psychical and bodily sides of a human being, and these also may by way of a simile be regarded as inner and outer sides; but it is just as impossible to see both sides of a circle from a standpoint in the plane of the circle, as to see these two sides of humanity from a standpoint in the plane of human existence.

As the open-systems model shows, the subject's inner processes can of course be mediated to him through the external senses (channel 2 in Figure 4.1) and accordingly have the same 'quality' for him as those of another's (channel 4 in Figure 4.1).

The duality exploited by the container metaphor has been appealed to by some recent philosophers as evidence for a substantial mind–body dichotomy.[60] Such appeals are ill-founded, however, if the open-systems model offered is appropriate. (This is a matter to be decided by the tests of experience, understanding and predictive power.) The intradermal central nervous processes which are directly accessible to the 'scanning' system of the individual whose nervous system it is (as 'mental' processes) are one with the processes accessible to any other individual observer via the sense organs (as physical processes). This identification is logically *contingent* precisely because the 'logical' division is grounded in the discernibility of qualities determined by the different channels of communication. What is philosophically significant is that the discernibles so identified have a common reference, viz. an ontologically unique physical process. There is no sanction, therefore, in the discernible qualitative division between mental and physical aspects of experience, for any claim for a substantive 'mind' or a uniquely psychic domain outside that in which physical processes have their being.

3.2.4   *Analogies of identity*
The open-systems model also illuminates some difficulties in previous formulations of an hypothesis of contingent identity between mental and physical discernibles. These have usually employed helpful and suggestive analogies which break down in crucial respects, and fail to represent precisely that qualitative discernibility which is at the root of the problem. This failing arises from the fact that analogies have been drawn from common domains of experience corresponding to the same information channels, whereas the problem arises from the qualitative distinction between experience of internal and external sense-mediated channels. The analogies have therefore been incomplete in this vital respect. For example, the identity holding between $2 + 2$ and 4 is a conceptual identity; that is to say, '2' '4' and ' + ' have a purely 'mental' status.[61] The identity holding between water droplets and clouds[62] is an identity of physical composition, both droplets and clouds being entities mediated by the senses. And the same goes for the 'morning star' and the 'evening star' identity.[63]

Perhaps the most helpful analogy offered so far has been that of the gene and the DNA molecule,[64] because 'gene' is a theoretical operationally defined term and DNA is an essentially observable substance. Even in this case, however, the gene concept is an inferential structuring of sense-mediated observations. None of these analogies in fact spans the radical division, which has been stressed since Descartes, between the experience we have of the 'other' which is mediated through external sense, and our immediate experience as privileged 'observers' of our own processes. By stressing the concept of access, and by using the open-systems communication channel model, it seems possible adequately to represent at the same time ontic unity and the orthodox discernibility of mental and physical aspects of experience as immediate and mediate modes of access to that unity.

4 SOME ASPECTS OF THE PHYSICALIST MODEL OF THE MENTAL

In order to elucidate the conceptual model briefly outlined above it may be useful to discuss a number of important related points.

4.1 *The Physical*

Much misunderstanding is generated among philosophers by talk about materialism and mechanism because for them these terms continue to have medieval connotations. For many, materialism and physicalism still mean stones and tables and mechanism means clockwork.[65] Even when a comparatively radical physicalism is proposed, it turns out that vestiges of these basic models are still operative. Sellars's conception of the scientific image of man which he suggests might displace the (orthodox) manifest image is a case in point. He contemplates the replacement of the person as the basic logical category by collections of elementary particles, as suggested by science.[66]

One important consequence of this is that he finds it necessary to invent and defend the status of 'sensa' as items in the scientific image against an adverbial theory of objectless sensings on the grounds that sensing is an anthropomorphic concept which is inapplicable to collections of basic particles.[67] But since a complete scientific image must include the phenomenal qualities of sense (to explain certain propositional attitudes, viz. talking about sensations), there must be sensory qualia predicable of the scientific image.[68] However, since he also maintains that a basic property of an aggregate must be a property of its basic constituents (i.e. there are no emergent spook-properties), it seems inescapable on this view that either spook *items* called 'sensa' are concocted or, even more dubious, that the basic particles of physics must have the basic 'sensed' property; i.e., because, being a primitive predicate, 'sensing redly' can be true collectively of wholes consisting of particles or nerve-cells only if it is true of them severally.[69] But none of this dubious metaphysics is required of the physicalist. To take a similar case: the concept of heat as elucidated by molecular kinetic theory and physiology does not require either 'heat sensa' or that each molecule be hot, but only that there be certain specifiable relationships between mean dynamic energy levels of collections of molecules and certain components of the central nervous system.[70]

The physicalist's problem with 'sensa' is salutory because it is resolved by recognising that sets of elements in interrelation (systems) may manifest properties in virtue of their systemic relations alone. The systemic relations are not occult properties. They are certainly intersubjectively perspicuous and they may well be mathematically determinable also. And it is precisely with the development of this systems-cybernetic model of the physical objective world that science acquires the conceptual capacity to describe adequately human behaviour and its mental determinants in physical terms.

'The systems view of the world' as adumbrated by von Bertalanffy, Laszlo and others does not find it necessary to draw a sharp line between animate and inanimate or between system and sub-system. Instead, based both on the primitive assumption that there is general order to be found in the universe and on the empirical evidence of the developing sciences, it postulates a hierarchical continuum of systems embracing sub-atomic particles, atoms, molecules, cells, multi-cellular organisms and ultimately societies. This terrestrial hierarchy of physical systems, it is suggested, provides the proper context for an analysis of human behaviour and mind.[71] When this mature conception of the physical has been developed, even the most cogent criticism of a physicalist account of mind as somehow identical with the brain (*qua* collection of billiard balls) is answerable, namely the appeal to contextual determinants of mental concepts (see Chapter V below, Section 4). This requires a considerable refinement of the supposedly primitive atomistic model of materialism, yet this can be achieved without contravening the essentials of an objective–physicalist model, namely realism, inter-subjective testability and lawfulness.[72]

As Spinoza has already recognised, even within a purely materialistic model, regardless of how highly developed the self-awareness and independent activity of an individual living system may be, only the universe (seen as nature and society) is an absolutely perfect cause unto itself. Therefore, individual systems such as the human body are related through a complex network of interconnections to the environment. The evolution of the brain coincides with the increasingly effective co-ordination of the processes of active adaptation to the environment.

In groups such as human societies the basic mediating link in the interconnections with the environment, and hence the leading link in the *internal* interconnections, is precisely the external and nervous activity of the individual. Individuals are separated from each other anatomically, but this is an illusory independence. The brain first developed as an organ of primarily internal interconnections and then primarily as an organ of interconnection with the environment. This augmented the dependence of the organism on far more distant and complex events in the environment. Kremanskiy employs the vivid metaphor of the brain coming to act as a Trojan horse 'by means of which the external environment penetrates into the very depths of the leading subsystem of the higher animal organism and from there, after having assumed the form of definite groups of its own internal impulses, directs its internal and external activity'.[73]

Among the most important constituents of the *human* individual's environment, of course, are the other human individuals with whom he participates in a community extending in both space and time. This community is a system of communication channels formed in terrestrial media (light, air, electrics, etc.) and is continuous with the synaptic pulses of each individual's nervous system. Against this background, Vygotsky's seemingly paradoxical thesis makes sense: that voluntary (as opposed to quantum–spontaneous or random) activity lies not within the individual but in the social history of the human community. The roots of voluntary action begin when the adult gives the child verbal instruction, progresses to (imitative) self-expressed verbal instruction and eventually reaches the stage at which behaviour is immediately subordinate to unexpressed instruction. At this final, mature, stage, the control previously exercised by others is internalised and regulates the higher forms of active behaviour which are thus social in origin, dependent on speech for their structure and 'voluntary' in their cause.[74]

The brain with which the mind is to be identified in the developed PO model is thus conceived not as a closed (cranial) system, but as a living, open, sub-system of a super-ordinate social system (or number of co-existing systems). Its development and functioning therefore embodies the neurally encoded constraints imposed through its complex superordinate relations.

Reductionism

What emerges from this discussion is that the PO model is not, as some theorists have maintained, committed to the dubious view that any set of physical laws adequate for a description of human behaviour and mental phenomena must be ultimately reducible to the 'Victorian' laws of elementary particle physics and chemistry.[75] Such extreme reductionism appears to derive from a residual positivist phobia about the occult together with the belief that once conscious states appear on the biological scene their occurrence alters the functional relations between neurophysiological variables in contravention of the ultimate *physical* laws of the universe. However, it seems likely that a non-reductionist approach based on hierarchical and general system principles is capable in principle of rendering an adequate account of human behaviour and the mental without departing from a fundamentally physicalist–realist conception.[76]

On this model the 'emergence' of mind is no Bergsonian spook principle: it is conceptually no more problematical than, for example, the systemic–hierarchical shifts from sub-atomic to atomic or atomic to molecular phenomena in the inanimate domain of physics. There, the dynamical structure of forces takes on different stable forms at different orders of organisation without the intervention of extra-physical factors other than *configuration* or organisation. As Laszlo has pointed out,[77]

> the concept of hierarchy composed of systems defined by invariant general properties does not connote reductionism and is well capable of accounting for the manifest diversity of functions and properties in nature. Fresh qualities can emerge in the hierarchy in the form of new transformations of invariant properties. Such nova are accounted for by a consideration that systems of each level contain systems at all lower levels, plus their combination within the whole formed at that level.

4.2 *Consciousness, Order and Hierarchy*

Many philosophers remain baffled as to how the quality of illumination termed consciousness could ever be thought to be a property of matter. As we have seen, they argue that, if consciousness is not a property of basic material particles or elementary combinations of these, then it is altogether inconceivable that it should be identical with a greater degree of something of which a lesser degree would be unconscious.[78] Against this view pious metaphysicians of previous generations (e.g. Locke and Spinoza) were satisfied to argue that if matter was created by an omnipotent God then there could be no limit to its powers. Such reliance on authority is not good enough nowadays.

The modern materialist's tack has been to show how purely material substance can manifest characteristically mind-directed behaviour. Examples of quasi-intelligent 'behaviour' are ready to hand even at comparatively rudimentary levels of nature. The *prima facie* teleology of rivers in navigating their course to the sea-goal, and the tropistic machinations of carnivorous plants are commonly cited examples. More often cited (and more often persuasive) has been the performance of artefacts. Descartes himself was impressed enough by the hydraulic automata at Versailles to formulate a mechanistic metaphysic of nature which stopped short only of man himself. His successors, beginning with La Mettrie, have pressed the analogy to include man himself also.

85

In recent times the artefacts have taken on an electronic form and achieved quite spectacular levels of performance such as chess-playing, pattern recognition and some complex operations requiring the execution of incompletely specified tasks. The arguments from physical artefacts to the physical basis of mind ('machino-morphism'), based on analogy and normal extrapolation of these facts, are well known.[79]

The objections to such arguments are equally well known and turn mainly on the truth that such artefacts are precisely that – artefacts: the artificial product of human intelligence, programmed to achieve humanly conceived goals according to logical procedures arrived at and precisely specified only after enormous analytical labour and test by *human* persons.[80] It has been said that with present methods the sophistication of an ant would probably require the whole of Britain's computer resources. So whither Artificial Intelligence?[81] But all that this need indicate is that the apostles of 'machino-morphism' have chosen inappropriate models.

The proper orientation towards this question is indicated by von Neumann's distinction between what we ordinarily take to be logic and mathematics (i.e. that of the designer and the programmer) and the intrinsic logic of the central nervous system. The latter must be relatively imprecise, and yet out of its integrative action is generated the exactitude of the logic (or logics) of conscious awareness. On a physicalist thesis some sort of invariancing and integrative-fusion processes are presumably involved, to be discovered by a future neuropsychology of logic. It seems likely that until the relationship between the intrinsic logic of the central nervous system and the ordinary logic of computer hardware and software is established, then nothing that can be called a truly artificial intelligence will be developed to justify the more zealous philosophical arguments from machine intelligence to a mechanistic account of mind. But to conclude from this that an essentially physicalist account of the mental is unwarranted would be mistaken.

Some recent work in genetics and artificial intelligence, based upon quite different premises from the conventional hardware/software *design* approach, suggests a possible basis for the relation between intrinsic and conscious logics. First of all, the commonplace and commonsense idea that nothing structured can grow spontaneously out of disorder has been seriously questioned in a thoroughgoing way. It has always been open to metaphysical doubt (viz. the PO root model); and with, for example, Miller's organic synthesis from inanimate materials, it has been open to scientific doubt also.[82] However, the evolutionary gap between the spontaneous precipitation of certain amino acids and the appearance on the biological scene of regenerative intelligent organisms is considerable. It has been commonly supposed by natural scientists that this gap can be filled in in terms of the basic PO model and *chance*, because the intervening period was very long and conditions very favourable. Furthermore, magical occurrences aside, the facts stand as pudding-proof that something of the sort took place. It probably did, but there has been growing doubt about whether even the large time scales undoubtedly involved are alone adequate to account for evolution by random mutation and natural selection.

Kauffman has now shown this doubt is probably warranted. There is reason to suppose that a fortuitous evolutionary history has not selected only highly ordered genetic regulatory circuits which alone ensure metabolic stability. Living things are not akin to precisely programmed automata selected by evolution. However there is good reason to believe that stability is to be expected of randomly interconnected regulatory circuits. Living things are akin to randomly assembled automata whose characteristic behaviour reflects their unorderly construction, no matter how evolution selected the surviving forms.[83] He has demonstrated that a completely random tangle of two input/one output logic elements quickly adopts stable patterns of behaviour when subject to structured patterns of input. Whereas such a random tangle of, for example, 1000 logical elements would be expected, on a completely random–equiprobable basis, to have behaviour cycles of 10^{150} states (compared with an estimated age of the universe of 10^{23} microseconds), in fact there is an immense restriction of behaviour to cycles of a few hundred states in length.[84]

Kauffman himself has taken the two input/one output unit as an analogue of the biological gene, and on this basis has made accurate predictions of a number of biological phenomena including cell replication time in various organisms as a function of the number of genes per cell, and the number of cell types in an organism as a function of its number of genes. These results have been arrived at from genetic considerations, but the model is formally identical to nerve-net models. Aleksander, for example, has taken the principle that a tangle of logical circuits is *predisposed* to act in a stable and orderly manner to be the basis of intelligent behaviour in entire complex networks (such as the brain). Synthetic nets of this kind, with inputs connected to photo-sensors, acquire short cycles of activity associated with classes of patterns applied during an initial 'training' period, patterns within each class being similar to one another. After training, such a net will enter one of a set of well-defined areas of state-activity. Aleksander has suggested that the net makes its own internal 'state-activity' model of its environment during training and enters these stable state structures as a sign of its recognition of its environment.[85] It is a striking fact that any design that brings about order in the net, such as insistence on special linear logical functions in the elements or the ordering of the inter-connections, (positively) tends to destroy the net's predisposition to stability.[86]

Apropos the controversy over machine intelligence, the parallel between learning nets and the human nervous system is obvious, and strikingly bears out the earlier hypothesis of Craik and Hebb already mentioned: that the neural basis of mentality lies in the formation of cell assemblies or neural analogues of the external world. The principle of structure emerging out of disorder in response to environmental stimuli provides a physicalist conceptual model of many cognitive functions (perception, memory etc.). The emergent nature of consciousness has recently been discussed in terms of the functional integration of processes which, when unintegrated, are unconscious.

4.2.1 *Functional integration*

Although brain mass and complexity are certainly decisive factors determining mental capacity, it is evident that even taken together they are not the sole determinants. This is graphically suggested by the fact that an assiduous post-mortem micro-dissection of Lenin's brain failed to indicate any neurone—anatomical basis for his extraordinary mentality. This might easily be accounted for by the further, dynamic, factor of *functional* integration. The concept of 'function' has been considerably elucidated in recent neuropsychology.[87] Notwithstanding the evidence for a significant degree of localised function, the old idea that control of complex cognitive and motor skills is vested in a single 'potifical cell' (or oligarchical group of cells) has given way to the central concept of 'functional system', that is a complex regulative system which establishes certain relationships within the organism or between the organism and the environment and produces some form of adaptive effect. It is now clear that seemingly discrete capabilities (e.g. simple limb movements) involve the integrated action of complex neural systems. In this way neural systems may be permutated and combined (functionally integrated) as sub-systems in any number of different superordinate systems, much as the units of speech are assembled into meaningful expressions or standard machine components are assembled into unique configurations such as a motorcar with its structural, mechanical, hydraulic, electrical and fuel systems.

Failure to appreciate this fact accounts for earlier confusion about the mental topography of the brain, since the integrity of superordinate neuronic systems underlying phenomenologically or introspectively discrete faculties might break down at any one of the links through its integrated but functionally independent sub-systems. The precise nature of the failure of the superordinate system would be evident only from the secondary symptoms attributable to malfunction of the failed subordinate system. Failure to understand speech, for example, may be due to failure either of retention (with malfunction of the temporal lobe), or of simultaneous synthesis of the speech elements into a coherent whole or logical scheme (with malfunction of the parieto-occipital zones of the left hemisphere), or of significance-analysis (with malfunction of the frontal zones), or of any combination of these. To the observer the manifest result is the same, yet the mechanisms are quite different.[88]

4.2.2 *Consciousness (as 'experienced integration')*

Consciousness, which is at the very centre of the mind–body world-knot, remains largely problematical, yet there is important general agreement on some important facts. Neuropsychologists seem agreed on Lawrence Kubie's claim that there is no action that we cannot perform in an unconscious state which we can do in a conscious state[89] (though it seems that we do not *learn* or *memorise* in unconscious or inattentive states). Since it is a central tenet of the prevailing evolutionary wisdom that nature would neither create nor tolerate gratuitously anything so prodigious and complex as consciousness, this thesis does seem paradoxical. It becomes more persuasive, however, if we recall such celebrated examples of unconscious or quasi-conscious machinations as Poincaré's identification of the transformations used to define Fuchean functions with those of non-Euclidean geometry,[90] and Kekule's formulation of the structure of the benzene molecule.[91]

The issues involved become clearer if they are formulated in terms of the concept of functional integration just described. Consciousness has to do with the functional integration of the brain's neuronic sub-systems into functionally superordinate systems. This involves interaction between three phylogenetically distinct brains, the reptilean (brain stem), the lower mammalian (sub-cortical system of the diencephalon), and the higher mammalian (cortex), initiated and sustained by 'recruiting signals' from the brain stem reticular formation.[92]

> It is the *congregation* of [such] activities within the nervous system that may be considered the physiological basis of consciousness and the congregation cannot legitimately be dissected into its components. The difficulty is not that in some vague and mystical way 'the whole is greater than the sum of its parts', but much more simply, that it is the *relation* between the various multiple activities that is of importance.

Human mentality and personality, dependent as it is on the integration of three phylogenetically distinct brains, has been vividly compared to a 1960s car with a 1940s carburettor and a 1920s generator.[93]

To pursue the earlier analogy between consciousness and meaning in speech: just as the significance of a statement lies neither in its symbols, nor words, nor syntax, nor semantics, nor context, nor form of life, but in the relationship of all of these within the functionally integrated whole which together they comprise, so consciousness is based in a congregation of brain activities. An analysis of this sort has the advantage of providing a causal account of the phenomenology of consciousness which includes as well as waking, normal sleep, the sleep-dream, the waking dream of psychotics, neuroses, multiple personality, double consciousness, etc., in terms of systemic integration and differentiation. This is in principle coherent with both the scientific description of brain physiology and a conceptual analysis of ordinary usage in so far as this reflects the phenomenology of consciousness.

Consciousness on this account is not to be conceived as a substantial or qualitative something which can in any literal sense be said to enter into the processes of the brain. Rather it is to be thought of as 'experienced integration', to use Fessard's term,[94] and as having an existential status analogous to that of, for example, the superordinate systemic function of complex molecules as distinct from that of the constituent atoms. With a final spin of the wheel of analogy, we should say that consciousness does not exist, only states of consciousness, just as 'disease' does not exist, but only diseased bodily states.

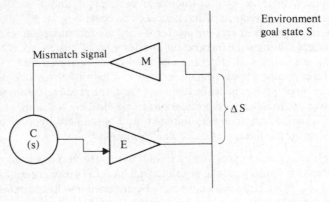

Figure 4.2

The general concept of 'functional integration' towards consciousness has been further elucidated in terms of hierarchies of neural feedback loops which are known to exist in the brain.[95] The loops carry secondary messages, that is to say messages about primary messages, or intradermal state changes reflecting reactions to extradermal state

90

changes. MacKay[96] has proposed an information flow model along these lines which with some modification is essentially as shown in Figure 4.2. The familiar elementary feedback control loop embodied in the thermostatic control is taken as a paradigm. The basic sub-systems interacting with the environment are an effector E (e.g. a heater), a monitor M (e.g. a thermocouple), and a comparator, or calculator, C. For any given environmental goal state S, the comparator embodies a corresponding sub-system state (s). Information received from the environment is compared with the represented 'goal-state' in the comparator. Coincidence or zero mismatch on comparison constitutes the environment's steady state. Finite deviation from this state ΔS, results in a mismatch between environment and goal state. This difference constitutes a primary reaction signal and activates the effector input to the environment in such a way as to tend to restore the equilibrium goal state. Of this basic picture Mackay has suggested that perception is represented by the activity of updating the conditional state to match current sensory data. The focus of attention has its correlate in the region of the field of incoming data against which the state of the system is currently being evaluated.[97]

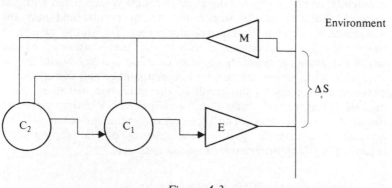

Figure 4.3

The model may be elaborated by introducing a second-order system (which takes as *its* environment the first-order comparator) as shown in Figure 4.3. As the first-order comparator C_1 senses state changes in the environment (primary signals), and thereby the effects of interaction through the effector, the second-order comparator C_2 senses state changes in the environment and the effects of interaction *through the first-order comparator*. In this way, the performance of the first-order comparator as well as that of the effector are subject to surveillance and regulation.[98]

It is easy to see that comparators embodying stable-state structures of the sort developed in the learning nets described by Aleksander are statistically self-organising systems of the kind envisaged by Mackay, and are capable of self-organising development under the influence of statistically ordered inputs from both the environment and lower-order comparators, in the way required for such hierarchical organisation. And as Mackay says:[99]

> If an organisation whose information system embodies an adaptive organiser may be said to '*know*' the fact to which the organiser is adaptive, then it would seem that one which embodies a motor-organising system on the foregoing lines could be said (other things being equal) to *know that it knows*. Obviously we can envisage an indefinite hierarchy of such learning nets or imitative organisers. This more than any other feature of our information flow model we might guess to be the main discriminant of systems capable of sustaining consciousness as we know it.

The concept of consciousness as the intrinsic self-awareness of certain functionally integrated feedback hierarchies also elucidates both the apparently simple quality of conscious phenomena (compared with the complex character of the underlying neural events) and also the emergence of mind in the natural hierarchies. The simple quality of given phenomenal experience is due to the fusion produced by the integrative action of neural hierarchies (a crude analogy would be the way an electric motor appears to rotate smoothly and continuously, although this motion is the result of the integrated action of many discrete phase-spaced induction windings transiently imparting momentum to the rotor). The emergence of mind in nature on this account is compresent with the emergence of the appropriately organised feedback hierarchies of neural nets.

4.3   *Adverbial Sensing (Objectless and Subjectless)*

Some at least of the mind–brain puzzles that have bedevilled philosophers are almost certainly the result of the basically static subject–predicate grammatical form. In English for example 'The sky is blue', whereas in Russian 'The sky blues' (i.e. dynamically). Even more striking is the oriental form. In English we say 'I see the red flower', whereas a literal rendering in Orientalese is something like 'seeing red-reflecting flowering in space near me-ing'.[100] In saying 'The flower is red' Chinese makes no translation of 'to be'. 'Red' as simple adjective meaning redness and as verb meaning 'to redden' is all covered by 'hong'. The idea of redness is well enough linked to flower by 'hong' alone.[101] It may be thought that its lack of clear word functions (here the verb–adjective overlap) could make Chinese a poor medium for logical and philosophical ideas where categories may be as important as what is expressed.[102] However, another view is that the importance attached to categories, and so to category mistakes, is a philosophical aberration endemic to Western philosophy as a consequence of the basic subject–predicate form of the Indo-European languages.

If so, and if the oriental forms express mental content more aptly, then Chinese would be on the contrary a rich medium for discussion of philosophy of mind. This opens up the intriguing prospect that before they can aptly express mental content Western philosophers must learn to think with the cyberneticians and talk with the Chinese! Certainly the dynamic or adverbial forms are conspicuously less likely than the static to trigger off ontological quests for blues or reds or blue or red domains; and what is more, they are consistent with the dynamic comparison–relation model of perception and cognition outlined above. The mere fact that such locutions may seem 'barbarous' to Anglo-Saxon ears because they are not the language game we usually play[103] is not reason enough for offering *a priori* xenophobic resistance to them, if they are less misleading or more appropriate for representing the phenomenal properties of conscious awareness.

4.3.1 *Sensing as objectless*

The problems of phenomenological language have long been recognised even by philosophers in the broadly analytical tradition,[104] and locutions closer to the oriental have been proposed to represent phenomenal properties. It is along these lines that the adverbial materialist account of sensations has been developed by Cornman among others.[105] An outline has already been given of this proposal (in Section 2.4.3 above), and it was argued then that, although the elimination of sensations (*qua* objects) from the ontological scene is important for the development of a PO model, phenomenal *properties* of sensings could not be so eliminated. In fact, although Cornman's 'sensing' is an ambiguous term, he fails to distinguish between anthropomorphic sensings (which Sellars, for example, apparently takes to be the only relevant sense) and the technological connotation which is already applicable *without* obvious anthropomorphic analogy to the functioning of purely physical sensors (thermocouples, optical densitometers, etc.). It is of course the latter that Cornman takes to be potentially reducible to or identical with material processes.

If we are to avoid denying the duality (or the plurality) of *properties*, as Cornman does, then some account of them should be available within the physicalist framework. The basis of such an account has already

93

been outlined in the biperspectivist model of the mental. Phenomenal properties on this account are intrinsic to the functioning of channels of communication as immediately experienced. Pepper offers as a vivid illustration of this point the case of the Penfieldian subject who is able to listen (with ears and temporal lobes) to a piece of music, while simultaneously watching (with eyes and occipital lobes) the hearing activity.[106] The temporal lobe activity is available to such a subject in two modalities: either *directly* (immediately), in which case the intrinsic phenomenal properties of his awareness are musical sounds (evident); or *indirectly* (mediately; mediated by the external sense of vision, as in any other observer), in which case the intrinsic phenomenal properties given (i.e. evident) will be those of vision, namely colours and shapes. That is to say, the immediate properties of vision mediate indirect perception of, are evidence for, the auditory processes in the nervous system which are immediately perceived as auditory properties; or rather, they *are* 'hearing' itself. In general, phenomenological properties are intrinsic to the experienced integration of the activity of self-scanning hierarchies of specific neural networks.

4.3.2   *Sensing as subjectless*

Just as the properties of conscious awareness (such as sensings) can be intelligibly construed as objectless, so they may be construed as subjectless also. This anti-Cartesian thesis derives from Gassendi who urged, against the *cogito* argument, that properly speaking the proposition 'I think' has no existential implication beyond that carried by 'thinking'. There is subsequently a thoroughly respectable tradition including Kant and Moore which denies the predicability of existence apart from the existence of predicables.[107] Mach for example quotes Lichtenberg with approval when he says[108]

> We become conscious of certain percepts that are not dependent upon us; of others that we at least think depend on us. Where is the border line? We know only the existence of our sensations, percepts and thoughts. We should say '*It thinks*' just as we say 'it lightens'. It is going too far to say '*cogito*' if we translate '*cogito*' by 'I think'. The assumption or postulation of the ego is a mere practical necessity.

If sentience and sapience are accountable in terms of ordered hierarchies of physical systems, the concept of the person (as the primary logical subject) becomes redundant. There is a transition to a concept closer to a neural–systemic locus in the universal mass–energy continuum, an epicentre of self-regulating and self-perceiving activities.

Such views are contrary to the OA root model of human individuality, according to which sensing, thinking, feeling and so forth (in short 'mentallings') are, *a priori*, the prerequisites of *persons*, to be expressed in personal categories.[109] It is appropriate at this point, therefore, to consider in more detail the question of personal identity: the nature of the perceiving subject.

4.3.3 Personal identity

The ontology of persons is fundamental to the OA–PO disagreement, and much metaphysical mileage has been travelled recently by the notion of the 'logical primacy' of *persons* as distinct from individual minds or bodies. Many of the problems that have exercised philosophers in this matter can be avoided, and the ontology of persons elucidated by a consideration of the phenomenology of personal identity together with what we had learned from neurophysiology.[110]

First, recall the wisdom of Hume's well-known analysis of the concept of personal identity.[111] He writes:[112]

> For my part when I enter most intimately into what I call myself, I always stumble on some particular perception or other of heat or cold, light or shade, love or hatred, pain or pleasure. I can never catch *myself* at any time without a perception and never can observe anything but the perception.

Recall too William James's endorsement of the same general view:[113]

> my personal identity is just like the sameness predicated of any other thing. It is a conclusion grounded either on the resemblance in essential respects or of the continuity of the phenomena compared. And it must not be taken to mean more than these grounds warrant, or treated as a sort of metaphysical or absolute unity in which all differences are overwhelmed.

The central significance of this principle has often been recognised. Compare and contrast, for example, the degrees of integration of the experience of Mach and Bismark: 'my ego appeared to me as one coherent mass only more strongly coherent in the ego' (Mach),[114] and 'Faust complained that he had two souls in his breast. I have a whole squabbling crowd. It goes on as in a republic' (Bismark).[115] Pathological cases of fragmented personality thus appear as different only in the degree of dissociation among differentiable states of consciousness.[116]

Here again, the neurological conception of functional integration will serve to elucidate the phenomenology of personal identity, just as it did the phenomenology of consciousness; that is to say, personal identity may be regarded as based in the functional integration of brain subsystems, a general hypothesis that is specific enough, yet flexible enough, to account for the variety of cases. In clinical neuropsychology, for example, the general concept of 'brain damage' proves inadequate to represent the variety and specificity of cognitive and personality defects observed,[117] which require something like a sub-system malfunction account. Dramatic corroboration of this is available from the evidence of clinical commisurotomy.[118] The philosophic importance of these empirical findings merits their consideration at some length.

Individuals with 'bisected brains', that is with the brain hemispheres surgically separated at the commisure (bridge) of the corpus callosum, are able not only to acquire dual (independent) memories, but also to manifest dual 'mind' and dual personality. Sperry reports how the 'right mind' and 'left mind' are not only distinguishable but may even be in opposition.[119] For example, motor acts directed by the left brain (e.g. pulling on trousers) may be directly opposed by motor acts directed by the right brain (simultaneously pulling off trousers) – the 'sinister left hand' syndrome. Similarly, verbal response directed by the speech-dominant left hemisphere to a question requiring right-brain information for a correct answer (e.g. the naming of an object identified tactually by the left hand) is random and erroneous but delivered with an expressive grimace of chagrin or disgust directed by the censorious, mute, but still motor-effective right brain. Strictly speaking, such cases are not 'individuals' at all.

The neuropsychology of clinical commisurotomy thus represents important *prima facie*, and possibly crucial, evidence against the concept of an individual 'mind' or 'logically' primitive person related to a particular body. For if a single personality is simultaneously initiating both of two opposing acts, then in what sense is it individual or primitive or unified? The most plausible account of this evidence is that there are manifestly two minds because there are two anatomically differentiated, independently functioning integrated neuronic systems, independent of any 'logically' primitive mind or transempirical person, and therefore possibly in opposition. The implication is that, since the purely physical subdivision of the physical brain alone is a sufficient condition for the subdivision of mind also, then the existence of an appropriately functionally integrated brain is alone a sufficient condition for mind (and consciousness).

This conclusion has been challenged on the grounds that a single decision system may still be directing both (mutually opposing) acts.[120] This is largely an empirical question to which some important answers have already been provided. Gazzaniga has reported experiments in which brain-bisected monkeys have eaten both green and black grapes with one hemisphere 'exposed' (and a patch over the opposite eye). With the second hemisphere then exposed and the other eye covered, the subject is given similar choices, but with the green grapes made bitter with quinine, and so learns to discriminate between the black grapes and the sour green grapes, which it avoids. When the eye patch is returned to its original position, the monkey continues to eat both green and black grapes indiscriminately.[121] In other words, there is no evidence that information or memory acquired by (with) the second hemisphere is available to any single decision system directing choices through *both* hemispheres. Rather, normal inter-hemispheric (physical) learning–memory transfer has been cut off with bisection of the callosal commisure.

In summary, the evidence suggests that mind and personality may be based only in the functional integration of brain sub-systems, so that, as the evidence of commisurotomy shows, anatomical duality entails functional duality, dual decision systems, dual memory and dual 'minds'. In any event, the remaining questions raised by commisurotomy appear to be empirical ones. The content of the prevailing orthodox concept of human personality is undeniably significant. But it has already been argued that no concept of this sort *can* have *a priori* validity. The issue is at the very least always open to the influence exerted by the osmosis of the empirical evidence and concepts of the human life sciences. Evidently, the properties of persons need not amount to anything more than the properties of relatively stable configurations of living neuronal nets along the lines indicated here according to IT. The phylogenetic and ontogenetic evidence, and the fact that fragmentation and functional dissociation of these physical configurations has manifestly profound effects on the integrity of personality, entirely corroborates this view. In this way person-predicates are predicates of bodies at a certain level in the terrestrial biological hierarchy. What is more, the resulting concept of the perceiving subject turns out to be very similar to the insights of traditions different to our own, but well established nevertheless.

Although the concept of subjectless sensings has a certain pedigree in Western philosophy which has been referred to, the *prima facie* barbarity of the appropriate locutions for ears attuned to the Hellenic–Judeo–Christian tradition is undeniable. From within the ethos determined by the logical grammar of the subject–predicate form, the Westerner confidently asks the rhetorical question, 'Is not the presupposition of all language and experience that there is an indubitable I?'[122] The simple answer, however, is 'No!' For we discover that the special emphasis given to the concept of the person in Western philosophy, including much recent analytical philosophy, is heavily culture-dependent. The oriental and particularly the Buddist tradition for example is very different. Alan Watts has written that:[123]

Zen asks us to find out 'who' it is that 'has' this mind (and does not

97

ask to be born before father and mother conceived us). Thence it appears that the entire sense of subjective isolation, of being the one who was 'given' a mind and to whom experience happens, is an illusion of bad semantics – the hypnotic suggestion of repeated wrong thinking. For there is no 'myself' apart from the mind–body which gives structure to my experience. It is likewise ridiculous to talk of this mind–body as something which was passively and involuntarily 'given' a certain structure. It *IS* that structure and before the structure arose there was no mind–body.

The agreement between Zen Buddist and the PO conceptions of personal identity is striking, and is further emphasised by a sutra which says[124]

It is only a grouping of elements which come together to make this body. When it arises only these elements arise. When it ceases only these elements cease. But when these elements arise, do not say 'I am arising' and when they cease do not say 'I am ceasing'.

4.4 *Dual Language*

Some theorists have advocated a move towards a utopian unitary language based on the wholesale extirpation from ordinary language of all terms with no purely intersubjectively determinable reference (that is, towards a scientific purge and reconstruction of the vernacular).[125] On the present view, however, such an enterprise is misconceived. The overwhelmingly decisive reason is probably the powerful and mundane one offered by Rorty, that of mere *convenience*. It is more convenient to talk about boiling kettles in the ordinary way than to talk about molecular kinetic theory, gas laws, evaporation points and so on. It is infinitely more convenient to talk about jealousy and forgetfulness and such like than to use a rigmarole of 'long Latin names that doctors know about' (Anscombe). And that's that, as far as the hey-ho and lack-a-day are concerned.

Notwithstanding the convenience of ordinary usage, however, there are still good reasons for developing a theoretical language of physicalism. First, if one of our unrepentant ultimate presuppositions is that, in spite of the labours lost and the labours unfinished of Ludwig Wittgenstein, there is, to put it bluntly, a difference between the way the world is and the way particular natural languages happen to slice it up, then the business of arriving at factual truths about the world is a different enterprise from getting the hang of the grammatical forms intrinsic to a particular form of life or ideological commitment. Nature has a short but impartial way with idiosyncratic language games: she recognises neither National Socialist Physics[126] nor Marxist–Leninist genetics.[127] Paradigmatically, the events at Hiroshima presented irrefragible evidence that the 'sciencing game' played out in the laboratories and testing grounds was according to rules intrinsic to a real, structured world. In general, technology is the effective proving ground of a hypothetico-deductive 'form of life' (science), the systematic purpose of which is precisely to discover such structure and rules.[128]

Second, the realistic assumptions implicit in science already entail a descriptive–predictive asymmetry with priority on the side of the physical–objective language of science against the convenient imprecisions of ordinary usage. Whereas the latter serves most purposes very well, nevertheless, where significant matters of dispute arise, ideas expressed in the vernacular concerning for example, water, lightning or matters of paternity are tested against standards expressed in statements about H_2O, electrostatics and the biochemistry of DNA. It is a matter of record that the intersubjective standards embodied in the language of science have been progressively extended, suggesting a possible continuum from subatomic physics to biology. The IT of mind and brain is the axiomatic foundation for the further extension of this continuum into the domains of behavioural and even introspective psychology at the level of human organisms. The final utopian extension would be to the level of sociology. These are persuasive reasons for developing a physicalist language to describe and explain ordinary experience.

However, to speak of a contingent identity between mind and brain does entail a kind of duality, which we have represented as a biperspectival *access* to ontologically single brain processes in the physical continuum. Consistency then requires that the duality of access involves duality of modes of confirmation and knowledge, and these we have characterised in terms of direct or immediate and indirect or mediate respectively. The duality is a *logically* necessary one, based on the numerical difference of individuals[129] such that it is logically necessary that one and only one (anatomically differentiated) individual should have privileged direct (introspective) access to the occurrence of his own central-state changes. It is this logical necessity that Austin spoke of when he summarised the problem of other minds as follows:[130]

a) Of *course* I *don't* introspect Tom's feelings;
b) of course I *do* sometimes know Tom is angry; hence
c) to suppose that the question 'How do I know that Tom is angry?' is meant to mean 'How do I introspect Tom's feelings?' ... is simply barking our way up the wrong gum tree.

The first two statements may be re-emphasised and amended, respectively, to bring out the logical entailment of the duality implicit in biperspectivist view, so that:

99

(a) of course *I* don't introspect *Tom's* feelings; and

(b) of course I do sometimes (*mediately*) know Tom is angry.

Once the duality of access or perspective is recognised along with the attendant duality of confirmation and knowledge, duality of language seems to follow. This is not to open the door to a dualist metaphysics but quite simply to reflect the mundane fact that to *undergo* a state change is different from the *observation* of a state change *undergone*: there is, one might say, a rudimentary difference between the token reflexive 'This' and the intersubjectively impeccable 'That'.

To illustrate, suppose for a moment that the utopian programme were implemented. Presumably children would be taught appropriate neurophysiological terminology instead of the old pre-identity mental terms. The meaning of the terms would of course change during education in the sciences, but this would be in the way of semantic enrichment. No ontological barriers need be crossed as is now the case.[131] However, the distinction between processes as *undergone* and as *observed* would still be required to be drawn in some way. Even if observation reports included specified co-ordinates within an objective space–time framework, these must 'hook-on' to some reflexive token: perhaps a prefix might be employed for this purpose. First-person forms generally might be indicated by the addition of some convenient modifier to the objective expression, say '*a* ...' = 'this ...'. A reformation of ordinary language along these lines would then be capable of properly reflecting both the nature of the world perceived *and* the mode of perception. Feigl's utopian fantasy expression '17–9–6–53–12' with neurophysiological references would, he speculates, replace the introspective 'tense-impatient-apprehensive-yet-hopefully-expectant'. But we would still need to distinguish between '*this* "17–9–6–53–12"' and '*that* "17–9–6–53–12"' so as to indicate from which perspective the events or states are being reported, which itself is additional objective information. With this addition, however, the utopian expression '*a* 17–9–6–53–12' has the same sense, as well as the same reference, as 'I feel tense, impatient, apprehensive yet hopefully expectant'.

Terms and expressions of this latter sort Feigl terms 'nomological danglers': they dangle from the ('objective') nomological net formed by the utopian physicalist language of a unified science, which on the IT can be related to the corresponding neurophysiological terms by means of a 'dictionary' compiled from the correlation of first-person reports and observer reports. Some identity theorists reject the nomological dangler thesis, and deny the need for such a dictionary. However, it seems that these are necessary to reflect duality of access, and to correlate the senses of first- and third-person reports. In fact, the danglers do not so much dangle as form the strands of a nomological net reflecting the first-person perspective, which is translatable into (though not 'reducible' to) the physical objective language.

An analogy with translation between natural languages is particularly apt with respect to the need to have some ostensive footing in both languages (or forms of life) in order to understand a literal translation. The physiological reference of any mental expression is *ex hypothesi* open to the confirmation and knowledge of third persons. Yet third persons may not *understand* the translation from the third- to first-person language. It is perhaps the refusal to countenance this possibility that has led some physical realists to deny translatability and 'danglers' altogether. But this denial is both unwarranted and unnecessary.

The case of complex sensory and cognitive states is not different in this respect from logically similar but comparatively unproblematical cases. Every native is native of some native heath. He can fully appreciate the expressions indicating 'alien to this native heath' yet he cannot, *ex hypothesi*, directly know what it is to be an alien on his own native heath. Similarly, every normal observer can fully appreciate that the Olympic shot-put champion is champion in virtue of 'public' physical endowments, yet cannot immediately know what it is *to be* such a champion. It is true that the non-utopian dictionaries of alien states and Olympic mesomorphy can be compiled only with the co-operation of aliens and Olympians. However, there is no *metaphysical* problem about alien talk or Olympian talk. I can see no metaphysical problem about first-person introspective–psychological talk, either.

Summarily, IT is necessarily based upon the logical symmetry of the mental–physical duality, and a corresponding duality and translatability of language of some sort seems to follow. There is however an explanatory–predictive asymmetry in favour of the objective language once the perceiving–introspecting subject is incorporated into the hierarchy of natural systems. Explanations of human behaviour already, and necessarily, employ descriptions of observable physical behaviour. IT in principle extends the domain of application of the PO model into the realm of sense, emotion, memory, motives, rules and purposes.

V

OBJECTIONS TO
MIND-BRAIN IDENTITY
THEORY

1 SOLVED PROBLEMS

The programmatic justifications for an identity theory outlined in Chapter II (Section 3.2) are what might be called its intrinsic merits. The extensive debate about IT has dealt with many of the problems that arise when the theory is viewed within the OA framework, and the solutions it provides to these might be regarded as its extrinsic merits (Chapter III, Section 7). The extrinsic task of the identity theorist has been basically twofold: first, to show that a logically coherent account can be rendered of ordinary mental concepts in terms of ontologically neutral 'inner disposition states'; second, to suggest how these inner disposition states are identical with central nervous system or brain states.

Armstrong has gone far towards achieving the first, mainly conceptual, task, by giving an account of a wide range of ordinary concepts such as will, wanting, intention, emotion, knowledge and reason in terms of perception and belief, defining perception in terms of belief (as acquisition of belief) and belief in terms of inner mental states 'apt for causing behaviour' which are contingently identical with central states. Although this account is far from being unproblematical or even complete (it is doubtful if it could ever be complete for reasons already given in Chapter IV, Section 2.4.2), it unquestionably demonstrates the intelligibility and coherence of the materialist–physicalist position, which has not always been appreciated.

The second task involves a wide variety of problems. Many of these have also been resolved and it is not necessary to rehearse them again here. Many ostensible problems have been shown to be due to confusion between identity of meaning and identity in fact, and are solved when this distinction is made.[1] Arguments from the (unique) privacy of the mental have been shown to have commonly conflated a number of distinct meanings of 'private', most of which are fully compatible with IT.[2] Similarly, the supposed logical primacy of persons has been shown to be not incompatible with the further thesis that persons are identical with their physical bodies.[3] The basis of many of the orthodox distinctions drawn between the mental and the physical do not bear examination, such as qualitative/quantitative, non-spatial/spatial, purposive/mechanistic, mnemic/non-mnemic, holistic/atomistic, intentional/blind.[4]

Linguistic objections have been advanced that IT is not false but is meaningless or unintelligible because ordinarily we do not mean by 'the mental', 'the physical'.[5] However, objections of this kind require a comprehensive semantic theory of natural language which will account for the fact that interpretation involves a wide range of extra-linguistic factors (such as scientific knowledge and theory). No satisfactory formal criterion sufficient for significance has ever been provided,[6] and, moreover, arguably never could be provided, *in principle*.[7] In fact, *prima facie* meaningless statements may become non-deviant in a variety of ways involving diachronic meaning shifts.[8]

Intentionality, of consciousness and the corresponding linguistic structure (supposedly) necessary to express psychological content, is another common basis for rejecting the identity hypothesis.[9] It has been amply demonstrated, however, that the linguistic criteria proposed do not, and probably no such criteria ever could, constitute either necessary or sufficient conditions for uniquely psychological expression.[10] Furthermore, the physicalist concepts of neural modelling and self-regulating, self-directed, 'information-flow' systems provide the basis of an adequate physicalist account of the intentional features of consciousness.[11]

Naive religious believers and moralists have typically been concerned about the threat that 'successful' scientific determinism, as is implicit in IT, poses for orthodox religious belief and morality.[12] Hume, long ago, provided a sufficient answer to such objections, that it is not certain that an opinion is false because it is of dangerous consequence.[13] In any event, the ascendancy of physical determinism has nothing like such calamitous consequences as has been supposed, as I shall try to show presently.

At another, more sophisticated, level attempts to argue from Gödel's theorem to an irreducible distinction between inanimate mechanism and human intelligence[14] have been shown to be mistaken; since, simply, as a number of authors have shown, no machine embodies intrinsic limitations to self-ascription not shared by human individuals.[15]

Finally, paranormal phenomena (precognition, telepathy, psychokinesis) have been canvassed much and often as evidence against physicalism.[16] If scientific circumspection is to be preserved it must be allowed that, potentially, they pose problems for the physicalist. However, even though paranormal phenomena may be 'a small black cloud on the physicalist's horizon', the evidence remains very flimsy and dubious when set against the evidence for the PO case.[17] This is assuming that there is a contradiction between psi-phenomena and physicalism, which is by no means necessarily so.

The arguments against physicalist accounts of the mental briefly mentioned above are the most persistent, persuasive and telling ones, which have been more or less refuted in the recent debate. It remains now to consider the most outstanding unanswered objections to IT and the PO model of mind.

It will be convenient to discuss the outstanding objections to IT under three heads: logical, epistemological and empirical.

2 LOGICAL OBJECTIONS

Although the distinction between identity of meaning and identity in fact has resolved many of the problems raised by claiming strict identity of mental and physical discernibles, the logical status of the identity relation continues to be one of the main obstacles to its acceptance. The putative identity can be further elucidated by considering in turn: (1) the terms; (2) the identity sign; (3) the identity proposition involved in statements of the theory.

2.1 Terms

It is necessary to begin by considering a rather surprising objection to IT. This is the claim that there can be no identity of mental and physical events because there *are* no events, events being merely the logical subjects of certain *statements*.[18] On this view the only significance attached to event statements is due to their status as answers to the question, 'What happened?' The physical realist might well settle for this piece of verbal reduction, if he is allowed to interpret the predicate 'happened' as synonymous with 'was a happening', because he can then identify 'happenings' instead of 'events'. This recourse is disallowed by the linguistic reductionist, however, on the grounds (1) that a complete answer to the question 'What happened?' can be given without mentioning the word 'happening', and (2) that the appearance of requiring that something be classified as a happening, which the

104

philosophical eye can see in the question 'What happened?', is an illusion.[19]

The substance of this argument, so far as I understand it, turns on whether the 'happening' in 'this after-image was a happening' strikes one as being all wrong or all right. Contrary to the objection thus argued, I shall assume that it is all *right*. But I take it that this is to suppose no more than the feeble truth that words like 'event', 'happening' and 'occurrence' are general terms denoting perspicuous state-changes, or states of affairs in some phenomenal field. It is not to run the risk of conjuring up an ontology of events, happenings and occurrences to roost among the birds and the bees and the cigarette trees.[20] I take it that the identity theorist wants to say merely that sensations, thoughts, memories, etc. (mental events for short), are precisely related to patterns of neuro-synaptic discharges (brain events for short) and that this relationship happens to be one of identity.

Nevertheless, much confusion does arise because of mis-understandings about what it is that is being identified. Critics persist with the idea that it is mental *objects* that are being identified with physical processes; they talk about sensations, thoughts and minds as though they were substantial objects or *things* of an immaterial sort such as sense data.[21] By making this assumption, refutation of an identity theory becomes child's play because it is obvious that an *object* cannot be identical with a process. However, the identity theorist does not interpret mental events as *objects* or state-changes in 'a mind' at all. There is no question therefore of identifying some*thing* mental with some*thing* physical, but only of identifying the mental *as* a subset of the physical taken under a (biperspectival) interpretation. More precisely, adverbial sensing, feeling, remembering, thinking, etc. (i.e. in general 'mentalling'), is the *having* of, or the *undergoing* of, a brain process of a particular sort. The terms of the identity relation, therefore, each refer to the attributes of a logical subject and the identity proposition is therefore at least logically coherent.[22]

2.2 The Identity Relation

The nature of the mental–physical identity has usually been elucidated by appeal to analogies with other recognised contingent identities arising in science such as water and H_2O, temperature and kinetic energy, lightning and electrostatic discharges, the gene and the DNA molecule. A quick consideration of these cases shows how contingent identity cannot be made *logically* perspicuous, because logical identity holds only in uninterpreted (i.e. content-less) formal expressions whereas identity-in-fact entails interpretation of facts.[23] This means that contingent identity is *empirically* perspicuous with all the indefiniteness that this locution suggests.

The virus theory of infection is a case in point:[24]

> What does virus reproduction mean and what does 'virus reproduction' mean? ... Since we recognise the virus only by its infectivity, observing virus reproduction actually means observing an increase in virus activity together with an increase in the number of certain particles in the field of the electron microscope. The question arises again as to how one might be certain that the particles before one's eyes are the virulent agents causing the observable lesions in the host organism. It is the question that Koch tried to answer for bacteria and to this day we must be satisfied with partial evidence yielding a measure of probability to the identity of physical particle and biological agent. For example, we can show that they have similar chemical and physical properties, but this clearly does not prove their identity; we can show that formaldehyde combines with virus substance *and* alters virus activity. ... Uncertainty remains, though in many instances it is shrunken small. *It is hard to doubt* the identity of a particle under study with the bearer of virus activity when the particle sediments in the ultra-centrifuge at exactly the same rate as the infection principle, the particle migrates in an electric field at the same rate as the principle, and the particle has the same diffusion constant and filtration end-point as the infection principle.

In general, recognition of a contingent identity follows from a close familiarity with a wide range of properties coincident with both terms of the identity, tending to put the relation beyond doubt, i.e. is as much a psychological as a purely logical process.

The parallel between the infection-principle–virus relation in biology and mental states–central nervous states relation in neuropsychology and behavioural science is obvious. Apart from the broad factors of phylogeny and ontogeny already referred to, the onset and termination of specific states of mind are simultaneous with the onset and termination of specific patterns of brain activity; changes of content in states of mind coincide with changed patterns of brain activity; the 'instant of awareness' is of the same duration as the unit cycle of the brain's self-scanning alpha rhythms, and so on. Certainly a reasonably diligent attention to the evidence seems strongly to suggest the possibility of an identity relation holding between mental states and brain states, although many philosophers have professed not to think so.[25]

In contrast, others have (apparently) been so concerned to establish parallels with already recognised theoretical identity relations that they have construed mental terms (e.g. sensations and intentions) as *theoretical* terms of ordinary language and behavioural science, the references of which could then be identified with the references of theoretical terms in neurophysiology.[26] This has led to the rather dubious view that the inner or directly accessible reference of mental terms, *thinking*, is a comparatively recent discovery in human history. Although this view does not deny thought, it does suggest that men were thinking long before they knew it: they talked, for example, about intending, but only *scientifically*, referring only to probability functions and behavioural dispositions.

To treat mental terms as theoretical terms in this way, to neglect the immediate sense of mental terms, is to overlook the unique nature of mind–brain relations and so the *unique* interpretation of their identity. It has commonly been supposed that the thesis of identity between the mental and the physical can be demonstrated only if it can be shown to be formally similar to *recognised* identity relations. (As though every sort of contingent identity after the historically first must conform to the same pattern.) There are two dubious assumptions involved here. First, it is supposed to be essential that terms spanning the identity sign be of the same logical type, both physical or both mental,[27] or both theoretical or phenomenal or observational, or etc.[28] Secondly, an identity must be purely logically perspicuous and must not depend crucially on an interpretation of the identity sign. A brief consideration of some of the commonly cited cases of recognised contingent identity, however, will quickly disabuse us of these unwarranted assumptions. Consider the following cases:

1 Clouds are (aggregates of) water droplets
        (observation–composition)
2 Water is H_2O
        (observation–physical chemistry)
3 Lightning is electrostatic discharge
        (observation–electrostatics)
4 The gene is a DNA molecule
        (genetics–biochemistry)
5 The infection principle is the virus
        (epidemiology–biochemistry)
6 Heat is mean molecular kinetic energy
        (thermodynamics–statistical mechanics).

2.2.1   Observation terms
If an observation term is one whose referent can ordinarily be seen (sensed) without the mediation of either instruments or hypotheses, then 'clouds', 'water droplets', 'water' and 'lightning' are observation terms.

2.2.2   *Theoretical–observation terms*

If a theoretical–observation term is one whose referent can ordinarily be confirmed with or without the mediation of instruments but not without the mediation of some scientific theory, then 'H_2O', 'electrostatic discharge', 'DNA molecule', 'virus' and 'heat' are theoretical–observation terms.

2.2.3   *Pure theoretical terms*

If a pure theoretical term is one whose referent is a mediating factor or postulate in some scientific theory but is not observable with or without the aid of instruments, then 'gene', 'infection principle' and 'mean molecular kinetic energy' are pure theoretical terms.

In the cases cited, then, we have the following combinations of terms in recognised identity relations:

1 'observation term'   =   'observation term'
2 'observation term'   =   'theoretical–observation term'
3 'observation term'   =   'theoretical–observation term'
4 'pure theoretical term'   =   'theoretical–observation term'
5 'pure theoretical term'   =   'theoretical–observation term'
6 'theoretical observation term' =   'pure theoretical term'

What is immediately obvious from these examples is, first, that the terms spanning the identity sign in recognised identity relations are not all of the same type, nor are both terms in any one equation necessarily of the same type (only (1) is, according to the criteria adopted here). In fact, the examples fall into three groups, namely identification of the referents of two different observation terms (1); identification of the referents of an observation term and a theoretical–observation term (2,3); and identification of the referents of a pure theoretical term and a theoretical–observation term (4,5 and 6). If heat is treated as an observational term we also have a case of identification of the referents of an observation term and a pure theoretical term.

Second, it is obvious that the interpretation of the identity sign varies significantly. Case (1) is an identity of composition. Cases (2) through (6) involve interpretations through various scientific theories (physical chemistry, electrostatics, biogenetics, biochemistry and thermodynamics and statistical mechanics). Although these theories have certain minimal common denominators, for example in *being* theories and in sharing a basis in atomic theory, beyond this there is no common formula for recognised cases of contingent identification.

No substantial precedent or canon of logic is violated *a priori*, therefore, if the unique nature of the identity between the mental and the physical is proclaimed from the outset. *A posteriori*, the evidence clearly

108

suggests that the case of hierarchically organised biofeedback systems capable of self-organisation and 'self-scanning' or self-information is in fact special in nature. The case of man is *most* special, because one of his functionally integrated sub-systems is uniquely concerned with the abstract symbolic representation and expression both of the processes he undergoes and of those he observes. This capacity *uniquely* allows both dual access to the central processes and duality of description, confirmation and knowledge. The mind–brain identity theory is thus a theoretical expression of the unique relation between the undergoing or having (i.e. the mental or immediate) and the undergone or had (i.e. the physical or mediated). The identification of the observer with the system is crucial: he is not merely an homunculus inspecting the interior of the system – he *is* the system.[29] It is through this *neuropsychological* thesis that the identity sign in the 'mental is physical' equation is to be interpreted.

2.3   The Identity Proposition

Having discussed the terms, and the identity sign, it is necessary now to consider the identity proposition. The line generally adopted by identity theorists has been that mental objects have neurophysiological properties, and vice versa, because they are in fact identical. The biperspectival interpretation of the mental–physical relation holds that each has phenomenal properties intrinsic to the modes of access or channels of communication concerned so that it is a mistake to claim complete interchange of all predicables in the way suggested by Smart, for example. This might be taken to concede all that the dualist asks. Not so, however, if we consider the common *reference* of mental and physical terms. The duality is merely one of *access* or perspective. That is to say, we have duality of sense but not of reference.

The substitutivity criterion seems to be violated nevertheless, and without substitutivity Leibnitz's criterion remains a problem for IT. It is doubtful if an analysis based on the predicate calculus can properly handle the adverbial account of subjectless and objectless sensings outlined above. What we have suggested is, not that a mental object (or event) is a physical object or event, but that a *mentalling* is the *undergoing* of a physical process.

This difference between 'brain process' and 'undergoing a brain process' cannot be over-emphasised, because in a statement of IT such as 'mentalling is a brain process' (taking now the preferred adverbial form) the thought expressed is 'mentalling is *undergoing* a brain process'.[30] I want to suggest that advocates of an identity theory *read* the first form as though it were the second; that is, 'brain process' is taken in its fuller sense as 'undergoing a brain process', whereas those who reject the identity do not take 'brain process' in the fuller adverbial sense. Instead they interpret it on the OA model, as referring to a physical object with physical predicates, contrasted to mental objects with mental predicates. A brain process as an object of mediated awareness can be fully described in the intersubjective language of a completed neuropsychology as 'that ϕ process', i.e. the reference or denotatum of 'brain processes'; but unless and until the description is filled out to indicate that it is the *undergoing* of 'that ϕ process', then the identity with 'this mentalling' – the object of immediate awareness – does not hold. In practice, however, when it comes to the substitutivity of mental and physical terms, the identity theorist's fuller sense of brain process as 'undergoing ...' is lost. As a result brain process terms are substituted in mental sentential contexts, generating absurdity that would not be generated if the adverbial form for mental expressions were used and if the complete sense of the physical terms of the identity relation were preserved. This in turn leads to the need to brazen out *prima facie* absurd predications by appeal to the 'contingent ignorance' principle.[31]

If what has just been said is true, then the claim that 'mentallings' have physiological predicates is coherent, but only if it is understood that it is the undergoing of the physical process referred to in the predication. For example, 'I have a red after-image' takes the adverbial form 'I am after-imaging redly', and is contingently identical with 'I am undergoing a (red after-imaging) brain process'. In general,

$$(\Psi)(A)[P(\Psi, A) \supset (\exists \phi)\{Q(\phi, A) \& \phi = \Psi\}]$$

where Ψ = 'mentalling';

ϕ = 'undergoing a brain process';

A = subject (self-perceiving system);

P = 'is experienced by';

Q = 'is undergone by';

$P(\Psi, A)$ = 'The mentalling Ψ is experienced by the subject A';

$Q(\phi, A)$ = 'The brain process ϕ is undergone by the subject A'

which will be read as: if someone is mentalling, then there is some brain process such that the individual experiencing the mentalling is undergoing the brain process and undergoing the brain process is experiencing the mentalling. Given this interpretation of the identity sign in '__ = __', then mentalling predicates are attributable to the physical (as undergoing) and physical predicates are attributable to mentallings (as the undergone) without the need for the 'heroics' involved in asserting mental predicates of physical processes *as observed*, or physical predicates of mentallings as undergoings.

110

2.4   Logical Possibility

It has been objected that, since the IT merely asserts a *contingent* relation, it is logically possible that the identification could be mistaken and *strict* identity thereby ruled out.[32] This raises the very large question of 'logical possibility', and the justification for a synthetic/analytic distinction which cannot be discussed here.[33] However, given a reasonably diligent attention to the considerable empirical evidence already available, philosophical talk about the logical possibility of disembodied mental processes, or the possibility that after all we might conceivably discover ordinary people with heads full of porridge oats or straw, or even nothing at all,[34] is so much at variance with the well-known facts that it strikes us as being rather Quixotic, to say the least. To assert such possibilities is to profess empirical ignorance, the true character of which should be made explicit with the addition to possibility assertions of the modifier: 'so far as I (we, anybody) can tell'.

The analytic/synthetic dichotomy is a logico-linguistic distinction and with the growth of empirical knowledge statements that were once synthetic may become analytic. To take one example,[35] the question of whether or not a lump of lead will float on water is *prima facie* open to the strictly *logical* possibility that it will, because, in the language of rustics at least, no self-contradiction is involved.

This logical possibility becomes drastically attenuated as the physical and chemical properties of lead and water are discovered and described within the framework of scientific theories, notably atomic theory, and especially as their structure is related to the periodic table of elements. Within this conceptual and nomological net the concept 'floating' takes on more definite connotations (which nevertheless contain the ordinary meaning), namely the relationship between the atomic weights, and so the specific gravities, of two substances. When 'lead', 'water', and 'floating' are located in the nomological net of atomic theory, then statements of the kind 'a lump of lead will not float on water' cease to be synthetic as they are when in contingent *ignorance* of the structure of the natural world, and become analytical statements about the relation of terms in the nomological net constructed by science as a more or less accurate symbolic representation of the natural world. (Note: in such cases it is the ignorance that is properly held to be contingent, not the structure of the natural world.[36]) Rejecting the analyticity of the claim that a lump of lead will not float on water then requires more than simple appeal to the fact that 'floating' and 'not-floating' are equiprobable alternatives to someone bereft of sound factual knowledge about the world. Rejection of the claim calls for the destruction of a whole scientific edifice, which is a very different and considerably more difficult enterprise.

In the same way, 'I think with my diaphragm' is a logical possibility only if we ignore or pretend to ignore neuropsychology and its manifold links with biology, cybernetics and chemistry. And just as 'floating' comes to mean something about relative specific gravities, so 'mentalling' comes to mean something about the activity of hierarchies of neural feedback loops.

> Iron sinks in water, but it could have been otherwise. Perhaps: *but how much else are we allowed to know?* It couldn't if it is still to be one of the transition metals with a place in the periodic table, but the periodic table could have been otherwise: it was not inscribed on the underside of the Mosaic Tablets: perhaps it could be otherwise; and perhaps there could be a world in which organisms are not functionally adapted to their environment. Well, perhaps, you never know: anything can happen. Nature is bountiful and full of surprises, and there's plenty more where that came from. 'Think Cornucopian'.[37]

Summarily: once the key idea is grasped, that what is being identified by IT is the *undergoing* of physical processes and mentallings, and this (unique) identification is seen to be coherent within a PO model of persons, then the main logical objections to IT can be met.

2.5 *Accounting for the Supposed Contingency of Mind—Brain Identity*

An important objection to IT has been raised in the form of a requirement to explain how two things that are supposed to be identical in some very strong sense amounting to necessity are nevertheless commonly thought of as only contingently identical.[38] The short answer to this objection is implicit in what has already been said. It is to say that statements of mind—brain identity, if true, are indeed necessarily true and not contingent at all. The arguments presented so far support the view that, at least for human beings, whenever there is some mentalling, there will be, necessarily, some corresponding brain process and without such brain processes there will be no mentalling.

It would be useful and more correct, therefore, to draw a distinction between the metaphysical categories, 'necessary' and 'contingent', and the epistemological categories, '*a priori*' and '*a posteriori*'.[39] In this way the usual formulations of identity theory in terms of contingent identity can be shown to be a misleading way of expressing *a posteriori* necessary truths. However, no serious logical harm need be done by this confusion because it is systematic. The analogies that are usually drawn with such cases as heat and mean molecular kinetic energy invariably represent the analogous cases in the same misleading way: as contingent truths, when they are really *a posteriori* necessary truths. The important principle argued for in both formulations, however, remains the same: that experience can yield knowledge of non-analytic, but necessary, truths. The point is that, no matter how they are categorised, mind–brain identity and other well-established cases of theoretical identity such as heat and kinetic energy are discovered in experience and not by logical or linguistic analysis. Even if there is no precise analogy between mind–brain and other cases there is reason to believe that none is really necessary; that mind–brain identity is unique in science and in experience.

The objection is not yet fully met however because it is said that the way in which analogous cases such as heat and molecular kinetic energy have turned out to be necessary truths does not seem to be the way in which the mind–brain identity could turn out to be either necessarily or even contingently true.[40] The explanation offered in support of this claim is illuminating and needs to be considered in some detail.

First, it is necessary to introduce an analytical tool. The argument turns on a useful distinction between rigid and non-rigid designators. A rigid designator is a term that designates essentially; that is to say, designates the same referent in all possible worlds where it occurs. A non-rigid designator picks out or fixes a referent under some non-essential description. For example, some individual might be picked out in two different ways: either as 'John Smith, first born son (1936) of James and Mary Smith', or as 'the man standing in the corner with a glass of champagne'. In the first case the description designates rigidly because unless the individual picked out satisfied the description he would not be *the* man in question. In the second case the description designates non-rigidly because the man picked out by means of it (John Smith) would still be the man in question, even if the description were false. (John Smith may be, in fact, sitting on a high stool with a glass of cider, and perhaps somebody else, James Jones, stands unnoticed somewhere in a corner with a glass of champagne!) The important point made here is that we should not confuse a description that identifies an individual essentially with 'accidental' descriptions which might be used to pick out the same individual.

Now if names or essential descriptions are rigid designators, then there can be no doubt that identities are necessary, because two rigid designators with the same reference will necessarily refer to the same individual. And there can be no situation in which an individual is not identical with itself.[41] There may be, for example, situations or possible worlds in which *the* Adolf Hitler is not identical with the *fuehrer* of the Third Reich, but there can be no conceivable situation or possible world in which *the* Adolf Hitler is not the third child of Alois Hitler and Klara Hitler (*neé* Potzl), born at half past six on the evening of 20 April 1889, in the Gasthof zum Pommer, an inn in the small town of Braunau on the River Inn which forms the frontier between Austria and Bavaria.

We are now in a position to consider the case of the identity between heat and molecular kinetic energy where we can see how, although the identity is *necessary*, people might be misled into thinking that it is contingent. Simply put, the argument is as follows. We use the terms 'heat' and 'the motion of molecules' as rigid designators for certain external phenomena. Since scientific inquiry establishes that heat is in fact the motion of molecules, and both the designators are rigid, it is *necessary* that heat is the motion of molecules. What gives us the illusion of contingency is the inessential or accidental property of heat (or molecular motion) that human beings sense it. We pick out heat and fix the reference of 'heat' under the description 'that which causes our heat sensation'. Such descriptions are, therefore, non-rigid designators of heat. They are only contingently true, if at all, of heat. It might have been that human beings have no such sensations, as with gamma radiation. Also, it might have been that with the same sensations, that is to say in the same epistemological situation, they might have identified something else by means of the sensations, gamma radiation perhaps. But heat would still be heat and identical with molecular energy.

The illusion that the identity between heat and molecular energy is contingent arises, it is suggested, from the contingent truth that human beings commonly pick out heat (and so molecular energy) by means of their own sensations of heat. It is *this* truth that is contingent, not the identity between heat and molecular energy. But because human beings can easily imagine that the sensation they call heat sensation was not caused by heat, but by something else, they mistakenly think that that which causes their sensation, *heat*, might not be heat and identical with molecular energy.

The case of mind–brain identity, which is commonly compared to the heat–energy case, is said to be significantly different and provides no basis for a similar explanation of why the identity is thought of as contingent. This crucial disanalogy is potentially fatal to IT unless it can somehow be explained. The disanalogy is argued as follows. By analogy with the heat–energy case, 'sensation' picks out its object – a mental phenomenon – by essential properties and so rigidly designates the mental phenomenon. Likewise, 'brain process' picks out its object by essential properties and so rigidly designates the physical phenomenon. According to IT sensations are brain processes, and since both the designators are rigid it is incumbent on the identity theorist to conclude that it is necessary that sensations are brain processes.

However, whereas in the case of heat–energy there is a *non*-rigid designator involved which accounts for the common view that the identity is contingent, it seems that there is no such possibility in the mind–brain case. Although we can say that we pick out heat contingently by the contingent property that it affects us in a particular way, we cannot similarly pick out a sensation, such as pain, contingently by the fact that it affects us in a particular way, that is to say by some intermediate process. On such a picture there would be the brain state and we pick it out by the contingent fact that it affects us as pain. This might be true of the brain state but it cannot be true of the pain. It cannot be said of the pain I now have that it is contingently a pain. There is no non-rigid designator for pain and no need of one.

This means that the common view or illusion that mind–brain identity, if it is true at all, is contingent cannot be explained by analogy with the heat–energy case where there was a contingent property whose description ('causing sensations of heat') served as a non-rigid designator for heat. And far from the identity being necessary, the common view is that we can easily imagine that there could have been mental phenomena without corresponding brain processes. What is required therefore is an alternative explanation of how these things, which many people can imagine, are not in fact things that can be imagined.[42] It is suggested that no such explanation is available and that is likely to be so because the mental and the physical are not identical at all.

One way for the physicalist to deal with this requirement is not to meet it, but to reject it as misconceived. For, on the view advanced here, 'mentallings' are construed adverbially; they are not *things* at all. Hence it is not part of the basic PO picture that there are two things that are rigidly designated, but only *one*, and that is a brain process. There is an interesting parallel between this case and the heat–kinetic energy case. The view that 'heat' rigidly designates something that has essential properties different from both kinetic energy and sensations of heat is highly dubious. If 'heat' is that which causes sensations of heat, then *ex hypothesi* it is kinetic energy: *there is only kinetic energy* which human beings have referred to as heat and picked out by what they call sensations of heat. If so, 'heat' cannot rigidly designate any *thing*, because there is no thing, over and above kinetic energy to designate. Similarly, in the sensation–brain process case, 'sensation' cannot rigidly designate anything because there is nothing over and above the brain process to designate. The identity is said to hold not between two *things*, but between a 'mentalling' and an 'undergoing of a brain process'. Thus, on this view the duality that is usually insisted on is, simply put, the difference between first-person (immediate) and third-person (mediate) access to the *same* thing. While it is true, therefore, that the mentalling is its own epistemic guarantee (for the individual concerned), this does not establish that there is something *else* to refer to over and above the *undergoing* of the brain process concerned. There is surely no case for an ontology of 'undergoings' over and above substantial processes undergone.

It might be said however, that there is more to the requirement for an explanation of supposed contingency that this argument admits. Let us therefore turn now to a closer consideration of how the illusion arises that mind–brain identity is contingent when in fact it is necessary, if true. It will be instructive first to reconsider the heat–energy case which is presented as the only model for explaining apparent contingency. In that case the argument assumes that there are, ostensibly, two things that are well known under two rigid designators, and that at least one of them is commonly picked out by a non-rigid designator in the form of a description in terms of some inessential property(s). In the heat–energy case the inessential property is of heat, namely 'sensed by human beings'. The explanation for the supposed contingency of the identity turns on the corresponding non-rigid designator. But that is not the only possibility. There is another more general consideration which is liable to be overlooked in the special case of heat where the supposed contingency arises in connection with the data of a special sense.

It is important to remember that identity statements, in general, cannot be made *at all*, let alone be known to be true, if there is ignorance about one term of the identity (or both).

Though heat may be, necessarily, kinetic energy, heat cannot be known to be identical with kinetic energy if heat and/or kinetic energy are unknown. But being *known* by human beings is no less contingently true of any feature of the real external world than being *sensed* by human beings is contingently true of some external phenomenon (such as heat). As with sensation of heat, so with knowledge of heat; heat would of course *be* kinetic energy even if no one *knew* it. The point, however, is that human knowledge of heat and (especially) knowledge of kinetic energy are non-essential properties of heat and kinetic energy. This suggests another explanation for the illusion of the contingency of the heat–energy identity: because it is contingent that heat and energy are known to human beings. What is contingent is the human knowledge of the identity, not the identity itself.

To summarise: criticism of IT has been based on the suggestion that, because human beings might not have sensed heat (that they sense it is only contingently true), they therefore, mistakenly, think that heat and kinetic energy are only contingently identical. No such account is available for IT. However, if the present view is correct, we can also say, more generally, that because human beings might not have known, say, about kinetic energy (that they know of it is only contingently true: they can imagine that they might have come to know something else or nothing at all), they mistakenly think that heat and kinetic energy are only contingently identical. It is as plausible to suggest the one as the other, but the more general, epistemic, case leaves room for a similar account in the case of IT.

The general point just made is that confusions arising from the (metaphysical) contingency of human knowledge do not necessarily involve acquaintance with the immediate data of some particular sense. This can be clearly shown in the cases of 'contingent identity' where there is no question of being misled by the raw data of some particular sense. One example of such a necessary identity which might (in the usual rubric of philosophical logic) be categorised as contingent is the case of radioactivity and spontaneous atomic disintegration. Far from radioactivity being picked out by a special 'radioactive' sense, its existence is known only by a fairly elaborate process of inductive inference against a background of well-established scientific knowledge and technique.[43] Even more than radioactivity, the phenomenon of spontaneous atomic disintegration can come to be known only by very elaborate and sophisticated models, theories, experiments and inferences which remove it very far from the raw data of any human sense.

The identity between radioactivity (as discovered by Becquerel and the Curies) and spontaneous atomic disintegration (as discovered by Rutherford and Soddy)[44] is properly speaking necessary (in the sense that whenever there is atomic disintegration of the appropriate kind there is, necessarily, radioactivity). Nevertheless, the identity would be regarded as contingent in the usual philosophical way of categorising things. In this case there is no obvious sensation and no non-rigid designator to explain the supposition of contingency along the lines suggested for the heat–energy case, but there *is* an explanation if we accept the more general argument from the contingency of human knowledge of the real world.

Another example of the same sort of identity might be the identity that is often (contentiously) said to hold between 'information' in the extraordinary technical sense developed in communications theory and the 'entropy' (or 'negentropy') of statistical mechanics.[45] In the same way as in the heat–energy case (and other cases such as mass–energy), the identity is suggested by a mathematical formula which is common to two fields of inquiry, in this case the Wiener–Shannon formula for information:

$$H = - \Sigma \, p_i \log_2 p_i$$

which (with positive sign) is Boltzmann's formula for the entropy of a perfect gas. As with other cases, the conjectured identity between them would, if true, be necessary, but categorised as contingent in the conventional philosophical rubric. Again, the explanation for this could not be the contingent truth that human beings *sense* information or entropy, for there is no such truth. It must be (and need only be) that human knowledge of information and entropy is contingent. There would be degrees of order and disorder in the world whether or not human beings knew it or even if there were no human beings at all.[46]

In the mind–brain case of course (leaving aside unconscious mental events) it is necessary that a mental event is known, at least to the person in whom it occurs. But it is only contingent that brains, as objects of external sense, are known to human beings. Since human knowledge about brains is only contingent, the identity holding between mind and brain may seem to be contingent. But, again, what is contingent is the human knowledge of the identity, not the identity itself.

Perhaps it might be thought that it is too implausible to suggest that brains are only contingently known to their possessors. The picture can be refined to accommodate this doubt by saying that *adequate* or *adequately sophisticated* knowledge of brains is a prerequisite for the identity to be known, just as an adequately sophisticated knowledge of heat and kinetic energy, or radioactivity and spontaneous atomic disintegration, are prerequisites for the respective identities between them to be (contingently) known.

Another example will both illustrate the need for adequately sophisticated knowledge and serve to introduce an important distinction that must be made between identities that can be established with no significant change in fundamental world-picture or root model and identities the establishment of which entail a significant shift in fundamental world-picture or root model.

Consider the case of Superman (the fearless worker of wonders for good and right), who disguises himself as Clark Kent (the mild-mannered and fearful newspaper reporter). Superman reveals himself only as the need arises. There is no doubt that 'Clark Kent' and 'Superman' are rigid designators for the same man: the identity is necessary. But either Clark Kent or Superman may not be generally known. It is necessarily true that Clark Kent is Superman, but it is only contingently true (of them) that they are known to be the same man. And that is why people may mistakenly suppose that the identity is contingent: *so far as they know*, the world might have contained both Superman and Clark Kent; they could have known something else or nothing at all. This is a similar case to the others just given.

The notion of 'epistemological situation' should be elaborated at this point. People in Superman's world (S-world) are presented only with limited data on Superman and Clark Kent. All anyone has to go on are their irregular appearances and co-ordinated reports and hearsay about their doings. This is the 'epistemological situation' of the inhabitants of

118

Superman's world. This situation is consistent with at least *two* possible alternative 'metaphysical' situations or possible worlds. First, there is the widely assumed one: that Superman and Clark Kent are really different individuals. Second, there is the alternative metaphysical possibility: that there is really just *one* individual. Now, although, as it happens, Superman and Clark Kent *are* the same individual, it would be only contingently true that they were known to be the same individual. And that would be sufficient to account for the mistaken view that the identity is contingent.

More than this, however, it would in this case be possible to specify an alternative reality or metaphysic which could give rise to an epistemological situation indistinguishable from that arising in the real situation. Thus in a perfectly respectable (metaphysical) sense of 'could' there could have been a different world (S_2-world): one consistent with all the universal laws of nature, which would be *epistemologically* indistinguishable from *the* Superman's world (S-world), but which contained two individuals, say Superman$_2$ and Clark Kent$_2$. Of course such a world would not contain either *the* Superman or *the* Clark Kent, but the distinction between *the* Superman/Clark Kent and the *possible* Superman$_2$/Clark Kent$_2$ is a distinction without any discernible (epistemological) difference. And this would be the basis of a mistaken belief that S-world could really be different to what it is.

There is no epistemological difference between the worlds, that is up to the point where there is sufficient evidence in S-world to establish the identity of Superman and Clark Kent. Up to that point it might understandably be thought that any identity would be contingent: afterwards, it must be seen that in S-world Superman is Clark Kent, necessarily. The new evidence provides new knowledge which transforms the epistemological situation. There is now a difference on which to base a distinction between Superman/Clark Kent and similar individuals in other possible worlds. It would then be (epistemologically) permissible to distinguish between the real S-world situation with *the* Superman (who is identical with Clark Kent) and other situations, such as S_2-world, previously believed or imagined to be real situations containing two different individuals altogether.

It is instructive to notice how the identity between Superman and Clark Kent might come to be known. In this case, quite simply, by coming across Clark Kent in some telephone kiosk removing a disguise and changing into Superman, or discovering Superman in some telephone kiosk disguising himself as Clark Kent. We come to know that Clark Kent is Superman by establishing the space–time continuity between them. We acquire new knowledge about them which serves only to fill in the gaps in what we already know. It would be *astonishing*

119

to realise that Clark Kent was Superman all the time, but no great upheaval in a world-view is necessarily required because in fact it would be realised that, for example, Clark Kent was never around when Superman was in action.

Consider now another fictional case, one where a fundamental change in world-picture is unavoidable when an identity comes to be known. Take the case of a small global world, Logica, with only one great mountain, call it Mount Kripke. The inhabitants of this world have a world-view and way of life that has four salient features for the present case. First, they believe that they live on a flat earth bounded at opposite ends by two great mountains, Kripke and Schmipke. In other words their root model of the world is flat earth. All evidence is interpreted in terms of this model. Second, they hold beliefs that forbid the climbing of the great mountains (that is to say, there is an explanation for why the mountains are never climbed). Third, they are forbidden to stray from the mountain-bounded or equatorial regions (that is to say, there is an explanation for why the mountains are never circumvented). Fourth, the Logicans spend half of their time each year at the foot of Mount Kripke; then they migrate to the other end of the world where they spend the other half of their time at the foot of Mount Schmipke (they therefore have knowledge, but only limited knowledge, of both Kripke and Schmipke).

One day some Logican commits sacrilege (whether from insouciance, curiosity, or to test a revolutionary world-view, it is not germane to the present issue to know). Someone either climbs or circumvents one of the mountains, say Kripke, to see what is on the other side and discovers there what he knows as Mount Schmipke. Kripke is Schmipke (necessarily). Yet knowledge of the identity is discovered in experience. It was a contingent truth about the mountain that it gave rise to the belief that there were two mountains. It is now a contingent truth about the mountain that it is known to be one mountain (and not two mountains as previously believed). Hence it might be mistakenly thought by Logicans that Kripke and Schmipke are only contingently identical.

Although previous knowledge of Kripke and Schmipke as such does not necessarily change (it is only extended in an important way), the new knowledge shows that Kripke and Schmipke are identical in a world significantly different from the one previously presupposed in Logica. In coming to know the identity there is a revolutionary shift in the culture's whole world–picture from flat earth to global earth.

In this case the contingent truth about the mountain (that it is known as one mountain) is complicated by the fact that there may be a world such as the one Logicans falsely supposed their own to be. Pre-revolutionary Logicans would, within the limits imposed by their world

120

view, culture and practice, be in an epistemological situation indistinguishable from that of the inhabitants of such a world. There is, therefore, a metaphysically impeccable sense of 'could' in which there could be a world such as the Logicans only imagined their world to be, and so far as pre-revolutionary Logicans could tell it *was their* world. This possibility would provide another explanation for why, although in fact on Logica Kripke is Schmipke necessarily, nevertheless Logicans might believe that it was only contingently true that Kripke is Schmipke and that their world is global and not flat: this is because those other things *could* have been true (given the previous epistemological situation). It is not that *this* world (Logica) could have been different and still be Logica, but that there could be a different world which presents its inhabitants with an epistemological situation indistinguishable from the one presented to inhabitants of *this* world Logica, in pre-revolutionary days. The identity between Kripke and Schmipke perhaps seems contingent to traditionalist Logicans because, given the previous epistemological situation, the world might have been in fact as they believed it to be.

To summarise and generalise: there may be in some world (W_1) an epistemological situation (ES_1) that is consistent with two (or more) metaphysical models or 'candidates for reality' (MM_1 and MM_2). Within the ontology of MM_1 there are two individuals I_1 and i_1. Within the ontology of MM_2 there is only one individual I_1 with two manifestations I_1 and i_1. It may be that one model (say MM_1) is preferred. Then, new evidence may change the epistemological situation (to ES_2). At this point it is apparent that I_1 is i_1. But the process of identifying I_1 and i_1 is not purely internal to the preferred metaphysical model (MM_1) but involves a shift in root model to MM_2. When this happens, there may be a tendency to (mistakenly) believe that *the* world (W_1) could really have been as it was previously imagined to be in some redundant root model, corresponding perhaps to some other possible world (W_2).

It will now be apparent that, in general, where the growth of knowledge significantly changes the epistemological situation by establishing a necessary identity, there may be a shift in root metaphysical model in relation to which the identity is necessary. In such cases the previously perspicuous or preferred model will become redundant and otiose, but there will be a tendency to regard the newly discovered identity as contingent in relation to the redundant model.

What light does this discussion throw in the mind–brain case? First, it shows that before mind–brain identity can be known it is necessary to have adequately sophisticated knowledge of mind and brain. Much of the debate about this problem has been concerned with the wrong issues: it has turned on the need to preserve the phenomenological autonomy and irreducibility of the mental side of the identity. However, it is contingent knowledge of the brain that gives rise to the problem. On the PO view and the biperspectivist version of IT advanced here, the autonomy and irreducibility of the mental has never been in dispute. (All that has been questioned is a picture of mentallings as *things* of some sort.) Knowledge of mind, therefore, is not in dispute.

What this discussion highlights is the importance of adequately sophisticated knowledge of the brain and its functions. Unless and until an appropriate model of the brain has been developed which is adequate to account for memory, consciousness, intentionality, purpose and other essential aspects of the mental, there will be no possibility of knowledge of mind–brain identity. This point is far from trivial. Knowledge of heat–energy and other such identities turns on sophisticated knowledge of the physical world.

Until adequate knowledge of the brain is attained, the epistemological situation will remain such that alternative models may well seem equally plausible. When the brain is believed to be essentially like a refrigeration plant, porridge oats or passive neural machinery, it will seem no more capable of sustaining mentality than a refrigeration plant, porridge or clockwork. So long as 'body' and brain are regarded so crudely that there seems to be no essential need to distinguish between the complex, dynamic, processes of living organisms and the inert stuff of corpses,[47] the possibility of conceiving and coming to know the identity between the mental and the physical remains infinitely remote and unimaginable. For, of course, inert stuff never intended or purposed anything. But, properly understood, spontaneously active neural nets, organised in hierarchies of functionally integrated feedback circuits, begin to look as if they might be capable of just those things. That is to say, when adequate knowledge *is* achieved mind–brain identity becomes perspicuous.

The second point to emerge from the discussion is that, in a changed epistemological situation, the identification of the mental with the physical is not likely to be an inference purely in terms of the OA–Cartesian model. What is involved is a root model shift from the OA to the PO model.[48] Understanding and acceptance of the identity involves the perspicuity and force of the PO root model. Whereas it is not unreasonable within the redundant model to speak of being able to imagine mental events with no correlate physical events, such claims are Quixotic within the emergent PO model.

The explanation of how there are things (such as disembodied human minds and thoughts) that many people can imagine is that such people have a root model of the world, and especially of persons, that permits such imaginings because they are not inconsistent with the categories of the root model. Indeed, by definition root models exercise a powerful influence by determining the intuitions people have about what is possible. And some people think that intuitions are powerful evidence for *anything*.[49] But as Ryle pointed out, ingrained hypotheses do seem obvious no matter how redundant they may be.[50]

It may be intuitively plausible to imagine disembodied minds and other such things in the epistemological situation existing before the development of adequately sophisticated knowledge of the brain. In the old epistemological situation perhaps the world might really have been as the OA model supposes it to be. Phenomenologically, brain-identical mind might in this situation be held to be indistinguishable from, for example, immaterial mind (much as *the* Superman/Clark Kent might in some epistemological situations be indistinguishable from $Superman_2$ and $Clark Kent_2$, if the world had been as it previously was believed to be). As in other cases, so in the mind–brain case; new knowledge shows that there is a difference on the basis of which to make a distinction between immaterial mind and brain-identical mind. The difference is to do with knowledge of the physical brain's workings which shows that, contrary to established presuppositions, the characteristic properties of the human mind and mind-directed human behaviour can be accounted for in the physical terms of the brain and its workings.[51]

Consequently, when it is loosely said that the things that are commonly imagined are not in fact things that can be imagined, this does not imply a straightforward heroic defiance of common knowledge of what people claim they can imagine. What is implied is that, in the now perspicuous PO model, such (OA) imaginings are logically incompatible with true knowledge. We can go on supposing the real possibility of what we can imagine only for as long as we make the assumptions implicit in the OA root model. But this model can be sustained only so long as the force of the PO model is unknown, ignored or discounted.

There is of course no logical guarantee that comprehensive knowledge of the PO model will render the OA model redundant and the related imaginables unimaginable. There is nothing so unthinkable that someone cannot be found who will testify to being able to imagine it. However, such people are not usually very knowledgeable about the real world, and their imaginings are a poor basis for serious argument. Nevertheless, not all such cases can be dismissed so easily as being due to scientific ignorance. There are other cases where there are powerful psychological or ideological reasons (such as deeply held religious convictions) that intervene in the full acceptance of the emerging scientific picture. In such cases as these, what happens is that the new scientific truth does not emerge by convincing its opponents and making them see the light, but rather that such opponents eventually die and a new generation grows up which is familiar with the new picture.

Finally, there is in all of this an explanation of why the mind–brain identity theory which, properly understood, is necessarily true, should be commonly thought to be contingent even by many physicalists. Knowledge of the brain and certainly adequately sophisticated knowledge of the brain is contingent. For this reason the identity of mind and brain may seem contingent, but what is contingent is human knowledge of the brain and the identity with mind, not the identity itself. Brains would be identical with minds even if nobody knew about brains, just as kinetic energy would be identical with heat even if nobody sensed (or knew about) heat–kinetic energy.

3 SCIENTIFIC–EMPIRICAL OBJECTIONS

Among the outstanding objections to an IT that are essentially empirical in nature, the most important are those from (1) inadmissibility, either as a scientific thesis or as justified by the evidence; (2) denial of mental–physical isomorphism, and (3) non-parsimony of laws.

3.1 *Admissibility*

The status of IT as a scientific hypothesis has been challenged on two basic grounds: first, the lack of a criterion; and second the lack of evidence.

3.1.1 *Criterion*
It is objected that some criterion for identifying the psychological and the physiological is necessary, both to distinguish between identity and mere systematic correlation and to allow the possibility of refutation. But no such criterion is available.

This objection is partly met by the adverbial theory of mentallings as adverbial aspects of physical dynamics. A spatial location criterion, for example,[52] is no longer pertinent, just as the location of a body's velocity is not a pertinent criterion for identifying its velocity with its dynamic relations, because velocity is not the sort of thing that has location over and above that of the body of which it is a vector property. Also, once homogeneity of phenomenal properties of *modes of access* (evidence) is no longer seen to be a prerequisite of contingent identity of *reference* (evidenced), then the need for homogeneity of criteria is no longer necessary,[53] so that first-person reports of immediate awareness are admissible as criteria (of the undergoing) along with third-person reports of mediated awareness (of the undergone).

Nevertheless, it is still arguable that a given first-person report is not intersubjectively confirmable in the way that, say, an instrument reading is.[54] But this truism is misleading. Even in the paradigm case of mutually corroborative instrument readings, different observations of two observing (observer) systems are involved. And when the laws are confirmed by universal repetition of the classical experiments, it is not considered necessary that the hardware and observers be numerically identical for each instance of confirmatory testing, only that repeatable conditions be met.

Strict repeatability is of course logically impossible but is not a special drawback of first-person 'introspection' reports. Certainly, the immediate quality of 'raw feels' is *ex hypothesi* unconfirmable, but the case of the introspecting first person is not essentially different from the observing first person. 'I feel a pain' ('there is a paining here') and 'I see the pointer reading x' ('there is a seeing pointer reading at x-ing here') are both first-person reports. In the general case intersubjective confirmation simply means that subjects in the same context will repeat the same experience. The context for OA science is assumed to be the *extradermal* environment exclusively, so that repeatability and intersubjective confirmation is achieved by substituting different observers in the same (external) environmental context. Comparable intersubjective confirmation of introspective reports by repetition, however, includes the possibility of interposing *intradermal* environments of different introspecting 'observers'. In both cases, however, confirmation is by normal observers in similar contexts.

The bogey of the logical separateness and unique perspective of first-person reports of immediate experience is laid once it is recognised that the scientifically vaunted third-person reportage is actually unique first-person-*plus*-context reportage. General *ceteris paribus* assumptions (i.e. of other things being equal)· and particularly the assumption of the normal observer are thus seen to be useful and commonly justified, but none the less misleading, surrogates for a proper account of the *intra*dermal contexts of observation. The confusion about first-person reports being inadmissible evidence for scientific knowledge claims arises from the mistaken OA assumption that the confirmatory context must always be entirely extradermal (a residual error arising from the model of man as in some sense outside the natural domain, and of 'sciencing' as merely an optional human pursuit). In brief, the relevant referential focus of third-person reports is extradermal (or mediate), whereas the relevant referential focus of first-person reports is intradermal (or immediate). It has often been pointed out, however, that first-person 'raw feels', unrelated to an intersubjectively confirmable context, have minimal epistemic content and can scarcely be regarded as *knowledge* at all.[55] First-person reports of 'undergoings' therefore derive their cognitive status from contexts; and the contexts and knowledge claims are (crucially) intersubjectively confirmable.

First-person reports are in fact already used in a wide variety of scientific contexts, particularly in psychology and medicine. A doctor, for example, might say – something like: 'About twenty seconds after we stop the radiation you will feel a sharp stomach pain. Don't worry. (*Ceteris paribus*) this always happens. It will last for about ten seconds and will gradually go away and be gone in about five minutes.' In doing so he employs an hypothesis about the immediate awareness that individuals have when undergoing exposure to radiation, and about the physiological state-changes undergone as a result of radiation. This hypothesis is based on repeated correlation of first- and third-person reports of precisely the kind disputed in philosophical arguments about the mental–physical relation. Practising medical scientists have totally disregarded, and apparently with conceptual impunity, those philosophers who have argued that 'enjoying or enduring phenomenal properties is not a physical affair'.[56] Fortunately, doctors correctly assume that to be in pain is *to be undergoing physical state-changes*, and that this most definitely *is* a physical affair. The fact that this conception of the state of affairs can be formulated, communicated and understood, and also that it leads to effective action, is powerful evidence that the underlying conceptual model is not fraught with impossible logical and/ or empirical muddles.

There remains the fact that the empirical evidence for identity is not different from the evidence for other, dualist, theories (parallelism, correspondence, double aspect and interactionist), but this is not different from *recognised* cases of contingent identity relations, and is not a decisive objection to identity theory.

Apart from the considerations already discussed, the refutability and so the scientific status of IT rests on three distinct assertions.

1 Mental events are (ontologically) the same as the undergoing of certain brain processes.
2 There is an isomorphic relation between the mentallings and the brain processes.
3 The physical–causal laws are sufficient to predict human behaviour.
   It follows that the hypothesis is open to refutation on a variety of testable grounds, principally:
1' demonstration of either the occurrence of mentallings in the absence of any physical process undergone, or the undergoing of physical processes of the patently mentalling sort in the absence of mentalling;
2' demonstration of a one–many relation between a given mental state and a number of formally and functionally dissimilar brain states, or

conversely a many–one relation between 'mentallings' and brain states;

3' the demonstration that radical discontinuities exist in the physical causal account of behaviour and that these discontinuities are accounted for in mental terms.

As with any other high-level hypothesis, refutation of an I-hypothesis on these grounds is not a straighforward matter of crucial experiments. In the event of ostensible disconfirmation, the hypothesis is sustainable through either the formulation of further explanatory hypotheses or the rejection of the disconfirmatory data. Nevertheless, although refutation by crucial test is not possible, refutation by an accumulation of disconfirmatory evidence undoubtedly *is*, and to that extent IT is a coherent scientific hypothesis.

3.1.2 *Evidence*

The second ground for doubting the scientific credentials of IT has been to question its very basis in the available evidence. Boring, for example, called the hypothesis 'metaphysical nonsense',[57] and philosophers have continued to raise doubts about the strength of the purely evidential support for the theory.[58]

The known correlations of brain processes with first-person reports have already been mentioned in Chapter III (Section 5.2.2), and it was remarked that these are much more extensive and detailed than most philosophers have credited. And whatever views philosophers may hold about the status of psycho-physical correlations, neurophysiologists certainly feel that the available evidence fully justifies, as a *modus laboris*, the assumption of a very close psycho-physical correspondence of the sort required by some form of IT.[59] Mountcastle for example has spoken of [60]

the neural activity set in motion by sensory stimuli which is successively transformed through successively interconnected populations of neurones, complexed against stored information contributing to and conditioned by those neural locales and activities concerned with set effect, [and how] these neural activities do themselves lead to *and in fact are the very essence* of the form of a discrimination, a localisation, an estimated magnitude, or a description of quality. Both private and public happenings are considered the result of the same chain of neural events.

The localisation in the brain of the activity associated with a variety of general classes of mental events such as the senses, fear, pleasure and pain has already been referred to. There is no *a priori* reason to believe that explanations of further specificity of function is beyond the scope of

127

biochemical, cell-assembly and learning-net theory, together with such holistic concepts as hierarchical order and systemic self-regulation as cited in Chapter III (Section 5.2).

3.2   *Mental–physical Isomorphism*

It is generally agreed that, if it were shown that a (completely specified) brain state were associated with more than one mental state, then IT would be falsified, for of course a one–many physical–mental relation would rule out identity. Some physiologists have, however, contemplated the possibility of a many–one relation,[61] and this possibility has also been construed by some philosophers as an objection against strict IT, which ostensibly requires a one-to-one correspondence.[62] Another, related, objection is that, even though it is possible to know that a mental event is identical with some physical event, it is impossible to know which one, in the sense of being able to give a unique physical description that brings it under a relevant law.[63]

3.2.1   *Many–one, physical–mental relations*
The argument for a many–one physical–mental relation has a number of aspects, only one of which is very important for the PO model. First, however, we can note that there is a sense in which it is trivially true that more than one configuration of active neural nets might give rise to a single mental state, and this is the sense due to the structure of the brain's functional sub-systems. The model is made clear by considering the directly analogous case of duplicative paralleling of functions in certain fail-safe systems in engineering, administration, etc., systems that are so arranged that when malfunction occurs the functional role of a malfunctioning sub-system is taken over by a similar system in parallel with it. Ordinarily, such parallel systems are not essential to the overall systemic function and so are redundant. It is well known that such redundancy exists in the brain, so that it is possible for an individual to sustain massive (redundant) cortex loss without significant loss of overall function. In this case each and every mentalling would be identical with a physical process of a given structure which may be (redundantly) replicated in parallel in the same brain.

Similarly, it is arguable that physical configurations quite different from the human brain might sustain mentalling processes indistinguishable from the human. An identity theorist need not scruple to concede this possibility: first, because it is irrelevant to his interest in *human* thought processes and their relation to the human brain: and second (and this applies to the redundancy case also) because the more general substantive issue is whether mentalling is sufficiently accounted

128

for in terms of physical processes in contrast with rival dualist accounts. So far as this central issue is concerned, it is a matter of indifference whether or not other physical systems fulfil the necessary and sufficient requirements for mentalling. In other cases (animal, extra-terrestrial, android, etc.) other-than-human mentalling would simply be identical with the undergoing of other-than-human physical-state changes.

The most substantial morphological objection to an IT, given the possibility of a one–many psycho-physical relation, is the possibility that some mentalling can be related to quite *different* patterns of neural activity, both in the same human individual at different times and at the same time in different human individuals. J. J. C. Smart's insight, that neuropsychology is closer to engineering than to pure science, is relevant to this point.[64] Consider the rudimentary case of bridge design. The same design requirements can be fulfilled by an indefinitely large number of physical configurations. In this sense, even though the formal bridge design fulfils a given invariant *function*, it is not identical with any particular design *configuration*. This analogy is illuminating, so let us pursue it. The fundamental or formal bridge design fulfils certain requirements such as, roughly speaking, overall dimensions, weight and distribution of load-bearing capacity, which will be common to *all* embodiments; that is to say, there are certain specifiable *formal* relations among the elements of any one configuration that are isomorphic with similar relations among the elements of other configurations with the same function. The bridge design might be said to be identical with the specifiable set of relations common to all configurations, expressed roughly as overall dimensions (span), distribution of load bearing capacity, etc.

In its simplest form such a set of relations is expressed in the equation for the bending of simply supported beams: $M = EI/R$ where M is the design bending moment, E is a relation between stress and strain (modulus of elasticity), I is the second moment of cross-sectional area about the axis of bending (moment of inertia), and R is the radius of bending of the beam under load. In a given case (i.e. for a given bridge function or purpose) the value of the design bending moment, determined by the loads to be carried over the span, will constitute one sort of constraint or boundary condition. The radius of bending will also be constrained for obvious reasons, a constraint on the manner in which the bridge function is fulfilled. Within the limits imposed by these constraints the bridging function can be fulfilled by an indefinite number of configurations using different materials (i.e. different bending inertias), provided the relation between E and I, specifically their product EI, is invariant.

Thus fulfilment of the bridge function is identical with the embodiment of the *set of relations* specified in the bending equation. A model appropriate to more complex functions, such as those of electronic systems, would involve correspondingly more complex formal relations, but would be essentially of the same form and exhibit the same 'morphology' in its functional–configurational relations. By analogy, high-order brain function (mentalling) might theoretically be fulfilled by any number of embodied configurations, but these configurations must each exemplify a set of relations that is isomorphic with that of all other configurations fulfilling the same function.[65] On this model, therefore, the identity theorist is identifying mentalling with the undergoing of physical processes that exemplify and embody a set of relations of a particular kind as well as being among elements of a particular (neurological) kind. As in the case of bridge configurations, so also in the case of cerebral configurations: the same function might theoretically be fulfilled by any number of configurations without diminishing either the fact that function is invariant with respect to formal relations, or the fact that in any *given* case conditions sufficient for fulfilment of function are completely satisfied by the *given* physical configuration with which, for the case concerned, the mentalling is identical.

The distinctions between three cases of psycho–physical morphology can perhaps be brought out more clearly by elaborating on the bridge analogy. (1) The case of redundancy in the brain's system is analogous to a number of bridges of the same type in parallel over the same span. (2) The case of different patterns of brain activity is analogous to different bridge design configurations. (3) The case of different sorts of embodiment (i.e. other than human) is analogous to the bridging function being fulfilled by means other than bridges, such as ballistic devices, aircraft, etc. As to the relevance of these distinctions for a putative identity relation: the crucial claim of IT is not undermined by the fact that numerous similar configurations of the same type (1) or even systems of different types (2), fulfil the same function; that is, to say of a system that a function is fulfilled in or by it is to say that the system in question embodies a set of relations among physical elements. Nor is the fact that the same function can be fulfilled by systems of *different* types (3) relevant to the fact that, for systems of a *given* type, to fulfil the function is to embody a set of relations among physical elements.

For human individuals, therefore, considered in general terms as cognising systems of a certain type, the function of mentalling is identical with undergoing a physical process exemplifying and embodying a given set of relations (i.e. of a certain pattern), and *ex hypothesi* these patterned processes happen to take place in the brain. Neuropsychology may or may not confirm that more than one actual configuration of neuronic or biochemical elements embodies the pattern of relations entailed by the mental–physical identity statement, just as the engineer finds several bridge configurations might embody the same overall pattern of relations fulfilling the same bridging function. It is highly probable that there *is* redundancy in the brain, and it is possible that there are also *more* complex forms of polymorphism. These are empirical matters to be resolved by looking, though biogenetic considerations would suggest that certain fairly narrow limits are imposed by brain anatomy and physiology.

The most significant conclusion to be drawn from the present discussion is, I believe, that there may be one–many as well as one–one relations between the mental and the physical and an identity relation still holds. This is so for each individual instance of mentalling, for the totality of instances, and also in the general, or categorial, case, provided it is clear that there is an isomorphism between a function, i.e. a mentalling (sensing, thinking, remembering, anticipating, etc.), and a *pattern* of physical events, exemplifying an invariant formal relationship. Again, crucially as always, the PO interpretation of the mental appeals to no other entities than physical elements and the dynamic structure of relations between them.

3.2.2 *The denial of law-like physical–mental relations*

It is said that, even if science should lead us to accept that every particular ('dated individual') mental event is, or must be, uniquely related to some corresponding, particular, brain event, there is still reason to deny that law-like relations could ever be established between them, that is invariant relations between *types* of mental and physical events. However, thoroughgoing physicalism which seeks to predict and explain mental events requires such laws because it requires that we know which physical event is identical with some mental event in the sense of being able to give a unique physical description which brings the mental event under a law.[66]

There are no strict psycho-physical laws because of the disparate commitments of the mental and the physical schemes. It is a feature of physical reality that physical change can be explained by laws that connect it with other changes and conditions physically described. It is a feature of the mental that the attribution of mental phenomena must be responsible to the background of reasons, beliefs and intentions of the individual. There cannot be tight connections between the realms if each is to retain allegiance to its proper source of evidence.[67]

This argument is based partly on an acceptance of Brentano's view that psychological phenomena are uniquely and irreducibly intentional, and the correlate view that psychological language has unique, non-extensional, features. There is ample evidence that this view is mistaken and there is no purpose to be served here by rehearsing the arguments.[68]

There is another point to be made here on the basis of arguments advanced in Section 3.2.1 above. The objection is that we cannot give a unique description of a type of physical event that is identical with some type of mental event. We might, however, take the point made in the last section, that identity theory implies an isomorphism (a one-to-one correspondence) between types of mental events and patterns of physical events *which exemplify an invariant formal relationship*. On this basis there would be among descriptions of physical events a unique formal description of the invariant relationship, which is satisfied when there is some (identical) mental event, and this does not require the specification of the precise physical embodiment(s). Thus we can think in terms of an isomorphism between 'types' of mental events and 'types' of physical events that exemplify invariant formal relationships. On this view, the occurrence of a mental event of some type is identical with the occurrence of a token of the identical physical type. This is one sort of 'nomological slack' between mental and physical events that a 'type-identity' theorist need not deny. The case is analogous to that of bridge design, where a 'safe design' ('mental event') may have any number of physical embodiments ('physical events') without this undermining the law-like nature of the relation between safe designs and the actual bridges that embody them.

However, there remains the substantial objection that, in point of fact, the mental and physical realms are logically incommensurable; they are not 'made for one another'.[69] This claim, if true, may be a sufficient obstacle to a coherent physicalist account of the mental. Now this question is not one that can be settled *a priori*, by merely asserting that, to *allow the possibility of* psycho-physical laws at all is to 'change the subject'.[70] Clearly, this assertion entirely begs the question of whether the mental realm is amenable to law-like explanations. It is well to recall in this connection the case of the scholastic professors who wanted to insist that Galileo was 'changing the subject' from discourse in celestial–terrestrial categories to something else. The only difference between past and present situations in the history of science is that, whereas in the past it was bold of scientists to risk advancing scientific explanations against entrenched prejudices, now, because of the successes of science, it is considered bold of philosophers to risk denying the possibility of scientific explanations on the basis of *a priori* considerations. We must look, therefore, not to *a priori* presumptions about the possibility of psycho-physical laws, but to the reasons given for denying the possibility of precise psycho-physical laws.

The fundamental reason given is that, supposedly, mental

phenomena, and so descriptions, attributions, and explanations of them, are intrinsically and uniquely open-ended, whereas physical phenomena are not. The point is that when we use concepts such as belief, desire and intention we must always be prepared to adjust our theory about the mental condition of an individual.[71] So even if precise and complete physical descriptions are possible within a closed system of physical laws, identity with the mental will be difficult to *establish* if it is inherently impossible to determine with the same precision the corresponding mental description. This apparent problem can, I believe, be resolved when it is recognised that the interpretation and description of physical phenomena are not nearly so closed or, rather, are not closed in the way that is usually supposed by philosophers. When a more faithful conception is achieved of the appropriate pattern of scientific explanation of complex phenomena, it provides a model of the sort that is commensurable with the complexity of mental phenomena also.

First, notice how the claim that descriptions of mental phenomena are inherently open is presented. It is said that:[72]

> we make sense of particular beliefs only as they cohere with other beliefs, with preferences, with intentions, hopes, fears, expectations and the rest. The content of a propositional attitude derives from the place in the pattern. ... When we use the concepts of belief, desire and the rest we must stand prepared as the evidence accumulates to adjust our theory in the light of the over-all cogency of what must be an evolving theory.

Here we have a statement of the problem of interpreting human behaviour *in its full complexity*.

Physical systems are usually presented, by contrast, *in their most basic simplicity*. It is typically assumed that explanations in natural science are based *simply* on universal general law statements of the basic form: 'If/ whenever such and such, then so and so'. The process of interpreting natural events (supposedly) involves describing particular events in the terms of the general law statements, and then explaining, predicting and retrodicting according to the covering law schema: 'Given such and such, predict and explain the occurrence of so and so'; 'given so and so, retrodict such and such which, when confirmed, explains so and so'. There can be no doubt that this simple picture is the one being compared to the full complexity of interpreting human behaviour.

Typically, we are presented with a comparison between on the one hand a human being undertaking an intentional action on the basis of certain beliefs and desires, and on the other hand a body falling in a vacuum.[73] It may seem plausible then to suggest that there is no real comparison between even a truism like 'If a man wants to eat an acorn omelette, then he generally will if the opportunity exists and no other desire overrides', and scientific law statements about a body falling in a vacuum because, for example, in the latter case, but not the former, we can tell in advance whether the condition holds and we know what allowance to make if it does not. Likewise, it may *seem* plausible to suggest that there is no hope of refining the simple pattern of explanation on the basis of reasons into a quantitative calculus that brings all relevant beliefs and desires into the picture.

The fundamental error in all of this is the sweeping assumption that all natural scientific explanations conform simply to, or are logically trivial refinements of, the covering law formula: 'If such and such, then so and so', which is theoretically closed. From this assumption it is inferred that explanations that do not conform straightforwardly to this simple pattern are irredeemably 'open' and incommensurate with explanations of physical phenomena. There is no reason why we should take such cases as bodies falling under gravity as paradigmatic of scientific explanation of all natural phenomena. If what we are concerned with is the behaviour of particular human beings, the obvious thing to be looking at is the form of scientific explanations of the behaviour of individual systems of great complexity, not explanations of the behaviour of the most simple systems under laws of the utmost generality. When we do so, the simple distinction made between mental and physical explanation is much less plausible.

In fact, when we look into the form of scientific explanations of *actual*, particular, physical systems, even those of very modest complexity, we discover that interpretation, description and explanation are by no means so straightforward that we can tell *in advance* whether salient conditions hold and what allowances to make if they do not. A simple physical system such as a weighted spring, for example, seems to conform archetypically to the basic covering law formula because the law statement, 'If load such and such, then extension so and so', covers the case. It is noteworthy, however, that even when this simple formula does apply straightforwardly it involves a complex set of relationships between laws of universal application (Newton's laws); laws of limited generality (Hook's Law); empirical (spring-rate) constants; specific values of variables (i.e. suspended mass) and a schematic model of the system established by 'opportunistic' procedures, typically described as 'analysis' or 'inspection'. However, if, as may be, the system does not behave in a way predicted by the simple formula, it will be necessary to modify the weighting given in the model to known relevant factors because of such effects as acceleration (as in a vehicle), gravity (as in space), damping (as with viscous fluids), and changes in elasticity (as in heating). Also, it may be necessary to introduce entirely new factors and

134

considerations into the explanatory schema or model to account for deviations from the formula *in specific cases*: in the example given there may be such factors as electrical or electromagnetic effects.

It will be evident from even this cursory consideration of an extremely simple artefactual system that the process of describing and explaining its behaviour involves a substantial element of interpretation (analysis and inspection) and re-interpretation, possibly in the light of new evidence.

The continual need for interpretation and re-interpretation is even more obvious, and to the point, in the case of such natural systems as learning nets of the kind embodied in the human central nervous system. It is possible to show that, although the behaviour of such systems does conform to the basic pattern, 'If such and such, then so and so', nevertheless they are capable of behaving in a way that calls for continual interpretation and re-interpretation, because, overtly, the same physical system may (1) respond differently to similar influences ('same cause, different effect') and (2) respond in a simiiar way to different influences ('different cause, same effect'). It is largely on the basis of such *apparently* causally indeterminate patterns of behaviour that human behaviour is set apart from 'merely' physical–causal behaviour. This case will be discussed more fully in Chapter VII (Section 7.3.1), but the reason why the behaviour of manifestly determinate systems requires interpretation is pertinent to the present issue. The fact is that even extremely simple physical systems of the learning network type conform to the basic 'If such and such then so and so' formula only provided that the 'if such and such' part includes not only events impinging on the system at a given moment in time, but also the effects of events that have influenced the system at previous times (including of course its basic structure). For systems as complex as the human brain, and on the postulate of IT this means, as we would expect, that present behaviour depends upon the individual's 'memory', 'beliefs', 'desires', etc.

In other words, the process of describing the structure and function of such a physical system can involve interpretation and re-interpretation of its behaviour on the basis of available and new evidence about its past. This process, in fact, is the process of cybernetic modelling, analysis and interpretation of complex systems where the determinate system is incompletely observable.[74]

This last point raises another important matter which should be mentioned here: the modelling of psycho-physical processes that depends upon the comparable 'openness' of both psychological and physiological descriptions. The theory of automata has been used, not to design mechanisms that merely *imitate* observable human behaviour, but to provide a logical scaffolding for the development and testing of psychological theory. It has been said that we search nowadays for clues to the organisation of human personality in two widely different fields, the provinces, broadly speaking, of psychology and physiology.[75] These clues come expressed in characteristically different languages, and so, although we may believe that the data should help us, without a correlating schema we have little idea what to make of them.

Crude mechanical or even computer models we know will not do, and this seems to be the important truth advanced in the objection under discussion. However, as Mackay points out, the language of information and control in which the theory of automata is framed is conceptually indeterminate between those of psychology and physiology. It belongs to both fields in as much as questions of information transfer, communication and control arise in both. Automata theory, designed as a model of the human organism considered as an information flow system, provides a common meeting ground in which hypotheses can be framed and tested and progressively refined *with the help of clues from both sides.*[76] The task for the behavioural scientist is thus: against a background knowledge of physiology and human behaviour, to design a self-organising system with the same information flow map, as well as the same behaviour, as a human being. The process of developing and deploying such models will involve iteration (i.e. testing and comparison) between psychological and information flow hypotheses. Both psychological and information flow theories will be refined in the course of this process, but it seems possible that they may converge and that our understanding of psychological phenomena would be advanced.

It is evident from these considerations that explanation of physical systems, except the most simple ones subject only to the most basic universal laws, are not closed in any important respect to do with openness to re-interpretation by observers in the light of new evidence.

Explanatory schemata commensurate in complexity to the complexity of neurophysiological systems are not obviously incommensurate with the known complexity of psychological phenomena. Indeed, if IT is true we would expect nothing less. More than this, however, there is reason to believe that information flow and other cybernetic models already do provide powerful heuristic tools for psycho-physical research based on iterative methods which exploit the openness to interpretation of both psychological and physical phenomena.

Doubt about the possibility of formulating psycho-physical laws because of the inherent open-endedness of psychological descriptions entails doubt about the possibility, in principle, of translating mental and physical talk. The point, again, is that when we use 'mental' concepts we must stand prepared to adjust our theory about an individual's state of mind in the light of new evidence. But an arbitrary choice of translation schema would rule out such opportunistic tampering with theory. It is said that an adequate translation manual would only be acceptable in the light of all possible evidence, and this is a choice that cannot be made.

Now translation between two non-formal languages does not rule out the possibility that the statements translated differ from time to time. Indeed, what else do we look for in a translation schema if not precisely this capacity to handle different statements? By the same token it is immaterial to the status of a translation manual that different statements should in fact be revised, and/or expanded, descriptions of the same state of affairs, such as a state of mind. Epistemological and methodological problems of establishing the truth of empirical statements in a given language complicate but are not the same problem as the problem of translation between different languages. If there are epistemological difficulties in establishing the truth of statements in some language, this just means a corresponding difficulty in establishing correlations. It does not mean *a priori* the senselessness of claiming that there are such correlations. What then does the doubt about the translatability of the mental and the physical amount to? Is it not to say that statements in one language reporting or describing mental phenomena are liable to revision; and that, *therefore*, the status of the mental–physical *translation schema* must be forever in doubt; therefore, that such a scheme is impossible? Clearly this is a *non sequitur*.

There is no more reason in principle to question the status of a mental–physical translation manual, because a different intention or belief might be discovered or a different weight or significance attached to ones already known, than there is to question the status of a French–English dictionary because something different, or even novel, has been said, or insinuated, in French or English. In practice, of course, the sheer complexity and transience of the phenomena may prove an insurmountable obstacle to the production of a useful translation manual, but this is not the same sort of problem as a systematic confusion based on a categorial difference. As has already been shown, most natural phenomena in the physical world no less than the mental are of an order of complexity that (notoriously) defies completely accurate description and prediction, so mental phenomena are by no means unique in *kind* so far as these difficulties are concerned. However, it is all too easy to exaggerate the difficulty of knowing others' states of mind. Misunderstanding is commonplace, it is true, but understanding is, nevertheless, typical – especially when individuals themselves are communicative.

I conclude therefore that there is nothing in even the endless possibility of revising 'theories' about *particular* (i.e. 'dated individual') mental phenomena, or states of mind, to rule out, in principle, the possibility of compiling a translation manual for the mental and the physical. For example, I may come to believe that my anxiety about my wife's imminent death is based not, as I previously believed, on grief for a loved one's suffering, but on a purely selfish fear of the loneliness in store for me. There is nothing in this, typical, case to raise doubts about whether (1) there are such definite and typical states of mind as grief for dying loved ones and fear of loneliness or (2) when such typical states of mind occur they cannot often be definitely known, or (3) there are physical correlates of these states of mind and these might, in principle, be identified, and typified.

3.3   Non-parsimony of Laws

Among the principal advantages claimed for IT is the claim that it extends, in principle at least, the domain of application of the invariant physical laws of science, and is therefore parsimonious of laws. It has been objected that the principle of parsimony of empirical laws does not hold, because the dualist psycho-physical laws are retained to relate neurological descriptions with the 'nomological dangler' descriptions in the first-person language.[77]

Although some advocates of IT have argued heroically that the mental properties of neural events are in reality neurological[78] (or at most topic-neutral as between mental and physical), we have found no reason to deny the duality of properties on a biperspectival account. The inference from this ready admission to the non-parsimony of laws, however, goes too far. It is true that description and explanation in the scientific language require *translation* into the first-person dangler language using a psycho-physical dictionary, just as dualism does. The parsimony achieved by IT is of a different kind, however. It lies in the possibility of eliminating *competing* accounts of human behaviour. For there is an important distinction to be drawn between alternative or *differing* accounts and *competing* accounts.

The distinction can be quickly illustrated by considering the case of combustion. Combustion might be accounted for in a number of ways. One version is the ordinary common-sense account in terms of heat generated by, for example, a fire causing a substance to burn. Another account is the accredited scientific account in terms of atomic theory, oxidation and the thermodynamics of chemical combination, etc. A third account is in terms of the obsolete phlogiston theory. Other accounts might be rendered in terms of supernatural agencies and so on. Of the first three accounts, the first (ordinary language) account and the second (scientific) account are alternatives differing only in degree of specificity. The second and third (phlogiston) accounts are *competing* accounts, since phlogiston theory requires that the combustible *lose* something whereas oxidation theory requires that the combustible gain something. The ascendancy of oxidation theory after Lavoisier was parsimonious of *competing* explanations of combustion, though the ordinary and scientific accounts remain as alternative but compatible accounts.

The parallel to be drawn with psycho-physical laws lies in the fact that dualists since Socrates (whether ontological, epistemological or linguistic) have commonly regarded the existence of bifurcated accounts of behaviour (generally the difference between physical–causal accounts and accounts in terms of reasons and motives) as *competing* accounts in some sense. It will be useful for the present purpose to distinguish here between *competing* explanations as *contra*-causal, and explanations that do not compete with physical causal explanations as *non*-causal. There is a peculiar ambivalence about the status of rational explanations of action in recent philosophy. They are sometimes treated as non-causal (and so avoid conflict with physical determinism), and sometimes treated as contra-causal (and so establish free-will against physical determinism (see Chapter VII below, Section 4). The behaviour of human individuals (or the 'actions of persons', in the preferred argot) is taken to be regulated by motives, reasons, intentions and purposes that are supposedly *not embodied* dispositions or in any way describable in physical–causal terms. These explanations are sometimes held to be of a different order *altogether* (i.e. non-causal), and yet at the same time are held to justify denial of the necessity attached to the explanations and predictions of human behaviour based on deterministic physical laws and mechanisms, that is to say are regarded as contra-causal in the sense defined. Such contra-causal explanations compete with physical deterministic explanations over the determination of human behaviour.

An IT however, interprets dispositional concepts *causally* and thereby proposes to translate motives, reasons, intentions and purposes into physical terms in a way similar to that in which ordinary concepts such as burning and heat are translatable into the terms of oxidation theory. In so far as contra-causal explanations are opposed to deterministic physical–causal explanations, there is parsimony of competing accounts of behaviour. In so far as non-causal explanations are *not* opposed to deterministic physical causal explanations but are 'convergent' with them,[79] then, like the ordinary accounts of combustion, the non-causal accounts of behaviour in terms of motives, reasons, etc., remain as alternatives to the deterministic PO account and for most ordinary purposes will be both more useful and more convenient.[80] However, the pursuit of thoroughgoing scientific understanding and explanation is an *extra*-ordinary purpose which gains in scope and predictive power through the psycho-physical translations offered by an IT.

Summarily, IT makes no more demands on scientific objectivity than does any well-established scientific methodology that depends on supposedly objective observations, and its form and content render it refutable by erosion, if not disproof. It therefore stands as a coherent scientific hypothesis which is also, in fact, sufficiently well supported by the available empirical evidence to allow it serious credence. The question of psycho-physical morphology (i.e. whether there is in *general* a one–one or a one–many correlation) is seen to turn on whether there is an identity of mentallings and invariant formal ordering in physical systems. The possibility that the same formal order can be exemplified in physical systems other than human bodies is irrelevant to the main metaphysical and ontological thrust of IT. Psycho-physical laws are possible in principle, given adequately sophisticated law statements. Finally, IT offers a parsimony of competing accounts of human behaviours (though, of course, there is no real parsimony for physicalists for whom the competing accounts are not real alternatives at all).

4 EPISTEMOLOGICAL OBJECTIONS

The outstanding arguments against an IT that are of a broadly epistemological nature are based on appeals to alternative autonomous forms of explanation and understanding.

4.1 *The Problem*

Perhaps the greatest difficulties in rendering an adequate PO account of *all* human experience arise in cases in which the orthodoxy purports to offer alternative autonomous accounts; it holds that there are certain occurrences that completely escape physical descriptions and explanations because the relevant facts are not simply brute facts but more complex affairs such as 'institutional facts',[81] for which different sorts of explanations *altogether* are involved. A number of trusty examples of the sort of thing in question will bring out the distinctions clearly enough.

1 Explanations and prediction of the shots in billiards employ concepts internal to the game itself, namely the rules and the tactics, skills and plans of the players. Explanations involving these concepts are quite different from any description of the movement of balls on a table according to the principles of Newtonian mechanics.[82]

2 A householder forgets to put out the milk bottles, thereby breaking the conditions of contracted milk service. Explanations involving contracts, service and non-fulfilment of requirements presuppose the existence of an organised community (common language, shared

activities and a background of mutual purpose, activity and understanding). There can be no account of these circumstances solely in terms of the entities and laws of physics.[83]

3 A raconteur relates a jest, which the hearer, being as humourless as the sphinx, fails to grasp. He is puzzled about the speaker's purpose, and thinks perhaps it is an exercise in verbal abstract expressionism. A proper explanation of the hearer's predicament can only be given in terms of the concept of 'humour' and 'sense of humour' and has nothing to do with biochemistry, not to mention (Lord help us!) physics.[84]

4 A man attempts to present a formal argument but omits a vital premise. This defect in his argument is, of course, expressed in purely logical terms. There can be no physiological process corresponding to the omission of the vital premise and no physical explanation of the error.[85]

5 An automobile skids at speed at a bend in a rain-soaked road and crashes through a safety barrier. The incident can be described either in terms of dangerous traffic conditions requiring due care and attention, warnings, legislative action, etc., or in the engineering and ergonomic terms of physical science. Neither account excludes or includes the other.[86]

6 Man C. C. (with black hair, striking eyes and a clipped moustache) utters the words 'I declare war against Russia' with the result that millions die laughing. Man A. H. (also with black hair, striking eyes and a clipped moustache) utters the words 'I declare war against Russia' and millions die fighting – the difference between the two events cannot be explained in the physical terms appropriate to bodily and verbal behaviour. The latter event involving Adolf Hitler especially (unlike the former involving Charlie Chaplin) requires the non-physical concept of performative utterances for proper explanation.[87]

7 Finally, a well-known omnibus example: a man is hand-pumping water from a well. As he does so the movement of his shadow describes a perspicuous pattern on the ground and the squeaking of the mechanism takes on the melodic form of 'Beat me daddy eight to the bar'. The water is pumped into a tank from whence it is tapped for consumption by a visiting group of nasties. The water has been deliberately poisoned; drinking poisoned water will cause the desired deaths of the despicable nasties; the death of the nasties will make possible enlightened government by liberal saints: thence the millennium–teleologicum. Now physical descriptions suffice to explain the mundane mechanical pumpings, the movements of the mundane pumper (whose muscles have long latin names that doctors

know about), the consumption of water and the subsequent death of the nasties. Physical concepts and language however are quite ineffective for the purpose of describing the shadow-patterns and the syncopated squeaks and are *especially* ineffective in the case of the intentional elimination of nasties for the desired purpose of bringing about the millennium.[88]

4.2   Games: Analysis and Synthesis

The distinctions made here all derive from the idea common to the metaphors of 'logical geography' and 'language games' (the nature of the relation, or, more especially, the *non*-relation between games). In one of his most seminal passages for the examples cited here Wittgenstein writes:[89]

> And this is true – instead of producing something common to all that we call language, I am saying that these phenomena have no one thing in common which makes us use the same word for all – but that they are *related* to one another in many different ways. And it is because of this relationship, or these relationships, that we call them all 'language'. I will try to explain this. Consider for example the proceedings that we call 'games'. I mean word games, card games, ball games, Olympic Games and so on. What is common to them all? – Don't say: there *must* be something common, or they would not be called 'games' – but *look* and *see* whether there is anything common to all, – for if you look at them you will not see something that is common to *all*, but similarities, relationships, and a whole series of them at that. To repeat: don't think, but look. ...

As the examples cited indicate, this view has been widely influential among analytical philosophers, who have tended, however, to stress differences rather than to seek similarities and relationships between different linguistic forms. This trend obviously runs counter to the whole synthetic tendency in modern science, and also to the strong tradition of synoptic philosophy. To this extent it has exercised what might be the most pernicious influence in recent philosophy.

The scientific tenor, and indeed the tenor of ordinary thinking without which practical activity would be inconceivable, is to seek pattern among the multifarious and variegated phenomena of experience. It is almost trivially true of course that the search for pattern is discriminative as well as integrative, but there is no question that knowledge and understanding accrues in the direction of maximising the range of phenomena explicable with the minimum of hypothetical structure.[90] The epistemological (or metaphysical) status of what might broadly be called the presupposition of the order, uniformity and intelligibility of nature is beyond the scope of the present discussion, but Duhem's remarks on the subject are particularly apposite and contrast sharply with Wittgenstein's:[91]

> Diversity fusing into a constantly more comprehensive and more perfect unity, that is the great fact summarising the whole history of physical doctrines. Why should this evolution whose law is manifested to us in this history stop suddenly? Why should not the discrepancies we note today among the various chapters of physical theory be fused tomorrow in a harmonious accord? Why resign ourselves to them as to irremediable vices? Why give up the ideal of a completely unified and perfectly logical theory, when the systems actually constructed have drawn closer and closer to this ideal from century to century?

And this insight is still fundamentally sound.

There is no pretence that the commitment to the pursuit of pattern, invariance and synthesis has any kind of formal or inductive sanction but, as Einstein remarked,[92]

> Every true theorist is a kind of tamed metaphysicist. The tamed metaphysicist believes that not all that is logically simple is embodied in experienced reality, but that the totality of all sensory experience can be 'comprehended' on the basis of a conceptual system built on premises of great simplicity. The sceptic will say that this is a 'miracle creed'. ... Admittedly so, but it is a miracle creed which has been borne out to an amazing extent by the development of science.

Against the constructive pattern-discerning tenor of the integrative tradition, much recent analytical philosophy has seemed almost positively to welcome the creed of 'mess'[93] and 'hurly burly'[94] at the level of human affairs. Of course, Wittgenstein himself was not denying order, structure and intelligibility to nature, or even to human language (quite the opposite). But it must be said that his later conception of order is restricted. One key metaphor compares the pursuit of meaning to the mapping of a varying terrain. His rejection or neglect of the profit to be gained from *causal* accounts leaves him with diversity without intelligible unity, or, to persist with the metaphor, a geography without a geology. It is obvious that the approved Wittgensteinian conventions might be applied to the inanimate domain with the same justice (or injustice) and with the same limitations with which it is applied to language and cognition.

At the level of ordinary prescientific discourse, propositions concerning the moon's motion, the behaviour of tides, the paths of projectiles and the rise of liquids in narrow tubes are as widely disparate as (and perhaps even more so than) ball games, board games, Olympic games and children's games, and yet a few principles such as Newton's laws of motion serve to provide a unitary structure within which the disparate phenomena become intelligible as different manifestations of an underlying order and structure. With regard to language and explanation, the possibility of unitary principles underlying the various linguistic forms and modes of explanation is no less cogent: more so, when it is fully understood that human life is entirely within the natural domain.

Exponents of the twentieth-century analytical creed of irreducible linguistic polymorphism concede that the laws of nature are not the result of human fiat.[95] The point they seek to make nevertheless is that there are different *sorts* of laws and rules and that different sorts of laws and rules reflect *human* purpose and interest. But the important fact is that human life and the business of rule-making and game-playing (including philosophising) is *itself* a natural process, and subject to the very same natural laws that the analysts admit not to be the fruits of human fiat or imagination. Once this complete interpolation of all human activities into natural biological hierarchies has been effected, we can thereupon extend the domain of *causal* analysis in the hope of discovering an invariance underlying the multifarious superficial differences in linguistic usage which undeniably exist, and to which the analysts have rightly drawn attention.[96]

4.3 *Games and the Possibility of Synthesis*

Before considering the general problem of linguistic and explanatory synthesis it will be a useful preliminary to discuss the key metaphor underlying the polymorph's position. We are invited by Wittgenstein to consider discursively what might be common to all games, and we are quickly encouraged to recognise that no single feature or simple set of features *is* common or essential to all of them. But is this really so? Undeniably, if we restrict ourselves to *appearances*, only family resemblances are evident. But again, how much *less* evident even than these are the relationships between lunar trajectories, tidal motion, cannonfire and meniscus phenomena? The scientific spirit is imbued with the imagination, confidence and enterprise to disregard *prima facie* dissimilarities as being potentially quite misleading as to the nature of discoverable relatedness where other considerations indicate some underlying articulating structure.

What then *are* the common denominators that would indicate a basis for essential relatedness in the case of games? Wittgenstein himself suggests two: rule directedness and point.[97] Since we are treating the matter discursively we can quickly add a third essential criterion for a game: that is, its point should not be believed by the participants to be ultimately concerned with matters of survival, or at least not a matter of serious importance.[98] Now definition, the textbooks tell us, should both significantly *exclude* and provide positive formal criteria (i.e. necessary and sufficient conditions). So if exclusion and significant inclusion are satisfactorily achieved by the threefold criterion proposed, then we have suggested reasons for expecting unity, as quickly as Wittgenstein suggested reasons for *not* expecting a unity. First, consider what might be excluded from the concept of games. All preconscious and subconscious natural processes including anabolism and catabolism are excluded, and if we accept the substance of the perhaps dubious but commonplace distinction between laws and rules then all reflexive and 'appetitive' behaviour is excluded also; so are all accidental, idle and 'noisy' processes (stumbling, thumb-twiddling and sleep-talking) and all productive work, restorative rest and creative imagination. There is, it would seem, no lack of excluded activities to make the criteria significant, even though they are comparatively broad.

What of the positive value of the criteria for distinguishing games from non-gaming activities? Let us consider cases where activities either become or cease to be games, to discover if the same criteria are operative. Begin by considering what is being referred to by expressions of the sort 'He's playing games' and 'It's only a game to him'. We find that activities that are otherwise not games become games as the suggested criteria become operative. Hunting becomes a game when it ceases to be a matter of survival, and when coincidentally it becomes regulated by rules. Similarly, affairs of the heart become games when intentions cease to be a serious matter of deep-felt emotion and tribal herd propagation. A business transaction that is entered into merely with the object of 'seeing what happens if (such and such an arbitrary rule or principle is adopted)', without regard for the serious implications and risks involved, is regarded as 'playing games'.

Conversely, consider the cases referred to by expressions of the sort 'We're *not* playing games (you know)', and 'It's no longer a game'. The first expression indicates that an activity has become a serious matter of direct survival value. In this category is the important case of 'war games' involving the rehearsal of serious strategies that *are* games only so long as the outcome or point is not actively a matter of survival: for when it *is*, the activity is simply *war*. The same principle applies to professionalism in sport: to the extent that the rules of games are violated, and their point comes to be regarded as primarily a serious matter of livelihood or survival (economic, ideological, etc.), then to that extent do they cease to be games. So, to the discursive query, about what is essential to board games, card games, ball games, Olympic games and children's games, we have the discursive reply: rules, point and not being primarily regarded as a serious matter of livelihood or survival. No attempt has been made here to do more than indicate a plausibly coherent basis for unifying concepts that a man on a galloping philosophical horse might otherwise think were significantly unlike. However, this brief consideration of the influential games metaphor does at least suggest that it provides no decisive reason for abandoning the possibility of a unifying theory of language and explanation.

4.4 *A Unitary Approach to Language and Explanation*

Most generally, comprehension is the recognition of pattern or structure at all cognitive levels from sensory perception to abstract–universal symbolic representation. This is not to say that progressive synthesis excludes analysis. On the contrary, analysis is obviously a prerequisite of fruitful synthesis, as the whole history of science testifies. The periodic table of elements and evolutionary theory are examples of sweeping scientific synthesis which would have been impossible without the prior systematic analysis and classification of significant differences. The creed of linguistic polymorphism in this century goes far towards establishing such differences in the uses of natural language, so that, for example, interrogative, emotive, prescriptive, exhortative and performative uses are now distinguished as well as the central descriptive use presupposed in traditional logic and the propositional calculus. Unfortunately, linguistic polymorphs have neglected and even positively opposed the important role of synthesis when it has been mooted at all. Understanding why this has been so is not to the present purpose, but it *is* pertinent to the present thesis that linguistic polymorphism has been the basis of most recent denials of the conflicts between science and morality, and determinism and free-will. However, once human activities are brought within the purview of science, as being wholly embedded in the natural world, on the PO model, there is no longer any clear justification for excluding language itself and its descriptive and explanatory roles from the quest for a general synthesis.

4.4.1 *Different uses of language*
How then does the PO model help us to view synthetically the varieties of distinguishable linguistic usage and explanation, as a basis for rendering a physicalist account of all of them? Perhaps an approach can be made by way of a schema for the processes distinguishable in all intelligent thinking and behaviour. Luria, for example, has distinguished

six stages involved in normal intelligent human thinking and behaviour. For the present purpose the number of stages is unimportant, and so is the fact that it is individual human thought and action that has been considered. The stages are identified only to indicate the character of intelligibly *ordered* behaviour, and might equally well apply to other than human individuals as well as to social groupings of any degree of complexity or level of hierarchical organisation.

1 *Motivation*: the stimulus necessary for any sort of action. This may not, however (as Luria holds), involve systemically *problematical* situations, but may be merely, for example, the spontaneous activity of the system's sensory-motor sub-routines under unproblematical conditions. In this case 'motivation' takes on a very extended sense closer to 'disequilibrium', according to which, for example, a see-saw would be 'motivated' to fall at its heavier end.

2 *Investigation*: the communication of information about the conditions obtaining in the internal and the external environments.

3 *Planning*: the formulation of plans or blueprints for the future, including search-and-locate operations among alternatives.

4 *Method selection*: selection from among available alternative means of achieving the plan.

5 *Operation*: rehearsal, possibly internal, of the plan.

6 *Comparison*: comparison of the outcome of the rehearsal with the blueprint's specification.

7 Given, on cybernetic principles, the matching of rehearsal outcome and blueprint specification, then the cognitive stage of the task is completed, and the basis for systemic *action* arrived at.[99]

If we take this analysis to be at least functionally typical of the operations of an intelligent goal-directed system's behaviour, we are able to identify a variety of typical communication loops and modalities in the ordered cycle of operations.

For individual organisms the communication loops are mainly formed by neural networks, although, as we have seen in Chapter IV (Section 4.1), even at the individual level complete functional integration of even intradermal sub-systems depends on extra-cortical organisation through 'new' functional organs.[100] For *groups* of individuals the basis of communication is the general behavioural semiotic, but particularly language.

The distinguishable roles that language fulfils will correspond to the communicative–integrative functions involved in the regulation of social groupings. The proposed concept or 'root model' through which the multifarious uses of language are to be synthetically unified, therefore, is that of systemic integration and the co-ordination of overall systems behaviour of which language is the main co-ordinating medium.[101]

147

Consider for example, the following possible taxonomy of usage.

1 The primary *descriptive* use of language is to communicate 'brute' facts by informing individual sub-systems of the states of dispersed and anatomically differentiated co-systems, subordinate systems and superordinate systems (cf. Luria's stages 2 and 3 above).

2 *Emotive* usage is a form of descriptive usage peculiar to the individual sub-system's expression of its own states as immediately perceived (cf. stages 2 and 6 above).

3 *Interrogative* usage is the form taken by systemic information 'search-requests' concerning the internal and external states (by analogy with the central-processing model of individual perception, which involves directed searches among surface irritations based on pre-existing mnemic models) (cf. stage 2 above).

4 *Predictive* usage is the form taken in planning, rehearsing and selecting courses of action (cf. stages 3, 4 and 5).

5 *Prescriptive* usage is the form taken in communicating the principles regulating systemic operations according to inherent structure and selected objectives (all stages).

6 *Performative* usage is the unique form taken in communicating decisions about system–state selection in the case of the deciding subsystem (cf. stage 4).

7 *Imperative and exhortative* usage is the form taken in enacting decisions intra-systemically (cf. stages 1 and 7).

This is no more than a sketchy indication of a PO *orientation* towards a coherent account of the multifarious uses of language. According to this model, different kinds or levels of explanation reflect the individual's biperspectival *recognition* of different kinds and degrees of relatedness with the environment, other individuals and groups. And, according to IT, to 'recognise' is to have neurally embodied (encoded) structures corresponding to the systemic relations recognised (see below).

4.4.2 *The PO model and rules*

Each of the cases cited as a polymorphic, or contextualist, objection to an identity hypothesis is based on an appeal to the operation of some rule or principle that is not in general considered to be physical and in particular is not concerned with the brain. Arguments along these lines generally suppose that the processes of human perception, cognition and action including the formulation and following of rules and regulative principles is somehow or in some unspecified sense outside of natural causation. More especially, for some unspecified reason the 'physical' description of a context is more often than not supposed to be restricted to, at most, mere *mechanics*. Typically, in the examples cited above, the agents (i.e. the billiards player, the dairy customer, the driver, the water pumper and the *fuehrer*) might just as well be hollow as far as the exponents of the linguistic mysteries are concerned. This restriction serves the polymorph's argument very well, because of course complex principles do not have crude mechanical correlates. But even when the evidence of neuropsychology is directly addressed, we typically find the unsupported assertion that there can be no physiological processes corresponding to, for example, missing a joke or omitting a logical premise.

But, given all the evidence, we must demand to know why *not* indeed! The development of mentality – the capacity to recognise rules and principles – requires the development of neurophysiological structure, and is practically quite unthinkable without it. The following remarks about volitional behaviour are typical of the kind of blindness in question:[102]

> Now such a man, surely, can discover that his leg is paralysed can he not? And how else can he discover this than by trying to move it and failing? And such trying, since it can by hypothesis involve no bodily effort and no motion of any bodily part, must be a purely psychological effort or mental trying, must it not? *The only allowable thing to say here really, is that no one knows.* ... The paralysed man's subsequent sincere avowal, then, that he tried to move his leg but failed evidently *does not mean that he did do something called 'trying'.* It means only that upon being told to move his leg he found that he could not. 'I tried' then, does not in this context mean (A) 'I did something though not quite all that I meant to do'. It means rather (B) 'I didn't move my leg, but that is only because I couldn't' and *that* is surely consistent with one's having done nothing at all.

The point in question here is that, as experiments with U-tubocurarine have long since shown,[103] conscious 'mental' acts by such a subject are correlated with non-obvious central nervous activity as indicated by EEG measurements; that is to say, there is very good reason to believe that there *is* a vital and demonstrable difference between 'I did something though not quite all that I meant to do' and 'I didn't move my leg, but that is only because I couldn't'. The former report connotes a verifiable state of affairs which the latter does not, namely the motor-effective activity of the cortex and central nervous system, which is immediately apprehended as 'trying' and which is prevented by the action of the drug from causing limb movements in the usual way. In fact the paralysed man's sincere avowal (A) *does* mean that he did something, something was going on and that something is called trying.[104] So, although a certain construal of the latter paraphrased locution (B) may be consistent with one's having done nothing at all, the former would be consistent only with there being certain activity in the central nervous system that would normally be effective in causing the action in question. In short, the proverbial difference between my intentionally moving my arm and my arm simply moving is very probably based in differential central nervous activity.

More important for the present discussion is the fact that the almost pathological refusal of some philosophers to consider the available data on the neuropsychology of sensory–motor activity extends also to the more complex activity of the temporal and frontal lobes of the brain underlying memory and teleological behaviour. Now it *might* of course be said in a certain tone of voice that, for example, pleasure in sex, fear of the dark or memories of childhood depend upon factors such as personal qualities of lewd lascivious libidinousness, of cowardice or childishness, and the persistence of the primary 'person' respectively, and that these are not physical concepts. But who, after the labours of Olds and Ungar and Penfield, will say that *no* physiological process corresponds to lust, fear and memory? And if not, why be so particular about laughter and logic?

It has been suggested for example that the basis of humour lies, to speak psychologically, in the sharp juxtaposition or collision of two cognitive systems or matrices of expectation given rise to in one system and resolution effected in another.[105] If so, then there is no reason to doubt that this phenomenon can be causally explained in terms of something like a 'dissonance' or a-synchrony between different neural nets, one embodying expectation-set, with insightful resolution through 'closure' of a different stable-state set.

The logical premise argument is similarly illuminated by considering the case of the calculating machine or 'analytical engine'. A disengaged cogwheel or a fused circuit is quite enough to account for the non-appearance of a vital premise in the data printout of a computer proof or calculation (and *mutatis mutandis* its omission or misapplication in the process of calculation itself). And there is no reason on earth why the precise coincidence of machine malfunction and logical mistake should be treated as a contingent matter with no more than curiosity value. Precisely the same arguments apply to the analogous non-integration of *neural* cell-assemblies into the nets underlying the calculating and/or reporting processes in the human brain and nervous system. If so, then the neurophysiologist as observer might apply neurophysiology to the brains of logicians, much as an engineer applies the principles of electronic circuits to digital calculators. Now nobody suggests that in undergoing the processes described by the engineer the machine is not performing logical operations. Still, it is argued that the laws governing the machine operation, those appropriate to an *engineering* investigation into a mechanical fault, are not the laws of logic, and precisely *this* is the point of the objection.

But, according to IT, the human individual, like the artefact, *in undergoing* certain processes that are in principle discoverable and describable by the neurophysiologist, is performing logical operations; and, what is more, a logical performance is precisely the intrinsic or immediate awareness the logician has of the calculating processes of his own nervous system. The participant–logician's principles and *rules* correspond to the observer–physiologist's structure and *law*. Both regulate and explain the same behaviour. In the man-machine system the human sub-system is liable to be misled into thinking that what he perceives *immediately* – the logical rules regulating the process – is *totally* divorced from the physical processes he *mediately* perceives going on in the machine sub-system. But this is a mistake. He *too* is a biophysical sub-system interacting with the physical machine. But only he has, *ex hypothesi*, biperspectival access to the physical processes undergone.

4.4.3   *The PO model and contexts*
The attempt to elucidate the basis of the PO view of the relationship between rules and physical process also bears upon rules regulating human behaviour in wider contexts. Once we adopt the notion of the individual brain as a sub-system in a variety of superordinate systems (family or social groupings) it becomes clear that it is not rules as such that are said by identity theorists to be identical with brain processes, as some critics have supposed. Rules as such regulate the behaviour of the superordinate groupings, analogously to the way in which logical rules regulate systems of calculi rather than individual calculations. The main import of the biperspectivist model is that the individual's awareness of a rule *qua* rule is his intrinsic immediate awareness, as a *participant* sub-system, of the constraints exercised by the superordinate systems of which is he is part. Rules are lawful systemic constraints from the inside. It is the individual's *recognition* of a rule that is properly held to be identical with brain structure or process, and not the rule itself.[106]

There is already some clinical sanction for this sort of account. The work of Lev S. Vygotsky has already been referred to, and further support can be drawn from Eysenck's thesis about normal and delinquent behaviour. He has cited evidence that suggests that the autonomic nervous systems of normal individuals have a conditioned structure which can be detected and measured by a variety of standardised autonomic responses (breathing, pulse, skin conductivity, etc.) under conditions of stress, due to deviance (fibbing etc). Significantly, those who do *not* manifest such reactions tend to be the sort of people, such as psychopaths, who do not display normal 'social conscience'.[107] This is consistent with the general PO thesis that exposure to the surface irritations involved in censure and chastisement during infancy literally re-structures the nervous system(s) of the normal individual, and that this is normally both necessary and sufficient for non-delinquent behaviour. *Mediately*, the structure might be observed or tested by the neurophysiologist; immediately, it is present to the individual himself as his disinclination to commit delinquent acts – his social conscience.

Objections are commonly directed against theses such as Eysenck's because they mainly involve classical Pavlovian conditioning theory which is primarily to do with automatic or vegetative processes, whereas, it is argued, it is precisely human reason and volition that are at issue. Eysenck himself has argued positively that only autonomic conditioning can *predispose* individuals against deviance, that is account for the sense of revulsion at delinquent alternatives. However, such criticisms are adequately met in any case when the central nervous system and particularly the brain are imported into the processes of initiation, learning and re-structuring. Indeed, the evidence of the frontal lobe–medio basal syndrome instanced by the celebrated case of Phineas Gage (see Chapter III above, Section 5.2.2), suggests at least an equivalent central nervous component in the regulation of social behaviour.

Here also we have evidence supporting Kremanskiy's Trojan horse thesis concerning the assimilation of individual sub-systems into superordinate social systems, and for Vygotsky's thesis about the social basis of individual acts of volition. For without the restructuring of the nervous system in social environments, behaviour is merely the unregulated consequence of random primitive spontaneity or reflexive responses to external or internal stimuli, as witnessed by the history of feral children and other less extreme cases of sensory and social deprivation.

Since the sub-system–superordinate system relationship is *reciprocal*, not only is individual human 'sub-system' behaviour regulated by superordinate social environment(s) through rules, mores, customs and so forth; but the individual sub-system may also in turn be itself instrumental in formulating plans that are reciprocally communicated throughout the system and which may become a basis for further systemic regulation.[108] This is clearly what happens when, for instance, a discrepancy between actual and intended outcome is recognised and fed back into the system as a basis for the modification of its behaviour and regulative principles. Changes in the regulative constraints, either internal or external to the system, bring about changes in point or goal, reflecting changed circumstances or context. Finally, entirely novel goals or blueprints for the future may be generated by sub-systems that involve new regulative principles or rules intrinsic to new patterns of activity.

What must be made quite explicit is this: the participation of the brain sub-system in superordinate systems begins with the epidermis and includes any loop into the environment. In the case of the individual brain it has been noted that mental functions must be organised in concertedly working sub-systems, each of which performs a role in a complex functional system (see Chapter IV above, Section 4.2.1). The sub-systems of the brain may be located in completely different and often distant areas of the brain. It becomes perfectly clear that the historically formed devices for thought (external aids such as the knotted tie, mnemonic notes, log-tables, computers) are essential elements in the establishment of functional connections between individual parts of the brain, and that by their aid areas of the brain that were previously independent become the components of a single functional system.[109]

> This can be more vividly expressed by saying that historically formed measures of the organisation of human behaviour tie new knots in the activity of man's brain and it is the presence of these functional knots, or as some people call them 'new functional organs' ... that is one of the most important features distinguishing the functional organisation of the human brain from the animal brain. It is this principle of construction of functional systems of the human brain that Vygotsky called the principle of 'extra-cortical organisation of complex mental functions' implying by this somewhat unusual term that *all types of human conscious activity are always found with the support of external, auxiliary tools and aids.*

It is as 'extra-cortical organisation' through new functional organs that the individual's action upon extradermal systems of varying levels of complexity is to be viewed within the PO model. 'New functional organs' might involve anything from a paper and pencil for noughts and crosses through a chess board and opponent, a political pamphlet, a library, a research team or the population of a nation-state, depending on the individual's status and relations within the structural hierarchy of superordinate systems. The important point for the present discussion is that at no stage in the description of the extension of the extra-cortical organisation is it necessary to introduce any concepts beyond those of physical elements, their dynamic interrelation in time, and the biperspectival awareness of the human agent–spectator (participant–observer).

The foregoing account is again recklessly broad-brush and inadequate, but the important point in rendering it in the narrow compass possible here is to sketch an *orientation* within which an intelligible physicalist account of the contextualist dimension of the 'mental' can be given that does not commit the grosser Procrustean sins of more traditional materialist accounts. There is a heavy demand on the physicalist to give *detailed* and coherent accounts of the principles sketched here; or, rather, there is a heavy programme of work to be done before the full details of the present root model are filled out, but the paradigm and *principles* have already impressed themselves upon many able thinkers.[110]

4.5 *Discussion of Objections*

Returning now to consider the 'contextualist' objections to an identity hypothesis, we begin first by taking note of three principles. First different usage and even alternative explanatory accounts are not *a priori autonomous* accounts. Second, and in particular, an IT suggests that different accounts may reflect different modes of access to a unique physical process. Third, following on the previous discussion of the concept of the physical, the system undergoing the processes concerned may participate as a sub-system in any number of superordinate systems of differing complexity at different levels in the different hierarchies. These three principles provide the basis for a PO account of the contextual nature of some mental concepts.

The main line of the PO argument against the objections may be clarified by considering the omnibus example (example 7 above) of hierarchically structured levels of explanation, corresponding to the progressive extension of the circumstances or context involved in a given act.

At the level involving only mechanical pumping motions there is no disagreement about the capacity of physical science to give a satisfactory account of what is going on.

The case of mellifluous squeaking and meaningful shadows introduces the first level of disagreement, since melodies and shadow-play involve aesthetic and perceptual criteria supposedly outside of the scope of any objective physical inquiry.

However, if we pursue the physical state-description of the pumping-agent sub-system beyond the relatively gross bits with long latin names (that doctors know about) and into the nervous system and brain, there is very good reason to suppose that in the association areas of the occipital lobes there are cell assemblies (1) *the having of which* constitutes the individual's capacity for discriminating significant visual pattern and (2) *the undergoing* of the sensory stimulation of which is for that individual the perception of visual pattern. Similarly, there is good reason to suppose that in the temporal zones of the right cerebral hemisphere there are cell assemblies (1) *the having of which* constitutes the individual's capacity for discriminating significant sound pattern and (2) *the undergoing* of the sensory stimulation of which is, for the individual so constituted, the perception of sound-pattern.

Provided therefore that the PO account embraces a description of the cell-assemblies concerned, *and* that it is understood that the 'domain' of perception and aesthetics is the perspective intrinsic to the *undergoing* of the processes so described, then the PO account is quite capable of rendering a complete explanation of the situation: one that, according to an IT, is *translatable* into the first-person language.

The case of deliberate or intentional poisoning is the level of radical schism between the contextualist polymorph and the physicalist. We are assured that the intention is not an inner state which would causally account for the intended act. But, as is so often the case with contextualist objections, only the most perfunctory consideration is given to the neurophysiological and biperspectivist interpretation of 'inner state'. The possibility that an internal image of the intended victim lying dead from drinking poisoned water might somehow be involved is mooted, only to be promptly dismissed on the grounds that the same image might also and equally occur to someone who was both ignorant of the poison present and innocent of malicious intent. But this dismissal is far too hasty for the identity theorist.

As an aside, it is useful to rehearse a routine piece of philosophical-cum-phenomenological analysis by distinguishing between the *concepts* 'poisoning' and 'murder', and mental *images* of poisoned-murdered people. Now it is trivially true that the idea (or concept or image) of people–poison–death might occur equally to the murderer and the innocent alike while performing the same mechanical movements. But surely it is obvious *ex hypothesi* that in the latter case the idea (image, concept) occurs by way of incidental or idle reverie and plays no part in his pumping operation. By contrast, in the former case it is *central* to the whole operation.

This distinction can be drawn and elaborated upon with comparative ease once we reject the simpleminded and stubborn insistence characteristic of some recent 'action-theorists' that everything should be explained from the viewpoint of a neuropsychologically ignorant *agent* or an observer equipped only with the concepts and information an agent has about his own inner goings on (the agent's self-information). Neurology in fact gives us very good reason to expect that the neural mechanisms determining the *murderer's* behaviour include networks and/or micro-structures constituting his 'blueprint' for the death of his victims by poisoning which are crucial controller–mediators in the sensory–motor processes involved in the pumping. Indeed, it is entirely plausible that to 'intend to murder' would be to have such a current blueprint for the future which regulates current behaviour. Current behaviour on this account is then only an instrumental expression or consequence of a blueprint for a future homicide.

The case of Walter Mitty is quite different, of course: if he does imagine the people dead we do not expect to find any functional connection between (1) those structures and processes the having and undergoing of which is his imagining and (2) those the having and undergoing of which constitute his intention to pump.

It is therefore totally at variance with what neuropsychology leads us to expect to say that in the act of (intentionally) pumping poisoned water nothing in particular is necessarily going on that might not equally well have been going on if the acts had been innocent acts of pumping non-poisoned water.[111] This mistaken view is the consequence of supposing that 'all that is relevantly going on' means the same as 'as far as Joe Soap can see from where he's standing, with 20–20 vision'.

IT simply acknowledges neuropsychology. There is then a *world* of relevant difference in what is going on. As *observed* (or observable) by the informed neuropsychologist the difference is neural. As *undergone* it is the difference between *mens rea* and innocent daydreaming.

To describe the situation in terms already employed: the poisoner *recognises* a connection between his image-plan, his pumping and the deaths by poisoning, whereas the Walter Mitty figure does *not* recognise such a connection. Clearly, the *circumstances* of an act as seen by a third person are irrelevant to, and do not bear upon, an individual agent's intentions except in the case that the agent *recognises* them, understands them and is (causally) disposed to act accordingly,[112] and this is practically quite unthinkable without the appropriate neural embodiments. An identity theorist is suggesting that there is thus a functional–causal difference of a straightforward sort between intending murder *in* acting and imagining murder *while* acting, and that the basis of the difference is in the nervous system, though without neuro-technology only the behavioural expressions (if any) of these different dispositions are normally available as observable criteria for the distinction.

It will be obvious by now what interpretation the identity theorist places on the other contextualist objections enumerated above and not already discussed. A complete PO account of the billiards game should include the neural embodiment of the participant's recognition of the rules of the game, and the player's strategies, tactics and skills, and not merely those items covered by Newton's laws of motion. Similarly, neural embodiments of the *recognition* of the principles regulating service contracts and imminent dangers are involved in 'forgetting the milk bottles' and 'traffic accidents' respectively as well as the mechanics of bottle movements and the conjunction of factors involved in a motor crash. Finally, the different consequences following from the utterance of a similar declaration of war by different individuals reflects both their different roles as 'performing' sub-systems, within their superordinate social systems, and also the recognition of these roles by other participating co-systems.

In general, what the observer mediately observes, describes and subsumes under scientific laws the participant–agent immediately understands and acts on as the rules, principles, mores, etc. regulating his behaviour in social contexts. A further consideration of some of the issues all too briefly raised here will be undertaken in a later discussion of other-than-causal explanations of agency and acts. For the present I take it that the substance of contextualist objections to IT can be met within the PO model.

Summarily: I have considered a number of important objections to IT based on the thesis that *physical* explanations are inappropriate for many purposes. The philosophical foundation for these objections in the creed of linguistic polymorphism has been discussed and an important shortcoming suggested: that *a priori rejection* of synthesis is not only unwarranted, but is counter-productive. A possible basis for a programme of synthesis has been briefly sketched, based on the concept of human individuality as embedded in, and interacting in multifarious ways with, a hierarchy of natural systems. Similarly, alternative explanations of human behaviour may be thought of as reflecting the structure of the systemic relations involved together with the biperspectival status of the agent–spectator. I have suggested that the physical processes to be identified with the contextually determined mental concepts are the central-state embodiments of the subject's recognition (understanding) of the systems with which he interacts, and the systemic constraints imposed by them.

5 SUMMARY

The main outstanding objections to IT seem to arise from a failure to recognise that two competing root metaphysical models probably underlie the dispute, so that many of the objections turn on an appeal to the structure of the orthodoxy. But once the (supposed) problems with IT are seen to be due to a confusion of root models, their resolution can be sought in an appeal to the emerging root model within which it is formulated and is coherent. In this way the main logical objections are seen to be anchored in the language of a dualist orthodoxy. Scientifically based objections to IT are also clearly rooted in a misunderstanding of the PO root model and of the crucial importance this has for the status of perception and the objectivity of scientific observations, and also for the nature of the identity proposed.

The same misconception, that the human body and brain are supposedly in some important sense outside of the world observed, underlies the most important epistemological objections also. These are disarmed by appeal to the PO model of persons as embedded in a hierarchy of interwoven physical, biological and social systems.[113]

I conclude that IT is both coherent and perspicuous within the emerging PO model of persons. The implication that mind-directed behaviour is therefore (by interpretation) physical behaviour or a physical process raises two important questions. First, can mind-directed behaviour (action), like other physical processes (behaviour), be adequately explained in terms of physical causation? Second, if so, is human action subject to physical–causal determination, at least to the same extent as other physical processes? To these questions we can now turn.

PART THREE

The way in which the inevitable comes to pass is through effort.

Oliver Wendel-Holmes Jr (1964, p. 5)

VI

CAUSAL NECESSITY

1 INTRODUCTION

If the mental–physical relationship should turn out to be identity then the recently buried perennial questions about the relation of physical causation to 'mind'-directed human behaviour (action) are raised all over again. For if mental events are physical events then the implication is that mind-directed events are subject to the same causal categories as other physical events. It is the object of this chapter and the next therefore to consider some of the main issues involved in the application of causal categories to human action.

It will be necessary to begin by considering some fundamental aspects of the traditional philosophical view of causation derived from Hume. There are many problems with the Humean view and it is neither possible nor to the present purpose to discuss all of them here. Two issues, however, are especially relevant to the emergence of a PO account of human action and must be considered.

First, there is the traditional view that any sort of thing can cause any sort of thing provided only that there is regular succession to be observed between them. In its application to the mind–body problem this view provides all of the advantages of theft over honest toil. The second and main issue that must be discussed is causal necessity, along with a range of related questions concerning causal powers, causal laws and universal causation. These matters are fundamental to explanations of human action which are in turn closely connected with the perennial problems of free-will and moral responsibility to be discussed later.

The main thesis advanced in this chapter is briefly as follows.
1 The widely influential Humean analysis of causation is unsatisfactory in important respects.

2 The PO model of causation as productive connection is more satisfactory than the Humean account.

In the next chapter the argument will be extended to explanations of human action.

2   CONCEPTS

2.1   *Causality*

Causality is the dual principle of universal uniform causation. The universality of causality is expressed in the maxim, 'every event has a cause', which implies that all events are effects. The uniformity of causality is expressed in the maxim, 'similar cause, similar effect', which implies that causes can be categorised on the basis of their similarity in relevant respects. Causality is to be distinguished, on the one hand, from other varieties of determinism such as fatalism, logical determinism and theism, and, on the other hand, from the various types of indeterminism such as fortuitism and quantum mechanical uncertainty. The prevailing orthodox view that human acts that are explained by motives, reasons and purposes* are neither deterministic nor undetermined will therefore, according to the present taxonomy, be a-casual and a-deterministic. Causality, the principle of universal and uniform causal connexity, has been characterised variously as a universal principle of nature, an inductive generalisation, an *a priori* principle of human understanding, a prescription for science, a pragmatic maxim, a presupposition, and a pious hope, among other things. The line to be argued later is that it is a synthetic *a priori* principle and, as such, can be construed in some sense as meaning *any* of the things suggested above.

2.2   *Causation*

Causation is the principle of determinate connexity between contiguous events. The connections have been variously characterised as purely phenomenal succession, as the products of powerful particular entities in action, as continuous chains of events, and as evolutionary state-changes.[1] There has been a wider divergence of opinion about whether

---

* Hereafter for convenience where explanations of human action in terms of motives reasons or purposes are being contrasted with causal explanations I shall use any one of the terms (but mostly reasons or rational explanation) in a sufficiently cavalier way to embrace the others. In this way I hope to avoid both an excess of irritating acronyms and tedious repetition of these related terms whenever the intention is simply to make the contrast between causal and rational explanations.

causation is to be regarded as a general explanatory principle at all, that is one covering several distinguishable types of natural relations, or whether there is only one sort of causal relation. Aristotle's theory of fourfold causation (i.e. material, efficient, formal and final causes) is the best-known example of the former. It has recently been suggested that the view that there are varieties of causation is due to a confusion between the categories of causation and determination, such that other categories of determination (e.g. statistical, interactive, teleological, etc.) have been wrongly thought of as causal categories.[2] According to this view 'causation' is specifically the principle of 'efficient cause', the asymmetrical linear relation between external agents (which produce effects) and patients (on which effects are produced) as exemplified in the well-known paradigm of billiard ball collisions. This in fact is the paradigm adopted by Hume as the single paradigm for all natural causal relations. With Hume, however, there are a number of other crucial departures. For, as well as rejecting the Aristotelian taxonomy of causes, he also rejects the important idea of productive connexity with its important implications of the sortal relatedness and temporal asymmetry of cause and effect. By adopting the inanimate billiard ball paradigm for all causation, Hume is also at odds with those who have suggested that (deliberate and intentional) human action is a special case and/or one that provides the proper paradigm for the causal relation: that perception of inanimate causation is an extension of the perception of novel effects brought about by mind-directed human agency.[3]

The line to be developed later, in accordance with the PO model, is to suggest that it may be possible to follow Hume in adopting a general formula for the causal relation, but also to preserve (1) the important distinctions that others following Aristotle have wanted to make, (2) the principle of productivity and (3) the status of human action as a special case of causation.

In the next chapter the view is advanced that in the important case of causal explanations of *human* actions, the introduction of an identity hypothesis allows a coherent causal account of mental-directedness which does not require the extravagant and counter-intuitive Humean principle that 'anything can cause anything'.

3   HUME'S VIEW OF CAUSES

3.1   *Hume's Account*

Although Hume was not the first philosopher to propose a phenomenalist account of causation, that is an account based only on observed regularities not real connections,[4] it is undoubtedly his influence that has pervaded empiricist philosophy and science ever since the publication of his *Treatise*. The main argument is very simple. It presupposes that the only ideas and knowledge we have of the world come from our sense impressions. Distinct impressions are distinct existences. It is then asserted that there *is* no impression of a causal connection. The only evidence we have for a causal relation between events therefore is their contiguity and regular succession. Any other causal characteristic must be supplied by the mind of the perceiving subject himself. Thus productivity and necessary connection, two of the most important aspects of both the common sense and the PO conceptions of causation, are unwarranted elaborations of the human mind according to Hume. Another consequence of Hume's thesis is that *any* contiguous phenomena perceived in regular succession are thereby, and in virtue of nothing else, in a causal relation to one another. In other words, 'anything can cause anything'.

This phenomenalist account has remained largely unchanged to date and continues to exert a powerful influence through the writings of modern empiricists. Its influence is also felt especially in the philosophy of science, where it continues to be quite acceptable to characterise the scientific enterprise as being the formulation of *descriptions* of the functional relations between phenomena only. According to this widely received view science is non-explanatory, only descriptive.[5] Characteristically, therefore, causation has traditionally been treated by Humeans and neo-Humeans on the assumption that it is essentially a phenomenological, logical, epistemological and psychological matter to do only with observations, admissable inference, purely conceptual relations and habits of mind. Some recent developments within the Humean tradition have sought to remedy the widely recognised difficulties, and many conceptual and epistemological issues have been greatly clarified in the process.[6] Nevertheless there are a great many other outstanding problems (metaphysical, scientific, etc.) raised by the phenomenalist regularity account which have remained largely unexamined. One consequence of this neglect has been that, especially on the metaphysical issues, the philosophic account of causation has shown little real progress from Hume's time until philosophers have more recently revived the case for real productive connexity.[7]

3.2 *Problems*

That some progress is badly needed is quickly established by considering the numerous notorious problems generated by, but insoluble in terms of, the traditional Humean account of causation. First, there is the surprising claim that we have no perceptual impression of a causal connection or of causal efficacy.[8]

Second, there is the assertion that causation is not perceived in single cases but only after habituation to repeated experience of constantly conjoined impressions in succession.[9] Third, there is the neo-Humean view that causes need not precede their effects in time; the causal relation is temporally symmetric.[10] Fourth, there is the problem of induction; the view that it is impossible to provide a rational basis for the anticipation of future events based on past experience.[11] Finally, there is the principle that causation involves succession of phenomena only, not real productive connection.[12] This in turn leads to a number of notorious difficulties including the impossibility of distinguishing between merely contingent succession and productive connection;[13] the denial of real entities beyond or underlying phenomenal impressions;[14] the generation of formal paradoxes, most notably Clavius's paradox and the Hempel–Goodman Paradoxes;[15] and what might loosely be called 'the pandemonium principle', that anything can cause anything,[16] especially that mental and physical entities enter together into causal relations indifferently.[17] (This view has profound consequences for the mind–body problem and action theory and explains how the inherently in-coherent orthodoxy is sustained.) This inventory is not intended to be exhaustive, but is offered in accordance with the principle that any thesis that gives rise to so many profoundly counter-intuitive and widely different problems is likely to be fundamentally unsound.

It is not possible to deal at length with all of these problems here. Nor is it necessary because these and similar problems have been discussed extensively elsewhere by others.[18] The salient fact is that the Humean account of causation which is still very widely received wisdom among philosophers is in fundamental ways problematical.

For the present purpose it will be sufficient to discuss in some detail just two of the problematical aspects of the Humean view: the principle that anything can cause anything, and the denial of real, productive, necessary connections (or causal necessity) between causes and their effects.

3.3   The Pandemonium Principle : Anything Can Cause Anything

One main consequence of Hume's 'regular contiguous succession' formula for causation is that there are no a priori type or 'sort' restrictions on the phenomenal items associated together through the causal relation. The counter-intuitive consequence, that any (sort of) thing can cause effects on any other (sort of) thing, Hume recognised and explicitly accepted.[19] Of special importance is his view that motives and such-like entities from the 'mental' domain and physical entities enter together into causal relations indifferently.[20] Later Empiricists have likewise affected to regard the contrary view that there must be some kind of type restriction on causally related entities as a 'strange opinion'.[21]

Against this position it must be said that, if recent analytical philosophy has achieved nothing else, it has shown the dangers of type and category mistakes of the sort implied by this principle. Unless some explanation of cross-categorial relatedness is offered, as in such cases as temperature and kinetic energy, or mass and energy, then such relations are *prima facie* logically suspect. The 'anything can cause anything' principle is based on a view of causation as contiguity and regular succession alone, which is descriptive, but not sufficiently explanatory. Contiguity and regular succession may constitute good grounds for supposing there to be some further causal relation holding between the phenomena and necessitating their succession.[22] But unless and until such a connection is established (and this presupposes a type-relation of some sort), contiguity and succession alone are not sufficient to establish connection, that is causation.

It is important in all of this not to ignore the role of energy, energy equivalence, and, perhaps more important, the modern conception of information-as-order in all change, including human behaviour. Explaining how various factors make a difference to the outcome of events requires more than a mere description of them in terms of non-physical predicates. It is necessary to give some account of how the difference-making factors (logically) might, and in reality do, enter into the mass–energy information economy of events, no matter what other descriptions might be given.

This points to another dubious feature of Hume's view. If causation is nothing but a regular succession of phenomena, then the mind–body problem is not solved, but overlooked. Most philosophers since Descartes have been impressed by the seriousness of the problem of how to explain the manifestly productive relationship between phenomena which are, nevertheless, supposedly different in essential ways. Hume's view offers merely a description of regular relationships between certain mental and physical phenomena. It denies the possibility of or need for any further explanation of how this can be and is so. In this way Hume conflates and confuses two quite distinct problems: the conceptual problem of whether the supposed relations between mental and physical categories are logically coherent, and the epistemological problem of how we know causal relations between mental and physical behaviour. By arguing that all knowledge of causal relations is based only on regular succession of phenomena he avoids the conceptual problems of how categorially different events can coherently be thought of in relation to one another at all, and thus provides a solution to the mind–body problem which has the advantages of theft over honest toil.

This account of causation also proves to be positively misleading when the mind–body (conceptual) relation is repeatedly used by him as a paradigm for causal relations.[23] For, of course, if two things stand in an identity relationship to one another it is misguided to imagine that we might observe or experience in sense a necessary causal connection between them. But identity is clearly an inappropriate model for causation, where observing a causal connection or experiencing it in sense is a real issue. Hume, of course, denies that there are objective causal connections to experience, but this is just another problematical aspect of the Humean view. It is to a consideration of this that I now turn.

3.4 Causation and Necessity

3.4.1 The time-slice ontology

The Humean view of causation turns on the basic model of distinct impressions which are distinct existences and the principle that there can be no *a priori*, logically necessary, connection between distinct existences. We might agree that this principle is overwhelmingly plausible,[24] but it is irrelevant to the question of the necessary efficacy of causes. In the first place the necessity of causation is not logical necessity at all (either deductive or inductive), but *natural* necessity. The necessary connections in question are in the world, not features of legitimate patterns of inference. Indeed, they are what legitimate patterns of inference aim to be *about*. In the second place, the presumption that it is distinct impressions that are in causal relation to one another is highly questionable.

There is no overwhelming reason for accepting the metaphysical root metaphor of distinct and unconnected 'impressions' or phenomenal time-slices: quite the reverse. As a root metaphor the 'time-slice' must prove plausible, and in the last analysis must pay its way like any other by 'commanding allegiance' by virtue of its success in adequately ordering human experience.

The basic problem with it is that it presupposes what might be called the 'Cosmic Odeon Cinema' account of human experience or, in Flew's words, the Paralytic's Eye View of the world.[25] So long as it is supposed that phenomena are presented to passive sense, as in the billiard ball paradigm, then it is arguable that the cinema is a better metaphysician than common sense, physics or philosophy.[26] If Hume's 'poison principle' has once been swallowed, then it follows that we can have no knowledge of real causal connections in the world. The apparent success of the demonstration is due however to the fact that it proves only what it implausibly presupposes:[27] the conjuring trick is the very first move in persuading the audience that it has no experience of substantial powers and the effects they cause. However, if the perceiving subject is alternatively conceived of as integral with the world and interacting with it, the situation is seen to be fundamentally very different from this. For then the individual is not merely an observer of the world presented to him as shifting four-dimensional scenery,[28] but he also *accommodates* to the impressed forces of powerful particulars impressed upon him and *assimilates* them in turn, through his own effective powerful activity. By thinking of causality in this way as something like a sensori-motor schema or as a practical category before considering it as a concept or as a purely logical and epistemic relation, the pitfalls arising from phenomenalism can be avoided.[29]

If the basic time-slice ontology is rejected, then the requirement that there should be some discrete impression of causation (as an observable tie or quality) which will underwrite causal knowledge claims, is seen to be misguided. Only in the time-slice model is there such a requirement for something like an observer's snapshot. Hume's demand for evidence of an impression of causal efficacy and his repeated assertion that there is no such impression should, therefore, be seen against the background of his peculiar and dubitable ontology. There are alternative ontologies where causation is viewed, not in the framework of a procession of distinct and unconnected existences, but as a continuously evolving process of interaction between real objects. In such alternative models causation need not be tied to a discrete 'snapshot' like impression but might be known in other ways (such as immediate acquaintance by embodiment in real causal processes). Not only is Hume's basic model dubitable, however, his arguments are questionable also.

3.4.2 *Difficulties in characterising necessary causal connection*
Hume's first specific move against necessary connections in the Treatise[30] is to dismiss claims to knowledge of causal efficacy or necessary connection on the grounds that there is no uniform way of characterising the force and energy of causal powers, and that in any case the supposed properties in question are unknown or known only obscurely. Recent Humean criticism has followed Hume in rejecting talk of the efficacy of causal powers as obscure.[31]

Now, although difficulties in formulating satisfactory and conventionalised characterisations of the real world are not to be belittled, they provide no conclusive proof that the phenomena concerned are not real and commonly experienced. Perhaps the outstanding precedent in the history of science is the case of inertial motion. There was ample scope for Humean-style scepticism about whether there is really any such thing, in so far as pre-Newtonian philosophers spoke variously and obscurely about dispositions, impetuosity, accidental gravity, uniform diform motion, impetus and the like.[32] Yet the history of the origins of dynamics shows the discovery of only one fundamental principle, though owing to inevitable historical accidents it was expressed in many seemingly independent laws and statements.[33] There is no reason, therefore, to doubt that the efficacy of causal powers, no less than inertia, is a real phenomenon which is not to be dismissed on the grounds that it has proven difficult to characterise.

Contemporary Humeans, like Hume himself, claim that a clear characterisation of causal necessity requires more than the mere mention of such words as 'power' and 'productive connection'. But this is to misrepresent seriously the doctrine of causal powers and causal necessity as it has been explicated in terms of capacities, intrinsic natures and structures, intrinsic and extrinsic circumstances, enabling and stimulus conditions and related concepts.[34]

3.4.3   *The denial of a causal impression*
Hume is quite explicit that there is no impression of a necessary causal connection or of causal efficacy.[35] Taking the question of the causal impression at the purely phenomenological and psychological levels at which it is introduced by Hume, there is good evidence from the psychology of perception that he was quite mistaken.[36] Michotte has shown that the impression of a causal relation is something more than contiguity and succession (although certain precise collocations of factors such as absolute velocity, relative velocity, path orientation, body size and so forth are involved).

He has identified the phenomenon of '*ampliation*' as crucial in this connection, that is to say a three-phase sequential transition from an initial perceived state of 'patient' stasis, through a second transitional phase superimposing agent–patient motion on to the first static phase, to a third phase in which the original 'patient' has assumed a new state of motion. 'Ampliation' occurs paradigmatically in cases of 'entraining' (mutual motion of patient and agent in the third phase) and 'launching' (transfer of motion from agent to patient in the third phase), and these are archetypical, mechanical cases of causation to which Michotte suggests all other cases, including *emotional* causes, attach by some psychological mechanism of association. This criticism of Hume cannot be regarded as conclusive, for indeed Hume's view is unfalsifiable. Nevertheless, as Miles has said, it seems that Michotte has shown beyond any reasonable doubt that Hume's explicit claims about the non-occurrence of a causal impression as such was mistaken.[37]

It has been pointed out that Hume is not committed to denying that in some sense of impression we have an impression of causation, but this is only the impression that Hume attributes to mental habit based on prior experience of regular succession and the mind's propensity to spread itself on external objects.[38] Hume's 'technical' sense of impression would be a phenomenologically pristine object, uncontaminated by prior experience of regular succession of like causes and effects. Moreover, it is said that the essential point is a *conceptual* one: that A's being the cause of B is not the sort of thing that we could perceive directly without previous experience of the uniform connection of things like A with things like B.

These points are, of course, quite inconclusive. The 'conceptual' point is no more than a reiteration of Hume's peculiar definition of causation in the terms of his presupposed ontology. It really tells us nothing about our actual experience of causes. And since it is impossible to revert to pristine perception, uncontaminated by prior experience, it will, therefore, always be open to the Humean to say that impressions of causation are due only to prior experience of regular succession (rather than to veridical perception with developed capacities and competences). In this sense Hume is in an unassailable position. But there is no reason why this view must be accepted. On the other hand there are good reasons to believe it is deficient as an account of causation.

The fact is that, whereas Hume acknowledged only an *inner* impression of causal necessity,[39] Michotte has shown that there is a visual impression of our perception of external causation and specified some of the conditions for its occurrence. There is, however, stronger and more commonplace evidence for necessary causal connections than Michotte's and this will be discussed forthwith.

3.4.4 *Failed candidates for the impression of necessary causal connection*

Hume considers, in some detail, a number of candidates for the impression of causal efficacy, none of them the most obvious candidates. In every case he reiterates his basic claim that there is no impression, but only regular succession. First, in the case of physical objects he considers secondary causes or unknown qualities as the source of causal efficacy and cites the examples of billiard ball collisions, the neurophysiological causes of behaviour, the descent of heavy bodies under gravity, the growth of plants, generation in animals and nourishment of the body by food. In each and every case he simply reiterates the same basic, dubitable, claim that we only experience succession of phenomena. Second, in the case of the action of the mind on the body he stresses the ineffability of the connection between them. As we have already seen, however, if the relation between the mental and the physical is identity it is misguided to consider it as a relation of causation at all, and so unsurprising that there will be no impression of a causal connection between them. Third, in the case of purely 'mental' causation he considers how ideas give rise to other ideas and how we can sometimes wilfully control these processes. He also emphasises how we must learn in experience the scope and limits of such 'mental' causation. Again, in each and every case he reiterates the same basic claim that all we experience is regular succession, not a causal impression. He does not even consider the possibility that 'mental' causation might be known by similarity or analogy with physical causation, although he allows causal reasoning by similarity and analogy.[40] In a word, Hume's arguments against an impression of necessary causal connection are unsatisfactory and inconclusive.

Considering the profound consequences and wide influence of Hume's claim that there is no impression of necessary causal connection it is rather surprising to discover that he considers what are by far the outstanding candidates for causal impressions only parenthetically, in a footnote to the Enquiry. It will be instructive therefore to give due prominence to what he has to say about those cases. He says that:[41]

> It may be pretended, that the Resistance, which we meet with in Bodies, obliging us frequently to exert our Force, and call up all our Power; this gives us the Idea of Force, and Power. 'Tis this *Nisus* or strong Endeavour, of which we are conscious, that is the original Impression, from which this Idea is copy'd. But, *first*, we attribute Power to a vast Number of Objects, where we never can suppose this Resistance or Exertion of Force to take place: To the supreme Being, who never meets with any Resistance; to the Mind in its Command over our Ideas and Limbs, in common Thinking and Motion, where the Effect follows immediately upon the Will, without any Exertion or Summoning up to Force; to inanimate Matter, which is not capable of this Sentiment. Secondly, This Sentiment of an Endeavour to overcome Resistance has no known Connexion with any Event: What follows it, we know by Experience, but could not know it *a priori*.

Here we do have Hume considering the central case where the necessary efficacy of causal powers is impressed upon consciousness. Hume's dismissal of the case is really quite unsatisfactory and depends upon two dubious assumptions and a failure to make some other important distinctions. The two presuppositions are, first, the general assumption that all knowledge of the world is or is reducible to distinct impressions which are distinct existences; second, the assumption that to know some object has causal power is already to know, *a priori*, the effects that the power can produce.

Each of these assumptions is dubitable. In the first case, the view that experience of the world is essentially punctiform (composed entirely of distinct impressions) is purely speculative, and by no means more plausible than an alternative physical realist account. This point has already been briefly discussed. Second, the requirement that knowledge of causal powers entails, *a priori*, knowledge of their specific effects in the real world clearly fails to allow for the influence in real circumstances of complex *collocations* of causal powers and conditions. Precise '*a priori*' knowledge of specific effects of specific causes in the real world requires the prior specification of the other factors apart from a specific cause which might broadly be called the causal conditions of the case. It is also necessary to distinguish first between force and self-conscious exertion of force by human individuals, and second between awareness we have simply of applied force (as when we deflect a spring balance with a finger) and experience of extreme exertion which accompanies the strongest endeavour (as in a Promethean assault on a mountain in full pack), where there are additional psychological overtones of strain and fatigue.

Thus, when Hume argues that our immediate experience of exerting or resisting force does not support a claim to knowledge of necessary causal connection because we attribute force to a variety of other things where there is no question of exertion and/or awareness of exertion; we see that his argument is quite inadequate. First, although physicalists will regard the argument from God's omnipotence as antiquarian and otiose, there is an interesting point to be made even here. That is that, although (supposedly) God's will prevails necessarily, nevertheless, according to some well-known views at least (for example Spinoza's view of God as infinite substance), He works through the order of natural forces, with all that this entails in the way of the orderly interaction of forces and resistances in the natural world. The use of 'resistance' in this context is, therefore, ambiguous as between '(potentially) effective opposition' (of which, against God, there is none), and 'counterposed force' (of which, even in God's workings, there is abundance).

Second, as we have seen, the influence of mind over body and over other mental events has two separate components: (1) the mind–body relation which, properly understood, is not a causal relation at all, and (2) the relations between different (mind–) brain processes, and between (mind–) brain processes and overt behaviour. In the first case there is no causal connection to find. In the second set of cases, there is essentially the same basis for knowing causation as in all other physical processes including inanimate processes.

Third, the fact that subconscious and inanimate physical objects and processes do not *sense* the application of force in no way entails that forces are not exerted by and upon them. This is easily shown in a case such as enforced deflection of a calibrated spring weighing machine. (Experienced) force applied by an agent causes a spring ineluctably or necessarily to compress, as indicated by a dial. The same effect is produced by an inanimate object in the same manner. It is a perfectly simple matter of reasoning by similarity and/or analogy that the inanimate object *enforces* (naturally necessitates) the compression of the spring as indicated by the dial in the same way that agent force does, even though there is no question that inanimate objects have accompanying 'sentiments'. This example in fact provides a paradigm for the way in which experience of necessary causal connection constitutes knowledge by *acquaintance* of causation which can be extended by similarity and analogy to other observed cases of causation where there is no immediate experience of causal efficacy. This point will be discussed later (Section 4.3.1 below) in connection with the PO account of causation.

Also, in such a case it is quite clearly misleading to speak of enforcing as 'strong endeavour' because this terminology introduces additional psychological overtones peculiar to agency, such as awareness of strain and fatigue. It is misleading because, whereas it is perfectly intelligible and coherent to say that inanimate objects offer resistance and enforce effects without self-consciousness, it is logically contradictory to think that anything could be aware of the psychological strain and fatigue of 'strong endeavour' and not be conscious of it.

Again, Hume's argument is unpersuasive when he suggests that our immediate experience of exerting or resisting force does not support a claim to knowledge of causal efficacy because we only know by experience and not *a priori* what specific effects may be. In this case error arises from the two misconceptions already mentioned. First, there is the belief arising from the 'distinct existence' ontology that, if necessity is involved in causation at all, it must be logical or *a priori* necessity. In fact what is involved is not logical but natural necessity, and as we now know there are 'naturally' necessary truths to be discovered in experience, that is to say *a posteriori* necessary truths. These are the truths discovered by science about the essential structure of reality (see Chapter V, Section 2.5). The second misconception is closely related to the first: it is to suppose that knowledge of the efficacy of causal powers entails full knowledge, *a priori*, of specific effects which might be produced in reality without prior specification of all the other relevant causes and conditions prevailing in the circumstances in question. Provided these additional factors *are* specified, there is no reason why *a*

173

priori knowledge cannot be claimed of the (aggregated) effects of particular causes. But it is inappropriate to expect *a priori* knowledge of effects unless there is also prior specification of all the relevant causes and causal conditions. Usually, of course, there is not, except in the closed systems of controlled experiments. The real world is open in this respect. However, this does not belie the efficacy of causes and the natural necessity of the connection between causes and effects.

I conclude that there is no reason why we need accept either Hume's peculiar time-slice ontology or his dubitable assertion that we have no experience of causal efficacy and necessary connections. Further than this, there are many good reasons to believe that Hume's view of causation is mistaken. There is good reason to believe that causes necessarily produce their effects, the best reason being the evidence of cases where we have immediate knowledge by acquaintance of the efficacy and natural necessity (or ineluctable nature) of causal efficacy.

3.5 Causality and Necessity

In Hume's view causality, the principle that every event necessarily has a cause, is 'sunken' in the question of causation: whether individual events necessarily have necessitating causes.

According to the phenomenal time-slice ontology, experience is composed of distinct, unconnected impressions or appearances which are distinct existences. Each event in the world is thus conceived of as occurring in total isolation from any other event. On this view, therefore, there is no reason to suppose that every event is a necessary effect of some cause. Although every effect has a cause, necessarily, events do not necessarily have a necessary cause. For all anybody can tell, events might occur entirely *ex nihilo* (like the events depicted in the Tom and Jerry world of cinematographic cartoons); or again they might not.

3.6 Humean Causation, Causality and Causal Powers

In order to explain causal necessity within the framework of a phenomenal time-slice ontology, Humeans have developed highly sophisticated regularity theories of causation in terms of subjunctive and counterfactual conditionals, inductive laws and so on.[42] Regularity theories of this sort provide considerable insight into the structure of causal inquiry. Most of them are entirely consistent with a physical realist account of causation as real productive connection.[43] They are predicated, of course, on the basic Humean assumption that there is no experience of the efficacy of causal powers, or real knowledge of powerful objects and processes. There is great concern to confine causal analysis strictly to epistemology; to what we can know of appearances.[44]

It is instructive, therefore, to notice just how difficult it is for Hume and neo-Humeans to adhere consistently to the time-slice ontology and confine their analysis of causes to the regular succession of appearances without invoking other factors. Thus, whereas Hume declares in his (epistemologically) *ex cathedra* tone of voice that: 'Any degree ... of regularity in our perceptions can never be a foundation for us to infer a greater degree of regularity in some objects which are not perceived',[45] he elsewhere argues that:[46]

> that human Body is a mighty complicated Machine ... many secret Powers lurk in it, which are altogether beyond our Comprehension: ... to us it must often appear very uncertain in its Operations: And therefore the irregular Events, which outwardly discover themselves, can be no Proof that the Laws of Nature are not observ'd with the greatest Strictness and Regularity in its internal operations and Government.

Similarly, although modern Humeans may wish to discount as mere irony Hume's lapses into talk of causal powers and machinery and to dismiss such talk as utterly obscure, they also, like Hume, are liable to invoke other factors beyond regular appearances to explain otherwise inexplicable intuitions and characteristics of causation. Thus,[47]

> the dictum that 'the universe needs to know where to go next' may require some explanation and defence. I am suggesting that there is some truth in the notion that what happens next *flows from* what is there already. The immediate future is, so to speak, extruded by the present and the immediate past.
>
> Of course all that is observed and all that ever could be observed amounts to a vast and intricate collection of persistences, continuities and complex regularities. But there is perhaps also something more elusive. Ayer suggests that 'everything that happens in the world can be represented in terms of variations of scenery in a four-dimensional spatio-temporal continuum'. Represented, yes: but is the representation adequate? Does everything that happens in the world simply consist of varied four-dimensional scenery? I want to deny this but it is difficult to say just what the denial means. The notion of flowing from, of extrusion, would mean that there had to be some relations of the general sorts mentioned above – persistence, continuity, regularity – that what happens fits into such categories as the continued existence of objects, motion, change (which involves also some persistence), growth development, decay, composition, disintegration, but not – at least in most cases – annihilation or coming to be from nothing. I am not, of course, suggesting that the laws or regularities in

accordance with which things come about must themselves be intelligible, but only that if we are right to see the future flowing from the present we are justified in expecting that there will be some *ways* in which it flows.

Here we have clear intimations that the time-slice ontology and regularity theory of causation do not provide an adequate account of some of the most distinctive features of our experience of causation. Moreover, it is evident that what is lacking is an adequate account of persistent objects, their structures and their law-like powers for change.

Similarly, on the subject of causality, whereas Hume says that it is neither intuitively nor demonstratively certain that every object that begins to exist (i.e. every event) must owe its existence to a cause,[48] elsewhere he recognises that:[49]

> The Vulgar, who take things according to their first appearance, attribute the uncertainty of events to such an uncertainty in the causes, as makes them often fail in their usual influence, though they meet with no obstacle nor impediment in their operation. But philosophers observing that almost in every part of nature there is contained a vast variety of springs and principles, which are hid, by reasons of their minuteness or remoteness, find that it is at least possible the contrariety of events may not proceed from any contingency in the cause, but from the secret operation of contrary causes. This possibility is converted into a certainty by further observation ... From further observation of several parallel instances philosophers form a maxim that the connection betwixt all causes and effects is equally necessary, and that its seeming uncertainty in some instances proceeds from the secret opposition of contrary causes.

Again, although modern Humeans follow Hume in denying that we have any right to assume that the universe is deterministic[50] (that is to say denying causality), nevertheless they typically speak of assuming that events have *some* cause;[51] of an underlying regularity of behaviour[52] and of presupposing the uniformity of nature because the universe 'needs to know what to do next'.[53] An interesting clue to the real status and role of the principle of causality is given by what typically follows from failure to formulate adequate regular causal laws to cover cases. If someone takes the Humean view seriously there is, logically, no more reason to suppose that events have hidden causes than that they are totally uncaused.

Given Humean presuppositions, failure to discover hidden causes of events, in some cases after entire epochs of inquiry, ought, logically, to lead to the conclusion, based on sound inductive evidence, that such events *have* no causes to find. What happens in fact, however, is quite different. We see no reason to accept failure, however persistent, as evidence that the quest for causes is misconceived.[54] Typically, the quest for causes is persistently pursued beyond failure by extending the field of inquiry.[55] Since this process can be and, more important, typically *is*, indefinitely extendible, it is no argument against causal determinism to say that causality holds only for a limited field of inquiry.[56] For if no determining cause is found, the field is simply extended, indefinitely.

It is implausible to suggest, as Hume does, that the supposition that there are necessitating causes for every observed event arises from the inductive evidence of observed regularity acquired by individuals. Implausible, because, statistically, there are few events, even few *kinds* of events, for which individuals have complete and first-hand experience of the necessitating causes. Hume is surely correct to say that only vulgarians doubt that all events must have some necessitating cause(s). It is precisely this certainty that provides the rationale for scientists to inquire into the specific causes of particular events and typical causes of kinds of events. But Hume is surely wrong to say that this certainty is simply the result of induction from individual experience. Failure to establish certainty on inductive grounds has led to various transcendentalist accounts of causality, the best-known of which is Kant's. Understandably, tough-minded Empiricists have been reluctant to embrace such alternatives to uncaused events and inductiv-ist–regularity theories. They are justifiably reluctant to risk admitting idealism into theories of the real world. There is however at least one alternative, non-idealistic, account of causality, and a highly plausible one, to do with the natural history of human cognition. This is already suggested by neo-Humean references to the innate human tendency to assume causality[57] and the survival value of the capacity for accurate causal suppositions.[58] I shall return to this issue presently when a PO account of causality is discussed.

Summarily: it is evident that there are substantial deficiencies in the Humean account of causation and causality. The nature of the deficiencies is suggested by the way in which Hume and Humeans tend to depart from their *ex cathedra* position to account for common features of causation and causality that have no satisfactory explanation in terms of the time-slice ontology and regularity theories. These observations have been largely negative. It is necessary to go further in order to meet the challenge that Hume presents:[59] to meet Hume's criticisms of claims to experience of causation as necessary connection; to take up Hume's challenge to present a plausible alternative view to his own; and to explain how, if there is such experience and such an alternative view, Hume overlooked them.

4   THE PHYSICALIST VIEW OF CAUSES AND CAUSALITY

4.1   *Desiderata*

It might well be asked why, if the Humean view is so problematical, has it been so widely influential among philosophers and scientists? And, more important, need it continue to be so? One answer to the first question seems to be that it has been much *less* influential in practice than it has been 'officially'. For, although in their philosophical moments scientists have often professed allegiance to some form of radical empiricist principles, in *practice* they have usually conducted their scientific affairs as physical realists. This of course is a perfectly Humean position.[60] The answer to the second question is that there is no reason why the Humean view should continue to be so influential. In view of the many problems to which it gives rise the emergence of an alternative to the time-slice ontology and regularity view of causal necessity is to be expected.

It would be a mistake however, to suppose that a simple inversion of the Humean model will do. The extreme Humean position, which limits knowledge of physical processes to observable phenomena (appearances), is manifestly unsatisfactory because it leaves out real objects and objective causation. The opposite and equally extreme, epiphenomenalist, position is that impressions of consciousness are another sort of 'link' or 'dangler' at the end of objective physical–causal chains, but a causally ineffective and redundant one. This is as unsatisfactory as the Humean view, because it leaves out immediate (conscious) experience of objective necessary connection and mind–body interaction.

The kind of model that is likely to prove most adequate is already implicit in some of Hume's own remarks, cited above: it will need to account for the impression of causation; necessary connection; the law-like regularity of observed events; and the principle of causality. To achieve this and to avoid the deeply problematical aspects of the Humean view a radical shift of root model is indicated.

4.2   *The PO Metaphysic*

The most appropriate and indeed the most obvious model for causation is incorporated in the PO model of the world already adumbrated. It is really no more than the common-sense view as elaborately refined by scientific inquiry. According to this view the world is composed, not of shifting scenery, but of quasi-independent particulars which are enduring individual mass–energy–information systems. Individual systems are embedded and interrelated in a hierarchy of systems of increasingly complex structure and function. This hierarchy extends from the energy-wave packets and elementary particles of physics up through many levels of structural complexity: the atomic, the molecular, cellular, organismic and ultimately the supra-organismic levels of psychological and social phenomena.

At the centre of this view is an ontology of natural types (atoms, cells, generic and specific organisms, etc.), each with typical or intrinsic structures. In virtue of their structures and embodied energies (causal powers) individual systems act and interact as generative mechanisms of change. Because structures are typical and not infinitely variable the changes they generate individually and collectively are not infinitely variable either, but display significant uniformity and regularity. This is well illustrated by the periodic table of elements which is both a definitive taxonomy of elemental structures and powers and, thereby, a basis for systematic analysis and explanation of reactive chemical processes.

Causation is located in the *continuous* processes of transformation in the structures and functions of individual systems and the relations between them. These processes take the form of continuous mass–energy–information exchanges or interactions.

Causal interaction takes place both inter-systemically and intra-systemically; it also occurs at all hierarchical levels, which is to say that the nature of causal interaction is a function of the structure of the elements interacting and the corresponding mechanisms of interaction. For this reason it is clearly naïve to suppose, as philosophers often do, that the invariant principles immanent in processes at one level (e.g. the level of idealised point-masses appropriate to mechanics) should apply universally and indifferently to all other levels of systemic structure (e.g. the level of neural nets appropriate to human action).

Human life and action are properly viewed only as integrated into the context provided by the hierarchy of natural systems. Specifically, consciousness and mind are explicated along IT lines as the intrinsic character of processes at one particular level in the natural hierarchy, namely the highest, which is the level of self-regulating and self-monitoring systems.

4.3   Causation and Necessity

4.3.1   *Experience of necessary connection*
It has already been argued that Hume is mistaken to deny experience of causation as necessary connection. The point is of the greatest

importance, and further argument is now needed to establish the case for objective, necessary, productive connections between causes and effects.

Let us begin by recalling the Humean view, that the necessity of causation between objects themselves is nothing more than regular succession of like causes and effects. This goes with the force of psychological habit that observed regularity produces in normal observers by which they anticipate effects from observation of usual causes. Many philosophers have denied that causal necessity amounts only to observed regularity. One good argument is based on the plausible claim that Hume confuses intelligibility with observability. The fact is, we may sometimes know what we cannot observe, as when we know that, necessarily, an extended object or surface cannot simultaneously be two different colours.[61] According to this view, causal necessity is a 'boundary to possibility', not an observable phenomenon at all. Another argument is that we perceive causation paradigmatically in individual cases, in the *relation* of individual causes and effects, not as a consequence of their regular succession.[62] It is pointed out that, for example, we commonly and typically experience causation in such cases as avalanches destroying villages and the vegetation of the countryside; waves eating away the shoreline; and wind bending trees.[63]

There is something in all of these points, but none of them fully meets the demand for evidence of direct experience of necessary productive causal connection. The necessity that an extended surface should be monochrome is an inadequate paradigm for the supposedly productive relation of cause and effect. And whereas it is true that causation is a *relation* rather than an object or event such as the ones commonly cited, it is supposedly a *productive* relation, and it is difficult fully to meet the Humean denial of this by appeal to cases that can so easily be construed in terms only of contiguity and succession.

The burden of evidence that we *experience* necessary connection falls on those cases where we have direct, immediate experience of causation in the interaction between external forces and our embodied-selves. Once this order of experience is acknowledged nothing is easier than to give suitable examples of experience of necessary connection.[64]

> Our understanding, then, of the 'link between cause and effect' is basically an understanding of physical contacts in all their various kinds – jolting, pushing, gashing, rubbing, gnawing, scooping, severing, grappling, getting entangled with, absorbing, falling on top of, crushing, mixing, irradiating, and so on (it is to be noticed that our words for the various sorts of contact mostly indicate a pattern of motion and a degree of force).

> It is experience of this sort, particularly instances such as being blown

over by winds, capsized by waves and crushed by rocks, where the effect is experienced as *ineluctable, inexorable* or inevitable, which provides the direct experience from which our understanding of *natural* necessity derives. This is not to say, of course, that natural necessity involves massive over-determination. Nevertheless the same principle applies in cases of over-determination and in finer processes such as minute scale imbalances and chemical titrations: the principle that change is necessitated by the action of forces sufficient to bring it about. The straw that breaks the camel's back is sufficient for the breaking, for all the fact that a straw is merely a straw and not Mount Everest. We not only have experience of impressed external force (enforcement), but there are also paradigm cases of ineluctably enforced 'self-action' such as spontaneous muscular spasm and nervous reflex action, as in cramp, epileptic fits and delirium tremens. At the root of the notion of *natural* necessity therefore is the experience and understanding we have of the inexorable way in which causes that are sufficient for their effects produce or bring about their effects.

Understanding of the necessary connection between causes and effects in cases of which we have no immediate (that is, embodied, conscious) experience is by a process of similarity and analogy with cases where we do have such experience, along lines already suggested. We do not experience, let alone observe, the necessity with which a steamroller crushes a walnut, but the case is similar in relevant respects to our bodies being crushed by great weights, where the necessity is literally impressed upon us. We do not experience the necessity with which fire consumes paper, but the case is similar in relevant respects to our bodies being burned. We do not directly experience the necessity with which acid dissolves metals but the case is similar in relevant respects to our bodies being eaten away by acid. We do not directly experience the necessity with which electromagnetic forces and other agents of 'action at a distance' induce their effects, but the case is similar in relevant respects to the pull of magnets that we do experience. Perhaps most interestingly of all, we do not (consciously) experience the necessity with which spontaneous firings at neuronic synapses initiate and propagate chains of other firings and eventually produce overt behaviour, but the case is similar in relevant respects to the spontaneous spasms of reflex nervous action.

Finally, we have on the one hand knowledge of persistence and inertia, that is knowledge that things tend to endure unless caused to change, and on the other hand immediate experience of the ineluctable necessity of the changes enforced by causal processes. On this basis we commonly take the occurrence of an event as sufficient evidence of the prior occurrence of the necessary and necessitating causes that are sufficient to produce the event in question, and without which it would not have happened.

A Humean objection to the argument advanced here is that, although we might have some experience of causation in cases of the sort described (for example as we peel potatoes), we do not thereby experience a counterfactual conditional: that is to say, we do not perceive what happens if, contrary to fact, we are not enforcing the effect (e.g. peeling) and this is necessary for causal knowledge. The point is that (supposedly) an element either of imagining or of discursive thinking enters into what we would ordinarily call causal knowledge.[65] This objection is surely mistaken in supposing that, in a forceful act such as peeling a potato, we must imagine or infer by some elaborate discursive process what would be happening if we were not acting, in order to know that it is our enforcement that is productive of its effect. We pause in our peeling, there is a pause in the peeling; we accelerate our peeling, there is an acceleration of the peeling. If such things are not known immediately *nothing* is, including the sense data of observation.

Thus, more generally, it is a mistake to doubt that immediate experience of necessary connection is its own warrant and needs no further support from reason or other experience, however regular.[66] If a finger is severed by a knife we do not need first to *imagine* what would have happened if there had been no knife, or to become an indentured butcher in order to know that the knife severed the finger. Indeed, it is precisely the (epistemologically self-guaranteed) experience we have of causation and the causal powers of objects that underwrites claims to knowledge of causal necessity and thus counterfactual and subjunctive conditionals.[67] Further than this, unless there is categorical causal necessity in individual cases, there would be no natural necessity in the regularity of causes and effects. Induction from observed regularity warrants logical inferences; it says nothing of the necessary connections in the real world with which, as embodied beings, we are directly acquainted.

4.3.2 *Natural necessity, logical necessity and natural objects*

The experience of necessary connection described is the basis of our understanding of natural necessity, as the necessary or ineluctable productive connection between cause and effect. Of course, most of our scientific knowledge of the world is not given in immediate experience, but is constituted in an elaborate system of inferences, including similarity and analogy: first, from observation to the nature and structure of natural objects, second, from the nature and structure of natural objects to the results that we do experience and observe, results that they bring about or necessitate. The possibility of scientific *explanation* thus turns on a detailed, hypothetically adduced knowledge of the mass–energy–information structure of natural objects in virtue of which they generate and necessitate the infinitely rich panorama of the observable natural world. Naturally necessary connections between events in the real world, that is in the interaction between real objects, underwrite the logically necessary connections between terms in scientific explanations of those events.

It is important to notice in this process the relationship between natural necessity, logical necessity and the concept of natural object or individual. We typify and identify natural objects according to certain essential or defining properties, including certain powers to effect change (dynamite to explode), and liabilities to suffer change (hypochondriacs to feel ill). Thus, when an object manifests its essential properties it does so necessarily: to be lead is to be heavier than water (necessarily). And when an object fails to manifest its supposed essential properties in the appropriate circumstances we conclude that it is not the thing or individual we supposed it to be: the lump that ordinarily floats on water is not lead (necessarily); the hypochondriac who does not frequently feel ill is no hypochondriac (necessarily).

The essential nature of an object, without which it is not distinguished from other objects, limits the scope of what it is necessary and possible for the object to do. Lumps of lead ordinarily sink in water *necessarily*; it is impossible that they should float because, given the atomic structures of lead and water, the relative magnitudes of the natural forces of gravity and hydrostatic pressure are ordinarily such as to enforce or necessitate sinking. From this it follows that the statement, 'a lump of lead will ordinarily sink in water', is *necessarily* true, is a necessary *a posteriori* truth. By the same token the statement, 'a lump of lead will ordinarily float in water', is a contradiction in terms, a *logical* contradiction.

Humeans have typically denied that such statements involve logical contradiction because it is possible to imagine or conceive the states of affairs that would make them true. But the supposed ability to imagine or conceive the opposite of what occurs with natural necessity does not tell against natural necessity. It is now well recognised that even some truths of mathematics may be imagined or conceived to be otherwise, though, if true, they are true of *logical* necessity. And it is rightly said that if the conceivability of the contradictory does not disprove objective necessity in formal systems where proof is attainable by *a priori* reasoning, there is no reason to suppose that it disproves objective necessity in science or the natural world.[68]

The concept of necessity embodies the principle of excluded alternatives.[69] Logical necessity connotes the semantical elimination of alternative interpretations of certain symbols. Natural necessity connotes

183

the elimination of alternative patterns of relatedness among natural events, because of the essential natures of natural objects and forces and the constraints that they exercise on the interactions between objects.

It is not surprising that agreement about logical necessity is relatively easily established among the community of speakers, for it is they who mutually determine the interpretations of symbols. To arrive at an adequate conception of a necessary *natural* connection requires the more protracted and laborious process of eliminating '*possible*' alternative causal mechanisms in nature. In practice this can never be achieved with absolute certainty, because of the fragmentary nature of individual human experience and the complexity of events. But for the community of inquirers extended in time and space, an 'almost certainty'[70] can be achieved in science which approaches asymptotically, and to all practical intents and purposes is often equivalent to, the certainty attached to formal necessity. This involves the rational reconstruction of experience as institutionalised in scientific method, which is beyond both rational *a priori*sm and empirical sensationalism, but embodies both.[71]

> It is empirical because it starts with observations and returns to observations for confirmation, and it is rationalistic because it goes considerably beyond experience to logically postulated entities such as co-ordinate correlation co-efficient, mass, and many more. It brings empiricism into combination with rationalism. This method has proven to be tremendously fruitful. It has produced theories which have revolutionised our life. Its applications surround us on all sides. We are liberated from the bondage of immediate experience yet are not turned loose on the infinite paths of pure reason.

4.3.3 *Causal conditions and causal laws*

The discussion of natural and logical necessity in the last section made use of the notion of 'ordinary' conditions under which natural objects necessarily bring about certain effects, as when lumps of lead are placed in water they sink to the bottom 'under ordinary conditions'. Also, the pattern of necessitation under ordinary conditions takes on a law-like form as in: 'whenever a lump of lead is put in water it sinks to the bottom'. It is necessary now to say something more, but briefly, about ordinary causal conditions and causal laws.

The events in any closed system of interacting objects and forces will be the outcome or distillation of all the causally effective influences involved. Mill went so far as to suggest that the net sum of conditions necessary for an effect *is* its cause. In the paradigm case of a lump of lead sinking in water the causal system includes, obviously, the lump of lead and the water and, less obviously but equally necessarily, the Earth, which enforces gravitational attraction on the lead and water. It is the net sum of the interaction between lump of lead, water and Earth that ordinarily necessitates the precise sinking effect that occurs; this is to say, there is no more and no less than lead, water and the Earth's gravity to account for. Also, given the same ensemble of objects, *and none other* (that is by considering lead–water–Earth as a closed system), the sinking follows necessarily as if by law.

The first thing to notice is that not all causal factors are ordinarily speaking causes. Although most of the conditions ordinarily prevailing in a closed system may be *necessary* for the occurrence of extra-ordinary and so interesting changes or events, they do not, by definition, ordinarily bring about such extra-ordinary changes or events, and so do not ordinarily explain the extra-ordinary changes we may be interested to explain. Therefore, while it is true that in any closed system of causally interacting objects each object contributes to the mass–energy information economy of events in the system, it is usually misleading to describe the whole collocation of causal factors as the cause of any event in the system. We usually single out from among the collocation of causal factors that necessitate some effect the one(s) that, extra-ordinarily, bring(s) about the effect we are interested to explain. The identification of some causal factor(s) as 'the' cause(s) of some effect is arbitrary in the sense that 'the' cause is no more necessary to the effect than other causal conditions, and the selection of one factor rather than another is a matter of human interest, often to do with an interest in intervening in and *influencing* events. Provided it is borne in mind that 'the' cause is singled out on this basis and that it has no other special status in causal processes, there is no harm, and a great deal of convenience, in the usual way of thinking about causes.

Thus, for example, although oxygen, dry timbers and the absence of monsoons are all necessary conditions for a roof truss fire in a London home, we single out the occurrence of an electrical short-circuit and sparking as *the* cause of the fire. Other ordinarily prevailing conditions are causally necessary, but insufficient, to bring about the fire without this cause. In a situation where ordinarily prevailing conditions are different, as in a continually sparking electrical contact breaking system, the presence of oxygen might be singled out as the cause against a background set of conditions including sparking and combustible materials. Thus it is usual in causal analysis to speak of causes against a background of *ceteris paribus* assumptions about ordinarily prevailing conditions. This set of causal conditions can usefully be called the causal field.[72] We might follow Mill so far as to say that the cause(s) of some event together with the prevailing causal conditions or causal field are what necessitate the event.[73] Causes necessitate their effects in certain

185

circumstances defined by the collocation of prevailing necessary causal conditions.

The second thing to notice about the paradigm case of lead sinking in water is that, as Montesque puts it, laws are the necessary relations that derive from the natures of things.[74] The law-like necessity with which lead sinks in water under gravitational force is due to the molecular structures of lead and water; the necessary consequences these entail for the values of specific weights and hydraulic pressures; and the gravitational force exerted by the Earth. Given no more and no less than the collocation of factors, lump of lead, water and Earth, the sinking of lead follows necessarily. It is a fundamental mistake to think with Hume that lead necessarily sinks in water, if at all, *because* it regularly sinks in water. Rather, something like the reverse is true: if lead regularly sinks in water it does so because it necessarily sinks in water, and the collocation of lead, water and Earth occurs regularly. Lead *would* necessarily sink in water even if such a precise collocation of causal factors occurred only once, or even if, in fact, it never occurred at all. Something like this might be truly said in the proposition, 'Lead sinks in liquid helium'.

This view of the ontological order of things which puts the productive activity of natural objects before the law-like regularity of appearances is, of course, a reversal of the Humean picture. One of the main advantages of this 'Copernican revolution' in the Humean model of causation is that the perennial Humean difficulty of distinguishing between bona fide causal regularities and accidental generalisations is amenable to a clear and plausible solution. Briefly put, the only sure way of distinguishing lawful and accidental universal statements is to point out that in the former cases we see why the regularity must hold, while in the latter cases we do not.[75] The reasons why things must happen in a regular way (if indeed they do) has to do with the way things really are, that is with the actual natures and structures of objects and the relations between them. To take the traditional example used since Reid to show the distinction between (law-like) causal and accidental regularities: day and night succeed one another with law-like regularity, and the regularity itself is the only explanation Humeans can offer for why it must be so. But this is a famously unsatisfactory attempt at an explanation. Indeed, it is no explanation at all. Alternatively, given no more and no less than the nature of planetary bodies (their gravitational forces, solar energies, global spins, etc.) and the precise collocation of causal factors that makes up the solar system, day must follow night because of the 'distillation' of pushes, pulls and radiations prevailing in the system in virtue of the nature of the objects involved and the relations between them.

The move from descriptions of observed law-like regularities to the nature, structure and functional relations between real objects, which generate and necessitate and so explain the regularities, is typical of scientific explanation. The same pattern of explanation holds when the generative mechanisms invoked to explain the law-like regularities are transcendentally real hypothetical objects, that is supposed real but unobservable *objects*, as in such typical cases as Gas Law regularities explained by atomic particles and patterns of infectious disease explained by viruses. Sometimes the objects that enter the scientific picture as a feature of transcendental hypotheses, and as such are only 'candidates for reality', turn out to be as real as real can be; such cases as bacteria are typical. When this happens the explanatory strategy of invoking unobservable generative mechanisms is fully vindicated.

Observed regularities and empirical laws are thus dependent upon the enduring and typical natures of natural objects and their regular collocation into closed or quasi-closed systems of regular structure. It is unsurprising, therefore, that except for closed and very simple natural systems such as the solar system and the contrived and controlled systems set up in scientific laboratories, there are few actual systems for which natural laws can be easily formulated and applied. This is not because there is no objective necessitation of natural events; because the world is inherently 'mess' and 'hurly burly'. The reason why there are no obvious laws governing events in the real world is that the real world is very complicated. It is an open system in the sense that all of the relevant causal factors that influence events, that is the relevant natural objects and forces, cannot be specified *a priori*. It is by no means certain that the *regular collocation* of necessitating causal factors that are required for general causal 'laws' occur in the real world at all. Indeed, it is doubtful whether they do, and that is why controlled scientific experiments are necessary to establish the causal powers of objects. But this does not mean that the world is not composed only of uniform types of objects, the essential natures of which define the physically possible course of development of interactive processes. Nor does it mean that what happens is not necessitated by the interaction of causal factors.

It is a mistake of anthropocentric epistemology to suppose that uncertainty, particularly everyday common or garden uncertainty, about natural events entails uncaused, contra-causal, or a-causal processes in nature. Such a supposition also ignores or discounts the powerful evidence of the explanatory successes of science.

Certainly errors are committed, scientific laws fail (or rather law-*statements* fail to predict the outcome of events) and ignorance and mystery abound. But there is no reason to suppose that all of this is not attributable to human errors of formulation, observation and inference in the partial view.[76]

1 Errors of formulation may arise because:
   (a) hypothetical constructs may misrepresent or inadequately represent real objects and systems;
   (b) law *statements* (L_2) may be incomplete or inaccurate renditions of natural laws (L_1);
   (c) natural laws may vary as a result of the emergence of new systems not anticipated in law statements.

2 Errors of observation may arise because:
   (a) the system modelled may have been ill-defined or inadequately isolated;
   (b) there are errors in measurement;
   (c) insufficient parameters have been considered due to inaccessibility, etc.

3 Errors of inference may occur because of:
   (a) plain mistakes (false association, distractions, memory failures, etc.);
   (b) over-simplification of inferential procedures; unjustified presuppositions, etc.

With natural human limitations providing such a fruitful source of obscurity and mystery, there is no need to look into the bowels of nature for the origins of caprice and darkness. On the other hand, from the ever-present possibility that we *might* be wrong about the causes of events it does not at all follow that we *are*;[77] or that, when we are *not*, we cannot also *know* that we are not.

Having now said something positive (if too briefly and inadequately) about the PO metaphysic, experience of necessary connection, natural and logical necessity, causal conditions and causal laws, it is now opportune to set out PO views of causation and causality.

4.4   *The PO Model of Causation*

4.4.1   *Causation*

Causation on the PO view is the relation of productive connexity immanent in the processes of interaction between the quasi-independent mass–energic systems comprising the real world. It is the relation of necessary productive connection between the states of a system undergoing a process of change, where the change from the prior state to the later state is an event to be explained. The event so defined is brought about by, and therefore explicated in terms of, those elements in the prior state which are the necessary conditions for the *change* to the later state, that is to say the 'difference-set' in the state description of the system necessary and sufficient to produce the *change* in system state.[78]

Single cause For example, in the simplest case of the billiard ball model of mechanics, the 'event' to be explained is the state-change of one ball from rest to uniform motion and of another from a prior to a later state of uniform motion. The cause in this event is the difference-set (which is in this case the single difference) without which it would not have occurred, namely the contact on one ball of another ball possessed of momentum, some of which is imparted to the 'patient' ball and thereby bringing about, producing or affecting the changes of state.

It will be evident that the notion of cause as 'difference-set' avoids the objection that the description of the prior state as the necessary condition for producing the later state must include the state of the whole universe. For on this view only the relevant *change* of state constitutes the event to be explained: non-contiguous events, counter-factual states of affairs and the conditions that obtain (*ceteris paribus*) throughout this change of state are not elements causally productive of the effect as *change*.[79]

Plural cause To treat continuous states as non-productive conditions or causal fields does not of course entail that all causation can be represented in terms of a 'single difference'. A plurality of necessary causes – the difference-set – may be jointly sufficient for the production of an event that would not otherwise have occurred as the effect of any one of the differences acting independently. Consider, for example, the slightly more complex case of an event such as the failure of a machine part. When a component breaks, the breaking might be explained as the effect of a single difference in terms of a stress–strength ratio. But in most cases the effect is the net consequence of a variety of different causal factors, each of which constitutes a different and distinguishable aspect of the system's states which are represented as quasi-independent variables in the system state-description. So, for example, absolute load, fatigue (load reversals), thermal effects (e.g. creep), chemical effects (e.g. corrosion), metallurgical effects (e.g. hardening) and so on may together produce an effect – breakage – which none acting alone would cause.

4.4.2 *The taxonomy of causes*

This last example introduces the important question of the taxonomy of causes. We have followed Hume in proposing a *single* formula for causation, though a different one: namely the connection between two states of a system that produces the change from the prior state to the later state. However, we have also recognised that causes are not of a single type, such as Hume's 'association by repetition', but relate different types of system and different kinds of system-state through different kinds of mass–energic mechanism. The way is therefore open to follow Bunge in outlining a taxonomy of causal connections (other than external-efficient causation), which would correspond to the varieties of natural determination:[80]

quantitative self causation; e.g., the successive positions of a freely moving macroscopic body are uniquely determined by its position and velocity at any given instant of time;

interaction (reciprocal causation); e.g., the functioning of every gland of the human body depends on that of the remaining glands;

mechanical causation of consequent by antecedent, usually with the addition of efficient causes and mutual actions; e.g., forces modify the state of motion of bodies – but motion may exist before the application of the forces;

structural (or holistic) causation of the parts by the whole; e.g., the behaviour of an individual – a molecule in a fluid, a person in a social group – is determined by the overall structure of the collection to which it belongs;

teleological causation of the means by the ends or goals; e.g., birds build their nests 'in order to safeguard their young'. Needless to say, goal-directed structures, functions and behaviours need not be purposely planned by anybody. Also, needless to say, this view does not mean that the future determines the present, only that *present* states (desire, belief, perception, etc.) direct activity towards a future achievement of a goal inherent in the present states;

dialectical causation or qualitative self-causation of the whole process by the inner 'strife' and eventual synthesis of its essential opposite components; e.g., changes of state of matter in bulk are produced by the interplay and final predominance of one of two opposite trends: thermal agitation and molecular attraction.

The important case of *statistical* determination is treated here for the present purpose as a convenient practicable surrogate for complete causal determinism.[81] It is acknowledged that from certain standpoints this is a very cavalier assumption,[82] but in mitigation appeal is made to the arguments that stochastic determination of high probability is in practice tantamount to a complete determination;[83] that the probability *distributions* in a system at any time may be uniquely determined by the distributions of a prior condition;[84] and that, for systems of the macroscopic order of human individuals, statistical indeterminacy is not a significant factor anyway.[85]

4.5 *The PO Model and Causality*

4.5.1 *Causality as universal causation*
Causality, in the PO root model, is the principle that in any isolated (or quasi-isolated) natural system all events are changes of state that are

necessarily connected to, and follow necessarily from, the state of the system at any previous time. Strictly speaking, only the universe is a perfect cause unto itself, so that all of the systems studied by science are quasi-isolated systems. This should give rise to no problems provided it is borne in mind that predictability will be limited to the degree of validity of the postulate of isolation. Unfulfilled predictions commonly refute this supposition. Then the system boundaries are simply redrawn so as to warrant the postulate. And there is nothing irrational about that.

The programme for deterministic scientific explanation is then twofold: first, to establish the nature and constitution of natural objects that comprise the world, that is 'finding or imagining plausible generative mechanisms for the patterns among events, for the structure of things, for the generation, growth, decay or extinction of things and materials, for changes within persisting things and materials';[86] second, given the state of a particular system (that is, a given collocation of natural objects) at some time, to formulate an explanatory theory (law statement) that logically establishes a unique state for the system at any other time.[87] As Nagel has pointed out, such a general formulation of the principle of universal and uniform causation does not prescribe a particular definition for the state-description (such as the state-description of classical mechanics), nor does it postulate as the goal of science the development of theories possessing some special logical form (such as that of being expressible by differential equations). It does not proscribe the use of statistical or quasi-statistical variables of state, and recent developments in subatomic physics are therefore not in conflict with its directives.[88]

The *cognitive* status of the principle of *causality* has been the subject of much debate among philosophers and scientists, as has already been said. The view advanced here is that on the PO model it is a synthetic *a priori* principle.[89]

4.5.2 *The* a-priority *of causality*
In order to elucidate the *a priori*ty of the PO conception of causality here proposed, it is necessary to refer to the PO root model. As long as the perceiving subject as homunculus is seen, in OA fashion, to be in any sense outside of the natural world or as in some sense over against it,[90] then it will follow that any insight he achieves into the principles operating in the natural world will be the result of observation on the phenomenalist model and deductive inference solely, even when he is interacting with the world. Causality then on this model *could* only be an inductive generalisation; but notoriously, in fact, one that is not justified by experience. Faced with this fact, its cognitive status degenerates to that of an heuristic principle or maxim regulating

scientific inquiry, even to that of a mere resolve, or a pious hope of finding order where it is to be found. The alternative Kantian option, that causality is an *a priori* category of the human understanding, is more convincing and commensurate with the force attached to causality in rational thinking. Its drawback is that the principle is taken as a *given*, unexamined and unexaminable in *principle* according to the rational principles of which it is itself the very *a priori* form. Thus the rational investigation of causality itself, in the Kantian view, provides the spectacle of an eye trying to see itself seeing: a futile task, no doubt.

But the tradition from which the PO model of human individuality has developed does not regard the perceiving subject as a spirit, persona or homunculus outside of or set against a world he is appraised of only by passive observations and inductive inferences. Instead, the human individual, together with his perceivings, cognitions and actions, is regarded as completely integrated into the hierarchy of natural systems. Individual awareness of the principles regulating natural processes is accordingly rooted in the fact that individual awareness is in and of the natural processes themselves. Thus Spinoza says that:[91]

> Those things which are common to everything, and which are
> equally in the part and the whole, cannot but be conceived except in
> an adequate manner. Hence it follows that some ideas or notions exist
> which are common to all men: for all bodies agree in some things and
> those things are bound to be conceived by all in an adequate manner,
> that is clearly and distinctly. There will then exist in the human mind
> an adequate idea of the properties which are common to the human
> body and any external bodies by which the human body is generally
> affected, and are present equally in the parts and in the whole of them.

In the same vein, C. S. Peirce refers to the 'natural tendency toward the agreement between ideas which suggest themselves to the human mind and those which are concerned with the laws of nature',[92] and he argues that 'every scientific explanation of natural phenomena is an hypothesis that there is something in nature to which the human reason is analogous; and that it really is so, all the successes of science in its application to human convenience witnesses'.[93]

With specific reference to Kant's conception of the *a priori*, Lorenz has suggested that the relationship between the thing-in-itself and the *a priori* form of its appearance is determined by the natural history of adaptation of the perceiving organism. The perceiver and the perceived are part of the same reality. Specifically, the structure and function of the human central nervous system is adapted to the world with which man copes. Thus Hume is wrong to suppose that all that is *a priori* is derived from the sensory history of individuals. For the adaptive structures arise from the natural history of the phylum and so are prior to any individual experience.[94] This view is endorsed by Craik[95] and Piaget.[96]

According to this view, then, there is a universal principle of nature underlying the ceaseless universal processes of change. The concept of causality arises in human thought in virtue of the fact that thought is in and of the natural process itself, and is regulated by the same principles. Crucially, the principle is *a priori* in the sense of being prior to the experience of any given *individual*. To quote Lorenz, 'Mankind today lives by the function of the innate category of causality'.[97]

It may be objected that this view is a highly speculative one. But then, it can be said that *any* account of causality presupposes *some* root model. The question is not whether the explanation of the principle should be speculative or not, but rather *which* model underlies our conception. The view proposed here knowingly rejects the epistemic anthropomorphism underlying most other accounts. It is, *prima facie*, a plausible view and in the final analysis it stands or falls by the persuasion it can exercise by virtue of its success in ordering human experiences.

Another important objection is the claim that most human thought is manifestly *not* regulated by the rational principle that there is uniform connexity underlying the multifarious phenomena of human experience. Now it may be that innocents and primitive cultures do not apprehend causality in the developed scientific sense, but when for example thunderstorms are explained with reference to the wrath of Gods, thunderbolts and hammer blows, the explanatory *principle* is precisely the same as that of the meteorologist, namely that some causal agency is operating. Even belief in the apparent arbitrariness of events (where it exists at all) is attributed to the deliberate, if apparently capricious, actions of the menageries of anthropomorphic agencies. Another answer to this important objection is provided by Spinoza's distinction between the seemingly arbitrary collocations of impressions we derive from the common order of our experience (*imagines*), and genuine scientific knowledge (*ratio*). The former is a consequence of the (necessarily) localised fragmentary and idiosyncratic view the individual has of the vast panorama of the universal process, and the latter is based in the structure brought to this ordinary experience in virtue of the universal principles inherent in mature human thinking.

This last point brings us to a consideration of the importance of *maturation* in the recognition and development of the concept of causality. Hume's account of the once-off perception of causal connections leaves the notion unexamined, though his account is heavily dependent upon it. In view of this it is surprising that philosophers have not given this topic more attention. (Miles, for example, supposes the need for maturation only parenthetically.[98])

4.5.3   *The syntheticality of causality*

Whereas on the PO model the principle of causality has its roots in phylogeny and objective processes, *individuals* are not born with an apprehension of it. In fact, the process of physical maturation is parallelled by a corresponding development of the causal concept in the general direction of the objectification of causation. As Piaget puts it,[99]

> the elaboration of causality is closely linked with that of the universe and from this point of view it seems impossible to acknowledge a progressive transformation of the perception or the representation of the world without recognising the existence of a structural evolution of the relation which unites cause and effect.

Elsewhere he refers to[100]

> a sort of law of development of knowledge. ... The initial state is that of a universe which is neither substantial nor extended in depth, whose entirely practical phenomena and spatiality remain related to a subject ignorant of himself and perceiving reality only through his own activity. The final stage is, on the contrary, that of a solid vast world obeying physical laws of conservation (objects) and kinematic ones (groups) in which the subject places himself consciously as an element. From egocentrism to objective realism seems to be the formula of this law of evolution.

In offering this law of development of knowledge Piaget explicitly takes the adult world as informed by Western science as a datum, on the assumption that, even though the process of objectification implicit in this view has not resulted in a final veridical world-view, the process nevertheless manifests a general trend in this direction (accelerated also, it might be said, through 'a community in time'). Similar arguments can be drawn from evolutionary considerations, since the evolutionary process evidences a trend to the apprehension of more objective reality through the more numerous 'coping negotiations' involved in more evolved life forms.[101]

> So at the end of sensori-motor development the universe becomes a coherent whole in which effects follow causes which are independent of the subject and in the midst of which activity itself must, in order to intervene in the structure of things, submit to objective laws that are both spatial and temporal. Just as object and space, at first centred on a self ignorant of itself, finally transcend the self by encompassing it as an element, so also causality and time, at first dependent on internal operations unaware of their subjectivity are at last conceived as interconnecting external events or objects and as governing the subject who has become conscious of himself.

194

The evidence of developmental psychology corroborates what is already plain to common sense, that individual attainment of the concept of causality requires a process of maturation.[102] Hume of course fully recognised this, but he attributed it simply to the 'nature' of the human mind which on the phenomenalistic account is presented as something given, unexamined and in principle unexaminable. Within the PO model, however, the evidence is that biological and specifically neurological maturation involves the development of the neural mechanisms necessary for veridical causal perception, involving *ex hypothesi* the development of neural analogues of the structure *and function* of the external world. In this respect then the concept of causality is synthetic in the sense that it requires individual experience for its *realisation*.

It is true that we remain largely ignorant of the physiological foundations of this process of objectification of causality, and that we must therefore examine it, as we have done, mainly from the point of view of critical epistemology informed by biology and developmental psychology. Nevertheless the *coherence* of the PO model of causality as adumbrated here should no longer be in question.

With causality, as with so much else, the 'innate' versus 'experiential' dichotomy is not exclusive, but simply represents two aspects of a process that involves the experiential development of (phylogenetically predisposed) innate propensities. The principle of causality therefore in the PO account rendered here is both synthetic and *a priori* in the Kantian sense.

It will be evident how a principle that is both synthetic and *a priori* can generate a variety of accounts of its cognitive status, especially when rendered in terms of different metaphysical root models. In the special case of the Humean phenomenalist account, only the *experiential* component is admissible, and causality is represented as no more than a prudent habit. Later scientific empiricism represents it as a principle constitutive of (inductive) scientific investigation. The attempt to establish it by inductive inference inevitably fails because this recourse does not acknowledge the *a priori* status and force of the principle. Where the fragmentary experience of individuals has been contrasted to the universality and invariance of *logical* analyticity the principle has been regarded as nothing more than a pious hope. Kant's conception of causality as an *a priori* category of human understanding accounts for the universality and force of the principle as compared to prudential, constitutive and fiduciary accounts, but his doctrine that such principles are laws that the understanding 'prescribes to nature'[103] is an extravagant view of human mentality to say the least, even if 'nature' is construed phenomenally. The view presented here is more like nature prescribing to herself, or else recognising, her own principles. In general, if causality is a synthetic *a priori* principle in the sense outlined, then it gives rise to the variety of accounts that have been rendered of its cognitive status when divorced from the PO root model.

4.5.4 *The principle of causality as vacuous and uninformative*

It has been said that the expression 'every event has a cause' is vacuous and utterly uninformative because it would be impossible to describe any circumstance that would show it to be false.[104]

But this criticism of the causal principle presupposes that only experiental–inductive evidence is appropriate to its support. If this presupposition were true then the criticism would be justified. Taken in its *a priori* aspect, however, causality does not require a meaning criterion of this sort. (What, it might be asked, would count as a falsification of the falsification *principle*, if it comes to that?) On this view the suggested *a prior*ity of the principle of causality is contrasted unfavourably with that of the purely formal principles of logic,[105] especially with respect to the PO view that the concept of an event entails productive state-change and so causation.[106] Thus, it is argued that it does not follow analytically from the concept of an event that every event has a cause. However, according to the PO root model, to suppose otherwise is to adopt an (unjustified) anthropocentric epistemology. There is no reason to suppose that human failure to discover a cause is due to anything except the necessarily limited and fragmentary viewpoint of human individuals. On the other hand, the increasing success of the *hypothetico-deductive* method in science, in discovering both causes in cases and non-arbitrary natural laws, demands much more recognition and respect than it is allowed by philosophic obscurantists.

The spectacular success of scientists in formulating hypothetical models of natural objects and processes draws attention to the intrinsic affinity between human mentality and the natural objects and processes it apprehends. The affinity is a phylogenetically determined characteristic, and in this non-rationalistic sense is prior to individual experience. The principle of causality is, on this view, a general manifestation of the (phylogenetically) innate and thus *a priori* structure of human mentality. It is this *a priori* aspect of causality that puts it beyond question of empirical falsification in individual experience. In a word, the principle that every event has a cause has the sanction of millenia of evolutionary development. It is therefore unsurprising that it is immune to falsification by individual observations.

This last thought points to important similarities between the cognitive status of the logical principle of contradiction and the natural principle of causality.[107] We do not doubt, when we are confronted by a putative demonstration of valid self-contradiction, that some phoney assumption has been made, or that some fallacy has been committed, or that some plain mistake has been made. Within the context of formal discourse we are not prepared to abandon the principle of contradiction;[108] we reject all demonstrative argument to the contrary, and treat anybody who fails to do so as certainly beyond the philosophic pale and very likely a case of psychopathology and unfit to manage his own affairs to boot. But the proof of non-contradiction must presuppose non-contradiction.[109] Yet nobody supposes that non-contradiction should be abandoned because it would be impossible to describe any circumstances that would show it to be false!

On the PO model, causality, as a principle of nature inherent in human thought, has the same sort of *a priori* status as the principle of contradiction. It brooks refutation no more than the principle of contradiction. The individual whose conceptual schema is realistically rooted in the PO model will no more entertain the possibility of an event without a productive mass–energic state-change, that is to say without cause, then he would entertain the possibility of logical contradiction. It is simply not good enough to say that there are, or very well might be, some cases where there are no good grounds to be offered in support of a scientific (causal) explanation of an event, and to think that one might then continue to do the best that one could, with failure (and *inevitable* failure at that) accepted as a constant lurking possibility.[110] For if this were so, the scientist could never be sure that the immediate failures, which he typically takes to be arising from his fragmented perspective, were not the inevitable consequence of uncaused events. He would therefore have no reason ever to expect to find a necessary cause (i.e. an explanation). For only through surrogates for logical necessity can science proceed to explain natural phenomena.[111] This of course is the familiar problem of justifying induction and the apparent irrationality of science. But, as we are suggesting, that problem arises only within an inadequate (phenomenalist) metaphysical model anyway.

Within the alternative PO model the possibility of uncaused events takes on the incoherent aspect of valid self-contradiction, and is treated likewise as a psychopathological matter, quite outside the philosophic pale altogether.

5 SUMMARY AND CONCLUSIONS

The Humean purview is seen as the product of an unnecessary, and in the final analysis unjustifiable, anthropocentric epistemology and metaphysic. The Paralytic's Eye View is commonly represented as a tough-minded insistence upon the sanction of elementary sense-experience. But the experience Hume describes is a myth. Not only is the Cosmic Odeon Cinema a myth, but there is very good reason to believe that it is an *impossibility*. For it is now recognised that, without *active* assimilation and accommodation in the sense of these terms indicated by Piaget, even *perception* on the Humean model is impossible.[112] Perception requires the imposition of the universe on the individual in the sense that the organism is itself included within the whole mass–energic continuum, that is the domain of powerful productive relations (causation).

The PO model provides an alternative to the Humean view. Causation is then the relation of necessary productive connection as common intuition tells us. Causality, the principle that every event has a necessary necessitating cause, is established as a synthetic *a priori* principle of human reason; not in any transcendental idealist or obscurantist sense, but, plausibly, owing to the natural history of human beings.

The Humean challenge[113] to such views is met first of all by showing that Hume is mistaken to suppose that we have no experience of necessary connection. Second, a plausible alternative view is available based on an ontology of real natural objects which are the content of highly developed scientific theories. Such a view is fully consistent with the common intuition we have about causation and causality, un-contaminated by Hume's ontology. Third, a plausible explanation for why Hume overlooked such a view is that he was committed to a fundamental view of human experience as punctiform, composed of independent time-slices. Given this initial commitment the rest of the sceptical argument follows. But this view is much more implausible than the view that we have experience of real causation. The PO view is vindicated by the success of science in providing causal explanations, not just of events conforming to past patterns of regularity, but events predicted purely on the basis of knowledge of natural objects and the necessary consequences of their workings.

This discussion of causation leads to the question of causal explanations of mind-directed human behaviour or action. The questions that must now be considered concern the extent to which orthodox views about the explanation of action depend upon a Humean view of causation, and how far these views can be sustained if the Humean view is superseded by the PO view. To these questions we can now turn.

VII

HUMAN ACTION

1   INTRODUCTION

The last chapter set out to address the questions raised by the implication of IT that mind-directed human behaviour is subject to the same causal categories as other physical events. In order to appreciate the nature of the philosophical problems raised by physicalism for orthodox accounts of human action, it was necessary to consider the traditional philosophical view of causation derived from Hume and to compare it with the physical realist view implicit in the PO model. Specifically, the question was raised whether causation is (1) regular succession of phenomena only, as Hume suggests or (2) necessary productive connection. The importance of this question for explanations of actions is that if (1) is the case then it is possible to argue that, even if mental events cause physical events, it still does not follow that human action is *necessitated* or determined by mental events, because regular phenomenal succession does not imply determination as natural necessity. But if (2) is the case, and on the postulate of IT mental events are physical events 'from the inside', then IT implies necessary productive connection between the mental determinants of action and action.

The conclusion of the discussion of causal necessity was that there is no compelling reason to accept Hume's basic account of causation and that, indeed, there are good reasons to reject it. The physical realist view of causation is at least as plausible, *prima facie*, as Hume's view, and furthermore there are good reasons for accepting it. Not the least of these are that it accords with ordinary intuitions; it corresponds to the way that scientists typically think; and it proves practically effective and fruitful. It is now opportune to consider how far orthodox explanations of action can be sustained if the Humean view is superseded by a physical–realist (PO) view.

The view advanced in this chapter is, in outline, as follows.

1 The prevailing orthodoxy about the autonomy of non-causal explanations of human action is basically incoherent.

2 The orthodoxy has a spurious coherence because the Humean analysis of causation is presupposed,[1] the incoherencies in the orthodoxy and the errors in the Humean analysis being mutually cancelling.

3 The PO model of causation together with an identity hypothesis is capable of rendering coherent the incoherencies in the orthodox account of human action.

2   EXPLANATION OF ACTIONS

Causal accounts of other-than-human events are almost universally accepted as sufficiently explanatory of those events. Substantial divergence of opinion usually arises only in the case of human behaviour; more specifically the voluntary, deliberate actions of normal, conscious, adult, human individuals. These qualifying concepts are themselves somewhat opaque, but they convey well enough the relevant sense of the usual distinction. The main point of the distinction is that there are at least two main types of satisfactory explanation, namely causal explanations, which are appropriate in general to other-than-human events, and rational explanations, which are appropriate to the special class of events involving human (or other rational) agency. This important distinction was first made by Socrates and has persisted in some form to the present time. The first statement of it in the *Phaedo* is sufficiently important and illuminating to bear a closer scrutiny, in view of the crucial importance attached to the more recent versions of it formulated by philosophers who want to reject the possibility of exclusively causal accounts as sufficiently explanatory of *all* human behaviour. Socrates says:[2]

> I once heard someone reading from a book (as he said) by Anaxagoras, and asserting that it is mind that produces order and is the cause of everything ... and I reflected that if this is so, mind, in producing order, sets everything in order and arranges each individual thing in that way that is best for it. ... These reflections made me suppose to my delight that in Anaxagoras I had found an authority on causation who was after my own heart. ... It was a wonderful hope ... but it was quickly dashed. ...

I discovered that the fellow made no use of mind and assigned to it no causality for the order of the world, but adduced causes like air, and ether, and water, and many other absurdities. It seemed to me that he was just about as inconsistent as if someone tried to account for my conversing with you, adducing causes such as sound and air and hearing and a thousand others and never troubled to mention the *real* reasons: which are that since Athens has thought it better to condemn me, therefore I for my part have thought it better to sit here, and more right to stay and submit to whatever penalty she orders.

There is an interesting point about this translation which I think casts some light on the recent discussion of the matter. That is that *aitia* is rendered as both 'cause' and 'reason', so that in translation into modern English Socrates seems to equivocate between physical causes and real causes (mental causes or reasons). That is to say, mental causes or reasons are special, *real*, causes, namely final causes related to rational purposes and motives. Leibnitz cites Plato with approval; but whereas Socrates regards the physical—causal account as explanatorily absurd and at best merely a *condition* for a 'real' causal account with no right to the name 'cause', Leibnitz accepts the legitimacy of causal explanation in science and stresses the compatibility of causal and rational explanations.[3]

The problem presented here then is this. We explain events not involving rational agency in terms of causes. We explain at least some human behaviour in terms of reasons. The question is whether (1) following Socrates we either regard causal explanations of human acts as irrelevant (except as conditional) or even possibly incompatible with rational explanations, or (2) following Leibnitz we regard causal and rational accounts as harmonious, or (3) following Anaxagoras and the scientific materialists we disregard rational explanations of human acts as failing to explain in the approved (i.e. causal—deterministic) sense.

If it can be shown that causal and rational accounts of human action *are* compatible in some way, then both the extreme Socratic (rationalist) and Anaxagorean (causalist) positions will be shown to be mistaken. This is the orthodox view shared by most modern analytical philosophers. It is also the view implied by the PO model of human action taken together with IT. However, the orthodox view of the compatibility of rational and causal explanations involves serious incoherencies which are not involved in the PO model. This is the thesis that I shall now develop, because of its relevance to human action in its libertarian and ethical aspects.

3 · THE CONCEPT OF PERSONS AS PRIMITIVE ENTITIES

Before discussing the current orthodoxy about the compatibility of causal and rational explanations, it is necessary briefly to indicate the important background assumption underlying this orthodoxy. This is that, contrary to the views of extreme idealist and materialist metaphysics, and the spectrum of metaphysical views in between these extremes, it is not possible to analyse individual experience (in the reductive sense of 'analyse') into psychic or mental or physical components. The human individual or 'person' is neither a bundle of perceptions, nor a thought, nor a group of cognita, nor a set of relations among thoughts and between thoughts and bodies, nor an activity, nor the exercisings of capacities, nor a pattern of bodily states.[4] The person is a *primitive* entity. As Strawson puts it,[5]

> the concept of a person is the concept of a type of entity such that *both* predicates ascribing states of consciousness *and* predicates ascribing corporeal characteristics, a physical situation etc. are equally applicable to a single individual of the same type. And what I mean by saying that this concept is primitive can be put in a number of ways. One way is to (ask) the two questions ... (i) why are states of consciousness ascribed to anything at all? and (ii) why are they ascribed to the very same thing as certain corporeal characteristics, a certain physical situation etc?

The answers to the two questions are connected by the fact that the necessary condition of states of consciousness being ascribed at all is that they are ascribed to the *very same things* as certain physical characteristics. States of consciousness could not be ascribed at all unless they are ascribed to (embodied) persons. The person, therefore, has mental and physical aspects but is not analytically *reducible* to these aspects. We speak properly only of the thoughts *of* some person, and of the body *of* some person. Even more important perhaps is the range of properties that can belong only to persons, such as being the source and object of rights and obligations, or that which takes on roles in communities. It might be suggested that the Strawsonian person is just Cartesian-man but glued together firmly. A more apposite analogy has been suggested of the 'wavicle' from physics, which (according to one interpretation at least) is neither wave nor particle, but *both at once*. Perhaps this ontological solution to the vexing dilemma of wave-particle dualism in quantum mechanics, that of positing a primitive with dual but irreducible properties, is an apt model for psycho-physical dualism also.[6]

In relation to the present discussion, however, there is one problem about the (OA) concept of the 'person' as primitive which cannot be avoided and which is particularly important. That is that the purposeful actions of an agent are taken to be unanalysable either in terms of the agent's desires on the one hand or his physical states on the other. Because person-predicates include rational volition, moral responsibility and so forth, it is insufficient to show that actions, in so far as they involve bodily movement, follow from, and are in some sense caused by, 'inner' states, whether mental or physical: in order that behaviour should count as an action at all it should be the action of the person or the self, and this is irreducible to such 'inner' states.[7] Thus Melden argues that[8]

> It is futile to attempt to explain conduct through the causal efficacy of a desire – all *that* can explain is further happenings, not actions performed by agents. The agent confronting the causal nexus in which such happenings occur is a helpless victim of all that occurs in and to him.

Similarly Richard Taylor argues that 'no matter how detailed a physical account we gave of behaviour we should never describe it as an act until we state that some agent caused it',[9] and says that since rational explanation 'is an explanation which in no way refers to causes, it is consistent with the absence of such causes or in other words with the supposition that the action in question, as distinguishable from the bodily motion it accomplishes, is not caused at all, or is performed freely';[10] 'to say that a man's act is free entails not that there is no cause for what he does, but rather that there is no cause for him doing it.'[11]

It may be that the concept of a person is primitive in the appropriate trans-empirical sense within the prevailing OA model, so that, presupposing this model, it can truly be said that there are certain predicates such as states of consciousness and free action which we apply to persons but which we would not dream of applying to material bodies – but *only* presupposing the OA model. If the shift from the OA to the PO model occurs, then through the mutual modification of the concepts of persons and material bodies it is no longer inappropriate to predicate the so-called 'P-predicates' of physical systems of a certain type, namely *Homo sapiens*. And then, according to an I-hypothesis, states of consciousness and 'free' actions are (with due allowance for the metaphor) physical states and processes 'from the inside'. By extension, reasons, purposes and motives are likewise physical states or processes 'from the inside'. This last thesis has been rejected by proponents of the orthodoxy, but the supporting arguments offered have been singularly inadequate, whereas on the other hand the OA model within which they are formulated is basically incoherent. This I shall now attempt to show.

4 ACTIONS OF AGENTS: THE ORTHODOX ACCOUNT

I have said that the orthodox view of the relation between causal and rational explanation of human actions is that the two are in some sense compatible. This observation is true as far as it goes but it does not reflect an important distinction which can be made within the general OA model. This is the distinction between, first, the view that causal and rational accounts of human behaviour are compatible, and even complementary, but are mutually irrelevant; and, second, the view that compatibility takes a Humean form in that reasons, and 'mental causes' generally, enter into mutual relations with physical causes. Both these positions involve incoherencies. But before discussing these we must first consider what the positions represent and examine their justification.

4.1 *Mutual Irrelevance*

According to one influential school of thought,[12] when we explain human action in terms of reasons the patterns of explanation involved are different altogether from those involved in causal explanations. The difference has to do with the supposed fact that actions and events are essentially different sorts of things. The by now familiar rationale underlying this view is that we must look to the 'logical geography' of our explanatory forms and recognise that the form of explanation offered in any case must be appropriate to the particular case and to its context. Now causal explanations do have an appropriate domain, namely science, and the other-than-human domain generally, but they are not the only legitimate sort of explanations. In particular, the explanatory form appropriate to the domain of human actions is *rational*.

4.1.1 *Justification*

The main justification for this view depends on the appropriateness of the basic metaphor of 'logical geography'. Now in fact, beyond drawing attention to the *prima facie* differences in explanatory concepts and language, proponents of the view have not attempted to show why these necessarily entail the mutual irrelevance of causal and rational explanations. After a long innings without question, this failure to *show* the mutual irrelevance of the two accounts has been subject to increasing criticism.[13] In any event the invocation of the logical geography metaphor is not sufficient of itself to justify the claim of the mutual irrelevancy of causal and rational accounts.

Another recurrent justification for this position, related to the more general one, is the claim that the 'Why?–Because' locution involved in inquiry is misleading.[14] The suggestion is that, whether we seek to elicit rational explanations or causal explanations, our query is expressed in the same form, 'Why?' And the appropriate response in either case begins with 'Because ...'. It is said that this is a mere etymological accident, but one that has the fatal effect of misleading us into thinking that there is a common explanatory form when in fact there is not. But this line of argument is very unconvincing. For we are bound to ask how such gross confusion in forms of words could have come about in the first place, and how it is so pervasive in language, if, as the orthodoxy wants to maintain, the patterns of explanation are *altogether* different'. On the contrary, when we consider that most of the human actions we are interested in involve physical movements, then we would positively expect to find an account of explanation which accommodates *both* rational and causal elements.

4.2   Mutual Relevance ('Mental Causes')

According to this minority view within the broad orthodoxy,[15] human action is properly explained in rational terms, but acknowledgment is also made of the commonplace belief that reasons make a *difference* to behaviour; that is to say, 'mental' causes enter into the causal process and make a difference to physical events.

The justification for this ancient and common-sense view, in lieu of the type or sortal requirement for causal relations, is by appeal (though not always explicitly) to Hume's criterion of causation as succession only. Thus Davidson, for example, cites Hume's definition of a cause as an object followed by another and where all objects similar to the first are followed by objects similar to the second. He does argue, against Hume, that ignorance of competent predictive laws does not inhibit valid causal explanations and says that we are usually more certain of singular causal connections than we are of laws governing cases, so that I am certain the window broke because it was struck by a rock – I saw it all happen[16] (i.e. I saw the rock strike the window followed by the window breaking). Nevertheless the Humean formula of phenomenal succession remains the same. However, we have found reason to reject the Humean formula of 'phenomenal succession' and, unless we accept that anything can cause anything, this raises once again the sortal problem of causation for this sort of compatibility account.

This brief consideration of the two main versions of the OA conception of the relation of rational and causal explanations is sufficient to suggest that each leaves crucial questions unanswered. The mutual irrelevancy view fails to account adequately for the fact that the rational account explains the same *physical behaviour* that the causal account explains, and it makes too light of the implication in ordinary thought and language that *some* sort of common explanatory form is involved. The mutual relevancy account presupposes a dubious phenomenalist view of causation, without which the thesis that reasons are causes of actions is incoherent within the OA model, which distinguishes categorially between the mental and the physical. However, there is a (physicalist) way to remedy these deficiencies if, contrary to the orthodoxy, there are states and changes of states in persons that are agentless causes and which, because they are reasons as well as causes, make persons voluntary agents.[17] In order to prepare the way for a further elaboration of this pregnant thought, however, it is necessary to examine in more detail the large claim that the philosophically orthodox and influential account of the compatibility of causal and rational explanation is incoherent.

5 THE INCOHERENCE OF THE ORTHODOX ACCOUNT

I assume that no definitive refutation of a root metaphysical model is possible; therefore in order to show the incoherence of the OA account of human action I shall follow the same modest principle adopted to suggest the untenability of the phenomenalist account of causation: that, if a model systematically gives rise to a number of serious problems or entails strongly counter-intuitive consequences, then its coherence and adequacy are seriously called into question. Perhaps it is necessary to point out at this juncture, however, that the following arguments are not calculated to call into question the ultimate adequacy of other-than-causal explanations of human action, but only the OA account of such explanations in relation to causal explanations.

5.1 *Rational Accounts as Non-explanatory*

It has been suggested that explanations of human behaviour in terms of reasons, etc., may not be really explanatory *at all* in any philosophically (as opposed to psychologically) important sense,[18] because all explanation must be to some extent predictive.[19] In the extreme case, that of scientific explanation in terms of invariant law statements, explanation and prediction are symmetrical on this view.[20] That is to say, an explanation is explanatory only to the extent that it can predict, and prediction involves some statement in terms of a covering law(s) or model hypothesis within a more general nomological net, from which the explanandum follows uniquely. Whenever two mutually exclusive explananda follow from the same explanans, i.e. when the explanation is 'anomalous', then the explanation entails a self-contradictory formula and would therefore always be false.[21] Now this is the case precisely with the OA account of rational explanations of human behaviour. Explanations of this sort employ such concepts as the motive of patriotism. But this motive of patriotism might equally well be employed to explain quite different, and even incompatible, explananda such as 'He joined the army' and 'He joined the peace march'.[22] This is the unsatisfactory consequence of conveniently adopting broad concepts and descriptive terminology which 'sit loose' to instances.[23]

So far this objection seems counter-intuitive, since we do explain human action in terms of motives such as patriotism perfectly satisfactorily. The objection does tell, however, against the OA view that in interpersonal transactions, where reasons are involved, an account is potentially explanatory simply in virtue of the employment of the appropriate rational concepts alone. For if this argument is correct, much more is involved in the appropriate explanation than the use of 'interpersonal' categories. The fact would seem to be that, contrary to what many orthodox philosophers believe, some generalised law statements (or law-like statements) are implied, even by rational explanation.[24] The problem with the OA account arises because of an illegitimate inference from the correct observation that to have a particular motive or reason or purpose does not entail a particular action, to the conclusion that no law statements are involved in the explanation. The mistake is to think that specific state descriptions cannot be provided *in terms of* law statements, given appropriate initial and boundary conditions.[25] (Smart's analogy between engineering and biology is again apposite in this context.) Law statements are the basis of all 'explanations' with explanatory power. Precise state-descriptions (and boundary conditions) ensure relevance to the given case. And of course the states of any given system can vary from time to time. What this involves is nothing less than the preservation of rational explanations by abandoning the OA claim that rational explanations are not law-like in the scientific sense, which implies that the explanandum follows in some sense necessarily from the explanans. This is not counter-intuitive, and indeed Ryle, as one major exponent of the orthodoxy, recognises as much when he writes of 'law-like' propositions employed in explanations of motivated acts as 'inference tickets'.[26]

207

The orthodoxy offers two sorts of response to the conclusion that explanation entails law-like invariance, both of them inadequate. First, it is said that, in order to provide 'law-like' explanations of individual cases which are precise enough, the law statements required will become so narrow in application as not to guide us or to warrant a singular causal statement. The explicit assumption here is that, for law statements to be explanatory, they must link with broad generalisations such as those of common sense.[27] But of course a law statement may perfectly well apply only narrowly in fact, in the sense of representing only a few actual instances (or even only *one*.) In the perfectly satisfactory sense of 'law statement' meaning 'explanans entailing explanandum', law statements of narrow application are every bit as explanatory as law statements of more general application. For example, the fact that few, if any, individuals are born heart-deficient would not detract from the explanatory power of a general law statement based on a functional model of human biology which entails the death of such individuals. In general the difficulty lies not theoretically in the scope of application of law statements, but practically in the specification of the relevant initial and boundary conditions (the 'state-description'). Consider the case 'This car ran downhill because its brakes failed'. The explanatory power of this statement does not require the general law statement, 'If brakes fail then cars run downhill', any more than does the usual rational explanation of a given act entail a general law statement of the form 'same motive, same act'. But we do not draw from this the conclusion that the explanation of the cars running downhill is not in terms of statements such as Newton's laws. These are employed in the state-description of the system states at the relevant time.

This problem brings us to the second orthodox response, which is really another sort of argument: that the reasons why rational explanations are not generalisable law statements are that rational concepts are intrinsically fuzzy or umbrella concepts which actually cover a variety of concepts so that no 'same-motive-same-action' formula can be specified; and also that, in particular cases of action, clusters of motives, reasons, purposes, etc., are usually involved in influencing an act, in which case it would be necessary to quantify in some way the relative influence of each motivating factor.[28]

The answer to both these responses is essentially the same: an explanation of the occurrence of an event is explanatory only in so far as it is law-like in the sense that the explanandum follows from the explanans. In practice we interpret a rational explanation of particular cases in terms of fuzzy or umbrella concepts by eliminating irrelevant terms, i.e. by sharpening up the fuzzy conceptual focus or by throwing out terms from under the umbrella. This process draws on a whole pattern of known relations relevant to some purpose known to promote human interests,[29] much as a scientific hypothesis of narrow range draws on a broad background of well-established theory. What we are left with is an inference in the form of a law-like rational proposition. For example, in order that patriotism should constitute a rational explanation we should have to know a good deal about the circumstances of the case: the individual, the society and so forth. Patriotism would provide a rational explanation of the enlistment in the army of someone with a 'hawkish' conception of his country and its situation, but not a pacifist's. On the other hand it would equally provide a rational explanation of someone else enlisting in the flower-army provided 'hawkish' connotations of the word were eliminated from the explanans by interpretation.

In either case what is explanatory about the explanation is the entailment of an explanandum by an explanans. To the extent that the explanans is indeterminate, so is its explanatory power. There is an analogous case in physics, with the inherent inability of quantum mechanics to explain Newtonian phenomena.[30] The inherent indeterminacy of an explanans sets corresponding limits to the determinacy of the explanandum, i.e. its explanatory power. The problem presented by numerous rational factors influencing behaviour points to the same sort of conclusion. An explanation in terms of multiple rational factors is explanatory only in so far as relative significance and weight can be attached to the various factors by interpretation. Although such interpretations cannot be quantitative in the ordinary scientific sense, this does not rule out explanations in these law-like terms: which is no more than common sense would lead us to expect. Even purely scientific explanations require structural and functional as well as quantitative definition (in the sense of perspicuous order).[31] So in practice we are able to interpret multiple-rational explanations by allocating appropriate relative weightings to each factor, and perceiving some pattern of relations among them analogous to the relative and relational aspects of scientific explanations.

Consider how, knowing only the relative masses in a dynamic mechanical system, together with its structure and the functional relations this defines, an approximate – and for many purposes adequate – prediction of its behaviour would be possible without any quantification at all. We can predict that the heaviest end of a see-saw will go down without quantifying the weight differential. Something very like this goes on when we successfully explain behaviour as we commonly do in terms of multiple rational factors. Consider, for example, the case of Smith who yesterday believed, like everybody else, that his father was a great man. He was motivated to honour him, but for reasons of state he did not canonise his father. For example, as prime minister he could not canonise his father for the good reason that he respected the law against it. Today Smith has learned that his father was a blackguard, so he is not motivated to honour him; but even though there are good reasons of state why he can and should canonise his father, for example to prevent civil disorder, he has good reasons why he does not (although the law has been changed; it was his father who changed it, and he has no respect for the self-immortalising machinations of his blackguardly father, moreover, by now he does not care a tinker's curse for order anyway). Clearly, ordinary rational explanations can in this way allocate relative weightings to several factors and, even when quantification is not possible, can articulate their relations effectively in analogous fashion to the same sort of explanatory logic in science, i.e. explanans and specific state descriptions in terms of law statements, and explanandum entailed by explanans.

In short, the orthodox view that rational explanations are not law-like, in the sense that the explanandum is not uniquely entailed by the explanans,[32] would mean that rational explanations are not explanatory at all, because they involve self-contradictory, (i.e. mutually exclusive) explanantia. In so far as they are explanatory, then they are law-like in the sense defined. It is therefore possible that they are isomorphic with, or that they converge with, other law-like explanations – namely *causal* ones.

5.2 *Temporal Symmetry of Cause-Effect in Agent Acts*

Some proponents of the orthodoxy characterise those bodily movements which are actions of agents as movements that agents 'make happen'. According to this view, such actions of agents are basic: they are uncaused though they may themselves be causes. So the explanation of the action of moving an arm for example is just that an agent makes his arm move.[33] This 'action' is primitive and cannot be explained in terms of antecedent causes. On the contrary we are eventually driven to the profoundly counter-intuitive conclusion that certain antecedent causes may be themselves brought about by the agent's subsequent act. According to Richard Taylor, this comes about as follows:[34]

> [There] are certain purposeful actions the ends or goals of which seem to precede these actions. For example, if it is one's purpose to flex a certain arm muscle the only way one can accomplish this is by moving the arm. The arm is caused to move by the motion of the muscle, but the arm moved in order to move the muscle, not vice versa ... or consider the nerve impulses. Part of the cause of the motion of a

man's arm when he moves it is certainly a certain nerve impulse from the brain, but it is false that he moves his arm by means of the nerve impulse. It is the other way around. Thus if a man learns of these nerve impulses – and many go to their graves without ever suspecting they exist – and then has some occasion to produce one of them – perhaps for the purpose of some experiment in physiological psychology – he can do so only by moving his arm. The purposeful action in such a case, namely the man's moving his arm, is the means to a certain end: the production of a nerve impulse which actually precedes that action in time. And this incidentally is the only kind of case I can think of in which one apparently does something as a means to the occurrence or non-occurrence of some prior event. It is thus the only kind of case I can imagine of changing the past at will or of having some event in the past literally within one's voluntary control. *The example is frightfully puzzling however and I shall henceforth disregard it.* [Emphasis added]

However, far from disregarding such a puzzling and counter-intuitive consequence of the primitive agent-action model, what is clearly indicated here is a radical incoherence in the orthodox account of action and the need for a thorough re-examination of the basic agency model that involves such consequences. The basic problem lies in the categorial distinction that this view makes between the agent as primitive entity and his mental and physical states. Further discussion of this question will be undertaken later (Section 7.1.1 below). Meanwhile it is interesting to note, because of the light it throws on the matter, that doing something that causes my finger to move does not cause me to move my finger; *it is moving my finger.*[35]

5.3 Rational Factors as Making No Difference to Behaviour

The mutual-irrelevance orthodoxy emphasises the explanatory nature of rational explanations, and denies that motives and so on have anything to do with physical processes regulated by causation as such. The relevant distinction drawn is between sorts of explanations. Thus, it is said that to explain an action in terms of motives is not to infer 'occult' inner causes, but to *subsume descriptions* of the action under hypothetical propositions.[36] Similarly, descriptions of the difference between a man gabbling and a man talking sense are *rhetorical* and *logical* only, with no physiological basis.[37] An explanation of an action in terms of motives and reasons may have no connection *whatsoever* with its causes; indeed, on this account there may *be* no causes.[38]

Now against this view we would want to argue that it is not enough to establish that an agent has relevant reasons, motives and purposes, and that the agent performed some action. We are also concerned to know whether the agent acted as he did *because* he had those reasons, etc. 'Because' here must entail that the agent's reasoning, purpose and motivation were the *cause* of his behaviour. It must be the case that the agent's reasons *produced* his action; that they are 'not just left in the air so to speak'.[39] We want to say not only that reasons provide the basis of satisfactory explanations but also that they make a difference to what we *do*, to behaviour, to bodily movement. A reason for doing something may be just as necessary to the performance of an action as the crudest physical condition; and indeed, unless it were, there would be no useful sense in which it would *be* explanatory of it. Whether or not, and how, some act is performed (i.e. bodies moved) may depend on whether or not there is a reason that would make a difference to the bodies *not* moving, or to the manner of their moving. The very word 'motive' implies as much, and common sense assumes it also. But on the orthodox account reasons are nothing more than explanatory concepts, which refer to nothing in the physical–causal explanandum.

The radical incoherence of this mutual irrelevance view therefore lies in the fact that, whereas we are to distinguish between motivated and unmotivated behaviour, motives, etc., have no reference beyond patterns of behaviour; they do not make a difference to these patterns, only to descriptions and to explanations of them; supposedly nothing is necessarily going on in a motivated act that is not going on in an unmotivated act. But only an *a priori* philosophical commitment to a quasi-behaviouristic, linguistic or hollow-man ontology would ever suggest such a thing.

5.4 *Actions as Not Doing Something*

An interesting case closely connected both with the difference reasons make to behaviour and with many legal anomalies is the problem raised by the way we normally regard individuals as being positively involved in the occurrence of certain events when they have not done anything, just as much as in other cases when they have done something: namely cases where the person has deliberately omitted or failed to do something that he would otherwise be expected to do. If, following the orthodoxy, we take the action of agents as primitive ('making something happen'), then all actions are modelled as the creation of a dynamic. So when there is no bodily dynamic created the agent has not done anything: there are supposedly no ghostly inner events called omissions or not-doings, even less than there are ghostly inner events called willings and doings. In cases such as these it must be said that the agent has failed to fulfil expectations that others have of him; in other words the explanation for the person's involvement in the event is framed in terms that do not really involve what the agent has done at all, but instead involve the *expectations of others*.

This is a rather queer and unsatisfactory sort of account of acts of omission, which we often consider to be equivalent to acts of commission. Thus we would say: 'By not telling the man as he stepped through the door that the aircraft was then flying at 30,000 feet and was not on the runway, as you knew he mistakenly believed, you caused his death just as deliberately as if you had thrown him out yourself.' This anomaly is closely tied to the concept of the person as a primitive entity, and its resolution is closely tied to the clarification of certain confusions involved in that concept. These will be discussed later (Section 7.1.1 below). At this point it is sufficient to draw attention to the Aristotelian conception of dynamics underlying this conception of agents making things happen (i.e. *creating* a dynamic), in contrast to the Newtonian conception of a world *continuously* buzzing with activity, i.e. of an 'agent' participating in and modifying a dynamic.

5.5   Anomalies in Law

According to the orthodoxy, when we are explaining 'interpersonal transactions', whether in ordinary discourse or law or history, the appropriate explanatory logic is by appeal to reasons.[40] However, the difference between rational and causal explanations is by no means clear-cut, so that in law it is still common to talk about someone causing the action of another, or being caused to act by another, through the provision of reasons for action. One authority on penal philosophy has even defined intention in terms of a 'physical act'.[41]

In law, a rational explanation of human behaviour can be treated *as if* it were a kind of causation, and responsibility mitigated accordingly, when by means of deeds, acts, words, inducements or some form of compulsion, one individual (the persuader) brings about the action of another (the agent), where in general:

1 the agent knows and understands the deeds, etc., of the persuader;
2 the persuader's deeds, words, etc., provide the agent with his reasons for acting;
3 the agent forms his intention to act only after the persuader's intervention;
4 the persuader intends the agent to act as he did.

This general formula would cover such fairly clear-cut cases of causing someone to act as these: menacing movements with a weapon, and other threatening behaviour (e.g. preparations to abandon the home); offering bribes; and blackmail. In each case we should normally say that the agent had been caused or compelled or necessitated in some way to act as he did by the effects of the persuader's actions. But even a brief consideration of these criteria for treating behaviour as if it were caused by a persuader suggests that they apply equally to the ordinary influence that is brought to bear on an individual in the course of his nurture and education. The similarity is highlighted by a consideration of borderline cases.

Hypnotism is treated as borderline in law because, although there is no overt deed, threat, inducement or compulsion, neither is the influence brought to bear just advice or mere suggestion. On the other hand, the orthodoxy would normally want to maintain that subjection to, say, political or philosophical argument cannot be treated as causing someone to act. This is to be explained in terms of the reasons an agent thereby acquires for action. But upon what basis would we make a clear distinction between obvious cases of hypnotism and (say) exposure to the political–ideological rally speeches of Adolf Hitler? We do indeed make a distinction, but the present argument suggests that the orthodox account of it as categorical is an unwarranted and *a priori* one.

Consider again the very close similarity between certain equally satisfactory explanations of the same act. An individual might act because on the one hand he may (1) be subjected to threatening gestures, (2) bribed with promises or (3) hypnotised; on the other hand (a) he may be a deaf mute to whom the *only* way to communicate a warning is gestural, or (b) he may receive verbal advice about future prospects or (c) he may be subject to some kind of formative initiation (religious, political, etc.). The first set of cases (1, 2, 3) would tend to be treated in law as being *caused* to act, the second set (a,b,c) as a person having *reasons* for acting. And yet if there is a difference between the cases it is not at all obvious: they all basically involve influence through the stimuli of 'surface irritations' in communication. Certainly there is no clear-cut basis for deciding whether to exonerate a person on the grounds that he has been subject to 'causal' influences, or to blame him on the grounds that he is a responsible rational 'person'. The orthodox view that causal and rational explanations are of different types *altogether* seems to be quite mistaken.

Two clues to a resolution of the dichotomy between the two sorts of account are available in Hart's discussion of the matter. First, it is said that 'to be sure' that a person has been caused to act as he did by another is to establish his 'state of mind' at the time of the act[42] and to show that the others have provided him with a reason for acting 'in his eyes'. Reference to the persuader's bringing about an event 'through the mind of the second person' suggests mental causes and leads to the second clue: the suggestion that an agent's reasons might be *causes from the inside*.[43] This metaphor has already been alluded to in connection with IT. Wittgenstein rejected the idea, and Hart raises the possibility in connection with borderline cases of causal accounts of rational action, but without drawing a conclusion. It is along these lines that causal and rational explanations converge.

What emerges from this discussion is that the anomalies created in law by the categorial distinction between rational and causal explanations point to the basic artificiality of the distinction in so far as it is treated as categorial. The conception of 'reasons as causes from the inside' is suggested by a consideration of cases where agents are caused to act in some cases by being given reasons, etc.

5.6   The Language of Action

Reference has already been made to some important similarities between the languages of rational and causal explanations: that either sort of explanation can be elicited by the same word, 'Why?', and any response will be prefaced by 'Because'. It was explained earlier that the orthodox response to this fact is to dismiss it as an unfortunate etymological accident. The 'accident' story is not good enough, especially when it is necessary to repeat it continuously in the face of the pervasiveness of ambiguous rational–causal terminology. Thus 'event' applies equally to the action of human agents and to inanimate state-changes, and this also is considered 'unfortunate'.[44] Reference has also been made to the interesting cases, particularly in law, where giving someone a reason for acting is 'as if' to *cause* him to act. It should be noted that the attempt to distinguish between explanations of such actions and explanations of normally caused events in terms of 'the reasons being known independently of generalisation' is mistaken, since all explanation entails some law statement, law-like statement or 'inference ticket' of a generalised sort. Also, just as we can speak equally intelligibly of agent's actions causing and being caused, so we can meaningfully talk about the effect(s) of an agent's action as well as its 'consequences' or 'outcome', etc. We can say for instance 'the *effect* of his resignation was to spread despondency among his supporters', just as legitimately as 'the effect of the explosion was to spread stress-fractures through the structure'. 'Action' itself is a word that applies perfectly intelligibly and non-metaphorically to inanimate events as well as to the behaviour of agents: we speak of chemical action, servo-action and legal action. The word 'motive' itself connotes a mechanistic paradigm for human agency, as Michotte suggests, just as much as the reverse – and the rich variety of emotive idioms testifies to this: 'struck all of a heap', 'shaken to pieces', 'overwhelmed', 'transported', 'impressed', 'pierced', 'bursting', 'crushed', 'gotten-down', 'knocked flat', 'repulsed', 'stricken', 'shocked' and many others. Especially significant are the causal forms of words we commonly use in *rational* explanations such as 'compelling reasons', 'overriding purposes', etc.

The orthodox suggestion, that the deeply rooted and pervasive linguistic idioms common to both causal and rational explanations are nothing more than an unfortunate etymological accident, or merely metaphorical, cannot be taken seriously. Indeed, there is nothing so mere about metaphors when they are so pervasive. What seems much more likely is that there is some underlying explanation for the deeply rooted and extensive overlap of the idioms of causal talk and human-action talk.

6   THE SPURIOUS COHERENCE OF THE ORTHODOX ACCOUNT

Taken together, the six points made below indicate a basic incoherence in the orthodox account of the relation between rational explanations of human action and causal explanations, i.e. that they are categorially different. There is good reason to follow the venerable and common-sense view that reasons make a difference to actions and not merely to descriptions and explanations of actions, which are logically secondary to actions.[45] If so, however, the old Cartesian dichotomy is raised again and it is necessary to account for the *manner* in which the relevant difference is made. The orthodoxy relies on Hume's criterion of causation as 'phenomenal succession' to account for this. It is in this way that all of the incoherencies in the orthodox account of causation and human action indicated here, and I suggest other incoherencies we might think of as well, are rendered coherent, because Hume is either explicitly (cf. Davidson and Whiteley) or implicitly assumed.

6.1   *The Explanatory Power of Rational Accounts*

Given acceptance of the 'pandemonium principle', there is no reason why motives, etc., should not enter regularly into successive relations with certain bodily movements, which fact can be expressed in an inductively generalised law statement. This, with certain important (quasi-behavioural) qualifications, is the basis of the OA 'inference ticket' account of 'rational–dispositional' explanations.

6.2   *Temporal Symmetry of Causes and Effects*

Although the problem of temporal symmetry is not such a widely disputed issue in the orthodoxy as some others, it is evident that it is rendered much *more* coherent by the neo-Humean account of causation.

6.3   *The Inefficacy of Reasons as Causes of Behaviour*

The difference-making problem is, for obvious reasons, not explicitly discussed. It is regarded as a non-problem by those who hold a 'mutual irrelevancy' view of reasons and causes. But if we are correct, this view stands as irredeemably incoherent. The mutual relevancy view explicitly invokes the phenomenal-contiguity-and-succession criterion to render coherent the 'difference-making' incoherency.

6.4   *Acts of Omission*

The peculiar problem of the *attributability* of 'not-doings' as well as doings to agents is a consequence of the orthodox view of the person as a primitive entity, which is open to serious qualifications which will be made presently.

6.5   *Anomalies in Law*

The legal anomalies, which turn on the conception of one person *causing* another to do something (act) by giving him a *reason*, clearly reflect the underlying Humean notion of reasons as 'mental causes' entering into continuous causal chains together with physical events.

6.6   *The Language of Action*

The commonality of the languages of causal and rational descriptions and explanations likewise reflects an underlying conception of an explanatory model common to both sorts of elements.

In general, therefore, the considerations presented here suggest that the incoherencies of the orthodox account of causal explanations of rational human action are rendered coherent and plausible only if a background of Humean causation is presupposed. However, it has already been suggested that phenomenal causation is untenable for a wide variety of considerations. The OA account of causation and human behaviour is therefore in consequence untenable also. The suggestion here is that the alternative PO model of causation *is* appropriate for explaining all human behaviour, with certain crucial provisos.

7 THE CAUSAL ACCOUNT OF HUMAN ACTION

7.1 Reasons for Rejecting Causal Accounts

As a first step towards developing this thesis, it will be instructive to examine briefly some of the main reasons why the orthodoxy has *rejected* the possibility of a completely adequate causal–deterministic account of all human behaviour. Apart from the logico-explanatory considerations just discussed there are two principal reasons for this: first, the *a priori* assumption that the agent's perspective on action-events is logically primitive and epistemically primary, and second the assumption that human action is such as to render causal explanation impossible.

7.1.1 The 'person' and the primacy of the agent's perspective

The assumption that the concept of a person is logically primitive has its corollary in the notion that the agent's perspective on his actions is likewise epistemically primary. Thus, we have the view expressed earlier that an agent's making an event happen is primitive: an act may be at the beginning of a causal chain[46] as 'first cause' but is itself uncaused.[47]

But the agent-perspective is not an independent conceptual realm, because all individuals are both agents and spectators. The agent's perspective is isolated only analytically and therefore is primitive only within a certain contrived analytical framework. Certainly as an agent I have no clear conception of links between my initiation of an act ('making something happen') and the manifestations and effects of the act, such as bodily movements. But there is no reason why we should pretend that as spectators we are no better informed. As an agent, certainly, I am unaware of the neurology and physiology involved in moving my arm, but as a spectator I know (or can know) about these things. My actions depend on the inanimate action of my body;[48] and the attribution of any physical effect either in or out of my body to *me*, without at the same time attributing it to physical events in my body, drives us to denying that the effect has a physical cause at all, since a cause wholly outside of my body precludes attribution to me.[49]

The same basic situation exists in the case of those indispensable brain-events underlying deliberate actions, which as agents we have no awareness of, but which are open to us in principle as spectators. Again, there is no good reason why we should pretend that we are always agents or that as spectators our information about causes stops at the epidermis. The fact that it ordinarily does stop at the epidermis, however, goes far towards explaining the dichotomy under discussion. The orthodoxy offers no more than an analysis of the *ordinary* uninformed concepts of agency and action from the agent's perspective. Science tells us *more*. The philosophic task as I see it is not to insist upon the analysis of ordinary concepts while rejecting or ignoring science, but to examine how ordinary concepts of agency relate to the scientific information; which is, in any event, only a systematic extension of the ordinary spectator's information.

We have seen that the concept of a person as primitive precludes *a priori* the possibility that some 'inner' cause, whether mental or physical, could be the cause of the agent's action. This transempirical conception of the agent as cause, apart from the state changes within his body (or mind), is very odd indeed.[50] The supporting reasoning it provides involves a *non sequitur* of the following form: the agent is not identical with any one of his attributes; anything that is attributable to one of his attributes is not therefore attributable to the agent because he is not one of his attributes. (Compare: Newcastle United is not identical with striker X; the goal scored was attributed to striker X; therefore the goal scored was not attributable to Newcastle United, because striker X is not Newcastle United.)

The concept of the person-as-primitive in this opaque sense has been criticised by Nagel in the following terms:[51]

a puzzle arises from ... so construing the nature of [the] self that any trait or action which stands in relations of causal dependence to anything whatever is automatically cut off from being a genuine phase of the self. It is as if a physicist, in analysing the performance of a baseball and noting that the shape, the surface quality and the elastic properties of the ball are partly determinative of its behaviour when it is struck by a bat, were to declare that these traits do not properly belong to the ball but are as much external to it as the impulse imparted by the bat. ... Just how and where the boundaries of the individual human self are drawn may vary with different contexts of self-identification, and there may even be important cultural differences in this respect. But however they are drawn, they must not be so drawn that nothing finally can be identified as the self. They must not be so drawn that an insoluble puzzle is made of the fact that we conceive ourselves to be acting freely (i.e. without external constraints) even though we may recognise that some of our choices are the products of our dispositions, our past actions and our present impulses.

There is another recurrent argument against 'inner causes' that is closely connected to the last one and based on a similar elementary confusion. This is the claim that, since 'inner' states could be brought about by some extraneous means such as drugs or electronic implants, *therefore* any inner state change must be treated as extraneous to the self.[52] But from the fact that it is *possible* that, or we could suppose that, such changes are extraneously induced it does not follow that they always are, or ever are. In fact there is every reason to believe that the very opposite is true, i.e. that, like much human behaviour, much central nervous activity is spontaneous in origin in the sense that it is not 'externally' caused.[53]

This drives to the very roots of the OA versus PO dispute, since within the OA model the 'inner state changes' are only contingently connected with actions, so it is 'logically possible' that actions can occur without inner state changes. According to the PO model, however, such logical possibilities are merely the dud cornucopian fruits of the scientific ignorance attached to the arbitrarily isolated agent-perspective. Against the background provided by neuropsychology we would no more expect to find a human person without a nervous system (or some surrogate for it) initiating an action than we would expect to find a specific mass of lead that would float in a specific mass of water. If we did, we should no longer mean the same things by these words. The important point here is that neuropsychology does not radically change the concept of the person so much as fill it out.

Implicit in the PO account of agent action is the view that the unity of personality depends on a unified pattern of integrated central systems. Autonomous agent action on this view follows from the spontaneously initiated and 'self'-regulated (but determined) activity of such systems.

It is sometimes suggested, however, that this view must be mistaken because there is definite clinical evidence against it.[54] This is that individuals who have behaved in an apparently purposive way because of external stimulation or disturbance of the brain regard such behaviour not as something they have *done* themselves but as something that has *happened* to them. As Penfield says,[55]

> When a patient is asked about the movement which he carried out as the result of cortical stimulation he never is in any doubt about it. He knows he did not will the action. He knows there is a difference between automatic action and voluntary action. He would agree that something else finds its dwelling place between the sensory complex and the motor mechanism, that there is a switchboard operator as well as a switchboard.

However, against this OA interpretation of the evidence it can be argued that the unique character of personality resides in the pattern of central micro-structures unique to each individual, the operative notion here being the fine-grained micro-structure. Consequently, relatively gross physical disturbance of such complex systems, such as occurs in the operations cited, would naturally manifest itself as extraneous to the micro-systemic function. Penfield himself has said of such cases that electrode stimulation of memory is so gross, so lacking in dexterity, that it may be likened to the sound of a piano when the keyboard is struck with the palm of the hand.[56] There is no reason therefore why we should doubt that induced micro-disturbances, of the order that normally occur spontaneously at the neural synaptic and neural-net level, would not be subjectively experienced as if the behaviour were freely willed.[57]

All that is required to accommodate the phenomenology of action in the PO model is that the experienced difference between a willed act and involuntary behaviour should involve neural mechanisms operating in correspondingly different ways.[58] If so, then there is no more reason to suppose one mode of operation is any less causally determined than another. Voluntary action is thus construed as the spontaneous activity of a particular integrated control system which corresponds to or constitutes the 'self'. Volition and responsibility then become tied to the notion of self-determination, a familiar idea indeed. But if the nature of the self is construed along PO lines, then there is no person *over and above* central systems to whom central processes 'happen' and who does things over and above the action of central systems.

I conclude that it is not only desirable from the scientific–predictive–explanatory point of view, necessary from the PO point of view and reasonable from the common-sense point of view, but also (contrary to the orthodox view of the 'person') logically coherent to look for inner causes as explanatory of rational human action.

7.1.2 *The impossibility of rendering a causal account of human behaviour*

The widespread view among exponents of the orthodoxy is that scientific explanations involving law statements apply reasonably well to relatively simple systems and their behaviour, but that rational and purposive human behaviour is immeasurably more complex and, being purposive, is different in kind from the behaviour of any conceivable physical system. The underlying assumption is that all scientific explanation is roughly of the form 'same cause same effect', as exemplified paradigmatically by the billiard ball model of mechanics; and once granted that assumption, it is easy to think of human behaviour as a hurly burly of many criss-crossing contingencies with no discernible regularities of the 'same cause, same effect' form, unlike the solar system and billiard balls and the simple well-controlled systems examined in physics laboratories. Typically, Lucas argues:[59]

Two people from the same background, in the same situation, with the same arguments presented to them, decide differently. We ask 'Why?'. *No answer can be given*, except that the one [person] decided to do, and the other not to do. This is the point where there has to be an end to answering.

And Richard Taylor claims that: 'if human behaviour is purposeful then *it can never be understood* in terms of the concepts of physical science'.[60]

The essence of this sort of argument can be summarised as follows. Whereas scientific explanations of events generally take the form of 'same cause (necessarily) same effect', events regulated by *human* action are characterised by:

1 similar causes not producing similar effects;
2 dissimilar causes producing similar effects;
3 invariant goal directedness differing in *kind* from linear causation.

These criteria supposedly reflect the fact that human behaviour is not determined by causal factors alone. Human agents act because they have reasons for acting.

The task of rendering a causal account of human behaviour therefore has two main aspects: first, to show how reasons relate to, and enter into, the mass–energy–information economy of events; second, to show how mind-directed human behaviour can be described and explained in causal terms.

7.2 *Identity Theory and the Relation of Reasons to Behaviour*

The first main aspect of the problem of rendering a causal account of human action is to show how reasons, etc., relate to and enter into the economy of human behaviour. This question is answered with reference to the mind–brain IT, and in view of the preceding discussion it can be dealt with here relatively briefly. The formula suggested by the theory is that an agent's reasons are physical structures and processes 'from the inside': from his own *immediate* perspective he is the net sum of his reasons, etc., while from the spectator's *mediate* perspective he is the net sum of his bodily structures (especially brain structures). To be acting for a reason is to be undergoing physical state changes of certain distinguishable types. For a body to be undergoing brain processes of a certain type is to be making something happen for a reason.

It is perhaps necessary to repeat here a point made before in the discussion of IT: the need to avoid the intentionalist fallacy of supposing that to be undergoing a brain process must be to be consciously aware of the brain process involved as brain process, that is, to know that a brain process underlies the phenomena of consciousness.[61] Nowadays perhaps few people would deny that at least some aspects of the phenomenology of consciousness are identifiable as the undergoing of physical processes

222

which the subject is immediately unaware of as such, as in the case of pains. The same point is even better illustrated by the fact that a televisual image does not include the physical paraphernalia involved in its transmission though in a vital sense the processes of image encoding, transmission and production are physical processes. Equally, on an IT the phenomenal difference between awareness of acting for a reason and certain physical processes does not entail that to be so acting is not to be undergoing physical processes of a certain type.

To date, the agent's immediate perspective on his inner processes has been the only access we have had to many (or even most) of the complex physical processes and interactions with the environment we undergo. We understand and explain non-personal events readily enough in terms of causal chains. But our ordinary knowledge of the causal chains ends when the causal processes enter into the human body itself. Thereafter, of necessity, we are obliged to provide 'personal' explanations of human actions, even though these might be incompatible with accurate causal explanations of the observable phenomena. Moreover, the ordinary dividing line between acceptance of, even deference towards, causal explanations and disregard of them is just the difference between common-sense knowledge of causes and common-sense ignorance. Roughly speaking, it corresponds to the human epidermis.[62] Where the contingency lies, however, is in the ordinary limit to our causal knowledge at the epidermis, not in the relation between central structures, processes and mental states. But neuropsychology is rapidly improving on our contingent ignorance in this regard.

Our conspicuous success in understanding and explaining the 'mind-directed' behaviour of complex systems in the absence of detailed *causal* explanations involving intra-dermal processes is due to the fact that we are complex systems of precisely the sort whose behaviour we seek to understand and explain. Our ignorance of inner processes is not total. As agents ourselves we have immediate access to the inner processes of which as spectators we are ignorant. We thus have considerable knowledge of inner processes of a type we logically could not avoid even if we wanted to. It is not that we are inside the system as a homuncular 'person' in a container inspecting the inside, but rather that in a crucial sense we *are* such a system. Thus, simply by taking up the point of view of the agent or by taking up a point of view defined as that of spectator of an agent with such a point of view, one presupposes the presence of any conditions necessary for the existence of the point of view of the agent.[63] In this way our ignorance of an agent's inner processes is compensated for by putting ourselves in his place: the strategy is to *presuppose* the factors of which we are ignorant. This strategy, which continental philosophers call *verstehen*, avoids the necessity of having to find explicit, objective principles for ordering the welter of relevant psychological concepts such as consciousness, deliberation, intention and purpose, and also, we might add, the complex central state processes.[64] What cannot be described and explained as causes is thus 'shown' as motives and reasons. In other words, we do not have to wait upon the discoveries of human science for most practical purposes. We are immediately acquainted with the workings of the objects of human science because we are *ourselves* human beings and for most purposes this knowledge by acquaintance is sufficient.

This strategy permits the widespread and conspicuous success we ordinarily have in understanding mind-directed behaviour, especially when we share a common form of life and speech with agents of whose acts we are spectators. However, the strategy is based on a vital presupposition which, although it may be justified and may not mislead in most cases, nevertheless may lead us to overlook differences in inner state that are crucial determinants of the behaviour concerned. Nothing, unfortunately, is more common than for ignorant individuals to suppose that they *would* have acted differently to the agent had they been in his position. What is commonly overlooked is the fact that a strategy of the sort that ordinary life rests upon is not the best strategy for arriving at the structures and processes regulating individual behaviour: it is only the most practical in ordinary circumstances. There is therefore nothing at all *illogical* or incoherent about seeking the inner causes of overt behaviour. The inquiry could in principle establish what according to IT are the structures of those inner states that are reasons as well as causes (depending upon the access to them) and that are the necessary and sufficient conditions for deliberate action.

7.3 *Causal Explanations of Mind-Directed Behaviour*

The second main aspect of the problem of rendering a causal account of human actions is to show how characteristically 'mind-directed' behaviour can be described and explained in causal terms. We can begin by considering what conditions would have to be satisfied if both ordinary and scientific spectators were to be persuaded that a satisfactory causal account could be given of rational action. Three main conditions are suggested. First, there should be a satisfactory account of how reasons, etc., enter into the economy of human behaviour. This has already been discussed in the light of IT in the last section. Second, there should be a significant difference between the causal explanations of inanimate and animate events. Third, the causal accounts of rational behaviour should be consistent with the special status ordinarily attached to persons among other physical objects. The third condition

224

would guarantee what the second requires if the causal explanation of deliberate intentional action lies in just those central nervous events that are peculiar to human agents, and that are required for the agent's deliberating and intending to act.[65]

With regard to the second condition, mention has already been made of the naivety of assuming *a priori* that the behaviour of all physical systems, no matter how complex, conforms to the patterns of causal invariance regulating the behaviour of simpler systems. This observation is particularly apposite with regard to the difference between inanimate 'billiard ball' chains of linear causation and the human systems which, according to the PO model discerned by science, are the most complex quasi-independent systems. With regard to the third condition, there is clear evidence, both phylogenetic and ontogenetic, that the 'emergence' of mind-directed behaviour coincides with the development of the high-order brain structures underlying perception and memory and of goal-directed self-regulation. A brief consideration of two basic applications of the PO model of causation to human behaviour will be sufficient to show that the characteristic features of events regulated by human action can in principle be adequately described and explained within the PO model, with reference only to causation and such structures as that of the central nervous system.

7.3.1 *Same cause, different effect: different cause, same effect (some elementary properties of finite automata, including neural nets)*[66]

The theory of finite automata is generalised to cover all systems that have a structure and function describable by a logic such as Boolean algebra. Such systems have the ability to learn to 'think' and to solve problems. The human nervous system can be represented as a system of this type. In particular the neurone has properties that satisfy the requirements of a basic logical element in such systems. Such elements can be interconnected in various complicated ways subject to certain well-defined but simple rules which again normal neural sets satisfy.

First: an output must either contain an impulse or not contain an impulse at any instant in time (the bistable condition).

Second: inputs can be pulse-carrying at any instant of time and can have any pattern of 1's (which represent a pulse) and 0's (which represent the absence of a pulse) in a set of input fibres.

Third: inputs can either excite (represented →) or inhibit (represented —⊖) the receiving element's output pulse.

Fourth: each element has a firing threshold − a measure of its sensitivity − which must be exceeded by the net effect of the combined instantaneous input of excitatory and inhibitory pulses (represented by e.g. ②) before the output fibres.

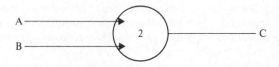

Figure 7.1

For example: an element with two excitatory inputs and a threshold level of 2 would be represented as in Figure 7.1. Thus for this elemental system to fire C at instant t, inputs A and B must fire at instant $t-1$. (In the causal terms already proposed, the firing of inputs A and B at instant $t-1$ causes the firing of C at instant t (the effect): the *event* explained is the state change from the element *not* firing at $t-1$ to the element firing at t.)

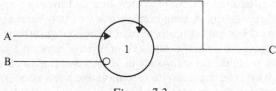

Figure 7.2

A loop element (Figure 7.2), once fired (by A), fires back on itself, so that unless a net inhibitory input (i.e. B without A) is introduced, it will go on firing indefinitely. It is assumed here, contrary to fact, that the threshold for every element remains constant. In the human nervous system, however, the threshold level is subject to substantial variations, owing for example to facilitation and metabolic, particularly endocrinic, influences. This calls for an elaboration of theory, but no change in principle. It has significant implications however for the naive rejection of the basic 'same cause same effect' formula for the explanation of human behaviour, and these will be discussed later.

Finite automata and conditional behaviour The manner in which finite automata, as exemplified by neural nets, acquire or learn conditioned responses to stimulus signals from the environment, can be quickly illustrated on the following simplified model of a neural-like network. (Figure 7.3). From 'rest', system state S1, (Figure 7.3(a)), if two input elements A and B fire together, C fires and then M (which stays 'live' because it is a loop element); and because this continuously excites element X, this reduces the threshold of X to 1. The system state is now S2 (Figure 7.3(b)), so that if either A or B fire alone thereafter, then X fires. But if this happens, either D or E is fired, which extinguishes M and starts L, which continuously *inhibits* X so that X then has an

226

Human Action

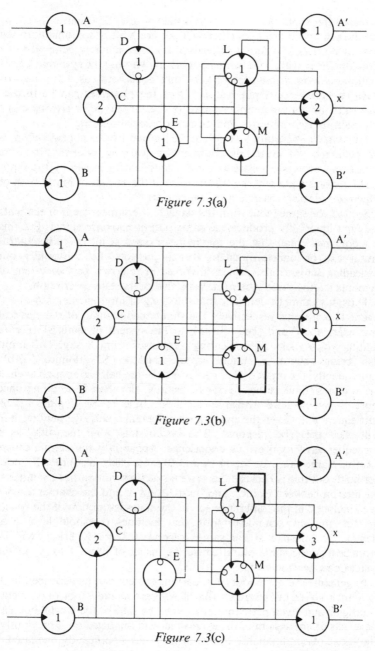

Figure 7.3(a)

Figure 7.3(b)

Figure 7.3(c)

227

increased threshold of 3. The system state is now S3 (Figure 7.3(c)), so that even A and B firing together will not fire X. It is not difficult to see that any number of different patterns of association can be generated in a similar manner within the same network, by varying the systems state of continuous loop firings, inhibitions, thresholds, etc., as a function of previous experience (input history). And the processes can be further elaborated by compounding systems of the same type to give memory extension, more numerous and complex associations, etc.

Two vitally important lessons can be learned from a consideration of the behaviour of even this rudimentary learning system. First, the transition from system state to system state is determined by the input signal configuration and the system state at the instant of input, both of which are sensibly discrete and determinate.[67]

Second, the same input stimulus signal to the same system of elements does not invariably produce the same output response signal. But this fact does not entail that the mediating process is intrinsically contra-causal and/or undeterminable. It only reflects the convenient but misleading semantical fuzziness involved in referring to the system of elements as 'the same system' irrespective of its state-description.

Thus, for example, consider that the firing of input elements A and B (event 1) represents respectively the simultaneous input of the classical Pavlovian 'food' and 'bell' stimuli to the system in state S1 (Figure 7.2(a)), which elicits a 'food-eating' response, firing X say. This input also brings about a system state-change to S2. (Figure 7.3(b)). Subsequently, the input of B alone (event 2) – the bell – is enough to elicit the system's 'food-eating' response firing X. But then in so doing once more a system state-change occurs, this time to S3 (Figure 7.2(c)). Subsequently not even the appearance of food and bell together (event 3) will elicit the food response. The system has gone 'neurotic' as a consequence of its previous experience. Apparently the simple causal formula 'same cause (as inputs A and B) same effect (as output X)' does not hold. But this is because the system state-description has changed in the interim between event 1 and (non-) event 3, and the change has not been included in the 'difference set' in the state-description of the *cause*. In fact, for any state-description that includes threshold level 1 at element X (substate s) the same response (effect), X firing, will be produced by the same plural cause, i.e. firing of input 1 to X: in the system changed to substate s.

In general: the behaviour of a learning system can be described in 'if so – then so' terms provided the 'if so' part includes not only events impinging at a given moment in time, i.e. the state of the world, but also the effects on the system of the events that had impinged on it previously. The range of conditionality of response is thus significantly increased.[68]

228

This example illustrates well enough, albeit in a very rudimentary way, how it may appear that the basic causal formula does not apply to the behaviour of systems of the learning net type, *if it is (wrongly) supposed that the state of the network remains constant.* But precisely this supposition is conceptually institutionalised in those philosophical theories that regard the concept of 'the person' as logically primitive. It follows necessarily from this supposition that the basic causal formula does not hold for the behaviour of human persons. But, as the present discussion suggests, there is no justification for making that supposition whatsoever. Indeed, there is ample evidence to the contrary, suggesting that the central nervous system is essentially a system of the learning-network type, though an especially complex one. Of course, there is no need for such detours into the elementary theory of finite automata to appreciate the basic points being made here. It is enough to cite the common knowledge we have that typically human behaviour varies from person to person (i.e. system to system) and from time to time (i.e. system state to system state) depending on genetics (inherent system structure), education and experience (i.e. acquired system structure, memory, threshold levels etc.) and state of health, (i.e. variable threshold levels). The appeal to automata-theory merely supports the general physicalist supposition that an observable difference in behaviour in itself indicates a difference in underlying causes and tends to undermine obscurantist, fortuitist and contra-causal arguments against complete causal explanations of human behaviour and actions.

7.3.2 Goal directedness as different in kind from linear causation (directively organised self-regulation by negative feedback)

The outstanding feature of human behaviour, that which has most consistently been held to set human action apart from purely physical and causally determined processes, is its goal-directedness. The ability of human individuals to persist in the pursuit of 'inexistent objects' (goals), against all impediments throughout repeated interruptions and for protracted periods of time, has been said to require explanations altogether different from causal ones, namely teleological ones. Teleological explanations in philosophy and ordinary discourse are explanations in terms of final causes, or purposes, which provide (in spectator parlance) the goal or, in agent parlance, the point of complex goal-directed behaviour or purposeful acts as the case may be. It is necessary therefore to examine in more detail the notion of goal-directed behaviour to see whether the orthodox claim can be sustained.[69]

Abstract criteria for goal-directed behaviour Sommerhoff has proposed general abstract criteria which distinguish systems showing objective goal-directed behaviour from those that do not; namely:[70]

229

action is directed towards a goal G when the following relations exist in respect of an arbitrarily chosen initial point in time, t_o (provided this precedes the action by a sufficient interval):

1 At at least one point of time t_k during the action, there exist two variables 'e' and 'a', defined on the environment and the action respectively, and a function F, such that $F(a_k, e_k) = 0$ is a necessary condition for the subsequent occurrence of G.

  This is to say how the necessary condition for achieving the goal may be satisfied by reducing to zero a relationship between a variable defined on the action and a variable defined on the environment.

2 a_k and e_k are mutually orthogonal (i.e. independent: neither determining the other at the same instant). Note that this condition rules out cases such as covariant properties of the same system such as pressure-volume of a gas[71] and rail-guided homing devices, since for example the rails connect values of action-defined and environment-defined variables.[72]

  This is to say that satisfaction of the necessary goal-achievement condition is possible by *altering the action variable alone*, whatever the value of the environment variable. The mechanism involved *brings about* goal achievement.[73]

3 The action is a function of the environment such that there exists at least one variable U_o defined on the initial state of the system, and a set S_o of values U_o (having at least two members) such that if
$$e_k = E_k(U_o)$$
and
$$a_k = A_k(U_o)$$
then for all U_o in S_o, $A_k(U_o)$ and $E_k(U_o)$ are bi-unique (one – one) and $A_k(U_o)$ satisfies $F[A_k(U_o), E_k(U_o)] = 0$.

  In this context 'system' means agent plus environment; and U is taken to be an *environmental variable*.

  This is to say that the agent in the agent–environment system satisfies the necessary conditions for *possible* goal achievment, i.e. there is more than one way for the agent to achieve the goal and the agent *would* produce an appropriately modified response under a variety of alternative circumstances (initial states).

The criteria here proposed, being abstract, are ontologically neutral as between mental (intentional–purposive) categories and physical categories.[74] Certainly the criteria represent the view that the variable defined on the action is an agent's intention; that the variable defined on the environment is some external state of affairs; that the necessary condition for achievement of the goal is that some state of affairs obtaining in the environment should coincide with the *intention* of action (the zero variance condition – (1)), that this can be brought about

230

through the agent's activity alone, irrespective of changes in the state of the environment (the orthogonal condition – (2)); and that the same goal *can* be achieved from a variety of initial conditions (the equifinal condition – (3)).

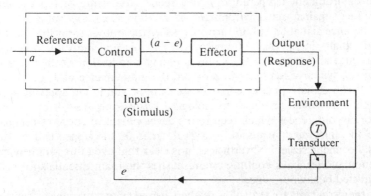

Figure 7.4

It is well known by now, however, that physical systems embodying mechanisms of negative feedback – roughly the regulation of input (from the environment) by coupling to output – display typical goal-directed behaviour, behaviour that satisfies Sommerhoff's criteria. A consideration of one of the best-known and simplest goal-directed feedback-regulated systems, the thermostatic control, will quickly establish this (Figure 7.4). The simple linear thermostatic control system depicted is composed of two interconnected subsystems: (1) the acting system, composed of a control element (comparator or subtractor) and an effector (an electrical power supply), and (2) the environment. The 'goal' of the system (G) is the attainment and maintenance of a given temperature T in the environment, (i.e. G is T in the environment). The control 'datum' or 'action plan target' for G is determined by the value of the control action variable a corresponding to the environmental temperature T. Note that the value of this analogical parameter is uniquely defined by the analogical nature of the system and its relationship to the environment: specifically by the value of transducer signal corresponding to the desired environment state T. The control sub-system compares and 'subtracts' the variable defined against the environment e from the variable defined against the action a. The resultant signal $(a - e)$ is the input to the effector system which determines the output from the acting sub-system to the environment. This completes the circuit. By means of an arrangement of this sort it is possible for the system to control the environment to G throughout

231

variation ΔT from T. As the temperature varies (ΔT) so will the transducer signal vary proportionately (Δe). The change, difference or 'error' will be reflected in the control-comparator (or subtractor) so as to alter inversely its output (i.e. the input to the effector). Thus a *reduction* in environment temperature T will reduce the value of the variable defined against the environment e, so *increasing* the value of the difference signal $(a - e)$, in turn increasing the output from the effector and finally increasing T. Conversely, an increase in the value of T will produce an increase in the value of e, and a reduction in the value of $(a - e)$, which value tends to zero and the maintenance of T, i.e. G.

It is necessary of course to exercise extreme caution in applying such simple automata analogies to biological systems because there are important differences which require the development of concepts peculiar . to the integrated forms of biological order at the upper end of the phylogenetic scale.[75] Nevertheless, it is clear that even this rudimentary automatic feedback control system satisfies the main essentials for goal directed behaviour, since:

1 the reduction to zero of a relation between two variables, defined against the environment e and against the action a, is a necessary condition for the attainment of G:
2 the variables a and e are mutually orthogonal, in that the environment state can vary independently of action state at any instant:
3 the agent–environment system is such that the response would be appropriate and the goal state would be achieved under a variety of alternative circumstances (initial conditions).

Feedback mechanisms of this basic type are widely recognised by neurologists and biologists to operate in a variety of forms and at all levels in the hierarchy of automatic controls regulating human behaviour.

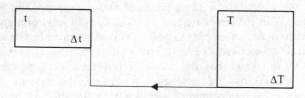

Figure 7.5

Feedback as circular causation Even the rudimentary process of goal-directed behaviour described above does not conform to the basic action–reaction model of linear unidirectional causation on the billiard ball paradigm assumed by Hume. On that model the effect of a change ΔT in an environmental temperature T would be to cause a corresponding change Δt on the connected sub-systems, directly proportional to ΔT. This situation is represented in the case of heater boxes employed in thermal conductivity experiments (Figure 7.5). Given this model, it is apparent that different causes, i.e. state-changes ΔT, will produce correspondingly different, but proportionate, final effects, i.e. state-changes Δt. In contrast, for different events in the *feedback-regulated* system different causes (state changes ΔT) produce the *same* final effect, i.e. the goal-directed regulation of the system to re-establish T in the environment. (Technically speaking, the activity of the system is 'equifinal'.) But this contrast is precisely the essential basis of the common philosophic distinction between physical causation and goal-directed behaviour.

The crucial difference between linear and feedback systems is in their structure or organisation, *not* in the mode of productive connexity between system states. Specifically, feedback systems embody circuits composed of links, and *the state-changing productive connection within each link is causal.* Thus von Bertalanffy has proposed the following criteria of feedback control systems.

1 Regulation is based upon pre-established arrangements ('structures' in a broad sense). This is well expressed by the German term *Regelmechanismen*, which makes it clear that the systems envisaged are of the nature of mechanisms, in contrast to regulations of a 'dynamic' nature resulting from free interplay of forces and mutual interaction between components tending towards equilibrium or steady states.

2 Causal trains within the feedback system are linear and unidirectional. *The basic feedback scheme is still the classical stimulus–response (S–R) scheme*, only the feedback loop being added so that causality becomes circular.

3 Typical feedback or homeostatic phenomena are open with respect to incoming information, but 'closed' with respect to matter and energy.[76]

Accordingly, successive states of the feedback-regulated system will be causally connected in a fashion determined by the system structure, i.e. non-randomly. In principle, then, a causal circuit will automatically generate a non-random response to a random event at that position in the circuit at which the random event occurred.[77] Goal-directedness, therefore, does not set human behaviour apart from the category of physical causation. The important difference underlying different behaviours is one of structure, as between linear–unidirectional structures and feedback circular, and perhaps other, structures. It is not necessarily to do with a difference between causality and a-causal relations.

It might be thought that the approach taken here, of examining goal-directed behaviour in terms of the concept of circular causation and feedback, does not explicate the ordinary, cybernetically naïve, concept of purpose.[78] It does however suggest how goal-directed systems work and what they must be like to act in a purposive way. In particular, the point of examining the cases of learning nets and feedback-regulated behaviours has been to show that the common assumption by philosophers that the category of physical causation is *in principle* incapable of explaining and/or predicting all human behaviour is based entirely on over-naïve ideas about causation. The argument here offered is not of course addressed directly to those who argue for a different, a-causal, explanatory *logic*. It is addressed to those who see human behaviour as radically different in kind to other physical systems, purely because of misconceptions about the power of causal explanations. Some overlook the significant increase in the range of conditionality of response that learning automata are capable of, and so envisage 'hurly burly' as the only physicalist alternative to Newtonian mechanics.[79] Others mistakenly assimilate the circular causation involved in feedback-regulated behaviour to simple *linear* causation,[80] which is significantly different.

7.3.3 *Summary*

A summary of the main points of the above discussion embodies the assumptions underlying the PO conception of human behaviour. These are that in principle a physical–causal account can be given of typically human behaviours that are characterised by:

1 apparently similar causes not producing similar effects;
2 dissimilar causes producing similar effects;
3 invariant goal-directness as opposed to linear causation.

This is possible when

a IT is postulated so that reasons are construed as causes 'from the inside';
b descriptions of an event include all of the relevant physical system states and state-*changes* involved;
c goal-directedness is seen to involve circular causation which is compounded of linear causation (through structure) and not categorially different from it.

Thus the concepts of access, order, structure, system and 'information' are crucial to a proper interpretation of the PO model of the mental and of 'mind-directed' behaviour.

8 PHYSICALIST RESOLUTION OF ORTHODOX INCOHERENCIES

It remains now to show how the incoherencies in the OA account of action might be resolved in the framework of the PO model. Of necessity this discussion will be brief, but it should be sufficient at least to indicate the lines along which coherent physicalist alternatives can be rendered.

8.1 *Law-like Rational Explanations*

According to the PO view, since reasons are causes from the inside, then rule-governed behaviour is behaviour regulated by functional invariances in central physical processes, that is to say the constraints or limits within which the self-regulating control systems operate.[81] If so, then such functional invariances depend on the physical laws holding in the system, together with the initial and boundary conditions defined by the system structure and state. Provided therefore that the physical laws are taken together with the system's initial and boundary conditions, human system behaviour follows the familiar predictive pattern: same initial and boundary condition, same final condition according to the laws holding in the system – or in cruder words, 'same cause same effect'. Where causes are a complex concatenation of motives, reasons and purposes, the precise initial condition will usually be correspondingly complex and usually cause more complex final conditions. But complex relations between 'rational' causes and effects will be no less naturally necessary for being complex. Reasons can be regarded as law-like inference tickets to action. Rational explanations are explanatory of action because they predict (i.e. the explanandum follows from the explanans); they predict because reasons are causes from the inside, and causes are natural necessary connections.

8.2 *Temporal Asymmetry*

In the PO view, natural processes are, in general, law-like mass–energic transactions. As such they are in accordance with the Second Law of Thermodynamics; that is to say, they are irreversible. The apparent reversal of the temporal order in the case of human acts of will and certain central processes (Section 5.2 above) arises only if the agent's immediate awareness of his willed acts is analytically isolated from the scientific observer's awareness of the central processes involved in the willing of the acts. If an act such as moving an arm is defined on quasi-behaviourist lines only as the arm's gross moving, then the logical illusion is created because the central micro-processes precede the gross movement which, according to the definition, is their cause. But clearly this 'frightfully puzzling' case is a physical absurdity and an abuse of common sense. It is purely the consequence of an arbitrary decision to define such acts behaviourally.

In the PO view neither the phenomenology of consciousness nor gross behaviour is logically prior to the temporal order of central and behavioural events. Accordingly there is no puzzlement generated if gross acts are not temporally prior to whatever is willed with them. What is implied by the PO model is that, if some state of affairs is willed into being, then there is some prior state of affairs that causes it, whether such causes are present to consciousness or not. Given IT there is no problem about this, because the central processes that cause gross behaviour can be included in the notion of the willed action, which is not just the gross behaviour willed, but the willing itself: in the adverbial form, 'he moved his arm wilfully'. Then the act of willing the central processes involved in the action involves no more than willing the action itself. For doing something that causes my finger to move does not cause me to move my finger; it *is* moving my finger.

It is perhaps worth mentioning here a problem that has often been raised about the temporal order of willed behaviour, namely teleology. It is sometimes argued that where behaviour is directed to some goal, then the goal to be achieved in the future determines and explains *present* behaviour. But as has frequently been pointed out, goal-directed behaviour requires only that a desire for some future state of affairs exists in the present, and that some present course of action is presently believed to lead consequentially to the desired future state of affairs.[82] Then, according to IT, it is an empirical question of identifying present desires and beliefs with central states and processes, which then become the neurally embodied plans or blueprints of the future, that structure and determine present behaviour.[83]

8.3   *Rational Factors Make a Difference*

The *sortal* problems of reasons entering into the economy of physical events does not arise if reasons are causes from the inside. A person's reasons cause or influence action because, quite simply, the physical processes he is undergoing cause and influence action.

8.4   *Positively Not Doing Something (Acts of Omission)*

The puzzle raised for the orthodoxy by acts of omission rather than of commission is readily resolved by the PO view. Whereas in the quasi-behavioural view an action is conceptually linked to bodily movement, so that without such movement it becomes incoherent to speak of an act at all, on the PO view the central processes, the undergoing of which constitutes willing, are regarded as part of the act, though they are normally unobservable. They constitute mental acts. Now in the normal case of acts of commission the sequence of events from central to behavioural processes will involve predominantly excitatory mechanisms. But it is well known that neural–synaptic action can have a net inhibitory effect. If so, then where the inhibitory central systems are causes that are also reasons, i.e. causes from the inside, the individual can be said to have deliberately inhibited an action, that is to say deliberately *not* done something. This simple account of acts of omission involves a more sophisticated and, as it happens, more realistic view of causal processes than is usual among orthodox philosophers.

The orthodox view of the causal efficacy of action supposes that bodily motion is created *ex nihilo* by the agent's action which is itself uncaused. This naive view persists with the essentially pre-Newtonian notion that *rest* is the norm and motion an abnormal condition brought about through special intervention.[84] The post-Newtonian insight is that *motion* is the norm and rest is brought about through the special circumstance of equilibriated forces and energies. In the post-Newtonian view therefore there is no difficulty about regarding null effects as positive, because rest is commonly regarded as the net effect of positive forces in dynamic equilibrium. Where inhibiting causes are also reasons the dynamic central process of inhibition constitutes the diliberate act of omission.

8.5   Resolution of Anomalies in Law

The anomalies created in law by the categorial distinction between reasons and causes, and between rational and causal explanations, are likewise resolved by introducing the notion that reasons are causes from the inside. There is then no problem about causing someone to have a reason for doing something. Whether or not a sequence of relations is regarded as rational or causal will then depend on whichever is most perspicuous in individual cases. This is particularly apposite in the case of mentally disordered individuals. The tendency to look for causal explanations in such cases is due to the opacity or inaccessibility of the rational basis of action. The usual procedures for interpreting others' actions breaks down because *ex hypothesi* the reasoning and central processes of such individuals are so different from those of normal individuals that the ordinary *ceteris paribus* assumption breaks down. But this does not justify the commonly expressed view that causal explanations are appropriate only in such abnormal cases.[85] It is rather that the usual ploys for obtaining rational explanations are ineffective, and causal explanations are then as easy (or easier) to come by as the deranged rationales determining deranged action.

8.6 *The Ambivalence of Action Language Reflects Biperspectival Identity*

Finally, the ambiguity of 'Why?' and 'Because' and related locutions such as 'compelling reasons', which defy the supposed categorial distinction between reasons and causes, is also explained if reasons are causes from the inside. This is a much more plausible view than the orthodox claim that language is permeated root and branch with a blatant category mistake of the most profound kind. On the PO view, for example, reasons are compelling reasons because the functional invariances in the physical brain with which, according to IT, they are identified, determine the manner and outcome of processing of information input: 'surface irritations' in the observer mode, reasoning in the agent mode.

9   SUMMARY AND CONCLUSIONS

In the last two chapters I have attempted to show that the orthodox view of the relationship between causation and human action is incoherent and untenable or at least implausible. Hume's widely received and often unquestioned account of causation is highly questionable from a physical–realist perspective (see Chapter VI, Section 3). Physicalism provides an alternative account of causation that is far more plausible in the light of what is known about human natural history (Chapter VI, Section 4). However, the orthodox view of human action, in so far as it admits causation at all, is based either explicitly or implicitly on Humean causation (Section 4 above).

The orthodox view of agent action is radically incoherent, as is shown by the numerous insoluble problems it gives rise to (Section 5 above). The radical incoherence of the orthodox view is not always apparent, however. One main reason for this seems to be that many of the fundamental incoherencies in the orthodox view of notion are blurred and compensated for by the suspect Humean view of causation, and in this way the orthodoxy achieves a spurious coherence (Section 6 above). An alternative physicalist account of human action can be given, however, based on the mind–brain IT, which is both more plausible in

238

the light of natural knowledge and at the same time meets the main requirements of an orthodox account of agent-action (Section 7 above). Furthermore, the physicalist model is capable of resolving the incoherencies in the orthodoxy (Section 8 above).

PART FOUR

A man does at all times only what
he wills and yet he does this necessarily.

Arthur Schopenhauer (1841, p. 98)

VIII

FREE-WILL AND DETERMINISM

1 INTRODUCTION

The previous discussion has tended to establish the coherence of the PO view that the mental is in some important sense identical with the physical, and that mind-directed human behaviour is subject to the same categories of causal determination as all other physical processes. This view is related to a variety of similar views expressed throughout the history of philosophy, such as fatalism, logical determinism, theological determinism and psychological determinism. Physical determinism however differs from these other metaphysical views in a number of vital aspects. The main difference is that it is firmly based in systematic science and supported by a rapidly accumulating body of well-attested evidence which has not been available until relatively recently.

Physical determinism has been aptly called an 'aggressor' concept because the domain of its explanatory power has been progressively extended at the expense of competing explanations, whereas it is rarely if at all that deterministic explanations are overturned, at least at the level of macroscopic events involved in human behaviour. In general, the tendency has been to show how more and more behaviour is explicable in terms of causal mechanisms. This fact alone would justify a re-examination of the issues traditionally raised in connection with meta-physical determinism.

The main problems raised by determinism are usually taken to be the challenge it represents to the traditional conception of human free-will and the related institutions of moral blame and punishment. It is almost universally acknowledged to be morally unreasonable and unjust to blame or punish someone for behaviour when the behaviour in question was inevitable.[1]

According to the version of physical determinism informed by IT, *all* behaviour, including mind-directed behaviour, is causally determined and so in this sense inevitable. Evidently it follows that physical determinism renders moral blame and punishment unreasonable and unjust. This quick statement of the problem indicates well enough the argument that has notoriously generated more quagmires, scandals and wasted ink than perhaps any other single philosophical issue.

The main question before us in this section, then, is whether the aggressive tendency of physical determinism could prevail and so render the related concepts of free-will and moral responsibility either empty or otiose.

Free-will Few serious thinkers of any metaphysical or ethical persuasion deny physical causal determinism as such. However, many do insist that there is a morally significant sense of 'free' in which an agent is free to do otherwise than he in fact does do, even if complete physical determinism is allowed. Indeed, they argue that an agent 'can do' or 'is free to do' otherwise than he do do in a number of highly pertinent senses.[2] It is clear then that the dispute over free-will and causal determinism cannot be settled without first establishing the relevant sense (or senses) of 'can' and 'free' in dispute.

Moral responsibility It is also argued that, even if causal determinism is granted (and often it is not), there are a number of perfectly proper senses of 'moral responsibility' that justify the claim that, when an agent was free, in some relevant sense, to do otherwise than he did do, then he is morally responsible, in some corresponding sense, for what he did do. So the dispute over moral responsibility versus causal determinism cannot be settled without first establishing the relevant sense (or senses) of 'moral responsibility' in dispute.

Consequences Finally, it has often been supposed that, should the thesis of physical determinism win wide acceptance, the effect on human affairs, especially on interpersonal relations and social institutions, would be serious, if not fatal. It will be important therefore to consider what the effect would really be.

The general aim of this chapter and the next, then, is to examine the proposition that as a consequence of IT the traditional conceptions of free-will and moral responsibility are rendered otiose. This aim will be pursued by considering:
1 how IT affects the concept of free-will;
2 how IT affects the concept of moral responsibility;
3 some of the supposed consequences of IT for moral and social institutions.

2   THE FREE-WILL PROBLEM

The traditional problem of free-will versus determinism springs from the *prima facie* incompatibility between the experience we have as agents making choices and initiating action and the view that objectively we are determined to do only that which we in fact do. Whether or not the determining principle is taken to be the logical rule of excluded middle, predestination, the omniscience and omnipotence of a divine creator, the unconscious fenaglings of id, ego and superego, or the automatic action of the central nervous system, the incompatibility is essentially the same. The evidence of neuropsychology is, however, especially persuasive and is the basis of the present discussion.

The determinist is wont to see his case with insouciant clarity, somewhat as follows. Suppose, contrary to determinism, that for a given agent some action (P_o) is an open option in a given situation (S): that is to say, the agent is supposedly free to exercise his will in choosing that option. However, causal determination of the agent's behaviour in S at a given time t uniquely produces P_b say (or in general $\sim P_o$). For the agent both to pursue the option and to satisfy the causal determination simultaneously in S at t requires $P_o. \sim P_o$, an impossible contradiction both logically and physically. But the weight of scientific evidence for the existence of causal mechanisms is overwhelming. Therefore the supposed option is not open in fact; that is to say, the supposition of free-will cannot be supported against the scientific evidence for determinism.

3   THREE POSITIONS

There are three positions that philosophers have taken on this basic problem.

First, the traditional *libertarian*[3] view is that there is at least an irreducible minimum of human experience, notably experience of moral choice, where causes do not operate. Essentially in this case the agent (person or self) exercises deliberate choice of action between genuinely open possibilities. This is achieved by a conscious act of will, typically though not invariably guided by regulative rational principles and usually against the force of strongest natural desire.

Second, the *determinist*[4] has traditionally argued that the subjective experience of 'genuinely open possibilities' is misleading because, objectively, various causal influences not of the agent's will are at work which completely determine not only the choice that the agent makes but the act of will itself, and so the agent is not 'freely' choosing and acting.

Third, various *compatibilist*[5] arguments have been advanced to the effect that free-will and determinism are not mutually exclusive since there is some relevant sense of 'can' or 'free' that is not only consistent with determinism but, it is frequently said, actually requires and pre-supposes determinism in order to be intelligible.

4   COMPATIBILISM

The compatibility of 'can' and 'free' with complete determinism in some sense of these terms has already been acknowledged, and further reference will be made to this issue presently. At this stage I want to suggest that, in so far as 'can' and 'free' are intelligible in a PO model and compatible with physical determinism, the senses of these words so involved are not those usually taken to be relevant to the peculiarly moral connotations of 'moral responsibility', namely: the wickedness, culpability and guilt of the agent, calling for moral blame, vilification and punishment.

The substantive dispute about free-will, then, I take to be between the views (1) that an agent P in a situation S at a particular time t could do, or was free to do, other than he did do at the time of the action in question, quite indifferently to the physical state of affairs obtaining, and (2) that a particular action at any given time is sufficiently accounted for by the physical causal factors inherent in the state of affairs obtaining at the time in question (and prior to it) which render the action physically inevitable.

5   PHYSICAL DETERMINISM

The problem of formulating the thesis of physical determinism in relation to human behaviour has been vastly compounded by the ambiguity of the key terms 'can' and 'free'. It will help therefore if we can cut through most of this discussion by stating as quickly as possible the issues raised specifically by IT. Fortunately the discussion can be limited straight away by showing that physical determinism does not call into question all ordinary senses of 'can' and 'free'.

5.1   *Two Levels of Determinism*

This can be done by introducing a distinction which has been made by a number of writers between two different levels at which the free-will dispute is conducted. First there is the level at which the ordinary unreflective man[6] addresses the problem. This level has also been referred to as the ordinary[7] or upper level,[8] the level of primary substitutibility of acts,[9] self-directedness[10] and second-order power.[11] For a person to be considered to be acting freely at this level it is sufficient that a variety of relatively easily established conditions be met. At this level a man can truly be said to be free to act otherwise than he does in a number of significant senses, such as: absence of external or inner compulsion or constraint; being consistent with well-known natural laws; permitted by law; having the appropriate opportunity; or as having the appropriate inclination, ability or power. None of the senses of 'can' and 'free' appropriate to this level is inconsistent with complete determinism. Much of the recent philosophical debate about free-will has been bent on establishing this fact, and there is nothing to be gained from rehearsing the arguments again here.

The physical determinist's case against free-will, however, is made out at the *second* level from which the problem can be addressed, that of the moderately reflective and well-informed man.[12] This level is also referred to as the special[13] or deeper level,[14] the level of secondary substitutibility of acts,[15] absolute self-directedness[16] and first-order power.[17] For people to be considered to be acting freely at this level it is not sufficient that the conditions appropriate to the more superficial level be met. Here the question is not 'Can I ever do what I want to do?' but 'Are there any exceptions to the rule that my wants are subsequent, constantly conjoined and necessarily connected to events that are not my wants?' The problem thus raised has been alluded to earlier and is essentially this: if the physical conditions obtaining in a given instance are not only necessary for the performance of an action but also, if the determinist is correct, *sufficient*, then the state change or changes involved in the action are naturally necessitated, physically produced or causally determined in the sense of these terms already indicated.

5.2   *Two Features: Structure and State*

Two features of causal mechanism and explanation corresponding to the two levels of discussion should be distinguished in order to clarify further the determinist's case. First, it is said that the general dispositions of the agent (in general his character) are determined by his genetic inheritance and his experience during development. The evidence of biochemistry, endocrinology and the neurophysiology of ontogenesis has confirmed what metaphysical determinists have traditionally maintained in this regard. These factors determine the *structure* of the physical system at the time of a given event. Second, whether or not a particular structure *functions* on any particular occasion depends also upon the *state* of the system at the time in question.

The essential point here can be made very easily in terms of a gun fitted with a safety catch. At any given instant, whether the gun fires or not may depend upon the position of the safety catch. The gun's structure is such that it can fire in a sense of 'can' that draws a significant distinction between systems of a firing type (e.g. guns), whether operative or inoperative (e.g. unloaded or with the safety catch on), and systems of a non-firing type (e.g. fingers, trees). This distinction between 'structurally can' and 'structurally cannot' is indispensible at the unreflective level. We might call it a logical distinction. But when the gun is in a state of having its safety catch on or being unloaded, then it physically cannot fire, that is, it is physically necessitated *not* to fire. Thus the gun both can (in virtue of its structure, or essentially) and cannot (in virtue of its state, or accidentally) fire.

An obvious parallel presents itself between this case and the basic case of automatic learning nets of the type (very probably) inherent in the human central nervous system. Whether or not a particular neurone or neural network 'fires' at a given instant depends not only on the structure of the system as it has developed up to that time, but also on the precise state of the system at the time. The central nervous system of an individual may be genetically predisposed to self-organisation along certain general lines, and may interact with the endocrine system in a genetically predisposed way. These predispositions may have been developed through previous experience to produce a structure capable of certain behaviour or responses, and in this sense the individual concerned 'can' or 'could' do other than he in fact does. But whether or not these dispositions (or capacities or powers) are realised in a given instance depends on a number of complex factors ultimately affecting synaptic firing thresholds at the instant in question. As even the crude example in Chapter VII showed (Section 7.3.1), it is possible for a human-type learning system with a given quasi-constant structure, and which in this sense remains the same system and structure throughout change, to respond differently to similar stimuli at different times in similar contexts, quite automatically as a function of state. What recent theoretical and experimental neuro-psychology leads us to expect is that a difference in network behaviour or response may reflect not only a difference in network structure (especially as between different individuals), but also a difference in state.

It is very misleading therefore to refer to the 'same' system where the state description is unspecified, since the difference in outcome as between states of the same system at different times in similar situations may be just as great as the difference between altogether different systems, i.e. different individuals. A thing that under strictly the same circumstances behaved in a different way could not be strictly the same thing – it would be different just in that it behaved differently.[18]

5.3 *Two Senses of Possible*

In the light of the distinction just made we can now profitably define two senses of 'possible' (and hence of 'can', 'able', etc.), and so resolve a most misleading ambiguity.

'Possible$_2$' is to mean 'physically possible' in a number of second-order senses such as 'consistent with natural laws' and 'within the repertoire of the agent's powers'. 'Possible' is to mean 'the one and only physically possible outcome in the event'.

To illustrate, suppose a system whose structure we know all about but whose current state we know nothing about: then we will *ipso facto* know the whole range of possible$_2$ outputs (possible in the second-order sense). But we will never be in a position to know what output is possible$_1$ (possible in the first-order sense) until we know the system's initial state as well as its structure; for only then can we eliminate all the second-order possibilities except one, namely the one determined by the system state at the time in question. Causal determinism renders impossible$_1$ all possibilities$_2$ except one, leaving as the one first-order possibility the one effect that in the event is causally determined by the antecedent state of the system: '(the one and only physically) possible$_1$ (outcome in the event)' applies only to the naturally necessitated effect of preceding causes.

5.4 *Reformulation of the Problem*

The problem of free-will versus determinism has usually been formulated in terms of the principle that to act freely implies that the act could, in some significant sense of that word, have been otherwise. The foregoing discussion suggests that the principle should be more closely defined in relation to the contradictory physical determinist case along the following lines: ' "does p freely" implies "can do Np" ' (where '*Np*' means 'something physically incompatible with p').

Now the determinist holds that for every act p of any agent, all acts incompatible with p are impossible$_1$; whereas the libertarian holds that some acts are free; that is (according to the reformulated principle), for some act p, some act physically incompatible with p is possible$_1$. Physical determinism therefore excludes free-will as traditionally conceived. So, if mind-directed human action is shown to be physically determined, then the traditional philosophical libertarian conception of free-will is untenable.[19]

Summarily, there is a common confusion of two different and significant senses of 'possibility' which gives rise to the errors and absurdities supposedly generated by physical determinism. These senses are possibility$_2$, meaning 'consistent with natural law and the agent's powers', and possibility$_1$, meaning '(the one) physical possibility (in the event)'. Possibility$_2$ involves general law statements and system structure. Possibility$_1$ involves system states, as initial conditions, in addition to general law statements and system structure. If a distinction is made between these two senses of possible, then errors and absurdities can be avoided and the case for physical determinism at the level of human action is supportable.

6 LIBERTARIANISM

6.1 *Central Concepts*

The libertarian view is firmly rooted in what we have called the OA model of human individuality and discussed at some length in previous chapters. It involves a conception of the self, person or agent that is essentially transempirical. Such a view of the self distinguishes it categorically and conceptually from the body's physical states, from the subject's 'inner' world of desires, beliefs and dispositions and, according to some philosophers (e.g. C. A. Campbell and Sartre), even, to a significant extent, from character and personality as formed by nature and nurture. But although undetermined in these empirically significant senses, agent action is nevertheless supposed to be neither random nor arbitrary. On the contrary, the transempirical agent exercises his will for a self-elected and self-directed purpose according to rational principles. The will as so conceived is supposedly a cause in the economy of physical events but is not itself caused. 'Action' is said to be logically distinct from the behaviour involved in performing it, and is distinguished by its rational and intentional determinants. Reasons and regulative principles are logically autonomous and irreducible explanatory concepts, and explanatory concepts only. They do not feature in any way in the logic of causal explanation and much less do they enter into the causal economy of physical events. This view probably goes with self-image involving an outline of vaguely bodily form within which the causal processes observable in the external world are suspended, at least where free action is concerned. Within this form the data of introspection hold exclusively. In short, the free actions of agents are inherent in a metaphysical model in which the concepts of persons, acts and reasons are primitive and contrast with the physical objects, systems, events and causes, which are primitive to a physical and scientific model.

Many of the shortcomings of the OA conception of agency have already been discussed. Ryle has evoked the underlying homuncular image very aptly and suggested how innocents might be led to transcend it. In his parable of the horseless locomotive, innocents are led to grasp the idea of motion without a mover, by being asked whether they imagine also that the supposedly hidden horse would in its turn have another hidden inner horse, or team of horses, moving each limb.[20] It must be said here again that the concept of the transempirical person borders on the unintelligible, especially when viewed in the light of the clinical evidence. In any event it is rightly said that the person so conceived is leading a very quiet life,[21] and, we might add, getting quieter all the time with every advance in the explanatory power of causal mechanisms in neuropsychology.

The previous discussion of IT, however, suggests a re-interpretation of the central concepts of agency within a physicalist model based on empirical evidence. To rehearse again this PO view: the uniqueness of human personality is admitted but is sufficiently accounted for by the uniqueness of genetic inheritance and development.[22] Actions can be usefully distinguished from *mere* bodily movements, but they are not (and cannot be) logically dissociated from the central processes and movements with which they are integral.[23] *Ex hypothesi*, this distinction is based in the presence or absence of determining micro-processes involved in intentionality. The characteristic purposiveness and the apparent irregularity of human behaviour may be unique in nature; but they are not necessarily outside the categories of causal determination when these are elaborated to include such concepts as circular causation and learning net theory. Consciousness, deliberation, reasons, motives and purposes are also acknowledged, but are interpreted as physical structures or processes 'from the inside'. The operation of will itself is construed as the immediate access or intrinsic quality of the brain's self-regulating and self-directing processes. Autonomy as spontaneous 'self'-initiated action is also allowed, but no more implies non-physical, non-causal categories and uncaused causes of behaviour than the spontaneous combustion of compost heaps does.[24]

Finally, rational explanations are not made *redundant* by physical causal explanations of the same events (described as bodily movements). But they are no longer necessarily completely outside the categories of causal determination: they are complementary to and converge with them.[25] In short, the central concepts on which the OA model of free-will is based, namely personal identity, action, purposefulness, irregularity, rationality and volition, can be adequately rendered in physicalist terms without going beyond the categories of physical determination.

6.2 Arguments for Free-will

The libertarian case cannot be rejected in this way without considering the main positive arguments for it, in the light of IT and its consequences as so far adduced. It will be convenient to consider seven main sorts of positive argument for free-will which are most commonly offered: the phenomenological; the linguistic; the empirical; the logical; the scientific; the epistemological; and the normative, or moral.

6.2.1 The phenomenological argument

The most obvious and striking evidence for free-will, it is said, is the immediate experience we have as agents in a situation calling for deliberate action and requiring the exertion of an effort of will. Typically, when agents are confronted with a choice between pursuing a more pleasurable or desirable alternative (the strongest desire motivation) and fulfilling some duty or obligation or generally pursuing some axiologically preferable alternative (the rational or moral motivation), they frequently decide on the rational or moral alternative. If determinism were true, it is argued, the force of the strongest desire would invariably prevail, but in fact it does not. That it does not depends upon the effort of will exerted by the agent which is present to him phenomenologically full-blown. The tendency to discount this pheno-menological experience is unjustifiable since it is no less indubitable phenomenologically than the immediate experiences upon which scientific predictions are made. It is not unreasonable therefore to take the phenomenological experience of natural choice between mutually exclusive alternatives as sufficient evidence for free-will.[26]

This long-standing argument is open to a number of objections. First, it is possible to reject the main features of the phenomenological analysis offered of the process of deliberation and choice. Just as Hume professed to being unable to catch a 'self' in the rich panorama of his introspecting, it is arguable that a thoroughgoing phenomenological scrutiny fails to locate a will or its acts. In situations calling for deliberate action, what is present 'to mind' is a range of alternative courses of action which may or may not be surveyed, dwelt upon, imaginatively explored for possible consequences, compared and so on. But the alternative to be pursued *presents* itself in the first instance spontaneously *as* the course of action to be pursued, and there is no willing by the agent of this selection to the pursuit of which effort may be applied. The first-order selection is made with deliberation and through the rational and intentional structure in which it is conceived, but the spontaneity with which it is made is like that of the emergence of an image on a photo-sensitive plate. It manifests itself to consciousness and makes manifest its consequences: it is not made manifest by something called an act of will, otherwise there would be an infinite regress of willings to will.[27]

Second, though it may be that even if we reject the concept of a 'will' over and above the processes of deliberation and selection, there can be no gainsaying that we do deliberate and select, and that as these alternatives are present to mind they frequently seem equally open to us. But we can accept the phenomenology of 'open possibilities' as manifest to the deliberating agent without validating the intuition as objectively true. The validation of any intuition involves its coherence with at least a substantial part of the rest of our experience. This holds at the mundane level of the perception of a 'bent' stick in water and at the grander levels of human action and cosmology. Thus determinists have frequently urged that the phenomenology of 'free-will' is illusory because it is incoherent with the rest of human knowledge. Typically, Tolstoy argues that, as in the case of the Copernican revolution, where we renounce consciousness of unreal immobility in space to recognise a motion we do not feel, so in the case of free-will we find it necessary to renounce a freedom that does not exist and to recognise a dependence of which we are not conscious.[28]

Third, although the question of whether we can act against a strongest desire requires a fuller discussion which will be undertaken later, two objections to the view that a transempirical moral effort influences the economy of mental–physical events can be mentioned here. It is arguable that, although one desire may seem strongest in some psychologically obtrusive sense to do with 'hot passions' (e.g. greed, lewd lasciviousness, fear, etc), the countervailing effort may be determined not by the putting forth of some transempirical effort of will at all, but merely by other mundane but 'cooler' passions (e.g. desire for public esteem, self-respect). Or again, and more profoundly, the (linear) metaphor of a tug-of-war between motives and passions of differing strengths can be abandoned altogether and a *systemic* model adopted which is more in keeping with the new knowledge we have of circular causation and its role in central processes. In this case, as Butler long ago recognised, the effort of will related to moral conscience is seen as regulative as between motivating forces, rather than a moral force itself.[29] The effort of will is thus at least analogous to the *norm*-determined activity of a self-regulating system. If this model is appropriate, then effort of will is indeed not a 'something' like a 'motivating passion' but neither is it transempirical. It inheres in the

253

organisation and function of hierarchically ordered and self-regulating systems.

Fourth and finally, the notion of an act or exertion of will presupposes an actor–willer over and above the physical processes involved, and we have found no reason to accept this transempirical concept.

6.2.2 *The linguistic argument*

A recurrent argument for free-will and against determinism is that the former is and the latter is not consistent with what we ordinarily say and presumably think about human action,[30] i.e. with the common stock of words that embodies all the distinctions men have found worth drawing.[31] For example, a well-known crypto-deterministic interpretation of 'I can' is 'I can if I choose', where choosing is, or at least may be, determined.[32] But according to Austin, on a proper analysis of the expression 'I can if I choose' in accordance with ordinary usage, the deterministic inference that 'If I cannot I do not choose' is illegitimate or at least 'curious'. This, he maintains, reflects the categorical or non-causal conditional interpretation of the connective 'if' in ordinary usage.

The assumption here, that there is a paradigm of 'ordinary usage' that determinism fails to conform to, is quite unrealistic. There have been many versions of what we 'really' ordinarily mean by 'can' and 'free' including absence of constraint,[33] ability,[34] unpredictability[35] and inexcusability.[36] It is better therefore to acknowledge that ordinary usage allows a variety of legitimate interpretations,[37] and that these quite likely reflect metaphysical commitment. Thus, in contrast to Austin's OA analysis of the connective 'if' in 'I can if I choose', the crypto-determinist offers a causal conditional interpretation. On this interpretation 'I can if I choose' is similar to 'I pant if I run'. The inference 'Whether or not I choose, I can' and 'I can *simpliciter*' are *illegitimate*, just as 'I pant whether or not I run' and 'I pant' are illegitimate. But the inference 'If I cannot I do not choose' is legitimate, just as 'If I am not panting I am not running' is legitimate. Austin objects that this last inference – that 'If I cannot I do not choose' – is very curious and so he concludes that the connective 'if' in 'I can if I choose' is not ordinarily interpreted as a causal connection, and the determinist's account of 'I can' is therefore illegitimate.

However, the determinist may mean literally and precisely what Austin finds so curious, i.e. that there is a causal connection between choosing and being able. The sense of able indicated here is first-order (able$_1$), corresponding to possible$_1$ above (Sections 5.1 and 5.3). Accordingly, it is not my ability$_2$ (i.e. 'capacity') but my ability$_1$ (i.e. potent state) that is said to be conditional on my choosing. This is the same form as Austin's paradigm of causal connection 'I pant if I run':

just as we might say 'If I am not panting I am not running', we can say 'If I cannot I do not choose' (or a more perspicuous paraphrase: 'If I cannot I am not choosing').[38] This interpretation is close to such familiar locutions as 'Well, if he can't do it, he is not (must not be, cannot be) trying'. And so we go round the mulberry bush. One man's antinomy can be another man's veridical paradox, and one man's veridical paradox can be another man's platitude.[39] In this case the libertarian's antinomy is the compatibilist's veridical paradox is the determinist's platitude.

Even if such a deterministic interpretation of ordinary usage were not possible, however, this still would not have been a decisive objection against physical determinism, because language and concepts are always subject to diachronic change, as has been repeatedly argued throughout the present essay.[40]

6.2.3 *The empirical argument*

Many of the most recent arguments for free-will are calculated to establish that it is objectively and empirically demonstrable that an agent has the ability or power to do otherwise than he does, and so demonstrable that he can do or is free to do otherwise than he does do.[41] These arguments usually take the form of showing that there are a number of standard evidential moves that are usually made when it is required to establish whether or not anything 'can' do something, and these apply equally when we want to establish whether anybody 'can' or 'could' have done something other than he does. The normal tests include: previous evidence of performing the same or closely similar acts, propinquity, circumstantial variety, agent similarity and simple frequency of performance.[42] If these conditions are well satisfied, as they frequently are, then the canons of inductive evidence for the hypothesis of freedom to do otherwise are as well satisfied in this case as for any other. Thus free-will is supposedly established empirically and determinism is disproved.

The main objection to this line of argument is that it misses the vital point, that it is not just a particular agent in a particular situation that is in question, but also the particular state he is in at the particular time in question. If the criteria advocated were adopted we might equally argue that a patently mechanical automatic pilot is free because its powers are such that it 'can' do other than it does in the sense that it has previously done so and in the relevantly recent past, in a variety of different situations, with essentially the same structure, and on frequent occasions. But nobody, and least of all the libertarian, wants to make this claim. The distinction previously drawn between possible$_2$ (as consistent with the agent's powers) and possible$_1$ (as a function of precise initial and boundary conditions at a particular time) shows that this argument, like other compatibilist arguments, is conducted at the ordinary unreflective level and so misses the determinist's essential point. At best therefore it establishes only what the determinist is not concerned to deny.

Empirical arguments of the kind mentioned may establish an agent's general capacities (possibility$_2$), but they do not touch on the vital question of precise initial and boundary conditions or states (possibility$_1$). Libertarian or compatibilist pronouncements consequently take on a bizarre form when this distinction is not made. Laymen might be forgiven, for example, for supposing that philosophy had entered a new age of scholasticism in the pejorative sense when they read such ambiguous pronouncements as these:

> 'He cannot act differently' neither entails nor is entailed by: 'There is no possibility of his acting differently'.[43]
> 'We are not entitled to argue that since Jones' being in condition K is physically incompatible with his walking away, the fact that he was in K shows that it was physically impossible for him to walk away.[44]

and

> The fact that the principle of causality does not annihilate or reduce our power to decide or act otherwise than we in fact do does not imply that in fact we have it in our power to decide to act otherwise.[45]

6.2.4 *The logical argument*

An argument for free-will has recently been derived from logical considerations, claiming to be a final blow for liberty and a decisive knock-down for determinism.[46] This is the argument from the logical indeterminacy of agent action.[47]

The argument from logical indeterminacy is based on the key point that if what a man believes affects correspondingly the state of his organising system, no complete up-to-date account of that organising system could be believed *by him* without being *ipso facto* out of date. The force of this argument supposedly derives from the fact that it is formal and does not depend on physical indeterminism. It allows that a super-neuropsychologist could in principle predict precisely an agent's future action on the basis of a complete state description of the agent's system, but only so long as he is not communicating (i.e. interacting) with the system whose behaviour he is predicting. Once this happens, as typically it might in the case of human agents, neither the agent nor the predictor could predict the outcome of a future action.

> If anyone tries to predict to us that we are about to choose porridge rather than prunes, no matter how scientific the basis of the statement, we can easily verify that he is simply giving us a fresh oppor-

tunity to make up our minds. ... The point is simply that the brain is always altered by receiving information so that the brain which has received a description of itself cannot possibly be in the state described.[48]

It is not that we are unable to ascertain the true description, it is that *for us there is no true description to ascertain.* For us the decision is not something to be ascertained, but to be made. In fact, any description of our decision as already certain to be of a stated form would be for us *logically indeterminate* (neither true nor false) because it would be self-referring rather like the statement: 'This sentence I am now uttering is false'.[49]

The main shortcoming of this argument is that it is explicitly based on the supposition that what people mean by free choice is a choice that nobody could (even in principle) describe to us with certainty in advance.[50] But indeterminacy in this sense is only a necessary condition for free-will; it is not sufficient. All that the argument establishes is that, while we are consciously deciding, when a decision is being *made*, we cannot be simultaneously predicting what we are deciding.[51] This carries no implication about whether or not our decisions are causally determined and so *inevitable*. The unacceptability of this view of free-will as the one involved in moral responsibility can be shown by the following case. Should the brakes and steering of a car unexpectedly begin to fail at the top of a mountain pass, the driver's immediate concern would be to avoid catastrophe by making decisions and acting on them. Still, he may be involved in a collision due to eventual mechanism failure. In such circumstances eventual failure, loss of control and collision would follow inevitably from the first incipient failure in that situation. Nevertheless on this Libertarian view a judge might say that the driver was morally responsible for the collision because he was free not to be involved in the collision with the other vehicle in the sense that he could not predict the (inevitable) failure and collision while he was concentrating on driving. But this would be manifestly perverse or a cruel jest.

The example illustrates another specious aspect of the logical indeterminacy argument, namely the claim that the agent could not believe the predictor's prediction and still pursue the same course of action with full freedom and so moral responsibility. The fact is that, (contrary to the thesis under discussion) it is quite natural for an agent in a concrete situation not to be influenced in his behaviour by a philosophically objective prediction, particularly when a deeply felt and pressing issue of some deep moral significance is involved rather than an indifferent choice as between porridge and prunes. Within the normative framework this is quite possible. Indeed, far from establishing, as MacKay suggests,[52] that an individual is morally *non compos mentis* when a given action is pursued in spite of his believing a highly probable prediction, such action might even prove moral virtue, in the commonly understood sense of that term. Stauffenberg's attempted assassination of Adolf Hitler and subsequent coup might well have been a case of this sort, where the agent is told beforehand that his failure has been reliably predicted, but this has not influenced his decision to perform a 'morally' justified action: obviously the 'moral' action itself in such cases might be completely determined by the agent's nature and nurture and the circumstances of the case.

Another peculiarity of this account of free-will is that it applies only to the agent's understanding of his own actions. It allows that a scientific observer could in principle acquire a complete explanatory specification of our physical state in sufficient detail to account for all our behaviour external and internal.[53] So it is only in the arbitrary case where the predictor communicates his prediction that a problem arises for the determinist. In the case of the uncommunicative observer the same problem arises as before: it is surely a joke to say that, although objectively a man's crime was inevitable, he is free and morally responsible so long as he is unable to predict his own future acts with certainty. This would also seemingly have the curious corollary that (isolated) objective observers, apprised of all the objective factors determining an agent's actions (e.g. moralists and jurors), could never in principle judge an individual morally responsible. Only the agent himself can do that, on this view!

Underlying this opaque view is the thought that two logical dimensions are involved in the two languages employed in agent and observer descriptions of the same act, and that these are complementary in some sense which makes physical determinism compatible with free-will. The argument is that in human action we are dealing with an 'irreducible mystery' which cannot be properly expressed in either description alone, and which makes it impossible in principle to give explanations of action that would be 'equally binding on us whether we believed them or not'.[54] I am not really sure that I fully understand what this unusual form of words is intended to convey, but according to IT there is no more of a metaphysical mystery about the relationship between our *undergoing* the physical processes involved in decision-making (i.e. deciding) and the processes objectively *observable* than there is between our *undergoing* the physical processes involved in a toothache (i.e. toothaching) and the physical processes as observable. It is true that in both cases there is a phenomenological difference between the undergoing and what is undergone, but in neither case does the duality of phenomena bear upon the inevitability of the succession of phenomena, which is based in causal mechanisms. MacKay concedes as much when he says that his argument applies when the workings of the brain are physically determinate.[55] If, therefore, the inevitability of successive events is not in question, then duality of logic and language as such has no bearing on the question of the rationality and justice of blame and punishment in so far as this requires that the behaviour in question is not inevitable.

To return to the curious corollary that only an agent can regard himself as free and so morally responsible: it is evident that this is an unacceptable basis for the institution of morality. To make any sense out of the present view we must suppose that the agent is judged (by others) from a normative interpersonal attitude, based on what Shutz calls the 'reciprocity of perspectives' or, more prosaically, looking at things from another's point of view. In this way others would be apprised of the agent's perspective including the intuition of freedom, choice and the related moral accountability; this would be the basis of the observer's moral evaluation of others. But if observers reciprocate perspectives with agents as a basis for morally evaluating their actions, the reciprocity must be complete and the observer's perspective embraced by the agent also. It has been argued before that the agent's perspective is an analytical abstraction, since every person is informed as an observer also. But then information about the physical determination of action is just as cogent for the agent himself as for others. The intuition of freedom based on logical indeterminacy should therefore be subject to the same validating criterion of coherence as any other intuition, as has been previously argued.

Finally, it can be shown that in a deterministic world it is possible to predict the behaviour of a learning system including the reaction of the system to information about the prediction.[56] This is a relatively technical consideration involving the problem of self-consistency of descriptions of predicted system states, and is beyond the scope of the present discussion. However, the foregoing arguments seem sufficient to show that the argument for free-will from the logical indeterminacy of agent action neither concerns the concept of free-will relevant to moral responsibility, nor succeeds in establishing the agent's intuition of free-will against objective knowledge of physical determinism. What it does do is provide an account of why we should think there is something 'queerly undetermined'[57] about the decisions we take while we are making them, even when these decisions are completely physically determined.

6.2.5 *The argument from scientific unpredictability*

Arguments have already been discussed which make some appeal to the unpredictability of events (the a-causality of decisions and logical indeterminacy). A number of philosophers have expressed the more general and perhaps widespread view that there is, at least *prima facie*, a basic unpredictability about even the macro-events of ordinary experience, which the advance of science does not affect and seems unlikely ever to effect.[58] This is the 'hurly burly' view of events that Austin expressed in the following passage:[59]

> according to *them* (the traditional beliefs enshrined in the word *can*) a human ability or power or capacity is inherently liable not to produce success on occasion, and that for no reason (or are bad luck and bad form sometimes reasons?).

Körner has expressed a similar thought more formally in terms of what he claims is the logical disconnectedness between scientific predictions and phenomenal events. The two are supposedly logically disconnected because the substantive terms in hypothetico-deductive statements are precise, whereas the phenomena they are made to designate are fuzzy. Because mathematical equality is not the same thing as perceptual indistinguishability, transitivity holds for substantive predicates in nomological systems, but not for perceptual predicates. In a word, events in the phenomenal world are irreducibly unpredictable because of the intrinsic fuzziness of the observations that are idealised in the exact terms of the predictive formal systems.

This kind of argument is open to objections on a variety of levels. First, it places great physical and metaphysical store in an irreducible minimum of epistemic obscurity. In doing so it ignores the kind of evidence already adduced against phenomenalism, particularly the simple fact that as observational techniques improve degrees of obscurity and fuzziness are reduced and predictions tend increasingly to be fulfilled more accurately. This is no trivial point, because it shows that we need look no further than the mundane difficulties inherent in observation to account for the difference between inaccurate (and so unconfirmed) predictions and accurate (and so confirmed) ones. The fact that predictions are possible at all is powerful testimony to the existence of a system of natural law (laws$_1$) which scientific laws (laws$_2$) ideally approximate to. Inherent in the 'hurly burly' view is the highly dubious crypto-Protagorean assumption that there is no objective order (law$_1$) beyond humanly perceived phenomenal regularity. Some philosophers even go so far as positively to insist upon an anthropocentric view of the world as the only appropriate view.[60]

Second, this last point raises a quite fundamental issue about the metaphysical implications of scientific hypotheses and predictions. Libertarians frequently argue that physical determinism could prevail only if the behavioural neurosciences produced exact and reliable predictions of specific normal human behaviour in ordinary circumstances based on hypotheses of great generality. Underlying this view is the quite mistaken lay belief that the established objective sciences, properly so called, have achieved that status by demonstrations of the prescribed kind.[61] It is true that physics for example is adequate for accurately predicting a wide variety of natural events. But when these are not the contrived and simplified affairs of laboratory experiments, they involve natural systems of very great simplicity such as the solar system, where the natural objects involved approximate to the idealised objects supposed by high-order hypotheses.

The fact of the matter is that the mathematical tools of physics are unable to handle with complete formal precision more than a small number of interacting 'bodies' (three or four) before the physicist is lost in conceptual and computational difficulties, and probablistic calculi are required.[62] Now the stage at which probability enters the scene is just the point at which mathematics becomes difficult; so to make an ontological issue out of probability is to take the quasi-Protagorean view that natural events have an intrinsic probability which nevertheless continuously and coincidentally shifts with human mathematical discoveries!

The main point, however, is that Newtonian mechanics is universally and properly accepted as adequate for explaining the behaviour of inanimate bodies *in spite of* the fact that it is forever impossible in practice (and so in a sense even in principle) to predict with complete accuracy the final state of even (say) a single avalanche on the North Face of the Eiger. The explanation for this is that it is now universally accepted that there is nothing about an avalanche that is outside the terms of Newtonian mechanics, except the mundane but insuperable practical difficulty of accurately establishing initial conditions and relations of a vast aggregate. Once it is accepted that we are dealing with objects that can be treated as in principle predictable by the theory, there is no feeling that actual unpredictability implies anything more than unmanageable complexity. In a word, if we cannot predict the trajectory and resting place of every particle that moved during an avalanche, this is not a reason for abandoning Newton and embracing 'hurly burly'.

Essentially the same holds true of the hypothetical models of neuropsychology. Though it is patently foolish to try to explain human behaviour in terms suitable for rocks and planets, there is no reason why we should not embrace *appropriate* models of comparable explanatory power to explain and predict behaviour. By this I mean that the concepts of system, feedback, hierarchy, analogical modelling and so on serve a

261

similar role in explaining human behaviour to those of mass, force, momentum and conservation in Newtonian mechanics. If these new concepts are capable of generating explanatory models that are testable in the same terms as the basic concepts of physics are testable along the lines indicated in previous chapters (Chapter III, Section 5.2, and Chapter VII, Section 7.3), then the impossibility of ever making a precise prediction of an item of normal human behaviour would be no more decisive against physical determinism at this level than a similar impossibility is at the level of mechanics.

In conclusion, it is worth pointing out again that unpredictability of the kind discussed is only a necessary, not a sufficient, condition for free-will in the sense we hold to be relevant to moral blame and punishment.

6.2.6 *The epistemological argument*

It is often argued that free-will is a precondition of true knowledge, and since we do have at least some true knowledge, this establishes free-will against determinism.[63] One version of the argument is that if causal determinism is true then all our beliefs, true or false, are causally determined: we would be bound to hold them anyway, whether objectively true or false, irrespective of any of the usual rational validating criteria. All of our beliefs are therefore suspect, including the belief in the truth of determinism, which is thus a self-defeating position.[64] Another version stems from, and appeals directly to, the OA metaphysic of a transcendental self.[65] This is that, unless the human experimenter were 'outside' of the physical system he investigates, manipulating determining variables by acts of free-will, there would be no guarantee that the changes brought about experimentally were due to the factors manipulated by the experimenter and not merely coincidental, causally determined, happenstance. This version of the argument thus even succeeds in construing the 'rational attractiveness' of the fundamental laws of physics as altogether belying materialism![66]

The basic assumption underlying this view is that physical determinism denies rationality and the rational validation of true belief.[67] But IT does have a place for rationality – only it is interpolated within the physical schema. The basic formula repeats itself again: rationally to validate a true belief is to undergo brain processes of a belief-validating kind. And there is nothing truer than truth.[68] It is of no epistemological moment that a true belief came about as an effect of causal antecedents, since the knowledge achieved is none the less reliable[69] and is subject to the usual validating criteria of coherence, correspondence, adequation and pragmatic consequences. Indeed, contrary to the 'transempirical experimenter' argument, the fact that the agent's action is in and of the world he is apprised of is the very best, and arguably the only, guarantee we could have that the models he forms of it and the beliefs he holds about it are not just passive cinematographic delusions. Eventually the libertarian himself must acknowledge that it is impossible for the agent continuously to think of himself as being not covered by any universal account he gives of the world.[70] Once more we see that the roots of disagreement lie in different metaphysical root models, with the orthodoxy supposing that rational insight is a transempirical property of persons and *in principle* outside of the causal categories.

6.2.7 The argument from normative experience

One of the most persistent arguments for free-will is based on the view that moral experience is logically autonomous and supports free-will because, unless the will were free, moral imperatives would be unintelligible.[71]

Ordinary experience often confronts us with situations in which we feel obligated to perform (or desist from) actions against even our strongest natural desires and inclinations. This, it is said, has nothing to do with natural processes, causal necessity and natural law. In such cases we act out of regard for right and wrong, that is regard for the precepts of moral law. When we do not, we feel guilt and remorse. And it is for the same reason that we may hold someone morally guilty who is physically powerless to do other than he does.[72]

Moral philosophers have taken moral experience of this sort to be unique, with no parallel in and no logical connection with the natural world of cause and effect. Hume's influential statement on the matter is usually expressed in the now celebrated dictum: 'you can't deduce an "ought" from an "is" '.[73] Kant follows Hume when he argues that, no matter how many natural forces may impel someone to will, they can never give rise to the 'ought' that forbids or authorises the will.[74] The most influential contemporary expression of essentially the same view is embodied in Moore's 'naturalistic fallacy', which purports to prove the essential autonomy of the realm of value and its irreducibility to the realm of natural facts.[75]

The moral imperatives that constitute the realm of value are intelligible only if agents have free-will to act in accordance with moral precepts and against naturally determined impulses to do otherwise. In a word, 'ought to do x' logically implies 'can do x'. Ordinary experience, moreover, is sufficient to establish the intelligibility of moral imperatives, since there is no more reason to question our experience of moral imperatives and moral choice than there is to question our experience of causal necessity. Since ordinary experience guarantees the intelligibility of moral imperatives, and since the intelligibility of moral imperatives entails free-will, it follows that ordinary moral experience supports free-will. Furthermore, because moral experience is autonomous and irreducible, scientific knowledge of the determinants of human behaviour has no logical implications for the free-will guaranteed by experience of moral imperatives.

The argument for free-will from normative experience turns, therefore, on the autonomy of moral experience and the support this provides for free-will against physical determinism and the evidence of science. It is appropriate therefore to consider the case for the autonomy of moral experience and whether it supports free-will as has been supposed.

It is not possible in the space available to consider all of the problems raised by supposing the autonomy of moral experience. It should be mentioned however that there is good (controversial) evidence that Hume's influential argument has been widely misconstrued.[76] If Hume believed that facts are totally divorced from values, as many of his successors have supposed, then his own naturalistic ethics, with its basic appeal to natural sympathy, sociability and human welfare, was certainly the first theory of morals to violate that very doctrine. Kant's account depends upon a highly dubitable distinction between the phenomenal–empirical realm of causal necessity and a wholly conjectural realm of 'noumena' or things-in-themselves. On Kant's view the person, as subject to moral law, is someone devoid of desires and motives, acting without a body, outside time and without extension.[77] It is not surprising therefore that philosophers have thought that such a person lives altogether too quiet a life to be a very instructive guide in the affairs of natural-born men.[78]

The most influential contemporary account of the autonomy of moral experience is Moore's, and this view warrants more detailed consideration. Moore sought to define the province of ethics in terms of a definition of 'good', which he regarded as the central ethical term. His well-known conclusion was that good is a simple, unanalysable, undefinable, non-natural property of natural objects, including human actions. On this basis he argued that the realm of ethics is *sui generis*. Any attempt to define moral values in terms of some natural property is doubly erroneous. It is a mistake to attempt to define the undefinable and it is a mistake to define something non-natural in terms of something natural, that is in terms of sense data, introspectable experiences, causation and substance.[79] Attempts to do so, such as utilitarian appeals to happiness or evolutionary appeals to survival and progress, commit the so-called 'naturalistic fallacy'. Moore's method of undermining naturalistic definitions of good is by an open-question argument. When a naturalistic definition of 'good' is proposed in terms of some complex property X, it may always be asked with significance of the complex so

264

defined whether it is good.[80] If so, then it is argued that X cannot be a definition of good since the question, 'Is "good" good?' is not significant. It is no exaggeration to say that the 'naturalistic fallacy' has acquired the status of a panacea for most of the strains imposed on the orthodoxy by naturalistic accounts of moral experience.

There are, nevertheless, so many shortcomings in Moore's argument that it is surprising that it should have proven so persistent and influential.[81] The fact is that naturalistic definitions of 'good' are not obviously fallacious at all in the proper sense of that word, meaning illegitimate inference. In any case, whether the supposed naturalistic fallacy is a fallacy is what is required to be proved, and cannot be assumed in the argument, as Moore and those who follow him do. The open-question argument, if valid, would be equally effective in undermining *any* definition of a word in terms of another word, which is to say it is not valid at all.[82] Moore's theory of meaning and definition is to provide an analysis of the complex term defined in terms of its simple atomic constituents. This account of meaning and definition is now widely recognised to be over-simplified and in some important respects positively misguided. The modern conception of meaning as use is opposed to Moore's atomistic enterprise, particularly for complex and abstract notions such as 'good'. Some of the errors in Moore's argument for the autonomy of ethics are instructive, however. Moore's most instructive error is to treat 'good' as a simple property of objects, like yellow. 'Good', of course, seems unlikely to be the same sort of thing as 'yellow'; or, in the preferred parlance of linguistic philosophy, the adjective 'good' does not bear the same relation to the substantives it qualifies as the adjective 'yellow' does. It is unsurprising, therefore, that neither Moore nor his successors have ever succeeded in making clear what kind of simple property 'good' is.

The error is instructive because it leads to the understanding that the reason why 'good' is undefinable in terms of natural or non-natural properties is not because it is some very obscure property which is neither natural nor non-natural, but because it is not a property of any description; it is a relation, specifically a relation between certain kinds of objects and the definition of the concepts under which they are apprehended and described.[83] In linguistic terms 'good' is not a descriptive adjective like 'yellow', but an attributive adjective, more like 'large' or 'real'.[84]

The significant property of attributive adjectives is that they are comparative terms; that is, to say that something is a large X implies that it is larger than most X's. In the case of the adjective 'good' there are specially close connections with the substantives it qualifies. To say that something is a 'good X' is to imply that it is a better X than most X's.

Further than this, it can be said that the meaning or definition of X determines the meaning '*good* X', for if objects of a certain kind fully satisfy the definition of the concept under which they are apprehended and described then they are, by definition, good of their kind. If the object in question is a human action, it will be considered good to the extent that it corresponds to the sort of action described. A good speech may be bad diplomacy. What this analysis suggests is that the supposed autonomy of ethics, or the categorical distinction between facts and values, is by no means as hard and fast as philosophical orthodoxy suggests. For, conceptual knowledge about what it is for something to be X, together with knowledge that something is in fact X, is sufficient to establish that something is a *good* X, at least for certain sorts of things.

The imperitival force of moral prescriptions has frequently been cited as a unique feature of moral discourse which is notably irreducible to facts. This claim introduces complex questions to do with speech acts and institutional facts, and more basic questions in the theory of definition which must be dealt with only briefly here. The relation between imperatives, such as those attached to the fulfilment of obligation, and matters of fact is perspicuous in the case of certain 'institutional facts', that is facts involving explicit social conventions and rule-governed procedures. Typically, in conventionalised social contexts, certain performances including utterances of speech, have the effect of *entailing* social and moral obligations which carry imperitival force. For example, in the context of a legal marriage ceremony a groom, in reply to the question put to him by the presiding officer about whether he undertakes to commit himself to a life with his bride, usually utters the words 'I do'. These words, and similar ones from the bride, are then confirmed by the officer's pronouncement that the groom is forthwith a man with a wife. Taken together these verbal utterances in that context *as a matter of (institutional) fact* constitute an undertaking on the groom's part to do certain things, which is tantamount to an obligation to do them. If someone is under an obligation to do something then he is obliged to do it, and this obligation in turn logically entails that he ought to do it; it is imperative that he does so.[85] Even this simple case is enough to suggest that matters of fact, describable states of affairs of a particular sort, namely social or institutional facts, are intimately bound up with values, including moral imperatives.

The case of institutional facts and social facts generally shows how Moore's analytical–atomistic theory of definition is an inadequate apparatus for capturing the imperitival character of moral discourse. The moral quality of an action is not some property of an agent or act, like yellow hair, or location, to be defined by analysis of a complex whole into its constituent properties. A more appropriate strategy is to seek the

266

meaning of 'good' in its use, that is in appraising, evaluating, prescribing and commending actions or sorts of conduct. To understand the meaning of 'good' then is to locate its use in the life of human beings. A salient feature of that use, as we have seen, is that it has to do with the relation between objects and actions and the concepts under which they are apprehended and described. An account of 'good', that is of values, might therefore be sought in the role played in the regulation of human life, by the comparison of objects and actions with concepts. We have seen that there is no reason to reject *a priori* the possibility that such an account can be rendered in terms of facts.

The main objection to the orthodox view of the autonomy of moral experience from the physicalist viewpoint is that it is based on a view of morality that seems to ignore or discount the plain fact that human beings and human societies are the products of biological evolution and that moral institutions exist in natural forms of life. Yet this important fact informs the views of so many of the great moral philosophers, from Aristotle to Mill and Kropotkin. Moore provided some grounds for rejecting pleasure, happiness and such things as the sole moral values, and these are certainly natural properties of human beings and their acts. However, Moore and the many philosophers who have followed his basic doctrine go much too far in rejecting out of hand *any* attempt to give a naturalistic account of moral experience, as if the enterprise were akin to squaring the circle. Viewed as defining the role that the comparison of conduct and concepts plays in regulating human life, there is nothing at all illogical in the enterprise, quite the opposite in fact. It is at least *prima facie* plausible that in this view there is room for prescriptions, imperatives, duties, obligations and the host of other ordinary moral concepts, without departing from the basic view that men and human societies are natural products of biological evolution, with all that that entails for non-naturalistic views of morals.

I take it that there is no *a priori* reason to deny the possibility of a purely naturalistic account of moral experience and that, on the contrary, there is reason to believe that a plausible naturalistic account might well be given. The information flow model of human behaviour[86] seems particularly apt for the process of comparison of objects and actions with concepts. If, as IT suggests, concepts have neural embodiments and perception is represented as the activity of matching or comparing such embodied concepts with incoming data from the real world, then human valuation itself, as well as perception, may be located in the special relationship that holds between human cognitive schemata and objects and behaviour in the external world.[87]

The information flow model might be deployed further to explain why only some objects and behaviours are considered 'good' when they fulfil the definition of their concept. The idea of a 'good' cancer or murder is, of course, bizarre. But this evaluative feature of some objects and actions can be explained by the fact that such things are positively disvalued; that is, they do not usually constitute a 'desired' goal towards which self-directed systems are directed. Instead, they are things to be avoided. This suggestion seems even more plausible when we notice that in cases where such things are desired, as for example when specimens of them are desired and sought for some purpose, pathologists and policemen may well speak elliptically of good cancers and good murders. Such expressions are of course mere ellipses for 'good specimen', because it is as specimens that cancers and murders may be desired and sought after. A film producer may speak in the same way of a 'good ruin' which is a bad building but a good film location.

It must be emphasised again here that a full account of the processes involved in moral experience must include, to put it crudely, the relations and communications between *groups* of brains. This point, important as it is, does not change the basic formula for normative experience suggested by IT: that is, to be evaluating is to be undergoing evaluating brain processes. The crucial consequence of community participation is to establish the recognition of norms by the individual (see Chapter IV, Section 4.1, and Chapter V, Section 4.4). This is the point of Vygotsky's thesis about the social origins of voluntary acts, according to which the overtly regulative function previously shared between two or more persons becomes a method of organising higher forms of active behaviour, which are social in origin and depend on speech for their structure.[88] What this suggests is that the evaluation of human behaviour involves the comparison between what is expected or desired (i.e. norms or ideals) and what is perceived. What is intended here is a quite literal physical sense of 'comparison' involving the cybernetic relation between established neural structures and perceived data from the external world. Clearly this basic model can be extended to cover purely *internal* comparisons of 'conjectured' patterns against norm-ideals.

There remains one potentially serious objection to such a naturalistic approach to values which must be tackled. It is that the autonomy of moral experience and moral discourse is a logical matter which is not resolved merely by establishing that moral experience is a feature of the social life of biological organisms. It is necessary therefore to say something about the well-known fact that 'ought' cannot be deduced from 'is'. It is here most of all that IT can illuminate moral discourse. The problem raised by the supposed existence of a logically distinct value domain turns out to be another aspect of the psycho-physical problem to which IT offers a solution. The same basic problem arises out of the conceptual and logical divide separating facts and values as arises out of the divide separating the mental and the physical. In both cases there is a problem about the relationship between two supposedly logically incommensurable domains which, nevertheless, seem to be closely connected in practice.

No amount of objective factual knowledge of the neurology of pain can inform us about the phenomenology of paining.[89] In the same way, no objective knowledge about the physical comparison relations between the neurology of cognitive schemata and the perception (or anticipation) of actions can inform us about the phenomenology of valuing, such as moral imperatives. But just as there is nothing unnatural or logically puzzling about the relation between 'paining' and the physical processes concerned,[90] there need be nothing unnatural or logically puzzling about the relation between the force of moral imperatives and the corresponding physical processes. The difference between sensing and valuing is not the difference between natural and non-natural processes, but the difference between the undergoing of two different sorts of natural process.

Our knowledge by acquaintance of sensings is not deduced from neurophysiology, though of course once sensings have been identified with physical processes of a certain sort we may infer, given the occurrence of one, that the other has occurred. The relation between moral imperatives and facts about the physical world should be seen in the same way. Our knowledge of imperatives is not deducible from neurophysiology, though if valuings were identified with physical processes we might infer, given the occurrence of one, that the other has occurred. The familiar fact that knowledge of moral imperatives cannot be deduced from factual descriptions does not, therefore, necessarily establish the autonomy of moral experience in any sense that undermines naturalism. This is because, on the relevant naturalistic view of moral experience, the relation between the facts and the moral imperatives is identity. Imperitival force, like sensing, is not the sort of thing that is deducible without knowledge of the processes involved under both descriptions.

There are important questions to do with the setting or creating of goals which define values and towards which imperatives are directed. I must leave these questions aside here. Their importance is considerable, but there is no reason to doubt that highly plausible physicalist accounts can be rendered of these things also.[91]

The foregoing argument has sought to show that there are good reasons for rejecting the view that moral experience is autonomous. Moral experience can be located squarely in the natural world, that is in the domain of substance, causality, sensation and human feeling.

Moreover, there is a plausible physicalist basis for explaining normative experience including the force of moral imperatives. It follows that the fact–value distinction no more implies contra-causal free-will in the sense relevant to moral responsibility than the physical–mental duality implies an ontological duality. In both cases the duality follows from the quite mundane natural difference between an objectively observable process and the undergoing of it.

I take it, therefore, that the argument from moral sense does not establish free-will against a possible naturalistic and deterministic account of normative experience.

It might be suggested that views such as the one advanced here are not naturalistic at all; that only those ethical theories that are refuted by Moore's naturalistic fallacy argument should be called naturalistic.[92] This device clearly begs the question of whether some account of moral experience can be given in terms of substance, causation, human sentiments and sense experience, that is a naturalistic account. The extraordinary tenacity with which naturalistic accounts of morals are resisted, in spite of the shaky foundations of the old arguments against them, has been attributed to the prevalence among philosophers of a deep-rooted desire to sustain a certain attitude to values which already sets libertarian strivings above all other considerations.[93] Certainly this explanation is consistent with the root model thesis advanced in this book. We shall argue in the next chapter that root models are defended not so much because they sustain values worth preserving, but because they define the values believed to be worth preserving.

7   SUMMARY AND CONCLUSIONS

Summarily, the central concepts of the OA view of human individuality underlying the traditional conceptions of free-will and moral responsibility have been examined and seen to be open to physicalist reinterpretation along lines implied by IT. The concept of free-will based on these concepts has no place in the PO model because it is inconsistent with the categories of physical–causal determination. The main positive arguments for free-will on phenomenological, linguistic, empirical, logical, scientific–predictive, epistemological and normative or moral grounds have all been found to be open to serious objections. The case for the traditional conception of free-will therefore has not been made out against physical determinism as informed by mind–brain IT.

To conclude this chapter, I take it that, although there are a number of other senses of 'can' and 'free' relevant to the evaluation and regulation of human action, the senses defining the traditional conception of moral

270

responsibility are embodied in the dictum 'does x freely' implies and requires 'not physically necessary that x'. According to physical determinism, this requirement cannot be satisfied in the case of mind-directed human behaviour, which on the basis of IT can in principle be explained completely within the categories of causal determinism. The positive arguments for free-will have been found to be inconclusive, and the OA concept of the transempirical agent underlying the traditional conception of free-will is inconsistent with the model that emerges from the life sciences.

It is evident from the discussion that the importance of instantaneous central micro-states as determinants of behaviour is vital to the physical determinist thesis. Similarly, the biperspectivist interpretation of these microstates offered by IT is crucial to the refutation of the libertarian's main arguments and to a re-interpretation of the phenomenal evidence for free-will along physicalist lines.

IX

MORAL RESPONSIBILITY

1 THE PROBLEM

The close link between free-will and moral responsibility in the traditional view is succinctly expressed by the maxim 'ought implies can'. If S ought to do x then (1) he is praiseworthy for x only if he could$_1$ have done $\sim x$; and (2) he is blameworthy for $\sim x$ only if he could$_1$ have done x. Thus 'ought to do x' implies both 'can$_1$ do x' and 'can$_1$ do $\sim x$'; i.e., neither x nor any alternative to x is physically necessary. But determinism says that either x or $\sim x$ is physically necessary, therefore determinism is inconsistent with the traditional view of moral responsibility.

As with free-will, the dispute about moral responsibility has been conducted in a smog of misconception and equivocation with the key term. For many of the disputants 'moral responsibility' has fairly precise and narrowly defined connotations. Since arguments can be readily found to show that physical determinism does not refute, or has nothing important to say one way or the other about, moral responsibility in some such favoured narrow sense, it is frequently (and wrongly) concluded that physical determinism does not refute, or has nothing of import to say about, moral responsibility in *any* sense. Again, as with 'free-will', the term 'moral responsibility' has a number of different meanings, so there is no paradigmatic meaning on which to base a trivial conceptuo-linguistic refutation of a far-reaching metaphysical thesis. One important and obvious distinction that is often overlooked is that between moral and legal responsibility. 'Responsibility' is sometimes used indiscriminately to mean either, and as a result both libertarians and determinists are misled into needless confusion, thinking that a denial of moral responsibility in one sense entails the denial of the basic social and legal institutions implied by another sense. Apart from this obvious confusion, however, there are a number of senses of 'moral responsibility' that are frequently offered as the real or the only possible meaning. Among the most frequently cited senses of 'morally responsible' are these:

1 having responsibility attributed;[1]
2 being the efficient or proximate cause;[2]
3 changeable by disapprobation and sanctions;[3]
4 acting in full knowledge of the facts and with intent;[4]
5 modifiable through foreknowledge of prediction;[5]
6 having no recognised excuse.[6]

It may be, and quite probably is, true that the semantic range of 'moral responsibility' covers all of these senses and many more. But it remains cogent to ask:

1' what it is that is attributed and according to which criterion;
2' why certain causal factors are singled out for attention;
3' what it is that is changeable and why we should change it;
4' what is special about these particular knowing, intentional acts;
5' why modifiability through foreknowledge and prediction is considered relevant and important;
6' what it is that the agent has no excuse for, and what he is excused from.

The answer to these questions is given by the sense of 'moral responsibility' that I take to be central to the traditional orthodox view, the one depending upon the concept of the transempirical person and free action. In Western cultures at least, other senses are logically secondary to this sense. This concept is rooted in the Judaeo-Christian mytho-poetic conception of wilful perversity, diabolical malevolence and the fall of Lucifer with its connotations of sin, illegality, wickedness, damnation, vileness and the *lex talionis*. To be morally responsible in this sense is to have freely done something that in some absolute sense is *wrong*, that is to say, something against some transcendental and categorical prescription and which is to a greater or lesser extent guilt-laden and justly deserving of vituperation, blame and punishment. As one great judge expressed it:[7]

> I am ... of the opinion that the close alliance between criminal law and moral sentiment is in all ways healthy and advantageous to the community. I think it is highly desirable that criminals should be hated, that the punishments inflicted upon them should be so contrived as to give expression to that hatred, and to justify it so far as the provision for means of expressing it and gratifying a healthy and natural sentiment can justify and encourage it.

273

Of course such antediluvian views are rarely clearly or directly expressed nowadays[8] – certainly not by modern philosophers. But there is a close and obvious connection between the fairly routine philosophical rejection of naturalistic accounts of moral experience and the baroque transcendental conception of moral wrong.

A consideration of excuses will shed some further light on the issue. The orthodoxy excuses misdemeanours by infants, lunatics and imbeciles largely because their abnormality is so generalised and patent that it is assumed there must be deep-rooted *causes* for their deviance, whether they are known or not. In such cases neurology, developmental psychology and psychological medicine merely fill in the details of a general story that educated men have commonly accepted. But the voluntary action of sane individuals is supposedly different in some categorical sense. There is no *obvious* abnormality in an individual who for most of the time behaves like everybody else. In such cases, where the presumption of abnormal causes is not pressed upon the observer by overwhelming evidence of general and deep abnormality, and where there is no detailed knowledge of particular causes, it is convenient to presume that there is no particular explanation of antisocial actions. There is no particular explanation, that is, unless wickedness and moral turpitude are explanations: and for the orthodoxy they are, because a transempirical person is not causally necessitated to behave as he does, and so antisocial acts are freely chosen acts of wickedness with malice aforethought. We see, then, that among other things the mythic concepts of wickedness and turpitude fill an explanatory role where knowledge of determining causes is incomplete. But 'moral responsibility' differs in an important way from other non-causal explanatory concepts, which the physicalist can construe as 'causes from the inside'. Moral responsibility in the central sense in question (i.e. explained by malice and wickedness) presupposes free-will in the contra-causal sense that any free act is such that alternatives are *not* physically impossible$_1$. Thus 'moral responsibility' in the important vituperative sense is *essentially* an attribute of transempirical and logically primitive persons who are free to do other than they in fact do.

The previous discussion, however, led to the conclusion that free-will in the sense presupposed by moral blame (etc.) is incompatible with physical determinism. The conception of moral responsibility that requires free-will in this sense is therefore also incompatible with physical determinism. (It is perhaps as well to point out again here that there are other senses of 'moral responsibility' that are compatible with physical determinism; and it is likely that moral responsibility in these senses is inherent in and prerequisite for social institutions. But, as will be argued later, once they are dissociated from the prevalent transcendental sense under discussion there is no obstacle to offering a naturalistic, and so a physicalistic, interpretation of them.)

2 THE NATURE OF THE INCOMPATIBILITY

Although numerous hard determinists have offered arguments to the effect that determinism is incompatible with the traditional concept of moral responsibility, there has been a great deal of confusion about the *nature* of this incompatibility. In fact, it would seem that few determinists have been very clear about the nature of their case against orthodox moral responsibility. One droll consequence of this is that scientific determinists frequently proceed from the argument that the concept of moral responsibility is otiose because it requires free-will in a sense that science refutes, to the conclusion that scientists have a moral responsibility (or duty) to inform the world of this fact. Thus Thomas Huxley earnestly maintained that 'volitions do not enter [at all] into the chain of causation[9] ... which in unbroken continuity compasses that which is and has been and shall be – the sum of existence',[10] and equally earnestly that: 'It is the plain *duty* of each and all of us *to try* to make the little corners we influence somewhat less ... ignorant [of this fact] than it was before we entered it.'[11] In similarly equivocal vein John Taylor has recently argued that: 'scientists carry a great responsibility to prepare society for the unwelcome conclusion of their work that free-will is an illusion'.[12]

Determinists have thus typically not been very clear about what perhaps is the true metaphysical nature of their position. As a result they have offered arguments that seem to give rise to such paradoxical conclusions that their case has seemed insupportable, and even incoherent. It will be useful therefore to discuss the nature of the basic confusion, and the way in which the main paradox arises from it, in order to show how apparent confusion and paradox can be resolved.

First the confusion. What determinists seem not to have been very clear about is whether scientifically based determinism renders the concept of moral responsibility meaningful but empty (i.e. without application) or meaningless and so otiose.[13] The most common scientific determinist view seems to be that, at the first-order level at which detailed scientific knowledge is vitally relevant, it turns out (or at least is highly probable) that there is no behaviour that cannot be explained causal–deterministically: all behaviour is excused on grounds of physical necessity, so no behaviour is morally responsible in the central orthodox sense of the word. That is to say, the concept is meaningful but empty if science can offer a complete causal account of all behaviour.

This interpretation of the determinist's position is supported by the frequent assertion by determinists that we ought not to blame, or that it is wrong to blame,[14] or that it is better if we do not blame, or that it is morally indefensible to blame, someone whose behaviour is inevitable (that is to say: everybody at all times). As Edwards succinctly puts it: 'From the fact that human beings do not ultimately shape their own character ... it *follows* that they are never morally responsible.'[15] Edwards himself suggests that 'follow' here means something like logical entailment.

But (and this is the paradox) it has often been argued that, far from there being a logical or quasi-logical implication that nobody is ever morally responsible on the deterministic thesis (or in other words that everyone is always excused), something like the opposite is true: all excuses, including excuses on grounds of causal necessity, logically imply excuse *from* something – and moral responsibility and moral blame are what one is excused from. So morally excusing arguments presuppose moral responsibility and therefore logically cannot be used to render it empty, otherwise they are self-defeating. In short, we cannot excuse *anybody* from moral responsibility if *everybody* is excused *a priori* on determinist grounds or any other grounds, because the very concept of moral excuse entails some application for the concept of moral responsibility.

The confusion revealed by this sound logical argument can perhaps be clarified by appealing to the metaphysical thesis advanced in the present essay, namely that there are two root models involved in the dispute. What determinism says is not so much that nobody is ever morally responsible in the sense of the term underwritten by the orthodox model, but rather that the whole (OA) metaphysical view in which this concept of moral responsibility functions is redundant. Such redundancy is not an internal logical implication of the redundant system itself but involves a metaphysical shift. Thus the major consequence of determinism for moral responsibility is not internal to the OA model (rendering it meaningful but empty) but external to it (rendering it meaningless and otiose), and this is because moral responsibility in the sense in question is outside of the explanatory conceptual schema for mind-directed human behaviour inherent in the successor PO model.[16] The determinist's case therefore is not based on a 'proper' interpretation of moral responsibility within the OA model which science renders empty (as a sense without a reference), so much as on the redundancy of the OA metaphysic of 'persons' and the related concept of moral responsibility that is rendered meaningless in the shift to the PO model.

Confusions must frequently arise in this way from the fact that two root metaphysical models may co-exist in the conceptual schema of the

276

same individual. In general, external metaphysical theses about the redundancy of metaphysical models may be confusedly construed as implying consequences within the value system defined by the redundant metaphysical system, whereas in fact the value system itself is redundant along with the metaphysic in which it inheres.

Another related matter that has been stressed repeatedly throughout the present book can be usefully repeated again here because it is sometimes supposed that metaphysical models are deliberately chosen, and chosen on the basis of the values they entail.[17] If this were so, then the OA model might be adopted precisely because it preserves values by preserving a sense of the importance of man's freedom and moral responsibility.[18] However, metaphysical models are prior to the value systems that follow from them, or rather values are implicit in root models. Consequently, not so much is the OA metaphysic attractive because it preserves a sense of the importance of man's freedom and moral responsibility, but rather the presupposition of man's freedom and moral responsibility are inherent in the metaphysic itself and thus are presented *as* the values that are believed to be worth preserving. The power of physical determinism, the reason for its successful aggression, is not that more and more people see it as satisfying certain values (on the contrary, it is often embraced only reluctantly[19]) but that science makes it increasingly perspicuous. IT thus has profound ethical significance because it is the basis of a perspicuous reconstrual of action in terms of physical determinist categories. This is a final extension of physicalist 'aggression' into the human value domain.

I conclude therefore that, as a consequence of IT, moral responsibility, in the sense of the term connoting guilt, blame, etc., is rendered otiose, and that the perspicuity of the PO model is not in the last analysis a matter for metaphysical choice based on value preference, but itself defines value preferences.

3 CONSEQUENCES

Many philosophers have contemplated the main conclusion drawn here and have supposed the most far-reaching and dire consequences to follow from a general acceptance of determinism. Human self-esteem,[20] ordinary and essential ways of talking about individual abilities,[21] the humane institutions of praise[22] and excuses,[23] ordinary interpersonal attitudes[24] and even the possibility of scientific knowledge itself[25] are just some of the most essential and valued features of human life as we know it which are supposedly put in jeopardy by physical determinism. McDougal went so far as to claim that the whole of civilised life was at stake.[26] Any thesis that appears to involve such far-reaching consequences as these calls for a closer examination. Some of these issues and several others have already been discussed, so just four of the most important ones will be discussed here. These are (1) human self-esteem; (2) the concept of responsibility underlying the practice of praise, blame and excuses; (3) interpersonal attitudes; (4) social and civil institutions. Perhaps this will be sufficient to establish what is justifiable and what the determinist does not seek to justify.

3.1 *Human Self-Esteem*

Among the most widely resisted consequences of physical determinism is the supposition that it downgrades, diminishes, deflates or demeans man's image of himself by making him out to be a 'mere' physical organism[27] and denying him uniqueness, rationality and choice.

This line of argument is essentially vacuous, for as Hume wisely said,[28]

it is not certain an opinion is false because it is of dangerous or dis-
agreeable consequence. And arguments of this type should be
foreborn as serving nothing to the discovery of truth, but only to
make the person of an antagonist odious.

Actually, as has been made abundantly clear already, IT does not deny uniqueness, rationality and choice but construes them in physicalist terms as, respectively, genetic and experiential uniqueness, causes from the inside, and 'self-causation'. There is, therefore, this much truth at least in Skinner's claim that nothing is changed by merely thinking about it.[29] Unless we are prepared to argue as well that man was in some important sense demeaned by heliocentricity and evolution, there is no philosophically important sense in which he is demeaned by IT, and physical determinism. On the contrary, if words mean anything at all, nothing could be more demeaning than to sustain comfortable and flattering superstitions against sound evidence to the contrary.

There is another and more substantial point that emerges from previous discussion of the orthodox concept of a person, and one that anticipates the discussion of jurisprudential issues to come. By logically relating the concept of the person (memories, dispositions, etc.) to the functionally integrated central system of his body, IT opens the way to an extension of a discernible historical trend towards more specific attribution of responsibility for 'immoral' acts.[30] In less developed communities moral responsibility for misdemeanours has been attributed to whole nations: offences committed by one were (still are!) held against all. Historically, with increasing enlightenment responsibility has become more narrowly distributed: to tribes, families, branches of families, and eventually to individuals. Or rather, what *counts* as an individual has changed, so that now only an anatomically differentiated individual – the social atom – is held responsible for an act he has committed.

But there is in principle no need for the rational process underlying the trend to stop here. It is frequently said that actions are performed 'against the inclinations of a better self', or that someone was 'not himself' when he committed an offence. We all understand the sort of thing that is implied here, though the concept of a person as logically primitive renders such locutions literally unintelligible. The problem for the orthodoxy raised here is the problem of how to single out for blame and punishment the supposedly 'free' self from all of the admittedly determined components of character. Though we may believe that an individual's delinquent actions are caused by some particular trait or disorder we condemn and punish the 'whole person'.[31] The physicalist avoids this problem by treating crime as the outcome of a relatively localised malfunction and not holding the entire (anatomically differentiated) individual to account; and in this he is merely continuing the trend towards an ever more precise attribution of responsibility for bad behaviour.

However, although this trend has its merits, it might be argued that there is a good deal of sense still in the old institutions of vendetta and blood feud, for a man's behaviour is determined not only by his nature but also by nurture; i.e., it also reflects to a greater or lesser extent the norms of the community in which he has been nurtured. So remedial measures directed towards the social sources of deviance (in general the supra-systems in which the individual participates) are as pertinent as those directed towards intradermal sub-systems. What such measures have in common and what gives them point is their role as natural regulators among hierarchies of integrated systems. But whether the causes of an individual's deviance are in his sub-systemic (i.e. inner, psychological, etc.) relations, his supra-systemic (interpersonal, communal, social, etc.) relations or (as is more probable) a combination of both, there is no ground for involving non-natural transempirical entities or transcendent criteria (except in the literal sense attached to group participation).

Summarily, the objection that human self-esteem is demeaned by physical determinism is insupportable, except in a trivial sense following from an inflated superstition. The 'person' is properly regarded as embedded in a hierarchy of natural systems, and not as absolutely unique and autonomous.

3.2 Responsibility: Praise, Blame and Excuses

A frequent objection to determinism since Aristotle has been that, if by denying free-will it denies the agent's ultimate responsibility for his actions, it undermines not only his liability to moral blame but his liability for praise as well, the assumption being that this is manifestly unthinkable. Similarly, some other philosophers have taken the obliteration of the traditional logical distinction between 'normal' (or rational) and 'abnormal' (or caused) behaviour to entail that actions that would be excusable within the OA model become inexcusable within deterministic models like physicalism.[32]

These two related arguments are both based in a failure to distinguish between different senses of the term 'moral responsibility', namely the evaluative and the attributive. Even if physical determinism does entail the redundancy of the *attribution* of moral responsibility in the central sense discussed above, it does not follow that evaluation or grading according to norms is called into question, because the evaluative sense still stands. Bearing this in mind, then, there are two aspects to each of the questions raised here. First (negatively), the vilificatory sense of 'moral responsibility' and the laudatory senses of 'praise' (e.g. eulogise, magnify, glorify) *are* rendered meaningless. On the PO view it is as vacuous to attribute responsibility for courage as it would be for eyesight, height or digestion. Each is the product of nature and nurture. But, given certain *natural* (including aculturated) preferences for some sorts of behaviour rather than others, an individual's behaviour may be evaluated or graded according to such preferences.

This concept of evaluation is the sort involved in evaluating other characteristics such as physical beauty or intelligence.[33] A person may be judged attractive or bright according to accepted and preferred norms without being thereby held responsible (i.e. praiseworthy), just as, conversely, a person may be judged unattractive or dull without being held responsible (i.e. blameworthy). Therefore, just as a person's behaviour can be judged to be incompetent or unacceptable according to some norm, and by the same token to be in need of change and improvement without being *morally* blameworthy in the vilificatory sense, so it can be judged to be competent and desirable without being praiseworthy.[34]

A common objection to this view was first offered by Aristotle himself when he argued that a person is responsible for his own character because his present dispositions have been brought about by his own past decisions. Paradigmatically, the sick man is responsible for his sickness because he failed to seek, or ignored, the doctor's advice. There are a number of counter-objections to this argument. First, it begs entirely the question raised by the case analogous to the man who seeks the doctor's advice and still is ill; that is, the case of the moral weakling and recidivist delinquent who, consistent with Aristotle's view, is presumably not responsible, but who according to the common libertarian's view (ostensibly held by Aristotle as well) is perhaps the most culpable of all.

Second, it has the preposterous consequence that we are most morally responsible in infancy and adolescence when the earliest character-forming choices are made. Third, and at the very root of the orthodox view, there is the supposition that the agent has a power that would enable him to acquire praiseworthy and desirable capacities if he only chose to exert it. But at this (first-order) level the determinist need only ask whether these powers are innate or acquired, and the libertarian is at once overthrown.[35] An infinite regress of innate versus acquired powers can be avoided only by posing the question in the context of the causal continuum within which the agent's unique character is genetically defined and experientially developed, that is to say determined by nurture but defined by nature. In short, the value placed on the institution of praising (in the sense of laud, celebrate and magnify) does not necessarily tell against determinism as Aristotle supposes, since it is quite possible and certainly consistent that both praise and blame, in the commensurate senses of the terms indicated here, are equally vacuous.

The supposed problem about the excusing game is resolved in a similar way. Should the categorial distinction between normal and abnormal be dissolved by physical determinism, this does not entail that the moral responsibility previously attached only to the concept of a 'normal' person is extended to those who would previously have been considered abnormal. The characteristically benign but suddenly crazy vicar does not become liable to moral blame where once he would have been excused. Indeed, something like the opposite is true, since if moral blame becomes otiose not only are those who were previously excused from it not subject to it, but neither is anybody else. Otiose is as otiose does.

The second (positive) point I want to make about praise and excuses concerns what is left of 'responsibility' once such connotations as 'guilt' and 'just vilification' have gone. For while in the PO view moral blame in the sense discussed does not attach to any behaviour, nevertheless some behaviour is quite naturally unacceptable in civilised communities, and as such it is natural that communal effort should be made to change it. If so, then delinquency in the sense of social incompetence or maladjustment may well entail responsibility in a number of relevant senses such as proximate cause, self-determination, fit object of sanctions, etc., which have been attached to other (vituperative)

281

connotations of the traditional term 'moral responsibility', but which are not logically dependent on them. The previous discussion of a naturalistic account of moral experience has already touched on some of the issues raised by this distinction, and they will be discussed later in connection with the social and legal consequences of IT. At this stage it is sufficient to note that physical determinism does not entail that all connotations of 'moral responsibility' are rendered otiose, only a certain mythico-poetic vestige.

A similar consequence follows from the elimination of excuses. The moral practice of excusing based on the distinction between normal and abnormal is eliminated if all behaviour is explained causally. As a consequence vituperative and magnanimous attitudes are alike rendered otiose; also, the concept of a 'normal' agent no longer marks a categorial distinction between two different logical forms of explanation, the rational–normal and the causal–abnormal. But the *phenomena* previously distinguished by these concepts are still distinguishable. Only now the distinction becomes one that reflects different types of causal mechanism. The crazy vicar's behaviour manifests a 'crazy' control system and the delinquent's delinquency manifests a maladjusted control system. The previously marked significant distinctions between differents sorts of behaviour are not necessarily eliminated on the shift to the PO model: only the explanatory concepts involved are affected.

3.3 *Interpersonal Attitudes*

One recent objection to determinism that has been much discussed is based on the thesis that the distinction between ordinary interpersonal attitudes and objective attitudes could not be sustained in a deterministic model.[36] The argument purports to show not only that determinism is inconsistent with ordinary interpersonal attitudes, but that this inconsistency refutes determinism because ordinary attitudes, such as resentment, are essential to our makeup, and it is useless to ask us to do what is not in our nature to do.[37] Finally, it is maintained that the adoption of 'objective' attitudes is not based on the thesis of determinism anyway, but on the supposition of the agent's incapacity.[38]

A sufficient objection to this view is that it makes an unwarranted *a priori* assumption about the permanence of a prevailing view and the possible (or rather the *impossible*) psychological effect on it of overwhelming evidence for determinism.[39]

But why should resentment not be suppressed or rendered otiose in the case of human behaviour just as much as in the case of inanimate objects or beasts? It is true that we may still rail in reaction against toe-stubbing rocks, recalcitrant locks and unreasonably crowing cocks, but we do not any longer, as human beings in other cultures have previously done, *resent* these things in the sense of the word held to be morally important. And should determinism prove persuasive at the level of human behaviour, as well as at these other levels, the same would presumably hold true there also.

But other objections can be raised against this argument. It is simply empirically false that a belief in determinism changes interpersonal attitudes drastically and for the worse. A lover's fervour is undiminished by a knowledge of hormones. In general, the fact that certain attitudes are associated with certain causal processes does not entail that knowledge of these processes entirely alters these attitudes from exclusively personal to exclusively objective. Indeed, far from this being the case, perfectly sensible human beings show a remarkable tendency to adopt interpersonal attitudes towards objects that they believe or know to be entirely determined, such as animals, and even artefacts. The claim that determinism (impossibly) requires or entails a calamitous change in our makeup and normal interpersonal attitudes is therefore groundless (in so far as it does not itself assume determinism!). Finally, it is difficult to see why normal attitudes are suspended when they are, unless it is because the resented actions come to be seen as following naturally and necessarily from (i.e. as determined by) some incapacitating *cause* such as the agent's unrealistic pictures of reality, or unconscious purposes.[40]

Far from guaranteeing normal interpersonal attitudes against deterministic objectification, the 'resentful makeup' thesis offers a conservative rationale for a commonplace pharisaical attitude which is in sharp contrast to the expansive views expressed by determinist sages throughout the history of philosophy. Thus Marcus Aurelius wrote:[41]

> How cruel it is not to allow men to strive after the things which appear to them to be suitable to their nature and profitable! And yet in a manner thou dost not allow them to do this, when thou art vexed because they do wrong. For they are certainly moved towards things because they suppose them to be suitable to their nature and profitable to them – But it is not so – Teach them then without being angry.

and 'If a man be mistaken, instruct him kindly and show him his error. But if thou art not able, blame thyself, or blame not even thyself'.[42] Spinoza wrote:[43]

> He who rightly realises that all things follow from the necessity of divine nature and come to pass in accordance with the eternal laws and rules of nature will not find anything worthy of hatred, derision or contempt, nor will he bestow pity on anything, but to the utmost extent of human virtue he will endeavour to do well, as the saying is, and to rejoyce.

The opening words of the oldest Taoist poem say:[44]

> The perfect way (Tao) is without difficulty
> Save that it avoids picking and choosing.
> Only when you stop liking and disliking
> Will all be clearly understood.
> A split hair's difference,
> And Heaven and Earth are set apart!
> If you want to get the plain truth,
> Be not concerned with right and wrong,
> The conflict between right and wrong
> Is the sickness of the mind.

The notorious materialist La Mettrie expresses similar thoughts in a more colourful vein:[45]

> If nature has made you a hog, go and wallow in the mire like a swine, for you are capable of no higher happyness and your remorse would only poison the only happyness of which you are capable without benefitting anybody.

And in this century the famous American attorney Clarence Darrow once addressed the prisoners in Cook County Jail as follows:[46]

> There is no such thing as a crime as the word is generally understood. I do not believe there is any sort of distinction between the real moral conditions of the people in and out of jail. One is just as good as the other. The people here can no more help being here than the people outside can avoid being outside. I do not believe that people are in jail because they deserve to be. They are in jail simply because they cannot avoid it on account of circumstances which are entirely beyond their control, and for which they are in no way responsible. ... You could not help it any more than we outside can help taking the positions that we take.

Finally, the last word on the determinist ethic was perhaps expressed by Tristram Shandy's Uncle Toby, who quoth of some confounded mess: 'they should have wiped it up and said no more about it'.[47]

3.4   Social Institutions

It has commonly been thought that physical determinism not only has consequences for man's self-esteem, praise and excuses, and interpersonal attitudes, but that the very fabric of human life would be affected should it prevail. Typically, the libertarian McDougal believed that a philosophy of physical determinism would be calamitous for civilisation,[48] and the determinist John Taylor has recently conjectured that 'the loss of free-will can only cause a complete alteration of the institutions that are now the pillars of society'.[49] This consequence supposedly follows from the removal of the supposed behavioural constraints associated with the concept of responsibility and depending upon free-will together with the downgrading of human self-esteem.

Underlying this view is the assumption that determinism renders otiose everything that the concept of 'moral responsibility' connotes. In fact, as we have seen, in ordinary usage the term has a very wide semantic range, most of which is retained and essentially unaffected by the metaphysical shift from the OA to the PO model, which renders only the guilt-laden and vituperative connotations redundant.[50] It may be said that this is rather an inconsequential mouse of a conclusion to draw from elephantine physicalist labours. But even if this were the only consequence, it is no mere bagatelle that people should be more understanding, more tolerant and kindlier to one another. And there is no special fairness (whatever else there may be) in blaming and punishing what the redundant orthodoxy calls 'morally blameworthy' misdemeanours – no more than there is in the case of any other, non-moral, variety of strict or vicarious liability.

Nevertheless, it is sometimes said that, unless physical determinism really did have something like the dire social consequences that some philosophers have supposed, it is essentially an uninteresting position.[51] Hare has suggested for example that, so long as people need to ask the question 'What shall I do?', then moral freedom and responsibility are sufficiently guaranteed; so if the determinist does not deny this need, he is not saying anything consequential about moral responsibility. But this (compatibilist) assumption is profoundly mistaken if it is also supposed (as it commonly is) that no naturalistic account of moral experience is possible, even in principle, and that attempts to formulate a naturalistic ethics are on a logical par with attempts to square the circle.[52] It is argued that because we are the sorts of things we are, i.e. human beings, sharing common forms of life, regulative principles and prescriptions and obligations are indispensible. So far so good: this is entirely compatible with physical determinism, depending on what we mean by human beings and on how principles, prescriptions and obligations are construed. But the further supposition, that a naturalistic account of moral experience, in so far as it is coherent at all, must be based on a fallacy, is inconsistent with physical determinism. Therefore it is a significant consequence of physical determinism that it challenges the widespread philosophical supposition that ethical naturalism is impossible.

285

I have already defended the supposed 'naturalistic fallacy' against a number of attacks and sketched in a naturalistic account of moral experience from the IT standpoint (Chapter VIII, Section 6.2.7). Moral experience, it was suggested, can be construed naturalistically on the basis of such concepts as relations, norms, goal-directedness and developmental initiation or communal conditioning through verbal communication, taken together with the concept of biperspectival access implicit in IT. If the thesis of physical determinism can be extended into the value domain in this way by means of IT, then value inquiry can once again be tied to scientific knowledge. Biology, psychology and social anthropology are again vitally relevant to normative experience, but on a new basis: the concepts of cybernetics and general system theory (among others) promise to be sufficiently well articulated to render a thoroughly naturalistic but non-Procrustean account of it.[53] Notwithstanding the prevailing conventional wisdom that knowledge of causes can tell us nothing of motives, purposes and values, it is becoming increasingly obvious that systematic natural knowledge of human life and mores can be profoundly important for an understanding of normative experience of human relations.[54]

What this implies is that normative experience is natural and intrinsic to participation in human social groups. Regulative principles, prescriptions and so forth are physical systemic constraints 'from the inside' (Chapter V, Section 4.4). There is no gainsaying that human normative experience is probably special in nature, but this status is entirely natural, commensurate with the special status humans have in biological evolution. There is no need to suppose that there is anything irreducibly 'non-natural' about it. On the contrary, it is frequently observed, and as often demonstrated, that no regulative principle or law can prevail that does not reflect the natural sentiments and beliefs and inclinations of any community.[55] As many moralists have recognised, it is human *nature*, or as the physicalist would say biology, that guarantees communal life as well as normal interpersonal attitudes, altruism, truth telling and the like.

3.4.1 *Science and norms*
There is a close and illuminating parallel to be drawn at this point between the syntactical rules regulating speech and the normative principles regulating communal behaviour. Both sorts of rule are normally implicit, generative (i.e. do not require 'conditioning' to all cases), (presumably) biologically based, but culturally variable. Wittgenstein remarked that there is a way of grasping a rule that is not an *interpretation* but is exhibited in what we call 'obeying a rule' and 'going against it' in actual cases.[56] If rules involve the concepts of right

and wrong in this sense they would seem to introduce a normative aspect into human and social science that has hitherto always been avoided.[57]

This conclusion need give no cause for concern about scientific objectivity, if the biological basis of rule-following behaviour is borne in mind. In the case of language, for example, it is significant that a child acquires it from parents who, typically, cannot say what the formal structures that determine competent usage are, though of course some sort of prudential account in terms of the practical need to observe conventions could be offered. Otherwise, it is sufficient that the child be allowed to grow up naturally in an environment where language is used. Perhaps the same may be said of the principles regulating behaviour: that for a child to acquire a working knowledge of behaviour norms (behavioural syntax) it is sufficient that the child be allowed to grow up naturally in an environment where norms operate. Socialisation is imitation and involves the totality of the operations enabling the individual to subordinate himself to the precepts and demands of the group.[58] So the regulative principles of practical reason (moral values) are synthetic *a priori* principles: *a priori* because they are prior to the experience of any given individual (being phylogenetically determined products of biological evolution), and synthetic because the phylogenetically predetermined capacities are developed in individual experience. In a word, normative capacity is innate and genetically determined; actual norms are acquired and culturally determined. And values always involve some relation between the needs of human beings and the conditions that impose and satisfy those needs. Thus a naturalistic account of normative experience is not necessarily a conceptual muddle based on an elementary and easily detected logical fallacy. Far from undermining social institutions, physical determinism renders an account of them in terms of man's nature.

Now the increase in our knowledge of causal determination itself constitutes a new development in the human environment (a largely symbolic one). It quite likely calls for some adjustment in the relationships and interactions within human groups, as such changes commonly do.[59] The process of adjustment to a changed situation quite possibly involves the redundancy of once-important co-ordinating concepts and principles. But there is no basis in this for the conclusion that organised human life as such is necessarily threatened: only a readjustment is implied. The fact would seem to be that those philosophers who have supposed calamity or profound social upheaval to follow from a general belief in determinism have overlooked the very physical–deterministic account of human societies the acceptance of which is supposed: which is that human societies are a species of self-regulating biological system and as such they adjust to change by changing.

This last point is pertinent to the other extreme response, the conservative one, which supposes that the relationships, concepts, norms, attitudes and feelings prevalent at some particular time and place (usually twentieth-century England) must be paradigmatic of all times and places. Clearly this is a mistake. Our systems need to maintain their identity and their ability to support the self-identity of those who belong to them, but they must at the same time be capable of frequently transforming themselves.[60]

3.4.2   *Social self-regulation*

Something must now be said about the controversy surrounding control of the factors affecting social relations. I have already deployed several fairly routine arguments against completely behaviouristic accounts of human experience (Chapter III, Section 5.1). IT as developed here denies even the central assumption of behaviourism, i.e. that 'mental' states of agents can be ignored. Nevertheless, physicalism and behaviourism share the important credo that the factors completely determining human behaviour are amenable in principle to scientific investigation and control and change.

The suggestion that this possibility should be pursued along the lines of a kind of social engineering[61] has met with bitter opposition from orthodox philosophers and others. But the central assumption, which the present thesis supports, is simply that *whatever* behaviours are developed they all follow from nature and nurture, i.e. are causal consequents of genetic and environmental factors. The plain evidence of *Les Enfants Sauvages* suggests this with particular force. There are no liberal saints isolated in jungles. So if the autonomous behaviour of respected and admired individuals, whoever they are, is, as the thesis suggests, completely determined by nature and nurture, then what results is not the end of human society but an added incentive to search out the causal seeds from which those worthies sprang and to sow them, so far as we are able, at the expense of those seeds that are destined to flower into behaviour of kinds that have been abhorred at all times and in all human communities. It is Quixotic to argue, as is frequently done, that it is better to be made in God's image, albeit as an insufferable lout, than to be any kind of *merely* natural man,[62] and mistaken to think that the whole approach begs the 'moral' question of the values that are to be systematically pursued and also who is to decide and apply them.

In the first place, a fortunate genetic inheritance and a favourable upbringing are none the less genetically and developmentally determining because what they determine happens to be an autonomous

288

person. In the second place, social engineering need suppose no other values than already naturally exist and (what is more) are already pursued, however ineffectively, with all the available determining apparatus at the command of family, state and educational and social institutions.

It is perhaps necessary to explain what is meant by the use here of the term 'social engineering', which might otherwise be misunderstood as implying the advocacy of a Brave New World approach to things. First, it must be borne in mind that in the PO model human society and human culture are determinate products of biological evolution no less than basal metabolism is. Social and cultural factors, therefore, are to be included among the factors that, quite naturally, determine individual and group behaviour. It follows from this that knowledge of how such factors determine behaviour can be deployed (indeed, is now and always has been widely deployed) to influence human behaviour. Such intentional influencing of behaviour by changing its social determinants is aptly called social engineering, whether piecemeal or wholesale. Other more familiar and less alarming names for exactly the same thing are 'child development', 'education' and 'social policy'. Needless to say, none of this is at all inconsistent with the most liberal and democratic social and political institutions.

The physicalism advanced here will surely attract less odium and acrimony than radical behaviourism because a significant implication of IT is that, as a *central state* theory, it does not suppose that 'behaviours' are completely determined by environmental variables alone. Concepts such as deliberation, choice and self-initiated goal-directed action, which are central to the orthodox model of autonomous human behaviour, are retained within the PO model. In a very important sense we have not been (*could* not have been) thinking, talking and living complete nonsense all these millenia. But the OA assumption of some sort of categorially distinct, a-causal, normative domain of human action is no longer supportable.

3.4.3 *Moric responsibility and moral responsibility*
By way of conclusion to this section, let us speculate on what we might gain from a moratorium on the use of the term 'moral responsibility', if such a thing were possible. The term 'moral responsibility' currently has vituperative and non-natural connotations. So even if there should be a general acceptance of a PO model and these particular connotations became otiose, it is likely that the trailing clouds of etymology would continue to cling to the term and its usage. Indeed, something like this was suggested earlier in the case of those philosophers who reject the theistic and mythic basis of transempirical values, but who nevertheless

still persistently hold ethical naturalism to be fallacious. There may be some advantages therefore in digging up another etymological root to graft the expurgated semantic range of 'moral responsibility' on to, namely 'mores'.

The term 'mores' has thoroughly terrestrial connotations like 'folkways' and 'customs', which 'morals', with its religious associations and connotations of high virtue, righteousness and piety, does not have. At the same time the semantic range of 'mores' overlaps considerably with 'morals' in the sense of being so basic as to develop the force of law. 'Mores' also clearly connotes laws that are regarded by a social group as essential to its preservation and welfare, which 'morals' with its categorical connotations does not. Clearly, therefore, 'mores' is a more appropriate term with which to express the physicalist–determinist's systemic conception of values as involving relations between human needs and goals and the conditions that impose and satisfy them. 'Moric responsibility' suggests all that is intelligible about 'moral responsibility' on a PO model, without introducing any extraneous non-natural connotations, and so something might be gained from its adoption in a physicalist system (if such a thing were possible).

4   SUMMARY AND CONCLUSIONS

With the emergence of the PO model and the postulate of IT, the perennial metaphysical dispute about free-will versus determinism takes the substantive form of a dispute about the coherence and explanatory power of specifically physical determinism. Against a background of developments in such fields as neurology, learning-net theory and cybernetics, the physical determinist's case turns on the crucial role of instantaneous system states as determinants of behaviour. This follows a distinction often drawn by philosophers between two levels of determinism that have often been confused. Ordinary discourse and orthodox philosophy address themselves primarily to an indispensable but relatively naïve and superficial analysis of determination which discounts scientific knowledge of first-order central-state determinants of behaviour. IT, on the contrary, positively entails that central states and processes are involved as sufficient determinants in precisely those mind-directed actions that supposedly refute determinism. Once central states and processes are interpolated into the mass–energic continuum, then volition can only be construed (as indeed it has been since Aristotle's time)[63] as self-determination. The more or less novel feature of IT and the PO model in general is that it construes 'self' as rooted in the more or less invariant structural forms of the central nervous system and brain.

Accordingly, the libertarian view that mind-directed agent action is somehow outside the physical–causal continuum is inconsistent with the view that emerges from the human sciences. Given the distinctions between different levels of determination and different senses of 'possible' required by the PO model, the determinist position can meet the major objections that have been directed against it. Conversely, the main positive arguments advanced in support of the libertarian view are inadequate, and in fact the cogent evidence appealed to by the libertarian can be rendered coherent within the PO model. Central to the determinist's case is the notion of a shift from the OA root model of persons and their acts to the PO root model (IT version).

The consequences for morals of such a shift are not, however, so radical as has sometimes been supposed by both libertarians and determinists. This is because the present semantic range of moral terms is very wide. 'Moral responsibility' not only has the central and peculiarly moral connotations of 'guilt-ladenness' and 'fit object of vituperative blame', but also such connotations as 'accountable', which are more neutral and less closely related to the orthodox supposition of wickedness and free volition. So although a shift in root model from the OA to the PO would make these peculiarly moral connotations redundant, the point of most *ordinary* moral discourse is left intact. However, the consequences for *libertarian* moral discourse are profound, since the redundant connotations of moral terms are central to it because they are so closely related to the OA model of persons. The coherence of the physical determinist's case depends on the view that the orthodox model of persons and their acts and the related (central) connotations of moral terms are not themselves 'wrong' and immoral in the orthodox senses of these words so much as non-perspicuous and otiose within the emerging PO model.

Finally, opponents of the PO model have greatly exaggerated its consequences for (1) human self-esteem, (2) responsibility, praise, blame and excuses, (3) interpersonal attitudes and (4) social institutions.

1 It is true that the prevailing orthodox concept of persons tends to be deflated by the PO model; but since it is evidently an already inflated view (the last vestige of an extreme cultural anthropomorphism) this particular deflationary charge does not tell against the PO model any more than did similar charges against Galileo and Darwin.

2 Similarly, certain central aspects of orthodox conceptions of responsibility, praise and blame are liable to be rendered otiose. Again, this does not count against the PO model. But far from entailing that everybody is culpable and *blameworthy* in the orthodox sense because nobody is excusable, the PO model entails that not only are those who are excused not blameworthy, but neither is anybody else, in the

orthodox sense. This is because the orthodox categories of praise and blame, within which the concept of excuses functions, are otiose and redundant.

3 With regard to interpersonal attitudes there is no reason to suppose that physical determinism is more likely than any other metaphysical model to undermine what is intrinsically valuable, always bearing in mind that what is valuable is defined within the conceptual framework of a root model. Metaphysical and conceptual shifts can take place and we shall continue to be human.[64] Further even than this, there is ample evidence from the writings of philosopher sages to support the view that hard determinism is a potent antidote to the unimaginative pharisaical cant to which the orthodox view of autonomous persons all too easily gives rise.

4 The supposed consequences of a shift to the deterministic PO model for social institutions has been no less exaggerated than other supposed consequences. One potentially profound consequence of IT, however, is that it opens up the possibility once more that the human sciences can be made directly relevant to normative experience. If what 'is' can inform us about what 'ought', without reduction, within the PO framework, then the possibility of a scientific ethics becomes as real as, for example, a scientific linguistics (Section 3.4 above).

I conclude that, among the supposed consequences of physical determinism, some that are supposedly undesirable do follow but are not so undesirable as has been supposed, while others do not follow, and yet others are implied that promise a positive advance on prevailing orthodox views in the direction of understanding and evaluating human behaviour.

PART FIVE

Today we pity the insane who used to be burned. A day will come when delinquents too will inspire pity; which will not prevent us from protecting ourselves against their attacks.

Gabriel de Tarde (1912, p. 59)

X

PHYSICALISM AND JURISPRUDENCE

1 INTRODUCTION

The previous chapters have been concerned with a cluster of perennial philosophical problems in their contemporary form. Although questions of mind-directed action, free-will and moral responsibility have traditionally been central to discussions of legal responsibility, guilt and punishment, the implications for law of IT and physical determinism have not been discussed among philosophers. The prevailing view seems to be that philosophical questions of mind and free-will have few if any practical implications for most questions of guilt and blame.[1]

Nevertheless, just as the perennial questions of mind and morals remain with us in spite of the celebrated revolution in philosophy, so do the related legal questions. To cite one conspicuous example, the British Psychological Society, of its evidence to the Butler Commission (1975) on the law relating to mentally abnormal offenders, said that the present state of psychological knowledge makes nonsense of the current legal concepts of responsibility and guilt, and that it is time that the implications of this were examined for a medico-legal system that seems to be unaware of them.[2]

It is appropriate therefore to pursue the thesis that IT provides the key for a final foreclosure of physicalism on the domain of human mentality, rationality and purposefulness into the area of jurisprudence, and the criminal law in particular. The hope is that the foregoing discussion will illuminate some of the current legal problems arising from advances in scientific understanding of human behaviour.

The thesis advanced here is as follows.
1 The prevailing state of the law and in particular the disposition of offenders is unsatisfactory.

2 Much of the trouble with the law and the legal disposition of offenders arises from the differences in root models of persons which lawyers and scientists operate with. The law presupposes the obsolescent OA model, and scientists suppose an extreme objective model.
3 The differences between law and science can be reconciled within the emerging PO model of persons as informed by IT.
4 The shift from the OA model to a PO model in law is consistent with a well-established trend previously pointed out by Gabriel de Tarde.

2 THE STATE OF THE LAW

Before going on to consider some jurisprudential problems in detail it will be instructive to survey the state of the field we are about to enter. There can be no doubt that anomaly, confusion and downright iniquity abound.

First, anomaly: one man kills because of the effect of a brain tumour on his otherwise normal behaviour and is acquitted without qualification (and, so far as the law is concerned, presumably free to kill again), on the grounds that he is not insane and the killing was unintentional.[3] Another man with a substantially similar defect, a bone growth pressing on his brain, commits robbery with aggravation and is committed to prison for five years on the grounds that at the time of the offence he was not *totally* irresponsible for his acts despite clinical evidence that surgical removal of the offending bone transformed his previous belligerent disposition to one of normality.[4]

Second, confusion: in a case substantially similar to the previous two a man killed his wife because of the effect of arteriosclerosis cutting off the blood supply to his brain. The presiding judge after careful consideration specifically deemed him *not* to be suffering from a physical disease but a mental one and allowed an *insanity* defense.[5] Whatever the merits of this otherwise very sound judgment, within the orthodox model undoubtedly assumed by the judge in question (Lord Devlin; see Chapter XI, Section 2.2.1), there is manifest ambivalence about the relation between mental and physical disorder, and their relation to insanity and criminal responsibility.

Finally, iniquity: it abounds on both sides of the metaphysical divide. Exponents of the orthodox view of persons have typically had no compunction about criminally convicting and even executing individuals who, according to unanimous and highly expert evidence, are deeply disordered in a way that substantially affects their behaviour, on the grounds that, no matter what experts say, if a *jury* is satisfied that an offender is responsible, it is not for the courts of appeal to say he is not.[6]

Some of the consequences of the extreme objective, instrumental view of deviance, are just as atrocious. A recently notorious case in America involved a youth being committed to an institution where he was detained under psychiatric supervision for thirty-four years following theft of goods valued at five dollars.[7] Clearly, the present state of affairs in legal philosophy and practice is what might loosely be called a mess.

Many students of penal philosophy have lamented the present state of affairs in the law which seems to be worse even than the mess that all the other affairs of men are prone to. Some have drawn attention to the changing moral climate within which law is practised which affects the public's conception of the proper treatment of the convicted offender.[8] The general trend has been toward a 'soft head' or 'treatment' line in law, in keeping with the more general tendency towards the dissemination of scientific knowledge of the causes of deviant behaviour and 'hard head' scientific attitudes generally. But as already indicated, although this trend has tended to remedy some of the worst abuses owing to the worst sort of pre-scientific thinking, it seems to have brought about abuses of a different and equally deplorable kind.

Any satisfactory philosophy of law must reconcile the conflicts evident in the present situation. There is the need to resolve the practical principles of criminal law with the deterministic view of human behaviour emerging from science. Practically, there is also the need to reconcile reasonable social demands for tolerable behaviour with tolerable social liberty. In the past these diverse requirements have proven difficult to reconcile because of differences of purpose and operational logic separating the lawyer, the policeman and the judge from the scientist. It is increasingly apparent that there is a need for a common rationale within which these differences can be reconciled. As one writer has put it, we are in the midst of a profound re-examination of all our social structures, punishment structures included. We have a definite need for a new moral philosophy which can support a new penal code.[9]

Three ideas that are central to the thesis advanced in this book are important for understanding current disputes in jurisprudence. These are the idea of root model conflict, the idea of dual access to natural processes (biperspectivism) and the idea of eidescopic shift or change in root model.

3   ROOT MODEL CONFLICT

Traditional and current orthodoxy, especially among jurists, lawyers and the executive branch of the law, is overwhelmingly derived from what I have characterised as the OA model of human individuality: the autonomous (and more or less transempirical) person. Lord Radcliffe has observed for example that it has taken centuries for English judges to realise that the tenets and injunctions of the Christian religion were not a part of the common law of England.[10] But this observation is clearly premature and over-optimistic when at the same time another lord justice, Hodson, claims that even if Christianity be not part of the Law of England, yet the common law has its roots in Christianity;[11] and Lord Devlin goes so far as to define 'real' crimes as 'sins with legal definitions'.[12]

Forensic scientists and like minds, on the other hand, tend to regard the practical problems raised by deviant human behaviour in purely instrumental terms within the objective framework of the human life sciences. Typically (if abrasively), J. E. Macdonald has argued that:[13]

the concepts of responsibility in legal and psychiatric practice (are) theological and metaphysical anachronisms best relegated to the amusement of the religious and others of that kidney. All that matters in any case of anti-social behaviour is that appropriate action may be decided upon. Questions of 'mad' or 'bad' with their value judgements and emotional loadings do not arise. We are confronted by a person who has committed some action that is abnormal by its infrequency of occurrence and that has brought its doer into conflict with his fellows; we have to decide how to obviate or minimise repetitions of such conflict for the good of all concerned.

Macdonald himself seems to be unaware that his own view is itself rooted in another alternative metaphysical model, an extreme reductionist materialist one.

It is evident therefore from the expression of these extreme and typical views that disagreements in jurisprudence quite likely derive from differences in root model, along the lines already discussed previously in connection with theoretical disputes about the mental, human action and moral responsibility.

In particular, the criminal law has traditionally assumed, in the absence of evidence to the contrary, that people have it in their power to choose whether to do a criminal act or not, and that he who chooses to do such an act is responsible for the resulting evil.[14] Forensic–behavioural scientists on the contrary presuppose that, despite *prima facie* evidence to the contrary, human action is completely determined.[15] The point is not merely that there is a class of offenders who are (supposedly) mentally ill and whose behaviour is determined, but that the *entire range* of human behaviour is determined by potentially explicable and predictable processes. The issue raised in this book is the growing support for the view that this supposition is entirely warranted so that it is no longer merely a metaphysical assumption or the *modus operandi* of a sciencing game, but has implications beyond the domain of science. To be sure, penal philosophers who have addressed themselves to the problem of general determinism have found strong support in the empiricist philosophical tradition for the view that the metaphysical problem of free-will and determinism is irrelevant to the practical problems faced by the law, because according to this view freedom means just the absence of compulsion. The legal view tends to be that a criminal act presupposes will but not free-will in the metaphysical sense of the term.[16]

4 ANALYTICAL ISOLATION OF PARTICIPANT AND OBJECTIVE PERSPECTIVES

The typical juristic view is attributable to the fact that, in the main, judges and lawyers as a class are trained for the practical accomplishment of society's goals, not for generalised discussion of the meaning and import such goals have for life or their philosophical justification.[17] Unfortunately this is so even when prevailing views are wrong-headed, prescientific and otiose. Holmes for example argued that the *first* requirement of a sound body of law is that it should correspond with the actual feelings and demands of the community, *whether right or wrong*, and that the purpose of law is to put a stop to actual physical theft and murder: law and order are required above all else, even above equality and moral justice. All law is directed towards inducing external conformity to a rule, and individuals should be sacrificed to this purpose if necessary.[18] Lord Goddard confirmed this general preventive view when he expressed the opinion that the duty of the courts quite simply is to punish, and that reform of the prisoner is not the court's business.[19] The same view is expressed in a standard text on jurisprudence: that the object of criminal law is not to reform men's hearts but to stamp out courses of conduct that either offend the minimum ethic or are socially inexpedient.[20]

Now, the practical juristic view expressed in these remarks is similar in many ways to the scientific view as expressed in Macdonald's remarks quoted earlier. Both recognise a practical need to control anti-social behaviour. This common practical purpose is the basis for reconciling practical and scientifically informed views. Where the two views diverge radically is in their perception of the nature of the problem and their approach to its eradication. The law, with its roots in the orthodox model of persons, still sees delinquency basically in terms of

299

the orthodox categories of free-will, moral responsibility, guilt, blame and retributive sanctions. Crime is attributed mainly to old-fashioned personal immorality. Approved remedies include moralistic exhortation and denunciation, retributive sanctions, and deterrent threats. Such views seem to be a consequence of isolating the practical or participant's mode of experience from objective scientific knowledge of the determinants of human behaviour.

Forensic scientists are not concerned with traditional moral and legal categories of responsibility, guilt, blame and retributive sanctions, but with the objective categories of cause and effect. The tendency then is to assimilate deviant behaviour to the deterministic model of physical disorder. The problem presented by crime thereby calls for the objective formulation of explanatory hypotheses, the discovery of causal mechanisms and the development of suitable remedies by analogy with physical disorder, with the practical aim of eradicating disorder and restoring order. Thus, the British Psychological Society in its evidence to the Butler Committee on the law relating to mentally abnormal offenders expressed the view that:[21]

> The processes giving rise to 'normal', i.e. socially acceptable, and 'abnormal', i.e. socially prohibited or illegal behaviour are, ... in principle equally amenable to explanation and prediction.
>
> We therefore argue that it is beside the point to talk about degrees of responsibility for one's behaviour. This in turn makes it difficult, we think, to talk of culpability and hence punishability for socially proscribed behaviour. Instead, one should talk in terms of explanations and possibilities for change.

It seems appropriate to associate the extreme objective view of antisocial behaviour indicated here with the observer perspective in the biperspectival version of IT.

It is apparent that the current legal conceptions of the person, and of the nature of society, are still bedevilled by vestiges of metaphysical models that are essentially incompatible with the scientific conception of man as a product of biological evolution and of human societies as essentially 'family-herd' groupings of a highly evolved type. As a result criminal law is profoundly confused about such fundamental matters as the nature of the mental, mind-directed behaviour, the nature of human capacities and the logical status of normative principles. I have suggested that this confusion originates in an obsolescent metaphysical model, the OA model, which inflates human volitional capacities. The influence of the OA model is perpetuated because the law systematically isolates the participants' mode of social experience from objective knowledge of the causes of behaviour. On the other hand, scientists are equally prone to take up extreme reductionist positions as a result of analytically isolating the observer's mode of experience.

The PO model informed by IT thus suggests how both extreme positions are insupportable, and for the same reason, i.e. analytical isolation of insights which are naturally inseparable. What IT suggests is a physicalist account of human experience that reconciles practical demands of human life with theoretical insights of objective science. This is possible because the biperspectivist version of physicalism advanced here takes mind–brain identity seriously. That is to say, mind is not 'reduced' or 'eliminated', but enters into the economy of human behaviour because it is identical with certain brain processes. In particular, if to understand, to recognise and to follow a social rule is to be undergoing determinate physical processes that are systemically integrated with a physical–social environment (see Chapter V, Section 4.4.3), then the problem of rule-*breaking* can be regarded objectively as the breakdown in these natural processes *as well as*, from the participant's perspective, as 'delinquency'. The prospect therefore is that IT is the key to a moral philosophy that will support a new penal code so that, without requiring a totally independent moral system rooted in theological tradition, society can make moral demands on individuals and justify its sanctions against these individuals by an appeal to the code that was violated.[22]

5   EIDESCOPIC SHIFTS

More than sixty years ago Gabriel de Tarde pointed to a discernible trend in legal philosophy which is strikingly similar in many ways to the present trend in metaphysics away from the OA model of persons and towards the PO model developed by science.[23] Legal philosophy and practice, he suggested, has developed through three discernible phases characterised by three 'root models' of human society (to employ the terminology used before). These can be conveniently characterised as Divine Order, Capitalist Commerce and Fraternity.

1 *Divine order* According to this view society is a divinely ordained hierarchical structure and the principles of legal justice are defined by God-given law. Offences are sins against God and the natural law; penalties are penances determined with regard to the victim and the past offence and without regard to the future of the offender. The regulative principle underlying law in this system is 'To each according to his station'.

2 *Capitalist commerce* According to this view society is a network of industrial and commercial interests. The paradigms of invariable

contract law and 'fair price' prevail against the individual person's situation: 'business is business' is the rule. Just as work is evaluated independently of the workman, so offence is appraised independently of the offender. Penalties for offences are regarded by quite explicit appeal to a mercantile analogy as in the way of inverse salaries for disservices rendered or as costs.[24] The regulative principle underlying law in this system is 'To each according to his works'.

3 *Fraternity* The socialist principle, 'To each according to his needs, from each according to his capacities', is the prevalent view in the emerging conception of law. Whereas other views have been concerned to denounce negative qualities and have been backward-looking towards the offence, this view emphasises the need to encourage positive qualities and the forward-looking aim of rehabilitating the offender in the future. The principle regulating this system of law is 'To each according to his perversity' (or disorder).

Although these 'root models' have developed historically in keeping with other developments in human culture, it is evident that they can co-exist and that vestiges of former modes of thinking persist long after they have ceased to be fundamental to the mainstream of thought.

De Tarde's suggested 'Fraternity' model corresponds strikingly with the PO model of persons in several important respects. In particular, neither supposes a non-natural sanction for practical principles of law, and neither arbitrarily requires of individuals at their peril to do more than is physically possible for them to do. That is to say, neither adopts the principles of the Old Testament or the nineteenth-century Manchester school of economic materialism in criminal law.

Positively, the emerging view advances, against the still prevailing orthodoxy, the forward-looking aim of rehabilitating offenders, with due regard to their individual situations and capacities. This is not, of course, to say that because, on scientific grounds, offenders are not to be ritually denounced and punished, their actions must be condoned. Nor is it to say that, because villains are physically determined to behave as they do, therefore they should be given the freedom of the land. What it does mean is that the prevailing orthodox legal categories of guilt, blame and retributive sanctions are otiose in the light of developing scientific knowledge of human behaviour.

6   CONCLUSIONS

The sources of disagreement identified here will serve to illuminate a discussion of the current disagreements in the philosophy of law that reflect the impact of developments in the human sciences, especially mental science, and to which IT with its implications of physical determinism is profoundly relevant. The extent of the consequences for law of a thoroughgoing determinism derived from IT is quite imponderable, although the previous discussion of the consequences for morality suggests that its practical consequences will be much less drastic than many thinkers have supposed. For the present purpose it will be convenient to discuss two central issues in the ongoing debate which together suggest the wide range of practical implications for criminal law of a physical–deterministic account of mind-directed behaviour.[25] These issues are the criterion for criminal responsibility, the reasonable man, and the thesis that crime is disease.

XI

THE REASONABLE MAN

1 INTRODUCTION

In considering the consequences for law of a shift to a PO root model of
persons it is appropriate to begin by considering the implications of a
determinist view of human actions for the prevailing views of criminal
responsibility, guilt, blame and punishment.

The argument advanced is in outline as follows.

1 Current legal practice is based on the principle that criminal guilt and
  liability to punitive sanctions depends in the last analysis upon
  whether or not the offender incurs the disapprobation and moral
  condemnation of the community.

2 In the law relating to provocation in cases of homicide this principle is
  formally embodied in the criterion of the reasonable man and the
  objective test that applies it. That is to say, if an accused did not
  behave as a reasonable man would in the circumstances of the
  offence, he is deemed guilty and deserving of punitive sanctions. However,

3 The objective test of culpability using the reasonable man criterion
  takes no account of the fact that, within the meaning of the law, a
  guilty man is, by definition, not a reasonable man as the law requires
  him to be. A scientifically informed view as embodied in the PO model
  of persons would require that in assessing guilt and blameworthiness
  account should always be taken of the specific offender in the
  circumstances of the offence, that is a subjective test.

4 If, instead of the current objective test, the law recognised the model
  of man emerging from science and, accordingly, applied a subjective
  test, then, in consistency with the PO model, nobody would incur
  guilt or blame or deserve punishment in the traditional sense of these

304

words because all behaviour is physically determined. They may, however, be deemed criminally responsible in the sense of 'strictly liable' under other provisions of a criminal code which was fully consistent with scientific knowledge of human behaviour.

5 The implication of this is that, in consistency with scientific knowledge, courts should be required only to establish the facts as to whether defendants committed offences, and whether in so doing they acted unreasonably. Questions of the disposition of offenders should be removed from the courts.

1.1 Criminal Responsibility

Notoriously, there is great difficulty in defining criminal actions in a way that clearly distinguishes them from other sorts of actions. Public wrong, moral wrong, the 'guilty mind', punitive sanctions and legislative or executive proscription are factors that have commonly been used to define crimes. Underlying all of these, however, is the disapprobation and moral condemnation of the community, usually as formally expressed. Certainly, agents whose actions do not incur disapprobation and moral condemnation are not deemed guilty, blameworthy and thereby deserving of punitive sanctions. The difficulties raised for law by the PO model of human actions are the ones raised by Samuel Butler in the satirical novel *Erewhon*; they turn on the difficulty of reconciling recognition of scientific evidence that actions are physically determined with traditional views of criminal guilt, blame and punishment.[1] For if an agent's actions are seen to be inevitable because physically determined (no matter what other (physically) 'anomalous' descriptions might be given of them), they do not in consistency incur disapprobation and moral condemnation in the traditional sense of these words. The traditional view of crime as evil, guilt-laden and blameworthy becomes otiose.

Although the communities' disapprobation and moral condemnation lie behind all laws that claim rational justification and common assent, the law relating to provocation in cases of homicide is especially interesting and important because there the fundamental basis of law is made explicit and is formally expressed in the legal criterion of the reasonable man and the objective test for criminally culpable behaviour that embodies it. What is especially important about the law relating to provocation is that it deals in an explicit way with the causally necessitated behaviour of mentally normal individuals who intentionally commit criminal acts, and with the criteria and procedures for establishing innocence and exculpation or alternatively guilt and culpability. If it can be shown in such cases as these that the criteria for attributing guilt and assigning punitive sanctions are incompatible with the emerging PO model of persons, that would be sufficient to establish incompatibility in all other cases. For if the law is incompatible with scientific determinism in the case of mentally normal offenders who 'can' do otherwise than they did when committing crimes, it will be even more incompatible in cases closer to severe mental abnormality where mental disorder is so extreme that it can safely be presumed that there is a necessitating causal connection between the mental condition and the criminal action.[2]

Although the issues concerning criminal responsibility arise here specifically out of the law relating to provocation in cases of homicide, the implications of admitting the special circumstances of the offender into consideration of guilt and blameworthiness have very far-reaching consequences for the criminal law which have been clearly seen by some legal philosophers and jurisprudents.[3] It is this fact that warrants the special attention given here to the reasonable man criterion and the objective test in provocation law. The central principle embodied in the law relating to provocation, which has such far-reaching implications for all criminal responsibility, is that, if a reasonable man would lose his self-control as the agent did in the circumstances of the criminal act, then the agent is deemed in law not to be guilty, blameworthy and deserving of punishment. If, however, the reasonable man would have retained his self-control, then the accused is deemed guilty with all that that entails.[4]

The problem of the reasonable man criterion arises from a conflict between two commonplace assumptions.

1 Courts decide questions of responsibility for criminal acts on the basis of the assumption that in the absence of evidence to the contrary people are free to choose whether or not to commit a criminal act. As Ounstead has said:[5]

> free-will forms the only rock on which a sane structure of criminal law can be built. It underlies the law of contract as much as it justifies the demand of 'Guilty' or 'Not Guilty' in criminal cases.

This assumption underlies the law's condemnation of an offender who did not act as an 'ordinary' 'reasonable' man would have done in the circumstances in which the crime was committed. Offenders are thus routinely deemed guilty and blameworthy without due regard to any relevant idiosyncratic characteristics unless they are deemed to be certifiably insane or otherwise suffering from severe mental abnormality. However,

2 Contrary to assumption 1, it is commonplace to assume that in general different individuals are more or less predisposed by nature and nurture to respond differently to similar situations. Whether or not an

individual incurs disapprobation and moral condemnation depends very much upon knowledge about the offender and the circumstances of the crime. The PO model of human action supports this assumption, and goes even further in stressing the decisive importance of precise states at particular instants for questions of 'possibilities' of choice of action. The problem of the reasonable man criterion arises therefore from the conflict between assumptions 1 and 2. It seems at least unjustly to demand more self-control of some people than of others and, at worst, to require free-will and self-control against the evidence of science.

Now many philosophers will deny that the two assumptions are inconsistent since the free-will of which the lawyer speaks is not the metaphysical free-will of philosophical libertarianism.[6] The law follows common sense and ordinary language in presupposing only the absence of compulsion and the agent's capacity to do otherwise than he did in fact do.[7] If so, the problem of the reasonable man criterion is easily solved, certainly. However, according to the thesis of physical determinism, in order that an agent should be considered free to do otherwise than he did do on the occasion in question in anything other than a taxonomic or epistemic sense, it is not sufficient that the agent was not subject to compulsion and had the capacity to do otherwise, but it is necessary also that the precise *state* of his system at that time should have been other than it in fact was: that is to say, the assumption of free-will in question requires a physical impossibility of the first order (impossibility$_1$).

If acts are inevitable in the sense that their alternatives are physically impossible, then in consistency with scientific understanding they do not incur guilt, blame and punitive sanctions in the traditional sense. This argument applies not only to recognised cases such as loss of self-control under provocation, or cases of severe mental abnormality, but to all cases of physically determined behaviour. If IT is true, then *all* mind-directed behaviour is physically determined, including the 'voluntary', self-determined acts of mentally normal individuals, for an action is none the less physically determined for being non-pathological. Carried to its logical conclusion, therefore, IT and the PO model undermine the current concept of and basis for criminal responsibility. For as Glanville Williams has pointed out in connection with grosser cases, 'it may be laid down as a general proposition that where the law imposes a duty to act; non-compliance with the duty will be excused where compliance is physically impossible'.[8]

This briefly is the central problem raised by the emerging PO model of persons for the reasonable man criterion in so far as it is the basis of a supposedly objective test of criminal responsibility.

It is now time to turn to a more detailed discussion of the questions raised by the emerging PO model for the reasonable man criterion. I shall discuss these under three heads: the reasonable man criterion; the objective test; and the subjective test.

2   THE REASONABLE MAN CRITERION

2.1   *The Concept of the Reasonable Man*

The modern legal concept of the reasonable man seems to have made its first appearance in 1869, when Judge Keating declared that in a case of provocation 'it is for the jury to decide whether it was such that they can attribute the act to the violence of the passion naturally arising therefrom and likely to be aroused thereby in the breast of a reasonable man'.[9] Holmes writes:[10]

> The reconciliation of the doctrine that liability is founded on blame-worthiness with the existence of liability where the party is not to blame ... is found in the concept of the average man, the man of ordinary intelligence and reasonable prudence. Liability is said to arise out of such conduct as would be blameworthy in him. But he is an ideal being represented by the jury when they are appealed to, and his conduct is an external and objective standard when applied to any given individual. That individual may be morally without stain, because he has less than ordinary intelligence or prudence. But he is required to have these qualities at his peril. If he has them, he will not as a general rule incur liability without blameworthiness.

The reasonable man criterion was accepted by the Court of Criminal Appeal in 1914[11] and more recently incorporated into the Homicide Act of 1957 which determines that:[12]

> Where on a charge of murder there is evidence on which the jury can find that a person charged was provoked (whether by things done or things said or both together) to lose his self-control, the question whether the provocation was enough to make a reasonable man do as he did shall be left to be determined by the jury, and in determining that question the jury shall take into account everything both done and said according to the effect which in their opinion it would have on a reasonable man.

More recently there has been some recognition that the criterion of the reasonable man does not reflect the widely held belief, traditionally expressed in the doctrine of *mens rea*, that the state of mind of the agent is crucial in determining overall responsibility for criminal actions.[13]

Accordingly the Criminal Justice Act of 1967 makes a 'subjective' assessment of responsibility based on a judgment about the actual state of mind of the accused *permissible*.[14] These developments, although they are in the direction of a shift to the PO model, and while they no longer make the objective or reasonable man test mandatory, nevertheless do not make a subjective test mandatory either – only permissible. Also, the legislation applies only to capital crimes and there is not much evidence that defendants in other cases benefit from it.[15]

Finally, there is a need to distinguish clearly between two different questions posed in terms of the reasonable man criterion. First, there is the question of how the reasonable man would behave. This is really a question of determining the prevailing norms in any community. Second, there is the question of whether a particular offender could be expected to behave as the reasonable man would in particular circumstances. This distinction is of the last importance in understanding the current problems with the criterion, as will be evident presently.

2.2   Justification

The justifications for the reasonable man criterion fall into two main groups: the positive arguments, and negative ones such as those that appeal to the dire consequences of abandoning it. Each group will be considered in turn from the viewpoint of physical determinism and IT.

POSITIVE ARGUMENTS

2.2.1   The OA model of persons

The reasonable man criterion is a clear, practical expression of the orthodox model of the transempirical, free and rational agent, with its connotations of extramundanity, at least in the matter of moral decision and action. As Brett has expressed it:[16]

> The 'reasonable man' rules quite plainly assume a particular view of human behaviour. They treat a human being as basically a rational being who can control his activities and determine by an act of mind whether he will respond to a hostile provocative act and who, if he does respond, can control the duration of his anger and the extent of his response. This remains true even if one accepts the view that the real purpose of the rules is to set up a standard of behaviour which all persons including the individual accused are to be required to conform. For it is utterly senseless to set up a standard with which human beings are incapable of complying.

309

This metaphysical assumption is exhibited in numerous legal decisions, and Lord Devlin's judgment is typical: in the case of a woman accused of murder for killing her husband who had repeatedly and brutally battered her near to death herself, he expressed the view that:[17]

> It does not matter how cruel he was, how much or how little he was to blame except in so far as it resulted in the final act of the [wife], what matters is whether the girl had the time to say: 'Whatever I have suffered, whatever I have endured I know that "Thou shalt not kill" '.

The main objection to this view is that it ignores everything that science has shown us about the nature and causes of human behaviour, as elaborated on at some length in earlier chapters and referred to again below. If the PO model of mind-directed human behaviour prevails, therefore, it is obvious that this crucial support for the reasonable man criterion is removed.

2.2.2   *The appeal to convention*

Recently philosophers have used the (supposedly) metaphysically neutral paradigm case argument from ordinary usage in support of the reasonable man criterion. The central thought is that we do in fact make a practical distinction between those people we judge could have acted otherwise than they did (in a perfectly understandable ordinary sense of 'could') and those who for one reason or another could not. So long as this distinction is not being denied, it is said, then it is just a matter of fact that we decide on the basis of an ordinary conception of what was the reasonable thing to do in the circumstances in question. As Hart puts it with reference to liability for negligence:[18]

> there is no reason (*unless we are to reject the whole business of responsibility and punishment*) always to make the protest that it is morally wrong to punish because 'he could not have helped it' when someone who 'just didn't think' is punished for carelessness. For in some cases at least we say 'he could have thought about what he was doing' with just as much rational confidence as one can say of any intentional wrong doing, 'he could have done otherwise'.

One objection to this view is that it is based on the assumption that all that is relevant to the question of 'moral' responsibility is that the agent could have done otherwise in the sense that he had the capacity to do so.[19] If the previous distinction between first- and second-order possibilities is made, however, then this assumption is insufficient to establish 'moral' responsibility, even on the orthodox model. More to the point, the issue of 'moral' responsibility does not arise if the first-order level of determination is taken into account.

The further implication, that it would be unthinkable to reject the whole business of responsibility and punishment and so we can at least sometimes say acts could be otherwise than they are, is also open to question. To begin with, the argument does not distinguish between the different orders of possibility already distinguished, or the different distinguishable senses of 'responsibility'. Since the OA conception of (*moral*) responsibility supposedly requires that the agent could have done otherwise, for someone to argue equivocally that agents never could do otherwise than they do may appear to (impossibly) deny 'responsibility'. But, as here suggested, this need be no more than equivocation between different senses of 'could', to whit the capacity sense and the instantaneous state sense, compounded by an equivocation between at least two senses of 'responsibility', i.e. the moral sense and the legal accountability sense.

There is in fact no reason why an agent may not be held legally accountable without being morally responsible in the orthodox sense. It is the familiar case of strict liability. Also, there is no conceptual reason why we should not reject the whole orthodox business of moral responsibility and punishment as such for this would presumably follow from a shift from the OA to the PO root model. The commonplace practical distinction between those who *in general* could$_2$ and those who could$_2$ not do a certain thing (i.e. have the capacity) would still indicate a significant difference between the sub-classes of those who could$_1$ not do other than they do on a particular occasion. It is perhaps necessary to remark that Hart's argument is intended to establish that culpability for negligence could be established without introducing strict liability. However, his argument is by assertion and assumption only. Apart from *asserting* that it is (morally) justifiable to insist on objectively reasonable action, and *assuming* that general determinism does not hold, his contention is unsupported. As we have shown, it is unsupportable if physical determinism prevails and the assertion is denied. In short, legal accountability based on the reasonable man criterion is justifiable, but only on the principle of strict liability, that is to say, indifferently as to the agent's situation.[20]

2.2.3 *The standard-setting argument*

It is sometimes said that the function of the reasonable man criterion is to set standards that individuals are *required* to measure up to 'at their peril'.[21] It is precisely *because* men are backsliders and not in spite of it that the 'reasonable' standard is required; the harder impulses are to resist, the greater is the need for a deterrent based on a reasonable man criterion. As Judge Biddel said to one offender, 'If you cannot resist an impulse in any other way we will hang a rope in front of your eyes and perhaps that will help'.[22]

It has already been pointed out that there is a need to distinguish between, first, the question of what the reasonable man's behaviour should and would be and, second, the question of whether particular offenders can be expected to behave as the hypothetical reasonable man would. These two questions have frequently been conflated and the standard-setting argument is one example of it.

The standard-setting argument is clearly concerned with the first question. It expresses the practical viewpoint of the criminal law and in particular the need to set out and maintain desirable norms of social behaviour. But it is evident that this viewpoint is quite divorced from the objective scientific considerations raised by the second question. These have to do with the objective possibilities of particular individuals conforming to legal prescriptions. On all views of the nature of man and society, deterministic ones no less than others, there will be norms of desirable conduct to maintain. The question therefore is not whether there are norms to be maintained, but whether the manner of maintaining norms is consistent with scientific knowledge of human behaviour. Consequently the standard-setting argument, to do with the first question, does not rebut deterministic arguments against the practical application of the reasonable man criterion, which have to do with the second question.

It is not only defenders of the reasonable man criterion who have conflated questions about desirable norms with questions about objective possibilities. Critics of the criterion have made the same mistake, but with very good reason, as will be discussed later (Section 3.3 below). Problems have arisen in the application of the criterion because in disposing of offenders either the second question, about whether offenders could be expected to behave as the reasonable man would, has not been asked, or else dubious libertarian assumptions have been made in answering it.

Provided, however, that it is construed only as an expression of the norms prevailing in a community and not as enforcing standards which are undefinable theoretically and which practically are too high for the community, then the reasonable man criterion is supportable.[23]

2.2.4 *Desirable judgments*

Very often, in such cases as self-defence and necessity, the criterion of the reasonable man operates to the advantage of the accused. One such precedent is the judgment that a ship's captain is not culpable of illegal entry to a port under embargo, even though he knew such entry to be illegal, if he does so of necessity.[24] The controversy surrounding the criterion stems from the supposition that it is entirely pernicious in its application. But clearly this is a mistake. It is important therefore that criticism of the reasonable man criterion based on theoretical considerations should not overlook its merits in application.

NEGATIVE ARGUMENTS

2.2.5 *The bad-tempered man argument*
Some judges have strongly resisted abrogation of the criterion because, they argue, it would lead to the possibility of situations such as the exculpation of a bad-tempered man for an offence that a good-tempered man would be convicted for, which would be 'neither law nor sense'.[25]

The concern expressed in this argument is that the law should avoid inconsistencies and so injustices. Now some arguments have been offered to show that this fear is ill-expressed, since there would be nothing unjust or senseless about treating the bad-tempered man differently from another (i.e. exculpating him) precisely because the distinction is based upon a real and relevant difference in character, and is therefore justifiable.[26] But from the PO point of view this argument is acceptable only if *neither* is regarded as 'morally' responsible although *both* are regarded as legally accountable because of their illegal acts. The question of the difference between them is then relevant only to the measures to be taken in each case. As Plato pointed out, the angry man differs significantly from the calculating criminal in, for example, the important respect that he quite likely recognises and assents to the standards of behaviour he is violating, and therefore he is not in need of moral education in the way the 'moral degenerate' is.[27]

2.2.6 *The subversion argument*
The view is often expressed that to abandon the reasonable man criterion and to admit the particular circumstances of an offender into consideration of his culpability for an offence would have very far-reaching consequences with repercussions in other branches of law. Lord Hewart for example referred to the defence of 'irresistible impulse' as a 'fantastic theory ... which if it were to become part of our criminal law would be merely subversive'.[28]

This argument has nothing to do with the truths of science, but in any case it is entirely speculative, and we do well to recall that similar arguments directed against a 'necessity' defence in cases of theft succeeded in maintaining the death penalty in England for thefts valued at more than three shillings and sixpence until the nineteenth century.[29]

More to the point, the evidence available since the 1957 Homicide Act, which introduced the category of diminished responsibility, suggests that an individual approach to dealing with offenders as such has no effect on the incidence of convictions.[30]

2.3 Objections

2.3.1 The criterion as vacuous

The criterion has been objected to on the quasi-logical grounds that it is virtually circular, since a reasonable man would not do anything that would incur blame of equally reasonable men in a court of law. If an act were really one that a reasonable man might be expected to do it ought not to be a crime at all. In practice it is presupposed that the 'man on the Clapham omnibus' does not give way to the temptation to inflict death or grievous bodily harm even under extreme provocation. Therefore if the test were strictly applied it would never succeed as a defence.[31] It has worked in practice only because it is not strictly applied by the courts.

This absurdity arises from the prescientific assumption, implicit in the criterion, that there are at least some (in fact very many) agents who commit criminal acts when it was possible that they should not commit them because they are neither insane nor otherwise mentally disordered; as if acts were any the less physically determined for being non-pathological. It reveals the interesting paradox that, according to the reasonable man laws, such defendants are deemed to be reasonable men and are *therefore* being punished for their unreasonableness.[32]

2.3.2 Retributive interest

Many objections to the criterion are based on the belief that it arises from an undesirable, inhumane and pharisaical disposition to exact retribution from those who have violated approved codes of conduct, irrespective of the *causes* of the conduct.[33]

The public pronouncements of many Old Testament-style judges and neanderthal politicians leave us in no doubt that this objection is well made. Nor are such dispositions highly anachronistic or confined to a few harmless cranks. As recently as 1965, the present Archbishop of Canterbury, then Archbishop of York, publicly expressed the view that 'Society must say through its officers of law, that it repudiates certain acts as utterly incompatible with civilised conduct, and that it will exact retribution from those who violate its order code'.[34] It must be said here that the case for retribution has been reformulated in recent times so that the emphasis has shifted away from the vileficatory connotations of 'exacting retribution' to the more justifiable concept of 'retribution in distribution', as a safeguard against victimisation under a strict liability system. However, it is evident that there are, undeniably, vestiges of the prescientific rationale of tribal sacrifice implicit in the retributive motive,[35] which underlies much support for the reasonable man criterion.

3   THE OBJECTIVE TEST[36]

Apart from the problems of the reasonable man criterion as such there are problems arising from the formulation and application of it in the objective test.

3.1   *The Jury Verdict and the Objective Condition*

There are four obvious candidates for determining the standard of reasonable behaviour, that is the objective condition for exculpation or guilt; the legislature, the judiciary, juries and scientific experts.

The legislature might be said to stipulate the standards of reasonable behaviour in the law itself. In a strict liability system which was indifferent alike to scientific knowledge and to the vagaries of human character, temperament and circumstance, the law itself would be sufficient to establish the standard of reasonable behaviour. This has never been seriously argued for, however; for as long as the 'reasonable man' has been a feature of the criminal law there has been 'compassion for human infirmity' in the interpretation of the law by the courts in particular cases.

The judiciary have in the past substantially determined the standard of reasonable behaviour in so far as it was possible for a judge to withdraw from the jury a defence based on the reasonable man criterion, on the grounds that no reasonable jury could find, on the evidence given, that the reasonable man would have behaved as the accused did. Although the 1957 Homicide Act sought to remove the determination of reasonable behaviour from judges, they may still advise the jury as to the characteristics of the reasonable man.

At least since Judge Keating's first reference to the reasonable man in 1869, the jury has been charged with responsibility for deciding on reasonable conduct. Since the 1957 Homicide Act the main burden of deciding what the standard of reasonable behaviour should be has been expressly vested in juries. As section 3 of that act says, the jury 'shall take into account everything both done and said according to the effect which, *in their opinion*, it would have on the reasonable man'. This is consistent with the more general view of criminal responsibility in a secular democratic society expressed by Lord Devlin, that 'for the purposes of the law ... morality in England means what twelve men and women think it means – in other words it is to be ascertained as a question of fact'.[37] The 'objectivity' of the objective test therefore has its basis in the supposition that there is a common standard of reasonable behaviour in the community and that this standard can be determined by a jury. Although this orthodox view of the test for criminal responsibility based on moral condemnation is losing ground, it remains the predominant one in English law.

Many commentators would argue that lay juries are inadequately equipped to decide questions of how people would behave in given circumstances. They would prefer that decisions about reasonable behaviour should be determined by educated opinion, particularly that of behavioural scientists and medical experts. The central issue in law is usually seen as the need to establish in practice the distinction between self-controlled and so culpable behaviour, and behaviour determined by necessitating causes, as in cases of 'irresistible impulse'. The legal position on this issue is that in practice there can be no scientific proof of whether an action was due to an uncontrollable impulse or an uncontrolled one; or again, there is no way of telling whether an impulse is irresistible because of some mitigating factor such as insanity, or because of some culpable factor such as greed, jealousy or revenge. In the absence of adequate scientific evidence, the decision is left to the jury on the basis of the reasonable man criterion.

Not only is it maintained that there is no satisfactory scientific basis for a characterisation of a normal (and presumably average and reasonable) man, or how he would act in given situations, but it is held that, even if there were, it would be inadmissible as evidence in courts of law.[38] Indeed, one Canadian judge expressed the view that the admission of expert opinion on the behaviour of normal people would be a most dangerous innovation.[39] It is entirely for the jury to decide what constitutes a reasonable or average man.[40]

Common sense might suggest that juries could only decide what, in their view, a reasonable man might have done in the circumstances of the crime. The Attorney General confirmed, on the contrary, that the proper reading of the 1957 Homicide Act concerns what the reasonable man '*would*' have done and not what he '*might*' have done.[41] Thus it is evident that the objectivity of the 'objective' test is considered to be beyond question, and, notwithstanding the impossibility of scientific proof of the degree of irresistibility of a particular impulse, it is determined that lay juries can decide not only what a reasonable man *might* have done but what in the event he *would* have done.

316

3.2   *Justification of the Objective Test*

3.2.1   *The attributive argument*

The main positive argument for the objective test is that matters of guilt and innocence are *essentially* legal or moral matters, not matters for educated opinion or scientific experts on human behaviour to pronounce upon. The objective test is directed towards establishing the standards of behaviour acceptable to the community. Referring to the crucial question of whether an accused's mental responsibility is impaired, one writer has said:[42]

> More than perhaps any other question a jury is called upon to answer, this is one that calls for a *free emotional response* to the total situation. For responsibility is not a quality inherent in the accused but rather an attribute that is ascribed to him.

Much of the recent criticism of the objective test is based on the belief that it calls upon common sense to make good the deficiencies of science.[43] This criticism conflates the two questions posed in terms of the reasonable man criterion (cf. Section 2.1 above).[44] Lord Parker's view is that the question as to whether the accused behaved differently to the average man in the circumstances of the offence (the first question) is best answered by having 'average' men *put themselves* in the position of the accused at the time of the crime. This is an eminently arguable view, and until such time as there is a more precise and equally *practical* way of answering this question, the present arrangements are well justified. The procedure is perfectly in keeping with routine scientific practice, provided the jurors constitute a reasonably representative cross-section of the community and their judgment is substantially in accord, as the law in fact requires.

3.2.2   *The lack of a scientific criterion*

The legal position on the objective test is that, since there can be no scientific proof of whether an impulse was irresistible or not, this question must be left to the jury to decide on the basis of the reasonable man criterion. This argument is at least partly based on an appraisal of the present state of scientific knowledge of normal human behaviour. It should be carefully distinguished therefore from similar arguments derived from the assumption that judgments about responsibility are not scientific but legal,[45] or moral,[46] matters.

This argument provides a solution to the peculiar problem raised by the objective test, of having the jurors 'think themselves under the skins' of the accused.[47] It shows that the problem is no different from any other similar problem in socio-psychological testing. Indeed, it was argued in a

317

previous chapter that even the observations on which the vaunted intersubjective–objective science is based conceal inevitable subjective variations under a blanket of *ceteris paribus* assumptions about the essential similarity of observers. The reading of the minds of average men is unquestionably and profoundly more complex than other scientific investigations, even those involving the reading of the most complex instruments; but then, so also are the human 'instruments' employed in the investigation of human behaviour. Further than this, it is evident that any future scientific theory about the normative beliefs of average individuals could only be based on the reports of average individuals about their normative beliefs: that is to say, would be no better than its data, or in other words than what the average juror would be able to tell. In a word, the objective test is the best practical way of establishing whether or not a defendant has anything to answer for in the eyes of his peers in the community, which is not a matter for science so much as for his peers in the community.

3.3   Objections to the Objective Test

3.3.1   *Conflation of prevailing norms with objective possibilities*
It was previously pointed out that criticisms of the reasonable man criterion commonly conflate two distinct questions raised by the criterion, but that the application of the criterion in practice in the objective test has made this mistake an understandable one. The fact is that the law itself conflates questions of desired and prescribed norms with questions of objective possibility. It has not been content to establish that a particular offender acted on a particular occasion in a way that the average man would not have acted. It has usually gone further and *required* him to *have* acted otherwise than he did even though any number of non-average factors may have determined that he acted in precisely the way he did *when he* did: factors that were not of the agent's will. One notorious judgment will suffice to illustrate how the test has been applied in the courts.

An impotent youth of eighteen was deeply disturbed about his disorder. In an attempt to allay (or confirm) his worst fears he consorted with a prostitute. The prostitute ridiculed the youth for his impotence. The youth lost his self-control, and in this state killed the prostitute. The court found him guilty of murder, and rejected the defence argument that the special circumstances of the case were mitigating. The explanation given for the judgment was that a reasonable man would not have done as the youth did.[48] The same judgment has been repeatedly confirmed in other cases, on the grounds that for exculpation the criterion requires that the 'reasonable man would act as the accused acted'.[49]

318

It is evident, therefore, that the objective test conflates a legitimate need to ascertain standards of tolerable behaviour, with quite different issues to do with the determination of the behaviour of offenders. It puts juries in such absurd positions as having to consider the effects of taunts of impotence on a man who is not impotent. For this reason several commentators have suggested that the objective test be abolished and replaced by a purely subjective criterion.[50]

3.3.2 *Disregard of scientific knowledge*

One of the most telling objections to the objective test is that in application it *systematically* disregards scientific evidence: both evidence about the causes of human behaviour in general, and evidence relating to the behaviour of particular offenders.[51] As one writer has graphically put it, the motorcar with which the law is concerned is one that runs on rails and yet is able to move freely from one side of the street to the other, and one whose behaviour is in no way affected when its steering mechanism is out of order.[52] It is said that it is perverse of the law to ignore the teachings of science and absurd for it to doubt their validity. But if attention is paid to them, it at once becomes clear that the reasonable man of provocation law is a figment of the imagination.[53] Consequently, although there is no legal definition of the reasonable man, a profile has emerged of this ideal person out of cases of precedent, something as follows[54]:

1 He is not unusually excitable or pugnacious.
2 He is not mentally deficient or under the influence of drugs.
3 He is neither physically abnormal, nor impotent, nor blind, nor a dwarf, nor scarred by severe injuries.
4 If a woman, she is not pregnant.
5 If his self-control is lost in finding his wife in adultery or his mistress or fiancée unfaithful, it is not when he is merely told.
6 He retains his self-control in the face of words however abusive, except in the case of certain undefined extremes.
7 He remains unmoved if his nose is pulled.

It is thus not surprising that critics should think that, whereas a yardstick is at least a precise instrument of measure, the reasonable man is like a rubber doll.[55]

Notwithstanding the supposition of the potential 'reasonableness' of individuals who are not certifiably insane or otherwise (technically) 'mentally disabled', there is already abundant and well-documented evidence from the human sciences that an immense variety of causal factors enters into the determination of individual human acts – physiological, psychological, economic and sociological. It would be impossible to discuss these in any detail, and for the present purpose it is unnecessary. It is perhaps sufficient to indicate only a few of the plainly physical determinants. There is, for example, strong evidence to suggest that among other factors physique,[56] chromosomes,[57] rare and undetectable diseases,[58] the conditionability of the autonomic nervous system[59] (especially in connection with early nurture) and abnormal brain function as indicated by EEG measurement[60] are potent though non-obvious determinants of behaviour which an ordinary man has no way of accounting for in his ordinary judgments of delinquent acts.

The general argument seems to be gaining acceptance among jurists and penal philosophers that the law should be better informed about scientific understanding of human behaviour and that more account should be taken of it in assessing criminal liability.[61] It is recognised that it is absurd to refuse to make allowances for abnormalities and physical defects of an offender,[62] and seen to be questionable how long the doctrine of absolute responsibility for conduct can continue to be accepted in criminal law.[63] Nevertheless, there is a need to pursue the problems raised by determinism further, as I shall now do.

4   THE SUBJECTIVE TEST

Consideration of the reasonable man criterion and the objective test of provocation law have led us to the conclusion that there is a recognised need to consider the circumstances of individual offenders in assessing criminal responsibility, that is a need for a subjective test. Once the individual circumstances of offenders are admitted into consideration, however, the implications for law are far-reaching and certainly extend beyond the law of provocation. The question that must now be considered is whether the emergence of a PO model of persons undermines the whole basis of criminal responsibility as this is usually conceived in terms of guilt, blame and punitive sanctions.

An incidental point should perhaps be made here to avoid possible misunderstanding: many of the excuses already admitted in criminal law involve insanity and diminished responsibility, but of course, physical determinism does not entail that all responsibility is abrogated on the grounds of insanity: in what follows I draw attention to such cases only as being the clearest examples of excuses on mental grounds.

4.1   *Recognition in Law of Non-cognitive Disabilities*

It would certainly be quite wrong to suppose that the law has not often made allowances for the different sorts and conditions of men. The origins of the subjective test go back at least as far as Aristotle's notion of unnatural passions, namely those with objects that are not naturally pleasant, but give pleasure from some pathological cause such as congenital disorder or bad upbringing.[64] In Aristotle's view such passions do not warrant the charge of incontinence. In 1833 Judge Hayward expressed the opinion that if an accused murderer was deprived of self-control 'the law in compassion to human infirmity would hold the offence to amount to manslaughter only'.[65]

Among the more enlightened changes in recent criminal law has been the recognition that human beings differ not only in their intellectual capacities but also in their emotional temperament and willpower. Notoriously, the old McNaghten Rules of 1843 recognised only 'defect of reason' as an excuse from criminal responsibility in capital offences. It eventually came to be recognised that this restriction was based on an obsolete 'faculty' model of human psychology. Long before this was recognised by law, however, clinicians urged reform. In 1908 the Royal College of Physicians of London advised the Royal Commission in the Radnor Report that 'the concept' of insanity as an intellectual disorder solely should be superseded by the understanding that it is an inability by reason of mental (not necessarily intellectual) defect and disorder to manage oneself and one's affairs'.[66] Again, the Aitken Committee of 1922 urged that 'a person is irresponsible for his acts when the act is committed under an impulse which the prisoner was by mental disease in substance deprived of any power to resist'.[67] The appropriate reforms were not implemented until 1957 when the Homicide Act determined that:[68]

> When a person kills or is party to the killing of another he shall not be convicted of murder if he was suffering from such abnormality of mind (whether arising from a condition of arrested or retarded development of mind or any inherent causes or induced by disease or injury) as substantially impaired his mental responsibility for his acts and omissions in doing or being party to the killing.

The ambiguity of the expression 'abnormality of mind' in this formulation led to a test case in which the defence of 'irresistible impulse' was denied.[69] The court of appeal quashed the original decision and Lord Chief Justice Parker gave a definitive interpretation of the 1957 Act with regard to non-cognitive disorders as follows:[70]

> Abnormality of mind which has to be contrasted with the time honoured expression in the McNaghten Rules 'defect of reason' means a state of mind so different from that of ordinary human beings that the reasonable man would term it abnormal. It appears to us to be wide enough to cover the mind's activities in all its aspects, not

321

only the perception of physical acts and matters and the ability to form a rational judgement whether an act is right or wrong, but also the ability to exercise willpower to control physical acts in accordance with that rational judgement.

However, in admitting disorders of willpower as a legal defence Lord Parker also pointed out that[71]

the step between 'he did not resist his impulse', and 'he could not resist his impulse' is one which is incapable of scientific proof. *A fortiori* there is no scientific measurement of the degree of difficulty which an abnormal person finds in controlling his impulses.

The history of irresistible impulse in capital offences thus converges with the criterion of the reasonable man since, in the absence of scientific *proof* of the irresistibility of any given impulse for any individual on a particular occasion, the burden of *unscientific* judgment as to irresistibility is shifted to the jury on the basis of the 'objective' criterion of the ordinary and reasonable man.

Despite the developments in law outlined here it is only recently, and then only in the case of capital offences committed by persons suffering from severe mental disorder, that there has been any tendency to recognise the admissibility in law of scientific evidence relevant to the causal connections between states of mind and impulses to criminal action. Moreover, so far this recognition is based on the general grounds that the mental conditions included in the definition of severe mental disorder or illness are of such severity that the causative links between the offence and the defendant's mental condition can safely be *presumed.*[72]

From the viewpoint of the PO model developed here, the concessions to scientific explanations of human behaviour do not go far enough (they are rather like coming out in favour of apple pie and motherhood and peace). For the orthodoxy still supposes that, no matter how much scientific knowledge we have of human behaviour in general, there will always be a significant class of offenders for whom there can be no excuse in the ordinary sense of the word.[73] At any rate it is held to be very certain that science cannot *now* explain all of human behaviour even in general terms, and even clearer that it is impossible to give a scientific explanation of a particular person's particular act unless that person is suffering from some recognisable defect (and what is more, that the defect is demonstrably instrumental in bringing about the offending act). That being so, it is said, all that is entailed by available scientific accounts of action is a reduction of culpability, or at most of the class of culpable offenders, where the evidence warrants it.

Even those critics of the objective test who advocate its replacement by a subjective test usually seek no more than to allow for the different thresholds at which different individuals cease to be 'masters of their own minds'. Their point is that different individuals lose their self-control under different degrees of provocation, not that self-control should cease to be a criterion of criminal responsibility. Therefore, even if the subjective condition replaced the objective condition, on this basis normal offenders would still be held guilty, blameworthy and deserving of punishment if after due allowance for their character and circumstances they were deemed not to have lost their self-control at the time of the offence. For example; an 'average' man finding his wife in the act of adultery might wilfully kill her and her lover, and yet avoid the charge of murder if he killed in anger. However, if he were known to be an unusually cold man and if, say, he first read a lengthy moral sermon to the lovers before killing them, he would be liable to the charge of murder because he had not lost his self-control.

4.2   *A Radical Extension of the Subjective Test*

Physical determinists with an eye to IT will want to say that determinate physical causal processes are sufficient to account for all behaviour, including deliberate, mind-directed, self-controlled behaviour, and this will not be affected in the case of 'normal' offenders by a redescription of their acts in terms of motives, reasons and purposes, because these are causes 'from the inside'. Thus, the argument goes, even for those who are not suffering from 'mental defect' in the clinically certifiable sense, there will be a sufficient explanation of their acts in terms of physical causal necessity. Glanville Williams has seen the point and implications of this very clearly:[74]

> [if] regard must be had to the make-up and circumstances of the particular offender, one would seem on a determinist view of conduct to be pushed to the conclusion that there is no standard of conduct at all. For if every characteristic of the individual is taken into account including his heredity, the conclusion is that he could not help doing what he did.

In reply to the libertarian charge that current scientific explanations of action are just promissory notes, the determinist can point to the extensive evidence of cases where previously undetected physical abnormalities have caused acts for which the doer was held to be culpable. Two such syndromes that are now well known are Huntington's Chorea and Pick's Disease. These disorders are generally transmitted by single genes, though (unusually for genetic abnormalities) they do not manifest themselves until early middle age. Sometimes the

323

clinical symptoms of the disease are preceded by a phase in which the sufferer begins to have grossly antisocial ways for the first time in his life with the result that he is mistakenly held responsible for his conduct until the clinical symptoms appear.[75] It goes without saying that where the offence is a capital one the clinical symptoms never do appear. Cases such as these may give pause to the libertarian, but he will remain unconvinced, because he can (quite rightly) maintain that every pick-pocket, road-hog, tax-dodger and bully is not, and *patently* is not, suffering from organic disorders of this clinical type. This much can be conceded, however, since the crucial point is made that ordinarily we are almost totally ignorant of the material determinants of behaviour.

Taking his cue from such cases as the example just cited, the physical determinist can now venture a decisive move, and propose that socially disordered behaviour is symptomatic of a disorder of the social individual. Before proceeding very far with this argument, however, it is as well first to take note of the stock, and supposedly to knock down, logical objection to this move. This objection deserves to be called Molière's objection to dispositional explanations in terms of 'natural essences', since that French playwright satirised the scientists of his day by ridiculing their explanation of the fact that opium induces sleep, in terms of its 'soporific quality', where 'soporific quality' means power to induce sleep. For some inexplicable reason philosophers, who ought to know better, and others who perhaps ought not to know better, still seem to think that this is a merely verbal and circular device which explains nothing at all. To be sure, the explanatory power does not carry us far, but it is not entirely without force. This is quickly established in the similar case of brittleness.

Long before we knew anything about such things as molecular bonds and crystalline structures, we knew that certain sorts of objects broke relatively easily, and we called them 'brittle'. We explained their breaking in terms of that property that they have in virtue of which they break relatively easily, i.e. 'brittleness'. Notwithstanding the labours lost of Ryle and Wittgenstein, when we talk about an object's 'brittleness' we are not just referring to its tendency to break easily when dropped. We are referring to some property it has, which other objects do not have, which makes the difference between their *not* breaking and its breaking.[76] It may well be that this property word may have a sense without a specifiable reference, in which case we make do with *symptoms* as an indication of its presence. Later on, when we find out more about the previously hidden structure, we may be able to specify the reference and have no need to refer to the symptoms. Such is the case with 'brittleness' as this refers to a class of (ordinarily unobservable) crystalline structures.

The suggestion now is that disordered, mind-directed behaviour can be taken in the same way, without circularity or vacuity, to be symptomatic of disordered central self-control apparatus. This form of words has controversial overtones for some philosophers, but all that is implied here, however, is the harmless tautology that, whenever an individual's actions are not ordered in accordance with rules and norms prevailing in his community, then his behaviour is disordered in relation to these norms.[77] What this means is that the central nervous structures and states (control systems) that are necessary and sufficient for ordered behaviour are maladjusted, and that as a consequence of the maladjustment the behaviour they regulate is disordered with respect to the relevant norms. It is useful to recall Ducasse's succinct formulation of the essential point here; 'a thing which under strictly the same circumstances behaved in a different way could not be strictly the same thing – it would be different just in that it behaved differently'.[78] Accordingly, it follows that a criminal act is, in itself, sufficient evidence that it was not possible (meaning 'possible$_1$') for the agent to do otherwise than in fact he did do at the particular time, no matter how infrequently he may have so acted before or since, or how frequently he may have desisted from such actions before or since. This may seem less counter-intuitive if we remember that it is misleading (not to say sloppy!) to regard an agent as 'the same' from time to time without regard to his specific physical states at particular times (see Chapter VII, Section 7.3.1).

For the reason given some writers have been critical of the suggestion that criminal behaviour of ostensibly normal persons in itself is a sufficient criterion of mental disorder.[79] The debate over this problem has been muddled by an unfortunate failure on the part of all concerned to distinguish between significantly different types of disorder, in particular by the attempt to assimilate disorder to disease. But this question is not immediately germane to the present point, and consideration of it is deferred until the next chapter. For the present purpose it is sufficient to remark that on a physicalist thesis nothing else but disorder or maladjustment would or could cause disordered behaviour. The question then is not whether or not to look to such sources of disordered behaviour, but rather, given the evidence of neuropsychology, developmental psychology, sociology and so forth, to explain why anyone would take the curiously naïve view that nothing in particular different is going on when an arm is raised in greeting than when an arm is raised in anger; because there is every reason to suppose that all sorts of different things are going on, but that they are ordinarily buried out of sight, in the nervous system and the brain, or diffused throughout a complex environment.

The logical consequence for law of IT and the emergence of the PO model therefore is that, once all of the circumstances of individual offenders are admitted into consideration of their culpability for their offences, even normal offenders cease to incur guilt, blame and liability to punitive sanctions in the traditional sense. This is in keeping with the general trend of penal history, which is that principles that one generation applies to the immature and insane are sooner or later applied to the mature and sane.[80]

5   SUMMARY AND CONCLUSIONS

In discussing the reasonable man criterion of criminal responsibility attention has been paid to issues that are not directly affected by the question of physical determinism. This is desirable for two reasons: first, because the debate has often been conducted as though all that is at issue is the need for the law to take account of the findings of science; second, because in this case it is just as important to show what is *not* affected by physical determinism as to show the consequences that *do* seem to follow. These consequences fall into two main groups.

First, the consequences of a shift from the OA to the PO metaphysic would obviously undermine the main assumption underlying much of the justification that has been advanced for the reasonable man criterion. In particular, it challenges the assumption that a normal offender could have done other than he did at the time of his offence, in the sense of 'could' assumed for moral culpability. It would also by the same token vitiate the vituperative sense of responsibility as blameworthiness for criminal offences based on comparisons with the hypothetical reasonable man. The redundancy of free-will and responsibility in the sense of Old Testament guilt, along with the OA model, does not entail the redundancy of responsibility as strict legal accountability, however.

Second, and perhaps more practically significant, are the consequences that follow from a possible resolution through IT of the extreme practical-participant and theoretical-observer perspectives on human action. This resolution is clearly desirable, because most of the disputes over the reasonable man criterion have arisen from the mutual failure of jurists and scientists fully to understand each others' perspectives, or to appreciate that they may be reconcilable on the basis of common practical concerns, within the PO model. On the one hand, offenders have been held responsible, convicted and even executed who by the best attested scientific evidence were seriously disordered, because judges have deemed the scientific evidence irrelevant. On the other hand, forensic scientists, if they exclusively pursue determinist assumptions to their logical conclusion, must always deny, and increasingly have denied, responsibility in the traditional sense of the word. From this denial there arise the possibility both of acquittals that are 'as scandalous as they are logical'[81] and (paradoxically) of serious injustice and inhumanity.

The contradictions can be reconciled first of all by recognising that human communities are the products of natural evolution. Their forms of life involve regulative and determining constraints. Second, contradictions can be reconciled by interpreting the recognition and following of rules as the undergoing of determinate central processes of a regulative type. To experience the *undergoing* of these processes (i.e. 'from the inside') is to have normative experience. The function of law therefore is seen to be rooted in the regulation of anatomically differentiated but socially integrated biological systems.

Science on the other hand is confined to the observer's perspective on these processes. What the judge is concerned with as a participant in the social form of life is to communicate norms and regulate social behaviour. That is, he functions in the system he regulates. The scientist, as such, does not have a *regulative* function in the form of life, but he provides objective information about the mechanisms that regulate function and so his insights inform practice. To illustrate by a parallel: to a (participant) 'seer' vision does not manifest itself phenomenologically as neurological mechanisms interacting with the environment (this is the truth so laboured by the conceptual analysts); scientists, however, can determine that 'seeing is undergoing certain neurological processes interconnected with the environment'. Disorder of vision is thus logically connected to certain neural disorders. Rectification of, or compensation for, neural disorders (e.g. by surgery or prosthesis) *entails* the rectification of, or compensation for, disorders of vision. And there is no category mistake involved. It works.

At this point it might be as well to anticipate a discussion to come and recognise that the parallel drawn between behavioural and visual disorders could give rise to the (justified) apprehension that some more or less crass form of psycho-social engineering was about to be suggested as a parallel to surgical remedies for visual defects. These qualms can be allayed by acknowledging that, in human affairs especially (as well as in vision), it is often advisable to follow the injunction, 'Do not adjust your mind, there is a fault in reality'. But so to acknowledge that the individual as such may not be disordered is not to reject the concept of crime as disorder or maladjustment; it only raises questions about the ontology of disorder, and ultimately about the metaphysical status of the individual person. Specifically, it draws attention to the unique constitutive relationship human individuals have with others in their

327

community(s). Social 'reality' involves other participants in a common form of life, and the problem of crime is the problem of ordering reciprocal, i.e. *mutual*, relations. These remarks lead to the main practical conclusions we can draw from the discussion of the reasonable man criterion and the objective test, which are these:

1 The first question raised by the criterion has the *practical function* of establishing what would be a tolerable standard of behaviour in the community in relation to a particular rule, which is to establish in effect whether an accused has anything to answer for to his peers. This is best decided by his peers, as is the case in the so-called 'objective test'.

2 The second question raised by the criterion, as to whether a particular offender could in fact have acted at a particular time according to the prescribed norm, is on a PO model redundant since a disordered act is symptomatic of disorder. Establishing and assessing specific causes of the disorder and formulating measures for restoring order are highly complex matters which may require all the resources of the human sciences and are beyond the competence of most ordinary people. They are not then in the main matters for the offender's peers, but in the main for experts.

With some important practical qualifications to be derived from other considerations, these consequences seem to follow for the reasonable man criterion from the PO model of human behaviour as informed by IT. In practice it would mean that the courts would continue to decide whether there had (technically) been an offence; whether it was the accused who committed the technical offence, and whether technically committing an offence was reasonable or not in the circumstances. Beyond this, the courts would have no function. Establishing the causes of offences and making recommendations for disposal of the offender would be, in the main, matters for experts. This conclusion has the merit that cases such as necessity (in the legal sense, e.g. entering an embargoed port in a storm), accident, misadventure and overt physical compulsion (e.g. being used as a missile to break a window) would continue to be handled by the courts and not by tribunals of human scientists, as would happen according to some other proposals for revision of sentencing practices in line with developments in science.[82]

XII

CRIME, DISEASE AND
MALADJUSTMENT

1 INTRODUCTION

In the matter of crime, philosophical determinism has commonly been expressed as the view that crime is a kind of mental disease and criminal acts the symptoms of disease. This controversial view of crime was stated with convenient forthrightness by Rondeau as follows:[1]

> Anger is a passing fever, jealousy a mental delirium, the rapacity of the thief and the swindler a momentary disease and the depraved passions which drive man to sin against nature are organic imperfections – the murderer himself is a sick man like other criminals – the moment all crime is recognised as the natural product of some disease, punishment must become only a medical treatment.

In this chapter, the main reasons why such a view has been held will be briefly outlined and the main objections to it will be discussed from the viewpoint of IT and the PO model of persons. It will be argued that an important distinction must be drawn between the category disorder and the sub-categories disease and maladjustment. Finally, an account of crime as maladjustment will be advanced which meets the outstanding objections to a disease account without departing in essentials from the hard deterministic view implicit in the PO model.

2 THE CASE FOR CRIME AS DISEASE

There are three main arguments for the view that crime is, or is due to, a form of mental disease. These are: the argument from linguistic usage, the argument from symptoms, and the argument from analogy.

329

2.1   Linguistic·Usage

The general hypothesis that mental disorder is disease (and so by implication the more specific thesis that crime is disease) has been so widely accepted, it has been said, that the language now expresses what most people actually think. Thus Ausubel has argued that in current medical and lay usage the connotation of the term 'disease' is generally regarded as including any marked deviation, physical, mental or behavioural, from normally desirable standards of structural or functional integrity.[2]

This is the contention that has been so much disputed by recent writers. Even if the claim about ordinary language is not true, however, the determinist might concede both that in ordinary usage 'disease' does not connote mental disease, and that, even if it does, usage is unsatisfactory. All that is necessary for determinism is that some account of criminal behaviour can be sustained in terms of determinate disorder, and this, I believe, can be done.

2.2   Symptoms

Many people are impressed by the close similarity and even indistinguishability of the behavioural symptoms owing to, on the one hand, physical, and on the other putatively psychological, causes. Thus, as well as genetic disorders it is well known to doctors for example that the behaviour symptoms of clinically defined 'depression' states and catastrophic loss of self-esteem are commonly indistinguishable from those due to oedema in cardiac failure; those for hypermanic overactivity, elation and compulsive striving for unrealistic goals are indistinguishable from elevated white blood count in acute infections; and those of phobias, delusions and autistic fantasies are indistinguishable from those for pathological conditions like pneumonia.[3]

This similarity naturally suggests common causes of symptoms and so the idea of mental 'disease' as well as physical disease.

2.3   Analogy

The problem presented by criminal behaviour is closely analogous in many respects to physical disease. For example, each disrupts ordinary function, whether the analogy is taken at the individual or the social level. Criminals may be regarded as not leading normal 'healthy' lives, just as physically ill patients do not. Sick members of the community are like decayed body tissue and criminals are like parasites on the body politic, and so forth. In both cases the abnormality calls for action by practical men, and institutions are established to deal with them. The analogy view is clearly expressed by Karl Menninger as follows:[4]

The very word 'justice' irritates scientists. No surgeon expects to be asked if an operation for cancer is just or not. No doctor will be reproached on the grounds that the dose of penicillin he has prescribed is less or more than justice would stipulate. Behavioural scientists regard it as equally absurd to invoke the question of justice in deciding what to do with a woman who cannot resist her propensity to shoplift or with a man who cannot resist an impulse to assault somebody. This sort of behaviour has to be controlled, it has to be discouraged; it has to be stopped. This (to the scientist) is a matter of public safety and amicable co-existence, not of justice.

A very powerful factor in persuading people of the aptness of the analogy is the precedent of recognised mental disorder, since notoriously in the past persons who by all modern standards would be certifiably insane or mentally deranged have been treated as wicked and criminal and cruelly persecuted and punished.[5] The former treatment of lunatics resembles in many ways the present treatment of criminals, and the analogy between the two cases and physical disease is easily drawn, as Samuel Butler did so effectively in the novel *Erewhon*.

3   OBJECTIONS TO THE THESIS THAT CRIME IS DISEASE

There have recently been many strong objections to the thesis of crime as disease, notably by the psychiatrists Szasz[6] and Breggin,[7] the social scientist Barbara Wooton[8] and the philosopher Antony Flew,[9] though sometimes from very different points of view and for very different purposes. I will consider just three of the main ones here corresponding to the reasons given for holding the view. This should be sufficient to indicate how the controversy might be resolved without departing from the deterministic essentials of a disease thesis.

3.1   *Linguistic and Epistemological Objections*

Thomas Szasz has forcibly argued in a number of works that the concept of mental illness or disease in general and the case of crime as a disease in particular is rooted in a profound linguistic and epistemological mistake, that of taking the metaphor of physical disease too far in diagnosing and treating 'mental' disease. He says:[10]

The crux of the matter is that a disease of the brain analogous to a disease of the skin or bone is a neurological defect and not a problem of living ... a person's beliefs – whether they be a belief in Christianity or Communism or in the idea that his internal organs are 'rotting' and that his body is in fact already dead cannot be explained by a defect or disease of the nervous system ... the (epistemological) error in regarding psychosocial behaviour consisting of communications about ourselves and the world about us as mere symptoms of neurological functioning – is an error pertaining, not to any mistakes of observation or reasoning as such, but rather to the way in which we organise and express our knowledge. In the present case the error lies in making a symmetrical dualism between mental and physical or bodily symptoms, a dualism which is merely a habit of speech and to which no known observation can be found to correspond. ... The notion of mental symptoms is ... inextricably tied to the social (including ethical) context in which it is made in much the same way as the notion of bodily symptoms is tied to an anatomical and genetic context.

This passage contains the core of the linguistic and epistemological objections to the mental disease thesis. The first counter-objection that can be raised against Szasz's conventional philosophical view is that, when he asserts that the disease metaphor is a *mere* metaphor, he commits what Stuart Hampshire calls the Fallacy of Literalness,[11] the fallacy of supposing that, because words have roots of a more or less concrete–ostensive kind, any metaphorical extension of them into less concrete forms of expression must be mistaken and inadmissible. This in itself is a profound error, because language and thought live and grow on just such extensions. It is interesting therefore to point to just one example in the very passage in which Szasz expresses the objection, where he makes the same supposed mistake himself. He speaks of 'organising' knowledge which, if we were to be etymological about such things, is an epistemological error when we are talking about knowledge that has nothing to do with organs at all. We might, emulating Szasz, insist that living animals can properly be said to be organised living systems but that any other usage is precarious metaphor and leads to dangerous zoomorphic nonsense about political states being living entities with general wills and corporate rights; and so forth and so on. But of course, talk of government and business organisations is just as intelligible and legitimate as talk about organised bodies of knowledge and organised bodies (*simpliciter*). So to talk of mental disease or disorder is not to make an obvious conceptual, logical or epistemological mistake even at the metaphorical level.

More far-reaching objections can be directed against Szasz's position, however. First there is the matter of the criterion for psycho-physical identity, or what he calls 'symmetrical dualism' (which seems to be the same thing). He complains that no known observation can be found to correspond to the habit of speech that expresses it. The previous discussion (Chapter V, Sections 2.2 and 3.1.1) showed that the reason for this is quite simply that there *is* no observation that would correspond to it because it is not the sort of thing that one can observe; it is a relation, specifically an identity relation, something like that between heat and molecular kinetic energy, or between mass and energy, or between viruses and infection principles, and so on. As such it is interpretative and not observational. Like those other examples it involves a *theory* through which observations are interpreted as related, and specifically as being in an identity relationship.

At least the idea as usually advanced is propounded as a scientific and metaphysical hypothesis; but Szasz, in referring to 'a habit of speech', puts his finger on a more deeply rooted epistemological relation, one that gave vertigo to the master Wittgenstein and problems to his disciples ever since, including Szasz. This is the fact that the psycho-physical hypothesis does seem to be so very deeply rooted in the language and is implicit in ordinary thinking. It breaks out, as Wittgenstein saw, in the ambiguity of the question 'Why?' and in the fact that the logic of the ordinary responses, though supposedly categorially different, are yet equally appropriate to it: in short, motives and causes are *both* explanatory in reply to the question 'Why?', and unless there is some relationship between them this is a very very peculiar thing. Wittgenstein himself saw it merely as a regrettable fact of linguistic life, and Szasz follows him in dismissing it as a bad and pernicious habit. But this is just not good enough in view of both the pervasiveness of physical 'metaphors' in mental talk and the explanatory power of the physicalist view that reasons are causes 'from the inside'.

This last point is pertinent to the second of Szasz's points I should like to discuss very briefly, namely the experience that Szasz refers to as mental symptoms of the problems of living which are inextricably tied to social contexts. An elaborated physical–determinist view is that individuals and individual 'minds' can properly be regarded only as sub-systems of social systems, linked through channels of communication to others in the same system, and beyond to more all-embracing systems. There is no suggestion that individuals or individual brains function in isolation from their environment, whether (patently) physical, social or symbolic, but quite the opposite: that other people (as well as symbolism in its many forms) can be regarded as, among other things, the brain's 'external aids to thinking'. They form the 'ecology of mind'.[12] The Trojan horse model is apposite for the manner in which the environment, and specifically the human and symbolic environment, continually restructures the individual organism through its brain and central nervous system. According to this physicalist model the world of immediate individual experience is the undergoing of interactions between biological individuals and their environment. And from the participant perspective the integrated networks of causes *are*, that is are identifiable as, the social and ethical contexts of the common form of life of which Szasz speaks. According to this view, then, the problems of living, the trouble of getting along with fellow men, of how we should live, are the problems of organisms interacting with their environment but as seen 'from the inside' – because the organisms in question are, quite simply, *us*!

Before moving on to other objections to the disease thesis it is worth drawing attention to Szasz's peculiarly astigmatic view of mental illness. According to him (and radical psychologists and psychiatrists influenced by him) there are really just three categories of people who are commonly called mentally ill, none of them properly so-called:[13] first, there are those whose debility is organic; these cases are properly called brain illnesses; second, there are those who are simply emotionally upset, depressed and unhappy about problems of living (such as failure of personal relationships); third, there are those whose conduct is merely unconventional, disapproved of or feared by powerful social, political and economic or other orthodox institutions (this class includes many supposed criminals).

When we turn to classic cases in forensic psychiatry we wonder in vain which of Szasz's categories many of them fit into. For example, what of the man who assassinates a political leader under personal instructions from God? And what of the case of the man who reacts to a rejected proposal by murdering an old lady whom he has never met, whose breasts and genitals he then removes and cooks with onions and then eats during the next few days?[14] According to Szasz, unless such people voluntarily submit to psychiatric treatment they must be presumed mentally normal, plain lawbreakers, criminals who need to prove absence of *mens rea* or face the legal consequences of their actions.

It is cases such as these, however, that spawn the prolific variety of idioms that describe mental illness. Thus we speak of people as, for example, 'deranged', 'unhinged', 'twisted', 'demented', 'touched', 'frenzied', 'possessed' and 'raving'. Only slightly less laconically we speak of 'having a slate loose', of being 'soft in the head', 'round the bend' and 'bereft of reason'. Anybody even only mildly impressed by the jejune argument that ordinary language embodies all of the distinctions that men have found worth making must find this argument for bona fide mental illness from verbiage overwhelming.

3.2   Conceptual Objections

It is said that, unless there is some scientifically objective and value-free criterion that distinguishes between diseased and 'responsible' persons on the basis of symptoms of abnormality that are independent of antisocial behaviour itself, then it is improper to speak of disease at all; otherwise the notion of disease becomes circular or vacuous.[15] Barbara Wootton, for example, draws a parallel with fever, and suggests that, just as we distinguish the fever from babblings in fever, we should be able (if crime is disease) to distinguish between the putative criminological disease such as moral defectiveness, as in psychopathy, and its behavioural expressions in antisocial acts.

This argument has already been touched upon in the discussion of the objective criterion, where it was dubbed Molière's argument against dispositional explanations in terms of natural essences. It is not necessary to do much more than repeat our conclusion from that discussion: namely that, as in the case of brittleness, explanations of disordered or diseased behaviour (as symptoms) in terms of unspecified causal mechanics are not necessarily either circular or vacuous even when we are not yet certain what the mechanisms are.

It is worth pointing out that Professor Wootton's choice of example does not support her thesis either. What she speaks of as fever is no more than a collection of other symptoms, with no more claim to causal status than babblings; for high temperature, chilled sensations and sweating are all symptoms or manifestations of the body's reaction to viral infection. Now people talked perfectly sensibly about fevers before viruses were dreamed of, and no logical aspersions will make nonsense of the fact that we use 'fever' to explain a collection of symptoms like sweating and babbling, and when people babble and sweat we say they have fever, and said so even before the invention of the microscope. In the same way the neuropsychologist (neurosociologist!) need not be talking nonsense if he uses 'disorder' to explain a collection of symptoms like lying, thieving and violent assault, and, when people lie, thieve and commit violent assault, he speaks of 'disorder' even when he is in almost total ignorance of the precise causal structure and function of the disorders he presumes are involved.

3.3   False Analogy

Antony Flew has suggested that, in all the debate about crime as (mental) disease by analogy with physical disease, the structure of the analogy has never been properly analysed. When it is, he argues, it becomes apparent that there are significant differences between physical disease and crime

335

which in effect vitiate the analogy. According to Flew,[16] there are two crucial differences between physical disease and crime.

1 In physical disease the sufferer is always a victim, whereas the criminal is not, and may even be said positively to enjoy the fruits of satisfaction of his criminality.

2 In physical disease the sufferer is deprived of his volition in respect of the disease to which he is a victim, whereas the criminal is exercising his volition in the very criminality of which he is not a victim.

Flew also draws attention to another characteristic of physical disease.

3 Physical disease or malfunction is culturally neutral, whereas the criminal is criminal because he breaks rules and laws that are relative to cultures and ideologies.

Flew suggests that mental disorder could be regarded properly as disease only if these criteria were met, but that criminal behaviour in general emphatically does not meet them.

I will discuss the first two (supposedly) essential criteria for disease together first, and then the third separately.

3.3.1 *Victimisation and Volition*

Flew's analysis of the disease analogy derives a certain plausibility from the fact that we are likely to think of physical disease as something like a fever, tuberculosis, cancer or poliomyelitis. In such cases as these the patient suffers and seeks the aid of doctors for betterment. Flew is supported here by Szasz, who defines illness in terms of voluntary submission of the patient for medical treatment.[17] The patient in physical disease is incapacitated in various ways beyond his control, and in ways that materially affect what he can choose to do. By contrast, criminals (except in *Erewhon*) do not conspicuously suffer from their criminality; seldom do they seek help to save them from robbing with violence and such like. They are free to do as they do without constraint. But here we may be misled by the choice of cases, because there are other cases of physical disease that are closer to criminality than the ones that first spring to mind.

Perhaps we should characterise crime first, then seek a physical analogue, rather than the reverse, in order to test the analogy more aptly. What we should look for is some characteristic of crime that is also shared by some disease or class of diseases. To this end we note that the most conspicuous feature of most crime, and the one that sets it apart from most disease, is that generally the criminal does not suffer from the actual crime, whereas others do. The reverse holds true of most disease, but not all. In fact, there is an important exceptional case through which the analogy can be better developed and tested. The case of infectious disease, and particularly the case of the carrier, is in many ways like that of the criminal. First of all, the carrier does not necessarily suffer himself though others do. So infection-carriers do not satisfy the first test of disease proposed by Flew. Second, the carrier, like the criminal, does not suffer from any loss of volition on account of the disease. So carriers do not satisfy the second test of disease proposed by Flew either. Whether or not they positively derive pleasure or satisfaction from their condition is a debatable point. It is likely that many criminals derive particular satisfaction not from the actual criminality, but rather from its fruits. In this respect they may be like a man who enjoys spending the insurance money after an unpleasant illness or accident, so that enjoyment is hardly a vital difference between them. But even if we allow that, unlike the carrier, a criminal does in general deliberately commit his crime, there remain some important analogies to carrier diseases.

The Guinness Book of Records gives the case of Typhoid Mary Mallon from New York City who was the source of one epidemic alone involving 1,300 cases. Since she herself was only a carrier, she declined voluntarily to give up employment in which she handled food, so she was compulsorily quarantined for twenty-three years until her death.[18] An interesting parallel that can be drawn from this case is that between the criminal's freedom to suppress his predisposition to lie, cheat and steal and Typhoid Mary's equal freedom not to work in the kitchens. Here, then, we have a close parallel between crime and an important type of disease, namely between the habitual criminal and the non-suffering carrier of infectious disease. From the determinist's point of view neither is more culpable than the other, though their cases are different in some ways.

It might be said that carriers are not being punished for having the disease but for breaking the law against carriers working at certain jobs, in which case they are being punished for a criminal offence, not a medical condition. The analogy holds here also, however, since it is not the criminal's morbid internal state of mind that is prohibited by law, any more than it is being a typhoid carrier that is prohibited. What the law prohibits are anti-social consequences following from public actions *deriving* from morbid internal states, and that is precisely similar to the disease-carrier case. We might go further and argue that, if there is a disanalogy, it favours ordinary criminals, because their 'condition' affects their *will* to do the right thing whereas there is not the same obvious effect in the carrier case.

Summarily, then, instead of Flew's first two conditions for disease as a basis of the crime and disease analogy I suggest that crime is a disorder like some diseases in the following three ways.

1 It is a disordered state of the person which occurs through nature or nurture or both.

2 It does not affect the normal volitional capacities of the person.
3 It affects others with whom he comes into contact.

At this point it is opportune to draw attention to a highly significant, and perhaps crucial, omission from most analyses of the disease thesis, an omission that gives rise to considerable confusion and needless disagreement. Usually the crime–disease debate is based on the model of therapeutic medicine where, typically, individual patients suffer from some morbid condition, and the treatment involves the administration of serum, drugs or other individual therapy. Now this model is manifestly strained if, as often happens, it is extended to cover such cases as political dissidence.

However, we may observe that the field of preventive medicine and its interface with the institutions of public health is a branch of medical or para-medical inquiry and practice also. In fact, personal hygiene and sanitary engineering have probably contributed far more to public health than therapeutic medicine ever could (or indeed ought to): both are equally concerned to eradicate disease.

If the analogy between disease and crime is extended accordingly to include preventive medicine and para-medicine, we must then look to the causes of crime in society and culture as well as to delinquent individuals whose acts are determined by such causes as bad upbringing, prejudice and discrimination, unequal opportunity, injustice, indifference, inequitable distribution of wealth and property, unearned privilege, arbitrary exercise of authority, repression ... and so on.

One consequence of extending the disease analogy in this way is that we see how, contrary to the objections argued, and as the case of Mary Mallon shows, there is no essential distinction between physical disease and (so-called) mental disease or crime so far as the compulsion society is prepared to exercise in its control and eradication is concerned. The Public Health Act of 1936, for example, specifically the section concerning the detention of infected persons, states clearly that:[19]

> A justice of the peace on being satisfied that a person suffering from a dangerous infectious disease is in a hospital vested in the Minister of Health, may direct that he be detained in the hospital (and that) any justice may extend the time of detention as often as it appears to him necessary for preventing the spread of disease.

Notice that these very sensible (and so far as I know uncontroversial) provisions imply nothing about the patient's responsibility and blameworthiness for having the disease.

Another consequence of extending the disease view to the analogy of public health is that, contrary to what is usually presupposed by objectors, such cases as political dissidence and 'protest' delinquency do not necessarily entail, on the disease model, an individual therapeutic approach to delinquents. The disease model does not involve, for example, stereotactic surgery for political opponents and disaffected youth. This is clearly not so because on the public health model it makes at least as much sense to look to the social and institutional sources of crime as it does to take a therapeutic approach to individual offenders.

3.3.2 *Cultural variability*

The third objection to the disease/crime analogy is that the criteria of physical disease are objective whereas those of mental disorder and so of crime are value-laden or culturally dependent. This has an initial plausibility similar to that of the 'victim-loss of volition' formula for physical disease. For no culture would deny the debilitating effects of bodily disorders and disease. Functional disorder at the physical level could for this reason be regarded as an objective standard, even without a precisely defined criterion. In contrast, where putative mental disorder and disease are involved 'order and health' have neither well-defined objective criteria nor even universally acceptable tacit norms. Homosexuality is a case in point. Whether or not it is regarded as debilitating or a 'disease' seems to vary with cultures.[20] Even more to the point is the fact that homosexuality can be permitted or prohibited by law, and it will rightly be said that it is a queer sort of disease that has this aetiology. So, it seems, mental 'disease' differs in this vital way from physical disease, and the analogy breaks down.

Let us acknowledge at once that the legislative criterion provides strong and perhaps in the final analysis decisive grounds for distinguishing between crime and disease. It will be necessary to develop the deterministic view of crime to meet this point.

There are nevertheless a number of difficulties with the argument from cultural variability that merit serious consideration. It is open to question from two general perspectives. First, at the level of physical disease one may question whether the 'debility' criterion is as objective, universal and value-free as has been supposed. Second, from the wider perspective of the systems viewpoint one may question whether the 'disorder' criterion is as value-laden or 'relative' as has been supposed, and whether this matters.

First then, if everyone in a culture suffers, and has from time immemorial suffered, from the same chronic disease, then there is no way of telling what the contrasting healthy state would be – just as someone who has been in pain all his life without knowing it until the pain stops will then say 'I thought everybody felt like that'. But if everybody always *does* feel like that, or *look* like that, how, we may ask, can it be called disease? We might say for example, that, as survivors of the evolutionary process, we are the disease-ridden carriers of maladies that killed off untold generations of the phylum, but what would that mean? The point made here is that physical 'health' is relative to overall group norms and is therefore not objective in some absolute sense, independent of the group itself.

Such grounds for doubt about the universality of norms of physical health are well illustrated in the case of goitre, which is caused by iodine deficiency. Some areas of the globe are iodine-sparse and people who live there have iodine-deficient diets, and goitre can become prevalent. Before the end of the nineteenth century it was thought that the diseased thyroid was nothing more than padding designed to fill out the neck and make it plumply attractive. Goitrous individuals do not display a single set of symptoms, but they range from dull and listless to nervous and tense as well as more or less normal. It is quite conceivable therefore, for geographical, cultural–dietetic, ideological or religious reasons, that isolated communities of this sort could develop (and have done) a common 'goitric' form of life with men and women widely admired for the size and plumpness of their goitres.[21] Such forms of life would have adapted to their environment, and only those adapted to other environments (in place or time) will regard their permanent condition as morbid. So, even at the physical-disease end of the analogy there lurk cases of cultural variability. There is, in fact, no absolutely objective or value-free criterion of functional normality, even at the crudest physical level.

We can moreover adopt a more generalised systemic view than the purely vegetative physical one. Here the discussion about organic adjustment at the vegetative physical level can yield an important insight. It is said that there is universal understanding and agreement about what constitutes physical health and physical disease. Granted the qualification just made we can perhaps accept this as being generally the case. But the reason for this is not to be found in the fact that the human body and its environment is physical and *therefore* objectively determinable in structure and function (in the sense that all cultures substantially agree about it). This assumption is the crucial mistake usually made in this dispute. The reason is rather that, as a matter of fact, human bodies and their physical environments are essentially 'universal' in the respects relevant to bodily health. They form a complex system of interknit biochemical cycles of carbon, nitrogen, oxygen, etc. And give or take a pinch or two of iodine and so on here and there, this holds true for all human forms of life. So the individual human body is a 'token' of a single phylum-type adjusted to a single physical environment. Thus the universality and objectivity of the criterion of functional bodily order stems from the universal similarity of systems, and not from the fact that a special (i.e. physical) sort of system is involved rather than some other sort of system.

The case of cultures is quite different. In the (so-called) physical (but really vegetative) domain, systems exchange energy or matter with the environment. In the cultural domain the exchange is informational. The environment is symbolic and social. In speaking thus of the organism's symbolic and social environment the 'mental disease' theorist is not committing an epistemological *faux pas* on a physicalist view because physicalism, at least since Lucretius, is founded not only on the category of mass–energy, but also on the category of order or information, in modern parlance. Now in contrast to the physical–vegetative domain, in the symbolic social domain the organism's environment is *not* globally uniform. Whereas the Russian poet adjusts to the same carbon cycle as the American five-star general and the Tanzanian tribesman, there are important differences between their vegetative and cultural environments because vegetative environments are, and cultural environments are not, essentially universal for all men in relevant respects.

Most bodily organs process and adjust to only the mass–energic exchanges in the culturally uniform (vegetative) environment. The brain however also handles and adjusts to the symbolic and social environment. Unlike the tissues of any other organ, brain tissue possesses the unique property of making possible awareness of the adjustment to the world of sensory, social and symbolic stimulation. Hence, by virtue of this unique relationship of the nervous system to the environment, diseases of behaviour and personality may reflect abnormalities in personal and social adjustment quite apart from any gross structural or metabolic disturbance in the underlying neural substrate.[22]

That 'disease' of the mind should be culturally variable is not then in itself a factor against its being considered a disease at all, because the unique function of the organ in question is precisely to adjust to and effectively interact with a symbolic–social environment. One might as well say, assuming a brain criterion, that a kidney is not diseased unless it malfunctions in relation to a symbolic or social environment (or something of the sort) as to say, assuming a kidney criterion, that the brain is not diseased unless it malfunctions in relation to a chemical environment (or something of that sort).

We can now address the question of the supposed non-objectivity of culturally variable health or disease criteria. It has often been said that men are rational animals only in human communities. This truism provides a universal and objective *formal* criterion for human rationality, i.e. 'being an executive member of a communal form of life'.

341

But unless and until there is only one form of communal life for all rational men (as there is for vegetative forms), it would be misguided to seek for a substantive criterion of order or adjustment, which was objective in the sense of being universal to all men and in all communities. (We might just as well look for the objective standard of a good fit in shoes and give up the ghost because men have different sized feet.) Also, it is a mistake to suppose that a thieving Mick is any the less disordered or disorderly in Finchley merely because he would be a pillar of the community among the Dobu tribe. There is nothing *subjective* or arbitrary, therefore, about the judgment that the Mick is disorderly, because *for him* the culture of Finchley is as objectively given in the symbolic–social domain as the proteins and carbohydrates he eats with his fish and chips are in the physical–vegetative domain.

There is nothing scientifically disreputable therefore in, for example, the fact that Americans (whether they happen to be psychologists or not) consider that among the symptoms of mental 'health' in an industrialised urban community are such vestiges of Quaker prejudice as holding down a job that gives satisfaction, and making friends.[23] What *would* be surprising, and scientifically rather disreputable, would be any suggestion that the aspiration, say, to be president of a conglomerate industrial corporation would be a necessary sign of mental health in Tibetan Llamas, but nobody has ever suggested this.

Criticism of the notion of mental 'health' has even been carried so far as to ridicule the rather unexceptionable idea that being able to form *some* personal relationship is a sign of mental health,[24] as if this requirement were not seriously the very minimum general condition of any recognisably human life whatsoever, healthy or diseased. The question of criteria for disease and disorder will be taken up again presently. At this stage I suggest the tentative conclusion that the objectivity of cultural norms for natives to a culture is not prejudiced by the existence of different norms in different cultures. Provided it is borne in mind that norms and individuals interact mutually, with *mutual* accommodation and assimilation, as with all interacting systems, there need be neither disastrous consequences implied for individual social freedom nor violence to sound scientific principles.

I conclude that most of the influential arguments I have considered have not been sufficient to undermine decisively the thesis that crime is disease. What has been established, however, is the untenability of a strict disease thesis in the important point of 'legislation'; that is, bona fide disease is not the sort of thing that is brought about by statute, whereas crime is. However, this argument does not tell against a disorder model of crime as maladjustment.

In saying this, a most important distinction is now being drawn which has so far been overlooked or blurred in referring indiscriminately to disease, disorder, derangement and so on, as commentaries on this subject commonly do. What I want to go on now to suggest is that the outstanding problems raised by the disease thesis can be resolved without departing in essentials from the disease thesis by drawing distinctions between disease, and on one hand the more general category of disorder, and on the other hand another sub-category of disorder, maladjustment. On this basis the essentials of the disease thesis can be sustained, and in such a way as to be unexceptionable.

4   CRIME AS MALADJUSTMENT

4.1   *A General Taxonomy of Mental Disorder*

The debate about crime as disease has been greatly confused by a failure to distinguish between quite different states of affairs which must be clearly and properly distinguished. The main problem seems to be that so far no party to the dispute has distinguished sufficiently between the category 'disorder' and the sub-category 'disease'. Flew, for example, in some opening forays against the thesis that 'crime is disease', lines up his opponents by citing passages that do not in fact contain the word 'disease' *at all*, but only 'disorder'.[25] The same conflation is evident throughout the literature. Thomas J. Scheff, to cite another example, in his introduction to a book on *Mental Illness and Social Process*, equivocates in typical fashion when he writes:[26]

> The articles in this reader represent recent thinking and research on a topic that might best be called the social reaction to mental *disorder*. The theme that is common to most of the contributions is a concern with recurring patterns of behaviour among individuals and organisations attempting to cope with persons who are defined as mentally *ill*.

And Lord Denning said that:[27]

> any mental *disorder* which has manifested itself in violence and is prone to recur is a *disease* of the mind. At any rate it is the sort of disease for which a person should be detained in hospital rather than be given a qualified acquittal.

Now there is a variety of clearly distinguishable species of the genus 'disorder' which are commonly taken to be mental disorders. These include *hereditary disorders* of a type transmitted through many generations, including various sorts of retardation and abnormality; *congenital disorders* owing to non-hereditary chromosomal aberrations

343

such as the XYY type, which has been correlated with psychopathic criminality; *damage*, whether due to injury or degeneration; bona fide *mental disease*, both with (as in general paresis) or without (as in schizophrenia) well-known physical correlates. Finally, I suggest, there is *maladjustment*, which holds the key to an account of criminal behaviour that does violence neither to science nor to individual interests.

4.2 *Maladjustment*

The special features of the concept of maladjustment can be brought out in contrast with other types of disorder through a simple machine function analogy, say a motor vehicle. Each of the types of mental disorder just distinguished has a recognisable analogue in the case of different machines of the same design or machines of different designs with similar functions. Pursuing the analogy; hereditary defects correspond to design flaws resulting in the relatively poor performance of machines of one type compared with that of machines of other types with the same functions. Congenital disorders correspond to cases where the manufacture or assembly of a particular machine has been botched, for example where there are too many washers under the wheel-retaining nuts, which vibrate loose. Disorder owing to brain damage has obvious enough machine analogues. Disease 'proper' corresponds to a disruption of normal function (morbidity) owing to extraneous physical causes, which shows itself in abnormal performance. For example, for the case where a well-known cause exists, there are in the machine case such analogies as choked air or fuel filters, or rust. The case where there is no known physical cause is the lamentable 'lemon' syndrome, known to all car owners, of diffuse and undefinable 'bugs' for which there is no reason to doubt there are physical causes but which defy expert analysis for a time.

Now in the machine case there are disorders of function of the machines systems which are properly called *maladjustment* and which must be clearly distinguished from other sorts of disorder. A machine may be well designed, properly assembled – in the sense that it has just the necessary parts, assembled in just the necessary way; it may be undamaged and free from disorders with known physical correlates; and yet it may still not *function* properly because the precise machine *settings*, or in general the system's relations, are not properly functionally integrated – they are functionally disordered or *maladjusted*. Typically, in a motorcar the timing of ignition firing may be asynchronous with the crankshaft phase sequence.

It is at this point that the analogy becomes illuminating, because *maladjustment* in the machine case suggests a corresponding species of the genus 'mental disorder'. That is to say, an individual may be free from hereditary disorders and congenital disorder; he may be free from brain damage and from disease, and yet he may still be disordered in the sense that the central self-regulating systems involved in controlling his behaviour in relation to given norms are functionally disordered or maladjusted in relation to these norms. There is, of course, a long tradition of regarding delinquents as maladjusted, and there is a wide variety of well-known causal factors in maladjustment, such as maternal deprivation, broken homes, over-indulgent parents, patterns of parental care, personality, sibling relations and family size.[28] What this analysis suggests is the mode in which such factors are translated into the causal mechanisms influencing criminal behaviour; that is, through their influence on the development and functioning of physical central self-control systems. Of course, although we may usefully and truly think in this way of maladjusted self-control systems underlying delinquent behaviour, the precise nature of such maladjustment is almost wholly unknown at the present time: all that is known are 'symptoms' of such conjectured disorder. This does not detract from the plausibility of the maladjustment account of disordered behaviour, given what we already know about the structure, function, development and pathology of the human brain. The uncertainty about the precise nature of maladjustment that gives rise to the observable symptoms does, moreover, suggest other useful features of the analogy between machine and mental maladjustment.

For example, if the precise causes of disorder are unknown, it may in practice be impossible on the basis of symptoms alone to distinguish on the one hand between extraneously caused machine disorder and maladjustment, and on the other hand between diseased and maladjusted individuals. This is precisely what tends to happen in practice. In the machine case the 'lemon' syndrome owing to extraneous causes is often indistinguishable from physical maladjustment. Similarly in the mental case; behaviour owing to such obscure causes as Pick's Disease or Huntington's Chorea is often indistinguishable from behaviour owing to 'mental' maladjustment as I shall now call it.

Another close analogy between machine and mental maladjustment is that the symptoms of mental maladjustment are not very different from normal variations of type. Maladjusted behaviour in fact tends to be an extreme expression of normal behaviour, as by now the analogy would lead us to expect, since few of us are perfectly adjusted to our functions and situations, just as few ordinary machines are ideally designed and finely tuned. This last point suggests how the analogy can be further elaborated to include a correspondence between on the one hand the way in which individual machines can be tuned (or mistuned) to different functions (such as high-performance 'racing' adjustment, or low power-rated 'endurance' adjustments) and on the other hand the way that individual persons may be adjusted (or maladjusted) to different social roles or functions (such as self-motivating leadership or dependable routine service).

It goes without saying, perhaps, that what is being elaborated on here is an analogy that serves the purpose of pointing up the distinction between two significantly different sorts of disorder that are commonly conflated, with very unfortunate consequences. It is not, of course, being suggested that normal people are in any simple way like motor vehicles.

The analogy is nevertheless sufficient for the purpose of showing how one who is free from disease, or any number of other disorders, may still suffer from the disorder of *maladjustment* to his ostensible role and to his prevailing socio-cultural environment. And simple though the analogy drawn is, it is not difficult to accept that in the brain's vast tangled porridge of functionally and hierarchically integrated loops of self-regulating neuronic feedback control systems, *interacting with the environment*, the scope for maladjustment and asynchronous synaptic firings is rather ample and, perhaps, sufficient to account for the disordered behaviour that would be the symptom of it. The maladjustment suggested is offered as a frankly physical one, based on a physical analogy. But the analogy shows a functional similarity, so it is no *mere* analogy.[29]

IT allows us to construe physical maladjustment of a certain type as entailing psycho-social maladjustment also (and vice versa). Neurology tells us that, from birth, the individual is physically structured and is re-structured through his interaction with his environment. From his symbolic and social environment he acquires rules and norms: he is, in a relevant sense, 'programmed' for life in a human community. His recognition of the rules and norms is neurally embodied. His ordered behaviour and adjustment to his own situation and others is determined by neuronic order and adjustment (reasons 'from the outside'). His disordered behaviour and maladjustment to his own situation and others is determined by neuronic disorder and maladjustment, which 'from the inside' may well be present as malevolent perversity or, equally and more pregnantly, as a feeling that 'the way things are around here needs changing in view of the trouble it causes for me'. This is the case of: 'Do not adjust your mind; there is a fault in reality.' That is to say, the systemic thesis of 'maladjustment' is neutral as between two remedies: assimilation by and accommodation of, the individual (to use Piaget's terminology); either the environment can be assimilated by the individual (he changes it) or the individual can accommodate to the environment (it changes him) to resolve the maladjustment.

4.3   *The Ontology of Disorder and Maladjustment*

Let us turn now to the outstanding objection to the disease thesis, which is that, since disease, unlike crime, cannot be legislated into existence, crime cannot properly be regarded as disease. The taxonomy of disorder just outlined shows that a state that is not disease can still be a disordered state, namely maladjustment. Disordered mind-directed behaviour is symptomatic of disordered individuals. This suggestion has been objected to on the grounds that, for example, political dissidence might be regarded as symptomatic of mental disorder, which would be preposterous. In order to clarify this issue and to meet the objection it is necessary to question some presuppositions about the nature of human persons. What is in question is this: if criminal behaviour is symptomatic of disorder, who or what is disordered?

Given the orthodox view of persons, the question is superfluous because the implication is clearly that it is the autonomous person, self or centre of consciousness that is disordered. Nothing else could be, except metaphorically. Within the physical–deterministic model however the situation is much less straightforward, because according to this view the person is a complex physical system embedded in a hierarchy of subordinate biological systems and superordinate social systems. The person is a 'holon',[30] that is, a biological system that has the capacity to adapt to its environment both as an organic whole and as a societal part. Viewed thus, as Laszlo says,[31]

> living in society provides him with the structures to which to adapt
> his motivation and behaviour. This is not a passive adaptation, for
> man is not determined by his environment (alone) but by his own
> decision-making capacities. Thus the well adapted individual *chooses*
> the mode of action which is functional to the social system as an ex-
> pression of his self-determination – the self-determination of a
> relatively autonomous part within a larger whole. This does not mean
> that *every* social system is supported by its members as a function of
> their self-determination. Some systems constrain individual develop-
> ment and randomise social roles, others freeze them into inflexible
> bureaucratic structures. It is well to keep in mind, however, that a
> social system which stunts individual freedom is just as much an
> aberration from systemic norms as any other type of system which
> reduces the function of its parts below their maximum potential. The
> well organised social system is composed of relatively autonomous
> and differentiated, yet functionally integrated sub-systems. Systems of
> this kind stimulate the decision making capacities of their members
> and enable them to evolve with their full complement of properties
> and the freedom to exercise them.

Antisocial and criminal behaviour on this view therefore may be either a maladjustment of the individual as an anatomically differentiated organic whole, or equally and alternatively a maladjustment of the societal constraints themselves to the functional norms of its constituent members. The concept of *reciprocal* adjustment is thus implicit in all subordinate/superordinate, organ/environment interaction and is well expressed in Piaget's distinction between accommodation and assimilation; to the precise extent that one interacting system assimilates another, that other accommodates, and vice versa. To speak of 'mental' abnormality in this context then is to imply a social 'ecology of mind', in which the individual mind is an embedded sub-system. Individual criminal acts thus are not necessarily manifestations of the unique perverse and isolated wickedness of 'primitive' persons, but rather commutual maladjustments in the set of integrated systems including (of course) the agent.

Precisely this view has been suggested by some forensic scientists. Thus Thibaut has said that:[32]

psychotherapy should attempt not merely to heal the individual but to develop a healthy community basis of behaviour that will be effective throughout the organisation of man as phylum. Instead of merely 'adjusting' a non-conforming individual to any culture he happens to be in, there will be a shift in emphasis to the revision of culture as a whole. ...

Similarly, the Ministry of Education Committee on Maladjusted Children expressed the thought that:[33]

A man can develop his powers to the full and lead a happy life only if he achieves a measure of adjustment and harmony with those around him and with the circumstances in which he is placed. Not that he need be satisfied with his environment; some environments are so unhealthy that they ought to be altered. Without the characteristically human attitude of discontent with things as they are there would be no development either of the individual or of the community, but it is possible to combine even a burning ambition to right wrongs with mental balance and tranquillity of disposition. Adjustment however can never be complete; continual adjustment and readjustment are necessary throughout life.

In short, whereas disease cannot be legislated into existence, maladjustment can; but remedial adjustment or readjustment can involve either the agent or the norms (or both), and so the maladjustment view avoids the main difficulties raised by the disease view.

348

5 OBJECTIONS TO THE MALADJUSTMENT VIEW

5.1 *Abuses*

Among the most common objections to the thesis that crime is maladjustment, and to deterministic accounts generally, is the claim that it leads to abuses of persons and personal liberty. These abuses arise, it is said, because the appropriate attitude to maladjustment and its causes and remedies is an objective one, and an objective attitude is inappropriate to human persons as *agents*, that is to say as centres of consciousness and rationality, with rights and feelings.[34] If men lose sight of the personal identities of supposed offenders, and regard them merely as disordered bodies, then worse iniquities can follow from this than from the worst sort of retributive punishment. As Aldous Huxley has put it:[35]

> The problem today is one of regulating the exercise of power by men of good will whose motives are to help not to injure, and whose ambitions are quite different from those of the political adventurers so familiar to history.

Another writer has referred to the arrogance and insensitivity to human values to which men who have no reason to doubt their own motives appear peculiarly susceptible.[36]

Perhaps the best-known current abuse is the application of the notorious 'analogy principle', which was introduced in the Russian Penal Code in 1922. It instructs the courts to take measures against any action deemed to be socially dangerous, even when the action is not in contravention of any article of the criminal code, provided there is an *analogy* between the action in question and some article of the criminal code that seems most nearly suited to the actions of the supposed offender. This principle has come to be associated with the Vychinsky model of the Soviet citizen as a socially integrated man, whose duty and contract is discipline.[37] Thus political dissidents, by analogy with criminal psychopaths, may (all too likely) be deemed to be maladjusted or suffering from mental disease and committed to clinical institutions.[38] Against such 'disorder' models of crime it is commonly argued that even bad people are not by the same token experimental rabbits.[39] In this connection attention is sometimes drawn to another point of difference between physical illness and criminality which has already been referred to, namely that, whereas patients suffering from physical disease *volunteer* for treatment, the (supposedly) diseased criminals as a general rule do not. Since the law safeguards the individual's right to refuse treatment for physical disease, for example by preserving his right to

349

discharge himself from hospital, it should not deny the same basic human rights to criminal offenders.[40]

There are several different aspects of this compendium of 'abuse' arguments that require discussion. To begin with we must acknowledge that there are abuses, and that at least some of them may be attributable to an excessively instrumental attitude owing to disease or maladjustment models and an analytical isolation of the objective perspective. Abuse of persons is not however a necessary consequence of the PO model. It should be remembered that both a disinclination to cause suffering and a resistance to Draconian constraints that impose it are demonstrable facts of human nature. There is no reason to suppose that these perfectly natural dispositions are more likely to be undermined than reinforced by a general growth of knowledge about the causes of human behaviour. Quite the opposite. The short answer to the abuse argument is that practical abuse calls for practical disabuse, for control and safeguards, and not for the abandonment of a scientifically informed legal system. The proper response to abuses in physical surgery is not to give up the practice of surgery but to curtail the abuses.

Second, as to the objective attitude towards criminals as persons, it can be said that, supposing the PO interpretation of crime as maladjustment prevails, then our attitude towards criminals, though admittedly objective, is *justifiably* so. To the extent that adjustment (to the individual *or to norms*) is called for, an objective attitude as opposed to a moralising one often may be precisely what is required. But even when it is not, the 'participant' or interpersonal approach is consistent with the PO model also, on the postulate of mind–brain identity. If an objective attitude were adopted to antisocial 'centres of consciousness', it need have no more drastic consequences for human life than the same approach to (conventionally) physical disorder. There was a time, it is well to recall, when surgery was resisted and autopsies were forbidden because the human body, even in death, was considered sacrosanct. The same view survives still in the practice of some groups. But on the whole the doctrine that persons are being abused by routine medication and surgery or the demands of personal hygiene is a dead letter. Attitudes towards the treatment of mental and behavioural disorders could easily change, are indeed changing, in the same way.

The third aspect of the 'abuse' argument follows from the second, since a change in attitudes towards criminals and what to do about them is only one aspect of, or a consequence of, a general shift in the root model of human individuality. If the PO model prevails, and the transempirical self is a redundant category, then all that is coherent in orthodox talk about persons is reinterpretable as talk about physical systems. And once we accept IT, and with it the proposition that disorder of the neural basis of personality can result in behavioural disorder, it is logically consistent to accept the corollary proposition that other kinds of manipulation of the same neural substrate can conceivably have therapeutic effects irrespective of whether the ostensible cause of the mental symptoms is physical or psychological.[41]

But of course none of this implies stereotactic surgery for parking offences, since (on the PO model) official warnings or fines are by interpretation just as much physical facts as they are 'institutional facts'. They involve organised movements in space, surface irritations of the organism, restructuring of the nervous system and brain; and this may be (demonstrably *is*) sufficient to bring about the desired behavioural change in most cases. This manoeuvre and conclusion is an excellent example of the way that philosophy can change everything and yet leave it the same!

An important case in point is the way in which a shift to a maladjustment view of crime and a treatment approach to offenders is entirely consistent with the traditional deterrent view of the disposition of offenders. For the prospect of treatment for crimes might be expected to have the same socially desirable and salutory effect on potential criminals as the corresponding prospect of the need for hospitalisation now has on men careful of their bodily health.

Fourth and finally, it is a mistake to say that crime differs categorially from disease in the matter of the compulsoriness of the measures taken. As the disease-carrier example established, where the natural and legitimate interests of others are jeopardised, compulsory treatment or preventive measures are applied, even in physical disease, thus showing that the principle of tolerable order underlies the formal regulations of human communities, regardless of the metaphysical model of persons presumed.

5.2 The Good Nazi Argument

It is said that maladjustment is not an adequate account of crime because adjustment means adjustment to a particular culture or to a particular set of institutions, and some institutions, even whole societies, are themselves criminal. In this way, adjustment and so maladjustment becomes divorced from moral and social rectitude. The archetypical case is the 'good' Nazi of the Third Reich.[42] It is said that such a man may be well adjusted to and well integrated into his society, and derive deep satisfaction from it; and yet, far from him being without criminal stain, we should want to be able to say that he was, if anything, quite the opposite. This indeed was the principle of the Nuremburg trials for war crimes. If rectitude is not integration into a form of life made manifest in behaviour ordered in accordance with its norms, then criminal vice cannot be simply a failure to integrate into a form of life made manifest in behaviour that is disordered in accordance with its norms.

It has already been pointed out (Section 4.3 above) that the maladjustment view of criminal deviance is consistent with the possibility that social constraints themselves, including laws, are maladjusted in relation to natural norms regulating human development and behaviour. The case of justified deviance has already been considered. The good Nazi argument is based simply on the converse case of unjustifiable adherence to laws that are inconsistent with natural norms regulating human development and behaviour. Naturalistically inclined philosophers have typically referred in this connection to the natural sympathies and sentiments that human beings have for the welfare of others and the common good, and they have contrasted these with the 'artificial' virtues owing to enculturation.

Just as it can be argued that the maladjustment manifest in criminal acts may reflect upon inhumane laws rather than the criminal deviant, because the law is incommensurate with natural human sympathy; so it can be argued that legal rectitude in an inhumane system may constitute a crime against humanity.

It might be suggested that, if this view were correct and there are common human sympathies, then we should expect to find that even the agents of repressive regimes such as the Third Reich, provided they are sane, share the same common human sympathies and sentiments as others. But it may be doubted whether in fact they do. If they do not then the argument from natural human sympathy is indecisive if not demonstrably false. There are two points to be made here.

First, it seems likely that many agents of repressive regimes are not deficient in their natural sympathy for other people. What is problematical is their lack of awareness of the extension of the class of people. Persecuted groups are often discriminated against because they are thought to be deficient in some personal property and so sub-human. Discrimination between human and sub-human is typically made without due regard to the relevance of the difference on the basis of which the distinction is made. The problem in this case therefore is not that inhumane regimes are based on principles other than human sympathy, but that there is a failure to understand where sympathy is due.

Second, there is ample evidence in fact that there is no extensive lack of understanding of where natural human sympathy is due and what it requires. To cite just one example, towards the end of the Second World War, Himmler and Eichmann, with regard to the action taken towards the 'final solution' of the Jewish problem, told the Red Cross that they had wanted the Jews to acquire a sense of racial community through the exercise of almost complete autonomy.[43] There is therefore, unsurprisingly, reason to believe that repressive regimes commit crimes against humanity not in ignorance of human sympathy but in spite of it.

The case of the good Nazi therefore is properly construed as adjustment to a system that is itself maladjusted to the principles determined by natural sympathy and so perpetrates 'crimes against humanity'. The maladjustment view of crime is thus consistent with the possibility that 'criminal' individuals may be models of rectitude within a prevailing system of law.

The apparent force of the good Nazi argument may derive from the assumption that there is an absolute, non-natural standard against which adjustment and the systems adjusted to can be evaluated. The standard in fact applied to Nazis at Nuremburg was the sanctity of human life and human welfare. Now it must be said that values such as these are by no means absolute values in the sense that they transcend the biologically and culturally determined interests of human beings. For as le Compte D'Argenson replied to the Abbé who had excused himself from transgressions on the grounds that he must live, 'I do not see the necessity'.[44] There is no absolutely objective, non-natural basis for establishing the criminality of 'crimes against humanity'. This does not, however, entail that there is no standard that is independent of culture and against which cultural norms can be evaluated. There is no need for supernatural or other extramundane authority; all that is required is a standard that derives from the demonstrable natural sympathies and sentiments of men which presumably have biological origins and which are common to all cultures.

6 SUMMARY AND CONCLUSIONS

Determinism in law has frequently been expressed as the view that criminals are diseased and that crimes are symptoms of their diseases. This view has *prima facie* plausibility by analogy with physical disease and derives additional force from the indistinguishability of symptoms in certain 'mental illnesses' and some physical diseases. For these reasons the notions of mental illness and crime as disease have currency in ordinary usage.

The disease view of crime is open to a number of objections, the most important and influential of which are based on epistemological, logical and analogical considerations. Most of these objections fail or are seen to be misconceived when looked at from the viewpoint of physical determinism. Nevertheless, some can be sustained, most notably the argument from the legislative criterion (that crime, but not disease, can be directly legislated into existence).

There are, however, important distinctions to be made between disease and, on the one hand the more general category of disorder, and on the other hand another distinguishable sub-category of disorder, maladjustment. It is thus evident that, whereas disease, disorder and maladjustment are equally deterministic (and as such equally objectionable to the critics of the disease thesis), objections that tell against a disease thesis do not necessarily tell against disorder or maladjustment views. The maladjustment view is, in fact, especially apt for the delinquent acts of (so-called) mentally normal offenders. The deterministic thrust of the crime–disease thesis is thus sustained by a maladjustment view against the outstanding objections to the disease view.

We have here one of the most important consequences of a deterministic view of persons which renders otiose the most fundamental metaphysical assumptions currently underlying the criminal law. These are, first, that each normal human being is an autonomous psychic unit, a personality, set against his environment (like St George against the dragon); second that such human personalities have, categorically, freedom of the will. For according to the maladjustment view crime is disorder which is completely determined by nature and nurture.

There are, of course, certain rather obvious corollaries to the thesis that crime is, if not disease, then maladjustment. For example, if crime is seen as a kind of maladjustment then a punitive approach to dealing with it would be as perverse and bizarre as Erewhonian recriminations and sanctions against physical disease. Similarly, if criminal behaviour is regarded as having a complex aetiology of a purely casual deterministic type, the question arises as to whether courts are suitable agencies for deciding the appropriate disposition of offenders.

These may seem to be radical and perhaps to some even alarming practical implications of the emergence of a PO model of persons and their acts which mind–brain identity theory advances. On the basis of what was said in the discussion of moral and social institutions, however, we might expect the practical consequences for the administration of law to be far less drastic and alarming than it is often supposed they must be. But to show this here would carry us even further afield and make this book longer than it is already.

354

XIII

THE MENTAL AS
PHYSICAL : CONCLUSIONS

The traditional, and still the prevailing, orthodox view of man is that in virtue of his mentality he is in some important sense or other set apart from the rest of nature. Accordingly, human institutions such as morality and law are based on the presupposition that human reason, volition and purpose are outside the natural processes of cause and effect.

Opposed to this picture is the traditional deterministic view of metaphysical materialism and physicalism according to which human life, including mind and mind-directed behaviour, is entirely incorporated into nature, and the natural processes of cause and effect. Recent developments in science, notably neuropsychology and cybernetics, have given considerable substance to this view. Specifically, the thesis of mind–brain identity provides a basis for a coherent and plausible physicalist view of mentality and mind-directed action.

The increased and increasing plausibility of this view has the effect of eroding commitment to the traditional orthodox view so that there is a tendency towards a shift in the predominant 'root metaphysical model' of man. This shift has consequences for the traditional presuppositions underlying such institutions as morality and law, and so potentially by implication for practice.

This is the thesis that I have developed and sought to make plausible. In doing so I have made sweeping and perhaps reckless forays across wide areas of philosophical terrain occupied by both sides in the conflict. What I have tried to do is to test the physicalist thesis against the best arguments the orthodoxy offers, wherever they are to be found. Since the redundant view is (conjecturally) nothing less than the longest-standing 'model of man', and since it permeates our thinking and way of life root and branch, the best arguments are scattered widely. It is far too much to hope therefore that there are not flaws, gaps and positively gaping holes in the argument I have presented. Nevertheless I can still hope that, like any half-decent fabric, enough of the general thesis survives to testify to the force and coherence of a purely physicalist purview on human life.

No honest effort to get at the truth should end without a menu of confessed doubts, reservations and puzzles, and a programme for future endeavour. In my case such a 'peas under the mattress' postscript may seem more like 'rocks in the bed'. The main points at which I am least prepared to be truculent are these:

The 'biperspectival' account of mind–body identity I have sketched defines the physical domain in terms of communication through external sense. About this view I suffer my own Gestalt vertigo. Although it seems a straightforward enough basis for the distinction between perception of external objects and such patently mental phenomena as imaginings, memories and emotions, I am bothered by the fact that awareness of social and institutional facts requires communication through external sense channels also. Reassurance here lies in the notion of 'participants' perspective within a hierarchy of physical systems, some of which are of a higher order than individual human organisms. The idea may seem strange because there is still an established orthodoxy which *contrasts* the physical and the social. But from the perspective of biology communities of organisms differ from individual organisms mainly on account of the nature of the systemic organisation and communication channels relating systems and their constituent sub-systems.

Related to this point is the realisation that from the orthodox viewpoint the thesis advanced in this book will seem physicalist in name only and so a sort of counterfeit: this, because the concept of the physical has been extended so far that it covers what the orthodoxy means by social, cultural and other things.

Against this doubt I set the basic point that the business of giving systematic, objective, and space–time causal accounts of social and cultural phenomena involves the fundamental concepts of organisation and information (in the technical sense). And these concepts, though they may extend the orthodox notion of the physical, are none the less physical concepts: they were (embryonically) in ancient times and they are so now even to the extent of being a recognised part of a developing physics in the most orthodox sense. Moreover, it is only to be expected that a physicalism that really does have the resources to account for mind-directed behaviour will not be exactly the same thing that the orthodoxy presupposes, *a priori*, it *must* be; that is to say, confined to inanimate natural objects, billiard balls, clockwork and other artefacts.

About the orthodox view of agent action, frankly I can never convince myself that I have quite grasped the point of such distinctions as that between 'a cause for his action' and 'no cause for *him* acting'. I am almost sure that this is because I expect far more out of such arguments than those who offer them put into them. But, 'Can so much libertarian capital be made out of so little by so many?' I still ask myself. At the root of my trouble here is the logically primitive and transempirical person whose life, to my mind, is altogether too quiet to be comprehensible.

I am very impressed by arguments to the effect that the most practically *fruitful* explanations of social behaviour must be in terms of the agent's own reasons, motives and purposes. And I realise that social science has its work cut out for the next generation or two getting *that* right. But here I am reassured that others such as Rapoport also think that it may serve us well to seek for causal explanations for our own actions which will enable us to understand social behaviour in a new and enlightening way. The indicated programme here is to work out the nature of the 'convergence' between rational and 'circular causal' explanations of agent action and social process.

About the practical moral and legal consequences of physicalism I have few reservations in the long run except that I am easily persuaded that in the present state of the science—art there are many 'inexpert laymen' whose half-consciously and unconsciously acquired insights into human behaviour far exceed those of many supposed experts. But here the important factor is that we are still waiting on even the *climate* for the development of a science which will really set experts apart from laymen in the same way that even meteorology can now respectably claim to separate the weather forecaster from the fishwife.

This last point brings me to the last rock in the bed, and the largest. Some years ago Bertrand Russell said that the best minds among the young would not do philosophy but would find their greatest challenge in physics. Today I am sure that the great challenge lies in the application of cybernetics, information and systems sciences to the study of human experience and behaviour. This calls for all of the technical expertise that physics has ever done and more, but the difficulty is compounded by the constraints imposed by the need to define and explore the phenomenology of human experience itself. This demands talents that only a very few are likely to possess in fruitful degree. Ervin Laszlo has offered the reassuring thought that high expertise is not called for to philosophise fruitfully in the framework created by the new ideas; that there are key ideas, general principles and unifying notions that can be fruitfully understood and assimilated without the need for high expertise. This is what I should prefer to believe, and I do so (but frankly

357

uneasily). In any event it seems to me that, just as in the past philosophical developments can be seen in terms of some science in effect saying 'What do we make of that?' (e.g. geometry, heliocentricity, mechanics, evolution and quantum theory), so today in a context of the perennial problems about mind and action we look at the informationally determined, automatically self-regulated behaviour of feedback systems and ask, 'What do we make of that?'

NOTES AND REFERENCES

INTRODUCTION

1 Gustafson (1973).
2 Urban (1939).
3 Collingwood (1940).
4 Pepper (1942).
5 Emmet (1966).
6 Körner (1959).
7 Laszlo (1972c).
8 Pepper (1942).
9 Kuhn (1970).
10 Schon (1967).
11 Jones (1969–70, 1972); Wisdom (1972).
12 Feigl (1967, 1969).
13 Place (1956); Smart (1959); Armstrong (1968).
14 Feyerabend (1963a); Rorty (1965, 1970); Cornman (1970).
15 von Bertalanffy (1964).
16 Rapoport (1962).
17 Laszlo (1969, 1972b).
18 But see Crosson and Sayre (1968); Sayre (1976).
19 Lorenz (1962a).
20 Piaget (1955).
21 Bunge (1959).
22 Harré (1970, 1972, 1973); Harré and Madden (1975).
23 Madden (1969); Madden and Harré (1973); Harré and Madden (1975).
24 Davidson (1963).
25 Honderich (1970, 1971, 1973).
26 C. Taylor (1972).
27 Fitzgerald (1968); Brett (1970); Samuels (1971).
28 Black et al. (1973, 1974).
29 Black et al. (1974).

CHAPTER I CONCEPTUAL THINKING AND
PHILOSOPHICAL DISAGREEMENT

1 Carnap (1960); Cornman (1964); Körner (1959, 1970).
2 Bannister and Fransella (1971).
3 Kohler (1959).
4 Sawyer (1970); Lorenz (1962b).
5 Duhem (1954); Hesse (1953, 1966); Furth (1969); Harré (1972).
6 Sparkes (1972).
7 Whyte (1968); Schon (1967); Hesse (1966).
8 cf. Schon (1967, ch. 3).
9 see Kreisel, (1968, p. 360):
   behind the formal system are intuitive principles of proof and the conviction they carry. But it holds that such psychological elements do not per-
   mit a precise analysis; so to get anything definite one must *replace* them
   by formal rules and study the latter. Now as long as one (believes one) has
   complete formal systems it is perfectly sound to exploit this fact i.e. that
   the formal rules do replace intuitive principles as far as the set of true
   statements is concerned. Putting first things first one begins by ignoring
   more delicate questions of the *kind* of knowledge or convictions involved;
   these can perhaps never have quite as definite answers as purely extensional questions of truth.
10 Bruner and Postman (1949). Compare
   1 Hasdale's letter to Galileo, Georgio de Santinalla in Galileo (1953 p. 98):
   Magnini has written three letters, confirmed by 24 men of the profession
   from Bolognia, stating that they had been present when you tried to demonstrate your discoveries, and that you were saying 'Don't you see that,
   and that, and that?' and not one of them admitted he did, but all of them
   asserted that they saw nothing of what you pretended to show them.
   2 de Groot (1966);
   3 Grey-Walter (1954, p. 468):
   I would suggest that the mechanism of conscious awareness depends on a
   statistical sorting based on some built in or earlier acquired criteria. ... If
   in later life a criterion of significance is established, then suddenly a whole
   field of experience which has been stored in unprocessed form becomes
   available for significant assembly.
   4 Kuhn (1970, pp. 63–4).
11 Wittgenstein (1971, prop. 5.6 *et seq.*).
12 Krech and Crutchfield (1948).
13 Pepper (1942). Pepper identifies '*formism*' based on plan-exemplification
   categories, '*mechanism*' based on physical categories (location, primary
   qualities, laws, etc.), *contextualism*, based on the categories of the 'given
   now' (change, novelty, etc.) and *organicism*, based on process–
   system–teleology categories. Pepper and von Bertalanffy have recently
   endorsed the suggestion that the concept of a 'system' constitutes a fifth
   alternative root metaphor or model, and potentially the most adequate:
   Laszlo (1972a), cf. Pepper (1966, 1970b, 1972).

14 Emmet (1966, p. 201).
15 Castell (1965, pp. 94–101).
16 Körner (1959, p. 279); Ryle (1954, ch. V).
17 Chomsky (1968); cf. Bruner and Postman (1949); de Groot (1966).
18 Jones (1969–70, 1972); J. O. Wisdom (1972); McDougal (1973).
19 Collingwood (1940, p. 23).
20 Bacon (1958, p. 170).
21 Cornford (1912); Kuhn (1970); Child (1965); and refer to Stark (1967) for numerous references.
22 Coser (1968); cf. Stark (1967).
23 Warr (1970); Bannister and Fransella (1971).
24 Marx (1913, pp. 11–12).
25 Smith, Bruner and White (1967 p. 40).
26 Black (1962); Trigg (1973), Gellner (1974).
27 Pepper (1942, pp. 97–8).
28 Whorf (1956 p. 216).
29 Austin (1956–7; in 1970, p. 184).
30 Ryle (1954, ch. V, esp. pp. 75–9).
31 von Neumann, Goldstein and Burks (1962).
32 Armstrong (1970 pp. 67–79).
33 cf. Planck (1950, pp. 33–4): 'a new scientific truth does not triumph by convincing its opponents and making them see the light, but rather because its opponents eventually die, and a new generation grows up which is familiar with it.'
34 Körner (1959 p. 280).
35 Hume (1966 edn., pp. 124–5).
36 Galileo in a letter to Kepler wrote (cited Wynn Reeves, 1958, pp. 110–11):
    Oh my dear Kepler, how I wish we could have one hearty laugh together! Here at Padua is the principal professor of philosophy who I have repeatedly and urgently requested to look at the moon and planets through my glass which he pertinaceously refused to do. ... And to hear the professor of Philosophy at Pisa labouring before the Grand Duke with arguments as if with magical incantations to charm the new planet out of the sky.
    Nowadays the professors would call themselves 'descriptive metaphysicians'.
37 Hanson (1958, ch. 1); Burtt (1965, p. 137); Platt (1968 pp. 106–9).
38 see Kuhn (1970, p. 114).
39 cf. Kanmer (1973, esp. pp. 225–6). For a detailed discussion of the many issues only glossed here see Lakatos and Musgrave (1970).
40 cf. Hanson (1958, p. 11).

CHAPTER II   TWO INCOMPATIBLE MODELS OF PERSONS

1 cf. Sellars (1963a, pp. 1–40): Sellars distinguishes 'manifest' and 'scientific'

images which correspond closely to the OA and PO models proposed here, but there are crucial differences between Sellars's scientific image and the PO model which are discussed later (Chapter II, Section 2.4). He does not stress what I take to be the crucial *systemic* nature of the PO model. Also cf. Franklin (1968, pp. 8–9): he distinguishes traditional and deterministic concepts of man. This deterministic concept is not specifically physical. See also Chein (1972); Wilkerson (1974); Shotter (1975).

2 Moore (1962, ch. 1). cf. Strawson (1959, chs 1, 3). Strawson conjoins mental and physical categories into a Cartesian hybrid 'person'; i.e., 'the concept of a type of entity such that both predicates ascribing states of consciousness and predicates ascribing corporeal characteristics ... are applicable to a single individual of that type' (pp. 101–2).

3 Strawson (1959, pp. 115–16).

4 An orthodox distinction between animate (organic) and inanimate (inorganic) matter persisted until Wöhler's organic synthesis of urea from potassium cyanate and ammonium sulphate (1828).

5 McDougal (1928, p. viii).

6 There is a growing insistence by anti-behavioural psychologists on the same personal attributes. See, e.g., Chein (1972), Shotter (1975).

7 Sprenger and Kramer (1971).

8 Hallowell (1964, pp. 49–82).

9 see for example, Weyer's *De Praestigiis Daemonum* (1566) passage in Wynn Reeves (1958, pp. 269–70).

10 Harré (1970).

11 Hempel (1942), Hempel and Oppenheim (1948).

12 Ryle (1954, chs V, VI); cf. Grant (1952): 'The causal law is prescriptive in that it is constitutive of natural science; that is to say if we give up looking for causes we are no longer practicing science we are playing another game' (p. 383).

13 T. Huxley (1898a).

14 cf. Vartanian (1960 p. 136).

15 Bunge (1969).

16 Sellars (1963a).

17 The first systematic textbook on neurology was written by Moritz Romberg (1795–1873); Edvard Hitzig and Theodor Fritsch published the first work on electro-excitability of the brain in 1870.

18 Pledge (1959, p. 21).

19 Angyal (1941, p. 256).

20 cf. von Bertalanffy (1971, pp. 8–15).

21 McCulloch and Pitts (1943).

22 Rosenbleuth, Wiener and Bigelow (1943).

23 Wiener (1961, p. 8).

24 Lucretius (1969, pp. 88–9; emphasis added).

25 cf. Cannon (1932); Ashby (1940, 1952); McCulloch and Pitts (1943, 1947); Rosenbleuth *et al.* (1943); Rosenbleuth and Wiener (1950); von Bertalanffy (1950); Sommerhoff (1974).

26 cf. Sluckin (1954, pp. 35–6).

27 Northrop (1948 p. 416); cf. Deutsch (1951).
28 Laszlo (1972b), with von Bertalanffy, Thayer, Pepper and Burhoe.
29 e.g. Scriven (1958); Malcolm (1964); Taylor (1967).
30 cf. Schon (1973).
31 Malcolm (1964; in Borst, 1970 p. 174); Coder (1973, p. 289); Castell (1965, p. 96); Strawson (1962, pp. 197, 204); Scriven (1958, pp. 122, 126).
32 ref. Stern (1965, pp. 380 *et seq.*).
33 ref. Farrel (1968, p. 87).
34 Joske (1967).
35 Feigl (1967, p. 87).
36 Emmet (1945, p. 203).
37 Ryle (1966, p. 310).
38 Skinner (1973).
39 Monod (1974).
40 Piaget (1930, p. 235).
41 C. Taylor (1967).
42 I have been pleased to find the same point made by Ted Honderich; cf. *Punishment: the supposed justifications* (1971, pp. 126–7). See below (Chapter VII, Section 4) for other similar objections.
43 Gendin (1973, p. 109).
44 Strawson (1962).
45 cf. Butler Report (Royal Commission on Mentally Abnormal Offenders) (1975, 18.36, p. 229).

CHAPTER III   THE MENTAL AND THE PHYSICAL

1 Bain (1874); Lange (1925); McDougal (1928); Onians (1951); Wynn Reeves (1958); Frankfort *et al.* (1967); Crossland (1971).
2 Descartes, *Meditation* IV (1966, p. 99; emphasis added).
3 Descartes, *Meditation* II (1966, p. 66).
4 Descartes, *Meditation* V (1966, p. 903; emphasis added).
5 James (1958, p. 73).
6 cf. Epstein (1973, p. 121).
7 Eccles (1970).
8 Feigl (1969).
9 Castell (1965).
10 cf. Vesey (1964).
11 Ockham (1964).
12 cited Wynn Reeves (1958, p. 178).
13 Losciutio and Hartley (1963); Feyerabend (1965); Kuhn (1970).
14 Armstrong (1968, p. 73).
15 cf. Butterfield (1949); cf. Kuhn (1957).
16 Bohm (1952, 1957); Bunge (1959, 1968); Nagel (1961). (For the relevance of quantum uncertainty to Human Behaviour see MacKay, 1957; Rosenbleuth, 1970.)
17 Bergson (1965); McDougal (1928).

18 Child (1924, 1941).
19 Crick (1955).
20 von Bertalanffy (1950).
21 Okakura-Kakuzo (1919).
22 *Sunday Times* (17 December, 1972, p. 5).
23 Eccles (1970).
24 Penfield (1950, p. 64).
25 Lange (1925, vol. II, p. 159).
26 Ryle (1966); Wittgenstein (1953); Strawson (1959).
27 Place (1956); Smart (1959).
28 Skinner (1953, p. 26) (cf. Wittgenstein, 1953, paras 157, 158).
29 Skinner (1953, pp. 27ff).
30 Smith *et al.* (1947).
31 Pribram (1969c, vol. 1, p. 15).
32 see especially Koestler (1967), Shotter (1975).
33 Sherrington (1955, p. 209).
34 Anscombe (1971, p. 22).
35 cf. Wittgenstein (1953 par. 109) and Ryle (1966, pp. 74 *et seq.*).
36 see especially Laslett (1950); Wooldridge (1963); Science Journal (1967);
     Pribram (1969c); Luria (1973), Rose (1976).
37 Venables and Martin (1967); Brown and Sancen (1968); Lajtha (1968–71);
     McIlwain (1972); Schwitzgabel (1973).
38 *Symposia*: Delafresnay (1954); Eccles (1966); Morruzi, Fessard and Jasper
     (1963); also Pribram (1969c), Luria (1973); Karczmar and Eccles (1972).
     More synoptic lay accounts include: Wooldridge (1963); J. Taylor (1971a);
     Rose (1976).
39 For the evidence of comparative anatomy of phylogeny see: Bressler and
     Bitterman (1969); Sechzer (1970). For evidence of ontogeny see: Bennet,
     Rosenzweig and Diamond (1969); Conel (1955); cf. Hirsh and Spinelli
     (1970); Held and Bossam (1961); Stritch (1956); Hyden (1959); cf. Dingman
     and Sporn (1964); Ungar, Galvan and Clark (1968); W. R. Russell (1959,
     esp. ch. VI); Slater (1950); Pribram (1969c, vol. 3).
40 Sperry (1966, p. 307). See Kleist (1959); Wooldridge (1963); Penfield
     (1954a, 1966, 1967); Penfield and Roberts (1959); Olds (1956, 1967).
41 Luria (1973); Kubie (1954b, p. 502–3); Kubie (1968, p. 178); Fessard (1954,
     esp. pp. 200–4).
42 Grey-Walter (1954, p. 345); cf. Bremer (1954, pp. 158, p. 497); Fessard
     (1954, p. 201); Kubie (1954a, p. 450); Penfield (1954b, p. 492); Kubie (1968,
     p. 178).
43 Sperry (1966); Gazzaniga (1970).
44 Prince (1906); Thigpen and Cleckley (1954); compare also the views of
     Hume, Treatise, (vol. 1, pt 1) and William James (1961, p. 69) on personal
     identity, and personal testimony such as Bismark's (cited Wynn Reeves,
     1958, p. 145) and Mach's (1959, pp. 28–9).
45 Hoskins (1943); cf. Mottram (1960); cf. Hoskins (1933); Mottram (1960,
     p. 75); McCollum, cited Hoskins (1933, p. 110); Funkenstein (1957); Olds
     (1960); W. R. Russell (1959, p. 131).

46 W. R. Russell (1959); Luria (1973, ch. 7); G. Miller *et al.* (1960, ch. 14).

47 see especially Mottram (1960, p. 75); McCollum, cited Hoskins (1933, p. 110); Funkenstein (1957); Olds (1960).

48 W. R. Russell (1959, p. 131).

49 Jarvie (1954).

50 Harlow (1888). Compare the opposite case of Mr W. A. Brindle, cited J. G. Taylor, (1971a, pp. 55–6).

51 Craik (1943).

52 Hebb (1967).

53 Grey-Walter (1965).

54 MacKay (1956).

55 Bain (1874); McCulloch and Pitts (1943, 1947); George (1957); von Neumann (1957); Caianiello, (1961); I. Aleksander (1973, 1977).

56 Marks (1967, p. 248).

57 Rosenbleuth, Wiener and Bigelow (1943); Rosenbleuth and Wiener (1950); Wiener (1961); Ashby (1946–7, 1970).

58 Shannon and Weaver (1949); Pierce (1961).

59 cf. Wiener and Schade (1965); L. Stark (1968).

60 Weaver (1949, p. 117); cf. Crosson (1968); MacKay (1969b, chs 3, 7).

61 von Bertalanffy (1971); J. G. Miller (1955, 1965, 1971); Buckley (1968). For criticisms of General Systems Theory see Buck (1956). Critical discussion can be found in von Bertalanffy (1962).

62 Laszlo (1972a, 1972b); Gayer (1972).

63 *Science Journal* (1968); Cote (1967); Pask (1968, pp. 79–87); George (1971, ch. 3). An adversely critical review of the field has been given by Sir James Lighthill (1973). Compare Baker (1971). Aleksander (1977) advances a radically different approach to artificial intelligence (1971, 1977).

64 Grey-Walter (1957; 1965); George (1971, ch. 3) (cf. Blakemore and Cooper, 1970).

65 Zerbst (1969).

66 Brindling (1970); Donaldson (1970).

67 L. Stark (1968).

68 Caianiello (1961); Proc. Int. Centre for Theoretical Physics (1973); Aleksander (1971, 1977).

69 cf. Kordig (1971).

70 Rose (1976, p. 361 and *passim*).

CHAPTER IV   MIND-BRAIN IDENTITY THEORY

1 Spinoza, *Ethics*, pt II prop. VII and prop. XIII.

2 Kant, *Critique of Pure Reason* (1965, 2nd paralogysm A 359).

3 Robinet, 1761; cited Lange (1925, vol. ii, pp. 29–30).

4 cited Lange (1925, vol. i, pp. 329 *et seq.*).

5 Fechner (1860); cited McDougal (1928, p. 295).

6 Wündt, 1873/4; cited McDougal (1928, p. 176).

7 Borst (1970, p. 25).

8 cited C. I. Lewis (1960, p. 291); cf. Kneale (1961, p. 340): 'Terms are the same or coincident which can be substituted one for another whenever we please without altering the truth of any statement.'
9 Frege (1960, pp. 56–78).
10 Sellars (1963b, pp. 106–226); cf. Maxwell (1962); Smart (1963a).
11 Feigl (1967, pp. 85–6).
12 Platt (1968).
13 Pepper (1969).
14 Smart (1963a, p. 96).
15 B. Russell (1948).
16 Feigl (1967, 1969).
17 Pepper (1969).
18 Feigl (1967, p. 107).
19 B. Russell (1967, p. 13).
20 Nathan (1969, pp. 259–60); cf. Popper (1971, pp. 145–6).
21 cf. Platt (1962; 1968, pp. 77–82).
22 Place (1956).
23 Smart (1959).
24 Armstrong (1968). The appellation 'UFSAM' is due to Feigl (1967, p. 138); cf. Borst (1970, p. 16).
25 cf. Smart (1963a, p. 81).
26 Feigl (1967, pp. 143 *et seq.*); Rosenbleuth (1970, p. 103).
27 Armstrong (1969, p. 82).
28 Armstrong (1969, p. 82).
29 Kneale (1969); cf. K. Campbell (1972, p. 112); Polten (1973).
30 Armstrong (1969, p. 82).
31 Armstrong (1969, p. 95; emphasis added).
32 Armstrong (1969, p. 116).
33 Armstrong (1969, p. 144).
34 Armstrong (1969, p. 156).
35 Armstrong (1969, p. 310).
36 cf. Medawar (1969, pp. 97–8).
37 Farrel (1950).
38 Rorty (1965, 1970).
39 Feyerabend (1963a, 1963b).
40 Cornman (1970).
41 Feyerabend (1963b); in Borst (1970 p. 140).
42 Cornman (1970, pp. 185–90, 267–78).
43 Cornman (1970, pp. 121–4).
44 Cornman (1970, p. 271).
45 Cornman (1970, pp. 270–1).
46 cf. Oxford English Dictionary: 'property' – an attribute or quality belonging to a thing; 'description' – the combination of qualities or features that marks out, etc.
47 Rapoport (1972).
48 von Bertalanffy (1971, p. 37).
49 Jordan (1968, pp. 51–2).

50 Feibelman and Friend (1945).
51 von Senden (1960).
52 Ryle (1966, esp. p. 17 and *passim*).
53 Ogden and Richards (1960, p. 23).
54 Pribram (1969b, p. 15).
55 MacKay (1956); J. G. Taylor (1971a, 1971b, 1972a); Marks (1967, esp. p. 257–9); Leibovic (1972, esp. p. 279).
56 J. Taylor (1971b, p. 735).
57 cf. Farrel (1950).
58 B. Russell (1948); in Vesey (1964, pp. 280–1).
59 Fechner (1860, vol. i Introduction; cited in McDougal, 1928, p. 137); cf. Lewes (1877); Alexander (1920).
60 Probably taking their cues from Wittgenstein (cf. 1958, pp. 7–8), though Wittgenstein certainly does not suggest a substantial dichotomy, merely a difference in logical grammar. What IT attempts however is to elucidate the causal basis of the logico-grammatical difference.
61 Feigl (1967).
62 Place (1956).
63 Smart (1959).
64 Armstrong (1968).
65 Typically, Lucas (1970, p. 88) supports his assertion that human beings are totally unmachinelike with reference to the Wooden Wotans of Wagner's operas! Nowhere does he refer to neurocybernetics. cf. Wilkerson (1974, p. 89).
66 Sellars (1963a). A detailed discussion of Sellars's views is given in Cornman (1970, pp. 233 and *passim*).
67 Sellars (1968, pp. 166 *et seq.*).
68 Sellars (1965).
69 Sellars (1971). *Note*: I must confess that I have some difficulty following Sellars here. He denies that, on his thesis, sensing is a property of primitive particles, but, like Cornman, I fail to see how this consequence can be avoided, unless we are prepared to accept the real existence and irreducibility of sensa. But to do this would be to concede the inadequacy of basic physicalist categories for replacing the 'manifest image' of man with a 'scientific image'. These difficulties arise because it is assumed that a whole cannot have some property X which consists solely in the parts of the whole having properties other than X and standing in relation to one another (i.e. 'emergent' *systemic* properties) (p. 406).
70 Strang (1961).
71 von Bertalanffy (1971); Laszlo (1969); cf. Whyte *et al.* (1969).
72 Koestler and Smythies (1969); Laszlo (1972b).
73 Kremanskiy (1969, p. 141).
74 Vygotsky (1960). cf. Piaget (1955, pp. 360 *et seq.*).
75 Feigl (1967, p. 12); cf. Russell (1948, pt I ch. 5); in Vesey (1964, p. 274).
76 e.g. Whyte *et al.* (1969); Koestler and Smythies (1969); Laszlo (1972b).
77 Laszlo (1972b, p. 49).
78 Whiteley (1973, p. 97).

367

79 cf. *Science Journal* (1968).
80 Lighthill (1973).
81 Aleksander (1971, p. 494).
82 S. L. Miller (1953).
83 Kauffman (1969 p. 437); cf. Pask (1968 pp. 105–108).
84 Kauffman (1969, pp. 452–4).
85 Aleksander (1971; cf. 1977).
86 Aleksander (1971; cf. 1977).
87 Luria (1973, ch. 1).
88 Luria (1973, pp. 311 *et seq.*).
89 Kubie (1954b, pp. 502–3).
90 Poincaré (1952; p. 37 of Ghiselin).
91 Kekule (1865).
92 Grey-Walter (1954, p. 345; emphasis added); cf. Bremer (1954, pp. 158, 497); Fessard (1954, p. 201); Kubie (1954a, p. 450); Penfield (1954b, p. 492).
93 Kubie (1968, p. 178).
94 Fessard (1954, esp. pp. 200–4).
95 Deutsch (1951).
96 MacKay (1957, 1966).
97 MacKay (1966, p. 430).
98 cf. Powers, Clark and McFarland (1960).
99 MacKay (1966, p. 433); cf. Sciama (1970).
100 Platt (1968, p. 101).
101 cf. Newnham (1971, p. 84).
102 Newnham (1971, p. 85).
103 Zemach (1973, p. 55).
104 cf. B. Russell (1967, pp. 92 *et seq.*).
105 Cornman (1970); cf. Chisholm (1966, pp. 95–6; note p. 95 for further references); Sellars (1969, p. 235); Emmet (1966, pp. 43 and *passim*).
106 Pepper (1969, pp. 49 and *passim*).
107 cf. Castell (1965, ch. 3) for a number of sources of this view.
108 Mach (1959, pp. 28–9), in Vesey (1964, p. 178); cf. B. Russell (1967, ch. 7, esp. p. 108).
109 For example see: Chisholm (1966, p. 102); Strawson (1959, ch. 3); Malcolm (1964; in Borst, 1970, p. 180); Wittgenstein (1953, paras 281, 283); MacKay (1969a, p. 485); Shoemaker (1963); R. Taylor (1966); Shotter (1975).
110 Esposito (1976, p. 232).
111 Hume, *Treatise*, (vol. 1, pt I).
112 Hume, *Treatise*, (vol. 1, pt 1, pp. 301–2).
113 James (1961, p. 69).
114 Mach (1959, pp. 28–9).
115 Bismark; cited Wynn Reeves (1958, p. 145).
116 Prince (1906); Thigpen and Cleckley (1954).
117 Blakemore (1967).
118 Sperry (1966); cf. Gazzaniga (1970).

119 Perceptuo-motor function and brain anatomy are contra-laterally related; i.e., the left brain hemisphere controls right-handed function and vice versa.
120 MacKay (1970, p. 140) (compare McDougal, 1928, pp. 295–6).
121 Gazzaniga (1970, pp. 143–5).
122 Ramsay (1964, p. 61).
123 Watts (1957, p. 139).
124 Sutra Ku-tsun-hsü-Yü-lu, cited in Watts (1957, p. 143).
125 Feigl and Maxwell (1961).
126 Goudsmit (1947).
127 J. Huxley (1949).
128 A point made by Dorothy Emmet in discussion following a paper entitled 'Is all Thinking Ideological?' presented to a conference at Shap Wells, Cumberland, November 1972 (unpublished); cf. Langer (1959, p. 31); Gellner (1964, p. 80; 1974).
129 Ayer (1940, p. 138).
130 Austin (1946; in Flew, 1965, p. 380).
131 Feigl (1967, p. 103).

CHAPTER V   OBJECTIONS TO MIND-BRAIN IDENTITY THEORY

1 see Feigl (1967); Place (1956); Smart (1959; 1963a, 1963b).
2 Cornman (1970, p. 37 and *passim*).
3 Cornman (1970, pp. 32–6).
4 cf. esp. Feigl (1967, p. 29 and *passim*).
5 Malcolm (1964).
6 Marhenke (1952).
7 Katz and Fodor (1963).
8 Cornman (1962, 1970); Craik (1967, pp. 124–6); Farrel (1968, 1972); Feyerabend (1963a, 1963b); Haas (1973; as presented in Newcastle, 5 December 1972); Monro (1973, p. 167); Rorty (1965, 1970); Ruddick (1971); Smart (1951); Stern (1965, ch. VII); Shaffer (1961); Waismann (1952).
9 Brentano (1874) cited by Chisholm (1957, pp. 168–9); Chisholm (1957, ch. II; 1967); Wilkerson (1974); Davidson (1970).
10 Urmson (1968); Cohen (1968); Boden (1970); Scruton (1970–1).
11 Craik (1967); Wallis (1968, e.g. p. 104); Reichenbach (1966, p. 181 and *passim*; 1951, pp. 92–3); Boden (1970).
12 McDougal (1928, pp. xiii–xiv, 356–7), C. A. Campbell (1957); Castell (1965, pp. 4–5); Downie and Telfer (1969, p. 114); Schaeffer (1973).
13 Hume, *Enquiry*, Essay VIII (pt 2, p. 97).
14 Lucas (1970).
15 Scriven (1969, pp. 124–5); and Putnam (1969, pp. 142 *et seq.*); cf. Smart (1963a); Sayre (1968).

16 Beloff (1965); Polten (1973).
17 Tuckett (1932); Price (1955); Hansel (1966); Randi (1975).
18 Hinton (1967).
19 Hinton (1967; in Borst, 1970, p. 250n).
20 see Geach (1967) for an account of events as the objects of 'count nouns' without existential implications (and below, n. 23).
21 B. Russell (1962 p. 12):

> Let us give the name 'sense data' to those *things* that are immediately known in sensation: such *things* as colours, smells, hardness, roughness and so on. We shall give the name 'sensation' to the experience of being immediately aware of these things. Thus whenever we see a colour we have a sensation of the colour but the colour itself is a sense datum not a sensation'.

cf. R. Brandt (1969, p. 67): 'there are still *things* like pains, colours, sounds, smells etc. They are what they are and cannot be made to disappear by any alchemy'.

Vesey (1966, p. 39): 'The identity claimed is not that of a physical object apprehended in two different ways or of *anything* else apprehended in two different ways but of the states of *a mind* with those of a physical object.'

D. Locke (1972, p. 55):

> What is this red flash I see, not an external item, ex-hypothesi; not some*thing* in my brain for no red flashes occur there, so in a materialist scheme of things there seems to be *nothing* which this red flash, which has no objective existence but is undeniably seen, can be.

cf. Cornman (1970, p. 68).
22 cf. T. Nagel (1965).
23 Geach (1967) has argued along rather similar lines, that identity is relative to interpretation. According to Geach, to say 'x is identical with y' is an incomplete expression; it is short for 'x is the same A as y', where A represents some 'count noun' understood from the context of an utterance. Two objects are indiscernible only in terms of the predicables (possible predicates) that form the descriptive resources or *ideology* of a definite theory. He rejects absolute identity but admits as many as needed, two place predicables of the form '__ is the same A as __' where A is some count noun. For example, we can count the men in Leeds or, with a different result, the 'surmen' in Leeds (the classes of men indiscernible by their surnames). And as Geach says, Leeds does not contain surmen–androids as well as men on that account. It is just that we number the inhabitants of Leeds in two different ways.

Similarly, if we treat 'events' as count nouns within the terms of IT (ref. e.g. Pepper, 1969 pp. 52, 56) we can say that some 'mentalling' is the same *event* as some 'physicalling' and we do not thereby conjure up an *ontology* of events any more than Geach conjures up a race of surmen. I do not wish to press the parallels with Geach's argument further because I believe that there is room, within the terms of a *true* theory, to speak of absolute identity (for example by treating events as (physical) state changes). Furthermore, just as, given an apposite theory, discernibles may be

370

identical on interpretation, so, given an erroneous theory, identicals may become discernible on interpretation.

24 Beck (1961, p. 243; emphasis added).
25 Brandt (1969, p. 69).
26 Sellars (1958, p. 526; 1956, esp pp. 320–1). cf. Cornman (1970, pp. 98–100).
27 Vesey (1966, p. 47).
28 Cornman (1970, p. 63 and *passim*).
29 Laszlo (1972b, p. 153n).
30 cf. Kim (1972, esp. pp. 183–4).
31 Smart (1963a, p. 96); see Chapter IV, Section 2.3 above.
32 e.g. cf. Borst (1970, p. 23).
33 Quine (1963).
34 Whiteley (1973, p. 91).
35 Seddon (1972).
36 Kripke (1971, 1972).
37 Seddon (1972, p. 494).
38 Kripke (1971, 1972).
39 Kripke (1971, p. 149 and *passim*; 1972, p. 303 and *passim*).
40 Kripke (1972, p. 304).
41 Kripke (1971, p. 154).
42 Kripke (1971, p. 163).
43 Becquerel discovered the phenomenon of atomic radiation by 'accident'. He noticed the changes to photosensitive plates stored in the same box with uranium salts (ref. 'The radiation from uranium' in Hurd and Kipling. (1964, vol. 2, pp. 364–6))
    In eloquent testimony to the 'contingent' nature of human knowledge of radiation, Einstein's memorial statement about Marie Curie refers to her 'bold intuition [and] a devotion and tenacity in execution under the most extreme hardships imaginable such as the history of experimental science has not often witnessed': cited Hurd and Kipling (1964, p. 368).
44 'The Cause and Nature of Radioactivity', *The Philosophical Magazine* (1902): in Hurd and Kipling (1964, pp. 383–401).
45 Shannon and Weaver (1949); Wiener (1961). For criticism of the supposed identity between information and entropy see Cherry (1971, esp. pp 214–17).
46 Information theory was developed for human communication, but in so far as it is based only on statistical probabilities of signals relative to a transmitter and receiver, it can be generalised to all other systems in communication such as lower mammals where semantical questions of meaning and intentionality do not necessarily arise.
47 Kripke (1972, p. 334 n. 73).
48 cf. Kripke (1972, pp. 334–5).
49 Kripke (1972, pp. 265–6).
50 Ryle (1950, p. 76).
51 See Chapter III, Sections 4, 5; Chapter IV, Sections 4.1, 4.2; Chapter VII, Section 7.3.

52 Malcolm (1964; in Borst, 1970, p. 175).
53 Vesey (1966, p. 47 and *passim*); Mucciolo (1974).
54 Margolis (1971, pp. 214–15).
55 Peirce (1934, vol. 5, p. 310); Keller (1945, p. 38); cf. Feigl (1967, p. 109–10); cf. Feyerabend (1963a; in Borst, 1970, p. 151).
56 K. Campbell (1972, p. 112).
57 Boring (1933).
58 Ayer (1940, p. 225); Farrel (1950); Brandt (1969, p. 69); C. Taylor (1967; in Borst, 1970, p. 236); R. Taylor (1966, pp. 90, 96); Popper and Eccles (1977).
59 Lashley (1958); Mountcastle (1966); Rosenbleuth (1970, pp. 107 *et seq.*).
60 Mountcastle (1966, p. 85; emphasis added).
61 Sperry (1970, p. 587).
62 Borst (1970, p. 23), citing Putnam (1967).
63 Davidson (1970).
64 Smart (1963a, p. 57 and *passim*).
65 Deutsch (1962, pp. 10–16; in Glover, 1976, pp. 67–72).
66 Davidson (1970, p. 100; 1974).
67 Davidson (1970, p. 97).
68 see especially Boden (1970), Scruton (1970–71).
69 Davidson (1970, p. 93).
70 Davidson (1970, pp. 90–1).
71 Davidson (1970, p. 98).
72 Davidson (1970, pp. 96, 98).
73 Davidson (1974; in Glover, 1976, p. 104).
74 Ashby (1970, pp. 113–17).
75 MacKay (1956).
76 MacKay (1956, p. 31).
77 Stephenson (1960; in Borst, 1970, p. 87–92).
78 cf. Smart (1961a; 1963a, p. 96).
79 C. Taylor (1972).
80 C. Taylor (1967, 1972).
81 Anscombe (1958).
82 Ryle (1966, p. 74–8).
83 Malcolm (1964; in Borst, 1970, p. 176).
84 Sprague (1969 pp. 71–3).
85 White (1972).
86 C. Taylor (1967; in Borst, 1970, p. 235–6).
87 Borst (1970, p. 29).
88 Anscombe (1957, para. 23 *et seq.*).
89 Wittgenstein (1972, paras 65–6).
90 see for example Duhem (1954); Popper (1959); Putnam and Oppenheim (1958); Hanson (1958); Nagel (1961); Harré (1972); von Bertalanffy (1971); Sparkes (1972); Laszlo (1972b).
91 Duhem (1954, p. 296).
92 Einstein (1950a).
93 Barret (1970): 'On this level (at which as individuals we live and die) we

encounter a vast shaggy, amorphous mass of unpredictability on which our knowledge has made very little impression' (p. 54).

94 Anscombe (1971, p. 22).
95 Ryle (1966, p. 76).
96 Lenneberg (1967, pp. 1–2); Gardiner (1976).
97 Wittgenstein (1972, para 564).
98 Huizinga (1949); Peters (1966, p. 159); Suits (1973).
99 Luria (1973, p. 327 and *passim*); cf. G. Miller *et al.* (1960).
100 Luria (1973, p. 30 and *passim*).
101 cf. Cherry (1962).
102 R. Taylor (1966, pp. 82, 84; italics added).
103 S. M. Smith *et al.* (1947).
104 cf. Wittgenstein (1972, paras 615, 618).
105 Koestler (1964, pp. 93–4); de Bono (1969, p. 177 and *passim*).
106 Hoffman (1967, pp. 130–1).
107 Eysenck (1970, pp. 119–20).
108 Lilley (1974, pp. 6–7).
109 Luria (1973, p. 31; emphasis added).
110 Lévi-Strauss (1972); Bateson (1973); Lenneberg (1967); Buckley (1967); Laszlo (1969, 1972b); McCulloch (1965); J. G. Miller (1965, 1971); Vogt (1960); Weiss (1971); Wiener (1969); Gardiner (1976).
111 Anscombe (1957, paras 24 and 41).
112 cf. Hart and Honore (1959). These authors consider the case where the circumstances of an agent's act include the words or actions of a second person. They aver the causal irrelevance of such factors in the absence of the knowledge and understanding of the agent: p. 50.
113 In saying this I note the systematic ambiguity of the term 'physical'. That is as between (a) the orthodox sense confined to physics, which distinguishes between on the one hand physics, and on the other biology and (supposedly) non-natural systems; and (b) the sense I have previously (Chapter II, Section 2.3) argued can properly be attached to the term that embraces order/information as well as mass–energy. The salient point is that, once order or more technically 'information' is recognised as a fundamental physical category (and the pedigree for such an idea goes back at least to Lucretius), then biological, social and other systems can be regarded without absurdity as differing only in degree of hierarchical ordering and complexity from conventionally so-called 'physical' systems.

CHAPTER VI   CAUSAL NECESSITY

1 Margenau and van Fraasen (1968).
2 Bunge (1959).
3 Collingwood (1937–8); Stout (1935).
4 Popkin (1953).
5 Russell (1953a); Ayer (1940); Schlick (1949, p. 517); Anscombe (1971); see Bunge (1959, pp. 132 *et seq.*) for numerous sources.

6 See especially Mackie (1974).
7 Kneale (1966); Bunge (1959); Harré (1973, 1975); Bhaskar (1975).
8 *Treatise* (pp. 123, 211); cf. Hamlyn (1957, p. 77).
9 *Treatise* (esp. pp. 134, 181, 214).
10 Russell (1912b p. 194); Schlick (1949, p. 527); Ayer (1940, p. 170 and *passim*); Dummett (1954). (But compare Hume's own (opposite) view: *Treatise* (pt III, section II, p. 122); *Enquiry* (2nd ed. (1750) Essay VII pt II, p. 82n (n.b. deleted from later editions.)).
11 *Treatise* (pt III, section IV, p. 138; pt III, section XI, p. 154).
12 *Treatise* (p. 211); cf. *Enquiry* (Essay VII, pt II); cf. Braithwaite (1953, ch. 4). See Bunge (1959, p. 200 and *passim* for numerous references).
13 Reid (1895, p. 627); Ducasse (1969a).
14 *Treatise* (pt IV, section II); cf. Craig (1953, 1956).
15 Harré (1973).
16 *Treatise* (pt III, section XI, p. 224).
17 *Enquiry*; see Essay VIII (pt I, p. 94).
18 Ducasse (1969a); Bunge (1959); Harré (1973), Harré and Madden (1975); Madden and Harré (1973). For anti-Humean critiques of the problems mentioned here see also the following: first, on the perception of causality: Michotte (1963); Miles (1963); second, on the perception of single cases of causation: Claparéde in Michotte (1963, p. 262); Piaget (1955, p. 311); Madden and Harré (1973, p. 123); third, on the supposed temporal symmetry of causation: Bunge (1959, p. 46); Ducasse (1969a, p. 89); Flew (1954); Black (1956) fourth, on the problem of induction: Bunge (1959, esp. pp. 201, 76–7), cf. Ducasse (1969a, p. 89). Finally, on the denial of productive connection; Reid (1895, p. 627); Ducasse (1969a). On the denial of real entities; Warnock (1953, pp. 181–6); Smart (1963a, pp. 29 *et seq.*); Nagel (1961, pp. 134–7). Mackie (1974) accepts the realist view that there are necessary connections holding unperceived between kinds of events which we identify by their external features, but emphasises that the burden of Humean argument bears upon causation *so far as we know about it in objects* (p. 215).
19 *Treatise* (pt III, section XI, p. 224).
20 *Enquiry*; see Essay VIII (pt I, p. 94).
21 cf. Ayer (1940, p. 197).
22 Kemp-Smith (1918, pp. 368–9).
23 see especially *Enquiry*, Essay VII (pt I).
24 Mackie (1973, p. 139).
25 Flew (1954, pp. 49–52).
26 B. Russell (1953b, p. 123).
27 Shimony (1947).
28 Ayer (1972, pp. 10–11); cf. Hume, *Enquiry*, Essay VII (pt I, p. 69).
29 Piaget (1955, p. 228).
30 *Treatise* (bk I, pt III, section 14, p. 208).
31 Mackie (1974, p. 60).
32 Butterfield (1949, pp. 3–16).
33 Dampier-Whetham (1930, p. 17).

34 Harré (1970, 1973); Harré and Madden (1975); Madden and Harré (1973) (see Bunge, 1959; Bhaskar, 1975).
35 *Treatise* (bk 1, pt III, section II, pp. 123–4).
36 Michotte (1963).
37 Michotte (1963, p. 415).
38 Hamlyn (1957, pp. 76–9) (cf. *Treatise*, bk I, pt III, section XIV, p. 216).
39 *Treatise* (bk I, pt III, section XIV, p. 216).
40 *Treatise* (bk I, pt III, section XII, pp. 192–3).
41 *Enquiry*: Essay VII (pt I, n. 1a, p. 73).
42 Mackie (1973, 1974).
43 Mackie (1974 p. 215).
44 Mackie (1974, p. 215).
45 *Treatise* (bk 1 pt IV, section II, p. 248).
46 *Enquiry*: Essay VIII (pt 1).
47 Mackie (1974, pp. 225–6).
48 *Treatise* (bk I, pt III, section III, p. 128).
49 *Treatise* (bk I, pt III, section XII, p. 182); *Enquiry*: Essay VIII (pt 1, pp. 89–90).
50 Mackie (1974, p. 198).
51 Mackie (1974, p. 69).
52 Mackie (1974, p. 79).
53 Mackie (1974, p. 225).
54 Mackie (1974, p. 68).
55 Mackie (1974, p. 74).
56 Mackie (1974, p. 74).
57 Mackie (1974, pp. 115–16).
58 Mackie (1974, p. 55).
59 Mackie (1974, p. 85).
60 Mackie (1974, p. 215).
61 Kneale (1966, p. 78).
62 Ducasse (1969a, pp. 147–53; 1968, pp. 8–13).
63 Harré and Madden (1975, p. 53).
64 R. F. Holland, unpublished paper; cited Mackie (1974, p. 133); cf. Hart and Honore (1959, ch. II, section II); Anscombe (1971, pp. 8–9; Harré and Madden (1975, p. 54). Piaget (1955) has produced evidence to show that infants come to recognise at some time about the age of one-and-a-half years that the cause–effect relationship involves physical interaction. He reports, for example, how an infant who perceived a relationship between movement of 'chair-in-contact-with window' and window movement learned only from further (active) experience that movement of the chair did not produce window movement without contact and thus productive causal connection between chair and window (p. 302).
65 Mackie (1974, pp. 133–4).
66 Harré and Madden (1975, p. 50).
67 This seems to be the force of Honderich's objection to the suggestion that conditionals have no truth value when their antecedents are not established as true (Mackie, 1974, pp. 53–4). Honderich's view of conditional

statements is that they are 'decently self-revealing statements of fact' about the nature and constitution of the world (Honderich, 1977–8, p. 83).

68 Kneale (1966, pp. 79–80); cf. Kripke (1972, pp. 261–2). The example most commonly cited is Goldbach's conjecture that every even number greater than 2 is the sum of two primes. Although there is no known counter instance, neither has there been any demonstration of the truth of the conjecture. Consequently the attitude of mathematicians to Goldbach's conjecture is said to be that it looks like a theorem, so, if it is true at all, is true necessarily; but it may conceivably be false. Another example is Fermat's problem: to demonstrate that, if n be a number greater than 2, there are no whole numbers such that $a^n + b^n = c^n$. (For a history of this problem see Bell, 1962.)

69 Kneale (1966, p. 78); D. G. Brown (1968, pp. 76–7).

70 Bunge (1959, p. 322 and *passim*); Harré (1973).

71 Laszlo (1969, p. 19).

72 cf. Mackie (1974, p. 35). Mackie borrows the term from John Anderson's 'The Problem of Causality', *Australasian Journal of Psychology and Philosophy*, XVI (1938).

73 This is what Honderich (1977–8) calls causal circumstances as necessitating, where a causal circumstance is a set of conditions-and-a-cause.

74 Montesquieu, opening sentence of *L'Espirit des Lois* (1748); cited Bunge (1967, pp. 376–7).

75 Harré and Madden (1975, pp. 36–7).

76 Bunge (1959, p. 325).

77 Madden and Harré (1973, p. 129); Madden (1969, p. 82).

78 Ducasse (1970, p. 164; 1968; 1969a).

79 cf. Honderich (1977–8, pp. 72, 78).

80 For the purpose of this discussion I have closely followed Bunge's taxonomy of determination (Bunge, 1959, section 1.5).

81 de La Place (1951, p. 6); cf. Max Born, 'Chance can be understood only in regard to expectations of a subject', *Proceedings of the Royal Society*, 66 (1953) p. 503; cited Bridgeman (1970a, p. 67); Craik (1967); Suppes (1970, pp. 8, 32).

82 von Neumann (1955, esp. ch. IV).

83 Mogal (1949).

84 Sommerhoff (1969, pp. 175–6).

85 Schrödinger (1967); Heisenberg (1966).

86 Harré (1972, p. 125).

87 Nagel (1961, p. 361).

88 Nagel (1961, p. 361).

89 The account advanced here is by appeal to a physical realist metaphysic and epistemology. For another similar approach which draws more heavily on a reinterpretation of Kant's ideas see Burkholder (1974).

90 see Lucas (1970). Lucas has even gone so far as to argue (p. 63) that:
  Man *can only have* a true view of the universe and the laws of nature by excepting himself from their sway and considering himself over against

the universe not as a part of it but independent of it and not subject to its
laws. [emphasis added]

91 Spinoza, *Ethics* (pt II, prop. XXXVII, coroll. and prop. XXXIX).
92 Peirce (1933, vol. 1 para. 81).
93 Peirce (1933, vol. 1, para. 316).
94 Lorenz (1962a, pp. 24–5).
95 Craik (1967, p. 99):

On our model theory, neural or other mechanisms can imitate or parallel
the behaviour and interaction of physical objects and so supply us with
information on physical processes which are not directly observable to
us. Our thought then has objective validity because it is not fundamentally different from objective reality but is specially suited for imitating it.

96 Piaget (1955, p. 352):

such a universe ... is ... imposed upon the self to the extent that it com-
prises the organism as part of the whole ... [as] a sort of law of evolution; assimilation and accommodation proceed from a state of chaotic
indifferentiation to a state of differentiation with correlative co-ordination. Assimilation and accommodation are therefore the two poles of an
interaction between the organism and the environment.

97 Lorenz (1962a, p. 33).
98 in Michotte (1963, p. 415).
99 Piaget (1955, p. 313).
100 Piaget (1955, p. 219).
101 Piaget (1955, p. 220).
102 Gruber *et al.* (1957).
103 Kant (1953, p. 306).
104 Warnock (1965); Hampshire (1972).
105 cf. Schlick (1949, p. 521).
106 Kemp-Smith (1918, p. 397); cf. Meyerson (1964, ch. 1); Ducasse (1970,
p. 165).
107 Similar views to those expressed here were advanced by Whewell (1847).
Thus (pp. 166–7):

We assert that 'Every event must have a cause': and this proposition we
know to be true, not only probably and generally, and as far as we can
see, but we cannot suppose it to be false in any single instance. We are as
certain of it as the truths of arithmetic and geometry. We cannot doubt
that it must apply to all events past and future in every part of the
universe, just as truly as to those occurrences we have just observed.
What causes produce what effects; what is the cause of any particular
event; what will be the effect of any particular process; – these are
points on which experience may enlighten us. Observation and experience may be requisite, to enable us to judge respectively such matters: But that every event has *some* cause, Experience cannot prove any
more than she can disprove.

108 Hanson (1963).
109 Pepper (1942, pp. 23–4); Ducasse (1969a, pp. 61, 64).
110 Warnock (1965, p. 316).

111 Harré (1973, p. 376).
112 Held and Hein (1963).
113 Mackie (1974, p. 85).

CHAPTER VII   HUMAN ACTION

1 Wilkerson (1974, p. 98).
2 Socrates, *Phaedo*, 94B–98B.
3 Leibnitz, *Discourse on Metaphysics*, XIX, XX, XXI, XXII; Monadology, para. 79.
4 Castell (1965); see L. J. Russell (1935–6, p. 180 and *passim*) for an early contemporary account of the transempirical agent.
5 Strawson (1958) in Chappel (1962, p. 135); cf. Wittgenstein (1971, 5.631–5.641); cf. Polanyi (1958); Castell (1965); R. Taylor (1958; 1966); Yolton (1973).
6 Danto (1967, p. 133).
7 C. A. Campbell (1957, p. 160); Chisholm (1964a). Recent writers on action theory following Chisholm have revived an Aristotelian distinction between efficient ('transeunt') and agent ('immanent') causation, to mark the (supposed) distinction between causation and action.
8 Melden (1961, pp. 128–9).
9 R. Taylor (1966, pp. 108–9).
10 R. Taylor (1966, p. 142).
11 R. Taylor (1966, p. 141).
12 Toulmin (1948); Flew (1949); Ryle (1966); Anscombe (1957); Melden (1961); Foot (1957); Hamlyn (1953); Warnock (1953); R. Taylor (1966); Hart and Honore (1959); Urmson (1952); Berlin (1966); Dray (1957); C. Taylor (1964); White (1962); von Wright (1970); Milligan (1974).
13 Ofstad (1967b, p. 186); Honderich (1971, pp. 126–7); Sher (1973); C. Taylor (1972); Langford (1971); Lucas (1970, pp. 28–9); R. Young (1973).
14 Wittgenstein (1958, p. 16); R. Taylor (1966, p. 141).
15 Davidson (1963); Alston (1967); Whiteley (1968); Yolton (1973); cf. Goldman (1970).
16 Davidson (1963, pp. 696–7); cf. Whiteley (1968, p. 101).
17 Davidson (1963, p. 700).
18 Angel (1967).
19 cf. Chiaraviglio (1968, p. 381).
20 cf. Hempel and Oppenheim (1948).
21 cf. Harré and Madden (1975, p. 39):
    If something else than what must happen could happen within any system, then no explanation would ever be possible within that system, because one would not have succeeded in explaining the occurrence of one event rather than another. A genuine case of explanation is successful in precisely the way one who takes the Humean problem of inductive scepticism seriously denies, namely by eliminating all alternatives to the

coming into being of the referent of the explanandum as not really possible in the given circumstances.

22 Angel (1967, pp. 281–2).

23 An expression used by Hart and Honore (1959, p. 43).

24 Hart and Honore (1959, pp. 22, 44–8); cf. Lucas (1970, para. 9, pp. 34–43).

25 cf. E. Nagel (1961, p. 570).

26 Ryle (1966, pp. 86, 116–17).

27 Hart and Honore (1959, p. 44).

28 Davidson (1963, p. 697).

29 Hart and Honore (1959, p. 55).

30 Angel (1967). Compare Munitz (1970, pp. 81–2):

Any conclusions reached in accordance with the rules of inference specified by the theory are logically determined. Thus the principle of indeterminacy, among others, is part of a total physical theory that in its function provides determined results of a type *it* is competent to reach. If it proves successful in dealing with observational facts it is not because causality fails for small objects but because man's creative ingenuity has found one more means of dealing effectively through his inferences with the data of his experience.

31 Lorenz (1962b); Sparkes (1972).

32 D. Taylor (1970, pp. 54–5, 70–1).

33 M. Black (1970); Chisholm (1976). The orthodox notion of 'basic action' referred to here is not precisely the same as that developed by Danto (1973). The orthodoxy maintains that there is a categorical difference between agent's acts and causally determined events. Danto develops a notion of basic action which is compatible with physicalism (by identifying agent acts as complex events, with a neurophysiological series of events).

34 R. Taylor (1966, pp. 194–5); cf. Chisholm (1964b, pp. 619f); cf. von Wright (1970, p. 77).

35 Davidson (1971, p. 11; (emphasis added); cf. Danto (1973, esp. pp. 63, 71–2).

36 Ryle (1966, p. 49).

37 Ryle (1966, p. 50).

38 R. Taylor (1966, p. 144).

39 J. Wilson (1972, pp. 37–8); cf. Thalberg (1976 pp. 233–4).

40 cf. Hart and Honore (1959).

41 G. R. Williams (1953a, p. 31 para. 11).

42 Hart and Honore (1959, p. 52).

43 Hart and Honore (1959, pp. 48–9).

44 R. Taylor (1966, p. 282).

45 Ryle (1966, pp. 49, 50, 87); R. Taylor (1966, pp. 100, 140, 143). See above Chapter VII, Section 5.3.

46 Hart and Honore (1959, p. 39).

47 cf. Davidson (1971, p. 11; 1973, p. 141); R. Taylor (1966, p. 141).

48 D. G. Brown (1968, p. 56).

49 D. G. Brown (1968, p. 58).

50 The term 'transempirical' is borrowed from Ofstad (1967a and b). It

represents well the idea of a person or agent who stands apart not only from the physical determinants of behaviour but from the mental and social determinants also. It is the transempirical agent that the criminal law deals with, who is 'master of his mind'. Devlin in Duffy (1949) 1A11. E. R. p. 932. See below, Chapter XI, note 4.

51 E. Nagel (1960; in Dworkin, 1970, p. 76); cf. Ofstad (1961, pp. 236–7; 1967a).

52 R. Taylor (1966, p. 94):
It will always be perfectly possible, in other words, that my hand moves as the result of the occurrence of that physical event within me which we can suppose to be brought about by an electrical impulse, a drug, or what-not, but that I do not move it or have anything to do with it moving.

53 cf. Hebb (1967); J. G. Taylor (1972b).

54 Penfield (1950); Toulmin (1970, p. 15).

55 Penfield (1950, p. 64).

56 Penfield (1950, pp. 62–3).

57 F. Ogden in his book *The A.B.C. of Psychology* (1944) cites (p. 43) Harvey Cushing, the great American neuropsychologist, as having induced an 'experiended-as-voluntary' act in a patient by stimulating the association areas of his cortex. Flew (1973, pp. 85–6) reports inability to discover the original source of Ogden's claim. However, the present argument stands, even in the absence (as yet) of well-attested clinical support, which may have to wait upon further developments in psychotechnology.

58 Toulmin (1970, p. 15); C. Taylor (1972).

59 Lucas (1970, p. 171; emphasis added).

60 R. Taylor (1966, p. 124; emphasis added).

61 Malcolm (1964; in Borst, 1970, p. 178); cf. Smart (1959; in Borst, 1970, pp. 57–8).

62 D. G. Brown (1968, p. 145).

63 D. G. Brown (1968, p. 117).

64 cf. D. G. Brown (1968, p. 117).

65 cf. D. G. Brown (1968, p. 147).

66 George (1957, 1971).

67 The rudimentary model sketched here is complicated by the influence of spontaneous or random 'noise' generating discharges at neurone synapses, but the essential principles of net-behaviour remain the same: see J. G. Taylor (1972b).

68 cf. Rapoport (1962, p. 93).

69 There has been a resurgence of philosophical interest in goal-directed behaviour and teleological explanation, and a number of recent works deal with these problems more exhaustively than is possible here (cf. Sommerhoff, 1969, 1974; Woodfield, 1976; Wright, 1976).

70 Sommerhoff (1969, pp. 147–202; 167 *et seq.*).

71 Woodfield (1976, pp. 67–72).

72 R. Taylor (1950a, 1950b); cf. Sommerhoff (1969, p. 159 and *passim*).

73 Woodfield, in a very interesting and important book (1976, ch. 4) has rejected Sommerhoff's purely objectivist analysis of goal-directedness. His

main criticisms concern the principle of orthogonal variables. He suggests that it is impossible on this principle to discriminate between equilibriating systems behaviour and goal-directed behaviour. The crux of his argument is that an environmental variable and an action variable determined by it would not be orthogonal by Sommerhoff's criterion. By hypothesis, however, the goal-directed action variable in a deterministic system is determined by the environment through the structure of the agent mechanism and the laws prevailing in the system. Consequently the relationships between goal-directed system variables and equilibrium system variables are equally determined and so cannot be differentiated as required of the orthogonal criterion of goal-directedness.

My own view is that there is here an absolutely crucial difference between relationships determined by invariant, universal, general laws (such as, archetypically, general relativity theory and the basic laws of thermodynamics) and relationships determined by the structure and function of particular mechanisms. In the second sort of case we can do what in the first sort of case we cannot: suspend or interfere with the determining relation. We can conceivably, in principle, suspend the operation of individual mechanisms without suspending or interfering with the universal laws obtaining; and this, indeed, is how in practice orthogonality would most easily be confirmed. And it is precisely this possibility of isolating the functioning of a more or less discrete sub-system from its invariant law-governed context that gives rise to the need for teleological explanation in the first place.

The significance of this point can be shown in the only relevant counter-example Woodfield gives: the case of the primitive scientist for whom it is a basic law of nature that when a hungry lioness sees an antelope she runs after it. By hypothesis, if such a scientist invariably observed that hungry lionesses pursue seen antelopes it would be impossible for him to know (on the criterion of orthogonality) that the lionesses' behaviour was goal-directed. Now we may leave aside the extreme implausibility that even a primitive naturalist could have such unrepresentative experience of lionesses and consider only the criteriological issue. Sommerhoff's procedure (cf. 1969, pp. 159–61) would involve checking for orthogonality by such simple measures as restraining hungry lionesses in sight of running antelopes. This would quickly establish that, no matter how often, ordinarily, hungry lionesses pursued prey, there is no basic law of nature involved (such as the second law of thermodynamics), but rather a system that is (potentially) goal-directed upon antelopes. That is to say, the criterion of orthogonality would yield in such cases what is required of it, viz. the identification of goal-directed behaviour.

In view of Woodfield's criticisms there are two points worth making, however. First, if, after making suitable tests for orthogonality, the primitive scientist still has no reason to doubt that hungry lionesses pursue antelopes as a basic law of nature, then indeed he *would* have no reason to believe that lionesses are goal-directed systems *vis à vis* antelopes; no more reason, that is, than we have for believing that hot objects are goal-directed when they

381

cool to a normalised temperature in accordance with the second law of thermodynamics.

Second, logically we cannot avoid the conclusion that, in practice, what is believed to be goal-directed behaviour is relative to a given set of assumptions and known laws. This is just to say that what counts as goal-directed behaviour (the extension of 'goal-directed') will change with growing knowledge about the organisation of natural systems and natural laws. It is not at all, as Woodfield suggests (1976 pp. 70–2), *absurd* to maintain that a belief contrary to fact, that a system is goal-directed so far as available knowledge allows us to judge, can be a belief based on adequate objective criteria. No criterion of goal-directedness, including subjective ones, will render us immune from false beliefs about such things. There is no apodectic certainty about the truth of any empirical proposition, but this in itself says nothing about the propriety or objectivity of the *criteria* for asserting the truth. So if men erroneously impute malevolent intent to inanimate objects that have caused harm this is a factual mistake, involving the use of the intentionalist criterion of goal-directedness; it does not vitiate the *criterion* of intent *per se*. But by the same token, although in ignorance we may wrongly suppose events to be goal-directed (because we assume that no basic law holds and so that variables are orthogonal), this does not entail that there are no systems where variables are both orthogonal and goal-directed. And this is all that is required to bear out the assumption that there are teleological systems and that objective descriptions of them can be true (cf. Woodfield, 1976, p. 21).

Although Woodfield rejects the possibility of purely objective criteria for goal-directedness, he nevertheless endorses the view I go on to advance, that, in *fact*, goal-directed behaviour turns out to be determined by feedback mechanisms.

74 cf. Sommerhoff (1969, p. 157).

75 Sommerhoff (1969, p. 153). It would be highly advantageous here if some commonly agreed usage could be established which clearly distinguished between the general category of goal-directed behaviour and its various sub-categories including purposive and non-purposive as well as feedback and non-feedback-regulated behaviours. The term 'purposive behaviour' is best confined to certain behaviours of hierarchically ordered physical systems capable of sustaining conscious intentionality towards a goal. There is always a particular danger that purposive behaviour in this restricted sense is conflated with the more general category of goal-directed behaviour and with misleading consequences. For the present purpose, however, I believe that it is sufficient to show that goal-directedness, and so, potentially, purposive behaviour, is not beyond the explanatory resources of physical causation.

76 von Bertalanffy (1971, pp. 169–72).

77 Bateson (1967, p. 381).

78 Woodfield (1976, p. 193).

79 Anscombe (1971).

80 R. Taylor (1950a, 1966).

81 One analogy would be the case of automatic-pilot controls which regulate a number of aircraft-controlling variables so as to maintain some variable parameter(s), such as air speed, in fact constant or invariant during variations in other parameters (such as drag, ambient temperature, etc.). Ref. Scientific American (1957). Another analogy would be the eye's capacity to maintain invariant visual function (same objects, colours, etc.) with varying ambient light intensity (see L. Stark, 1968).

82 Ducasse (1949).

83 G. Miller, Gallanter and Pribram (1960).

84 Bunge has made the same point in a similar connection (1959, p. 181):

> The Platonic tenet that only the soul is self-moving whereas bodies are entirely passive ... is vital for Idealism but is inconsistent with modern science which shows that the spontaneity of the 'soul' (that is of the psychic functions) far from being its privilege, is rooted in the fact that every bit of matter is buzzing with activities.

85 Strawson (1962); Peters (1958, p. 61; 1973, pt II); Gendin (1973).

CHAPTER VIII FREE-WILL AND DETERMINISM

1 cf. Hart and Honore (1959, p. 105); Ofstad (1961, p. 300).

2 Aune (1967): Aune, for example, has identified no less than seventeen different senses of five different types, and the literature abounds with myriads more.

3 e.g. Reid (1815); Dostoyevsky (1864); McDougal (1928); Sartre (1948); C. A. Campbell (1957, 1967); Castell (1965); Downie and Telfer (1969).

4 e.g. La Mettrie (1747); Tolstoy (1869); Schopenhauer (1841); Darrow (1934); Broad (1970); Matson (1956); Edwards (1970); Hospers (1950, 1970); Smart (1961b); Honderich (1970, 1973).

5 e.g. Hobbes (1841); Locke (1690); Hume (1750); Mill (1843); Moore (1912); Russell (1929); Hobart (1934); Schlick (1939); Grant (1952); Raab (1955); Nowell-Smith (1956, 1960); Foot (1957); R. Young (1974). Also, advocates of the 'two domainist' account of reasons and causes usually argue for some form of compatibility thesis (see above Chapter VII, Section 4.1).

6 C. A. Campbell (1957).

7 Smart (1961b).

8 Hospers (1970).

9 Broad (1970).

10 J. Wisdom (1963).

11 Ofstad (1961).

12 C. A. Campbell (1957).

13 Smart (1961b).

14 Hospers (1970).

15 Broad (1970).

16 J. Wisdom (1963).

17 Ofstad (1961).

18 Ducasse (1969a, pp. 63–4).

19 cf. C. A. Campbell (1951).

20 Ryle (1950).

21 Ofstad (1961, pp. 113–14; 1967b, p. 189).

22 Mottram (1960); Eysenck (1967); cf. Skinner (1973, p. 204).

23 Honderich (1970, p. 197); R. Young (1973a, p. 45); Danto (1973, pp. 61–4).

24 Smart (1961b).

25 C. Taylor (1972).

26 cf. C. A. Campbell (1957, 1967).

27 cf. Matson (1956, p. 495); Edwards (1970, p. 121); Ofstad (1961, pp. 181–2).

28 Tolstoy (1968 edn, pp. 1454–5. *Note*: A very interesting example of false intuition being overridden by considerations derived from scientific theory and observation is the case of Lindemann's research into aircraft spin. In the early years of the 1914–18 war a plane that got out of control and began to spin almost invariably crashed and killed the pilot. Frederick Lindemann piloted planes to great heights, threw them into spins, memorised readings of air speed, time, number of turns and other essential experimental flight data, pushed the stick forward in spite of the opposite instinctive reaction, and, purely as a result of his own calculations, pulled the machine out of spin and into stable flight (R. W. Reid, 1971, p. 126).

29 Butler (1969, Sermon III, esp. p. 62 n. 2).

30 Austin (1956; in Urmson and Warnock, 1970, p. 231; cf. Flew (1956, p. 19); C. A. Campbell (1951); Black (1970); see also references above Chapter VIII, Section 4.1) for the orthodox view of human action.

31 Austin (1956–7; in 1970, p. 182).

32 Moore (1966, ch. 6); cf. Nowell-Smith (1956, chs 19, 20).

33 e.g. Hume, *Enquiry*.

34 Raab (1955).

35 MacKay (1957).

36 Nowell-Smith (1960).

37 Ofstad (1961, p. 175).

38 Compare Paul Ramsay's paraphrase of Jonathon Edward's views: 'In other words a man is free to do what he wills but not to do what he does not will' Ramsay (1957, p. 13).

39 cf. Quine (1968, p. 19).

40 cf. Honderich (1970, 1971).

41 Raab (1955); Hampshire (1959); Ofstad (1961, 1967b); Lehrer (1966); Ayers (1968).

42 cf. Lehrer (1966).

43 Hampshire (1965, p. 32).

44 Aune (1963, p. 412).

45 Ofstad (1967b, p. 200).

46 Another notable logical argument for free-will has been derived from Gödel's Theorem (Lucas, 1970; cf. Nagel and Newman, 1959). Gödel proved that any formal calculus sufficiently rich to contain arithmetic must contain at least one significant proposition which may be true but which is unprovable within the calculus. The argument for human free-will is

essentially that any rational being could follow Gödel's argument and convince himself that Gödel's argument, though unprovable in a logical calculus sufficiently rich to contain arithmetic, was for that very reason true. Therefore a human being cannot be represented by a logical calculus, and therefore cannot be described in terms of physical variables all of whose values are completely determined by the conjunction of these values at some earlier time (Lucas, 1970, p. 133).

This argument is unsound for a number of reasons, most of which have been advanced elsewhere (cf. Scriven, 1958; Sayre, 1968), so I shall not consider it at length here. The main shortcoming of the argument is that, if a human individual follows the Gödel argument and produces the Gödel formula for the calculus representing his own reasoning, the important thing is not that he produces it, and knows it to be true, but the fact that a Gödel formula can be produced at all establishes him as deterministic in the appropriate sense. On the other hand, inability to produce a Gödel formula for a calculus representing his own reasoning does not in itself constitute a difference between a man and a machine (cf. Sayre, 1968, p. 22 and *passim*; Scriven, 1969, p. 125). In any case, it is simply empirically false that a human being (*any* human being) can produce the Gödel formula for the logical calculus representing his ratiocinations or for that matter that for the system of even a non-trivial machine, let alone know it to be true. But even if someone could, this would not justify the inference that *all* rational human individuals, even 'morally responsible' ones, could do so.

47 D. M. MacKay (1957, 1960, 1969a, 1966).
48 MacKay (1957; in Vesey, 1964, p. 395).
49 MacKay (1957, in Vesey, 1964, p. 395; emphasis added).
50 MacKay (1957; in Vesey, 1964, p. 394).
51 cf. Blanshard (1970).
52 MacKay (1966).
53 MacKay (1969a, p. 485).
54 MacKay (1969a, p. 487).
55 MacKay (1957; in Vesey, 1964, p. 394).
56 Landsberg and Evans (1970); J. G. Taylor (1971b, p. 736); ref. J. G. Taylor (1971a; 1974 edn, pp. 243–4).
57 MacKay (1957; in Vesey, 1964, p. 395).
58 Austin (1956); Lande (1970); Körner (1964), Lucas (1970); Anscombe (1971).
59 Austin (1956, in 1970 p. 218).
60 Barret (1970, p. 51).
61 Perhaps even more than pure science, applied science and technology have been widely regarded as the hard-cutting edge of the 'scientific outlook' in general and mechanistic explanation in particular. The popular view of technology, one particularly prevalent among professional philosophers, is that it perfectly exemplifies the universal, uniform and invariant character of natural law. The standard formula, 'same cause, same effect', is believed to apply without caveat or qualification to the standardised objects of engineering.

385

It is salutary therefore to contemplate the considerable chagrin and irony about this among engineers and technologists themselves. One of the best-known laws in engineering, but one never discussed in academie, is Sod's Law (sometimes called Murphy's Law or Finagle's Law), which states that: 'if anything can go wrong it will' (anon.: 'The Contributions of Edsel Murphy to the Understanding of the Behaviour of Inanimate Objects', *Electronics Today International*, October 1972, pp. 697–8: Jones, 1968, pp. 470–7).

62 Ter-Har (1958, pp. 1–2).

63 Haldane (1927); Blandshard (1970); R.Taylor (1966); Honderich (1971); Lucas (1970).

64 Blanshard (1970); Honderich (1970, p. 210 and *passim*).

65 Lucas (1970, p. 63).

66 Lucas (1970, p. 104).

67 e.g. R. Taylor (1966, p. 162); Lucas (1970, pp. 110, 115, 145); Boyle, Grisez and Tollefsen (1972).

68 Honderich (1970, p. 213).

69 Grunbaum (1952; in Ulrich *et al.* 1966, p. 9); Young (1973b).

70 Lucas (1970, p. 114).

71 Kant, *Critique of Pure Reason*, esp. B575 – B576; *Critique of Practical Reason*; cf. Reid (1970, p. 92); C. A. Campbell (1957, ch. 9, 1967b); Lucas (1970, pp. 49–50).

72 Ofstad (1967b, p. 200).

73 Hume, *Treatise* (vol. 2, bk III, pt 1, section 1: 1966 edn, pp.177–8).

74 Kant, *Critique of Pure Reason*, B576 (1965 edn, p. 473).

75 Moore (1968).

76 MacIntyre (1959).

77 Körner (1967, p. 204).

78 Ofstad (1961, pp. 113–14; 1967b, p. 189).

79 Moore accepted Broad's definition of 'natural object' or characteristic as one that either (a) we become aware of by inspecting our sense data or introspecting our experiences, or (b) is definable wholly in terms of characteristics of the former kind together with the notions of cause or substance; in Schilpp (1942, pp. 62, 592).

80 Moore (1968, p. 17).

81 Edel (1963, pp. 115–20).

82 Prior (1949, ch. 1).

83 Hartman (1958–9, 1967).

84 B. Williams (1973, pp. 52–61); cf. Geach (1956).

85 Searle (1964).

86 MacKay (1956).

87 cf. Hume 'so that when you pronounce any action or character to be vicious you mean nothing, but that from the constitution of your nature you have a feeling of sentiment of blame for the contemplation of it. Vice and virtue therefore might be compared to sounds, colours, heat and cold, which according to modern philosophy are not qualities in objects but perceptions in the mind, and this discovery in morals, like that other in physics is to be

regarded as a commendable advancement in the Speculative Sciences'
Treatise (vol. II, Book III, pt 1, section 1: 1966 edn, p. 177).
88 see above Chapter IV, Section 4.1.
89 see above Chapter IV, Section 4.4.
90 see above Chapter IV, Section 4.4.
91 Craik (1967); MacKay (1956); Miller, Gallanter and Pribram (1960); Luria
    (1973); Aleksander (1977).
92 Hare (1970, p. 82).
93 Edel (1963, pp. 121–4).

CHAPTER IX   MORAL RESPONSIBILITY

 1 Black (1970); Hart (1965); Hughes (1959); Glover (1970)
 2 Schlick (1939).
 3 Schlick (1939).
 4 see Ofstad (1961, ch. V).
 5 MacKay (1957).
 6 Nowell-Smith (1960).
 7 Stephen (1883, vol. II, pp. 81–2).
 8 But cf. Barry, cited Smith and Hogan (1973, p. 7); Coggan, Archbishop of
    York; *Hansard Lords*, (26 October 1965, col. 536).
 9 T. Huxley (1898a, p. 241).
10 Ibid.
11 T. Huxley (1868, in 1898b, p. 163).
12 J. G. Taylor (1971b, p. 738).
13 cf. Hook (1958 in 1970, p. 187).
14 Honderich (1970, p. 215).
15 Edwards (1970, p. 125).
16 Honderich (1973, p. 210) has made a similar point:
    It seems impossible first to give a characterisation of the responsibility in
    question which is independent of the statement about [the] actions being
    an effect and then proceeding to display an inconsistency with that state-
    ment. Rather a characterisation of the responsibility in question *is essen-
    tially* a characterisation of something as inconsistent with actions being
    effects. In the end responsibility is described as that which cannot exist
    given certain causal sequences. [emphasis added].
17 Franklin (1968).
18 Franklin (1968, p. 301).
19 see cases cited by Schopenhauer (1960, p. 78 and *passim*).
20 Hook (1970b); Hintz (1970); Castell (1965).
21 Ayers (1968, p. 95).
22 Aristotle, *Ethics* (bk III, ch. 1).
23 Aune (1967, p. 20).
24 Strawson (1962).
25 Lucas (1970, p. 63).

26 McDougal (1928, pp. xiii–iv).
27 McDougal (1928); Hook (1970b, p. 189); Hintz (1970, p. 178); Castell (1965); Lucas (1970); see Skinner (1973) for numerous references.
28 Hume, *Treatise* (vol. II, bk II, pt 3, section II, 1966 edn, p. 122).
29 Skinner (1973, p. 208).
30 Maine (1887).
31 cf. de Tarde (1912, p. 139).
32 Aune (1967); Raab (1955, p. 67).
33 Smart (1961b).
34 Wootton (1963, p. 30) has offered the interesting suggestion along these lines that the currently prevalent concept of a 'meritocracy' would be better termed 'cephelocracy' since there is no significant merit in inheriting high intelligence.
35 Matson (1956, p. 495).
36 Strawson (1962).
37 This is clearly itself an argument from determinism, however.
38 Strawson (1962, p. 294).
39 cf. Honderich. (1971, p. 135).
40 Strawson (1962, p. 198).
41 Aurelius, *The Meditations*, VI: 27.
42 *Meditations*, X: 4. 1951 edn.
43 Spinoza, *Ethics* (pt IV, prop. L, note: p. 221).
44 Seng-ts'an, Hsin-hsin Ming; cited Watts (1957, p. 135).
45 La Mettrie (1748; cited Lange, 1925, vol. ii, p. 75).
46 cited Dworkin (1970, p. 1).
47 L. Stern (1967, p. 336).
48 McDougal (1928, pp. xiii–iv); cf. Berlin (1969, p. 113).
49 J. G. Taylor (1971b, p. 213).
50 cf. Smart (1961b; in Dworkin, 1970, p. 209).
51 cf. Strawson (1962, p. 197); Hare (1972, p. 63 and *passim*).
52 Hare (1970, ch. 5).
53 Laszlo (1972b, ch. 13).
54 Rapoport (1974, p. 37):
    What is important to establish here is that whether or not purpose is seen to govern a chain of events depends not on the events themselves, but on how we view them. When we view our own actions 'from the inside' they may seem purposeful to us, that is, guided by a future envisaged goal. When we attribute similar feelings to other living beings (or even non-living ones) purpose seems to govern their behaviour also. But, if we examine a chain of events, each a consequence of the preceding, or even if we can imagine such a chain, explanation in terms of goals and purposes no longer seems necessary. In fact explanations dispensing with purpose have frequently been found for events originally supposed to be governed by wills and purposes. Thus it may serve us well to seek such causal chain explanations for our own actions, specifically actions involving conflict. Frequently this shift of point of view will enable us to understand conflict and its relations to environment in a new enlightening way.

55 cf. Holmes (1881, p. 38); Hart (1970, p. 114); MacNiven (1944; in Morris, 1966, p. 411).
56 Wittgenstein (1972, para. 201).
57 G. A. Miller (1969, p. 81).
58 Piaget (1955, p. 361).
59 Benedict (1963, chs, VII, VIII); cf. Rapoport (1974, part 1).
60 Schon (1973, p. 57).
61 Skinner (1973).
62 see e.g. C. S. Lewis (1953).
63 Aristotle, *Nichomacean Ethics* (bk III, ch. 1).
64 Honderich (1970, p. 196).

CHAPTER X   PHYSICALISM AND JURISPRUDENCE

1 Strawson (1962); Hare (1972, pp. 59–63); Brandt (1970, pp. 149–54).
2 D. A. Black *et al.* (1973, 1974).
3 Charlson (1955 1. All. E.R. 859); see Smith and Hogan (1973, p. 135 *et seq.*) for criticism.
4 cited J. G. Taylor (1971a, pp. 55–6).
5 Kemp (1957) 1, QB 399; cf. Kemp (1964) 2 QB 341.
6 Lord Goddard: Rivette (1950) Crim. App. Rep. (p. 94), cited G. R. Williams (1953a, pp. 295, 299); cf. Davies (1971).
7 Dennison v. State (1966), 49 Misc. 2d, 533, 267 N.Y. State 2d. 290; cf. R. V. Ford (1969) 1. W. Law Repts. 1703. Two accused pleaded guilty to the same offence. One was regarded as incorrigible and sentenced to twelve months; the other was given a longer sentence in the hope that there would be time for reform. On appeal the longer sentence was reduced to twelve months.
8 Allan (1964; in Radzinowicz and Wolfgang, 1971).
9 Gerber and McAnany (1967; in Radzinowicz and Wolfgang, 1971, p. 135).
10 Lord Radcliffe (1961, p. 12).
11 Lord Hodson; cited Wootton (1963, p. 45).
12 Lord Devlin (1969, p. 27); cf. Denning (1953, p. 112).
13 Macdonald (1955, pp. 75–6); D. A. Black *et al.* (1973).
14 Smith and Hogan (1973, p. 5).
15 D. A. Black *et al.* (1973, p. 339, 1974).
16 G. R. Williams (1953a, p. 16).
17 cf. Radzinowicz (1966, pp. 101–2).
18 Holmes (1881, pp. 38 *et seq.*).
19 Lord Goddard, *Observer*, 5 May 1963.
20 Patton (1973, p. 359).
21 D. A. Black *et al.* (1973, p. 339).
22 Gerber and McAnany (1967; in Radzinowicz and Wolfgang, 1971, p. 134).
23 de Tarde (1912, pp. 494 *et seq.*).
24 Hart (1970, pp. 109 *et seq.*).
25 There are of course other important issues that are closely related to these, which cannot be discussed here. These include, particularly, the question of

whether a treatment approach is more appropriate than punishment in a scientifically informed criminal law, and, correspondingly, the appropriateness of established sentencing practice.

CHAPTER XI THE REASONABLE MAN

1 Fitzgerald (1968).
2 This formula is the one used to characterise severe mental abnormality in the Butler Report on *Mentally Abnormal Offenders* (1975): 18.29 (p. 227); 18.36 (p. 229); 18.37 (p. 230).
3 cf. G. R. Williams (1953a, p. 52).
4 The 'classic' form of words used to specify the principle of provocation is interesting in view of the previous discussion of IT and the PO model of persons. As Lord Devlin put it (Duffy, 1949, 1 All. E.R. p. 932):

> Provocation is some act, or series of acts, done by the dead man to the accused, which would cause in any reasonable person and actually causes in the accused a sudden and temporary loss of self control, rendering the accused so subject to passion as to make him or her for the moment *not master of his mind*. [emphasis added]

It is interesting to notice here the implicit assumption that in any criminal act there is a person over and above not only the body but also the mind, which supposedly masters or fails to master its mind–body. Here we have the ghost in the machine and the transempirical person with a vengeance, and displayed in conspicuous legal trappings.
5 Ounstead cited in De Reuk and Porter (1968, p. 183); Castberg (1957, p. 93); Fitzgerald (1968, p. 365); cf. Brandon (1969).
6 Flew (1973, pp. 105–6).
7 cf. Hart (1968b, p. 156).
8 G. R. Williams (1953a, p. 588).
9 Welsh (1869) 11. Cox C.C., p. 336; Smith and Hogan (1973, p. 238).
10 Holmes (1881, p. 51).
11 Lesbini (1914) 3 K.B. 1116.
12 Homicide Act, (1957), Section 3.
13 Law Commission (1967).
14 Criminal Justice Act (1967), Section 8.
15 Morris (1976, p. 45).
16 Brett (1970, p. 635); cf. Castberg (1957, pp. 93 ff).
17 Lord Devlin: Duffy (1949) 1 All. E.R. 932.
18 Hart (1968b, p. 152; emphasis added).
19 Hart (1968b, p. 156).
20 In a similar connection Sir James Fitzjames Stephen, commenting on the special circumstances of a crime committed on instruction from God, said 'My own opinion is that if a special divine order were given to a man, I should certainly hang him for it, unless I got a special divine order not to hang him!' (Stephen, 1883, vol. 2, p. 160, n. 1)
21 Holmes (1881, p. 51).

22 Creighton (1909, p. 349).
23 cf. Holmes (1881, p. 76).
24 The William Gray 29 Fed. Cas. 1300 No. 17 694; cited Smith and Hogan (1973, p. 157); (cf. Aristotle, *Nichomacean Ethics*, bk III, ch. 1). Moral philosophers would do well to ponder this case since this was not a case where the ship was driven willy-nilly by the storm but where the captain made a deliberate choice to break the law in order to avert a greater evil.
25 Lord Cooper, Royal Commission on Capital Punishment Report (1953, p. 42).
26 See Smith and Hogan (1973, p. 240).
27 Laws: IX 865 a1 869 e5 ff., 1971; cf. Saunders (1973).
28 Lord Hewart: Kopsch (1925) 19 Cr. App. Rep. 50, at p. 51.
29 cf. Koestler (1956, p. 30).
30 Hart (1968c, pp. 109 and *passim*).
31 Smith and Hogan (1973, p. 244).
32 cf. D.P.P. v. Smith (1961) A.C. 290.
33 cf. Wootton (1963).
34 Archbishop of York: *Hansard* Lords Debates (26 October 1965, col. 536).
35 Hart (1966, pp. 65–6).
36 see Smith and Hogan (1973, pp. 234–44).
37 Devlin (1969, p. 100).
38 Phipson (1970, para. 1296).
39 Chief Justice British Columbia. Lupien (1969) Can. Crim. Cas. 32.36; cited Brett (1970, p. 639).
40 Lord Goddard, Chief Justice: McCarthy (1954) 2 Q.B. 105 at p. 112.
41 R. Manningham Buller: *Hansard* House of Commons Debates, 15 November 1956, vol. 560, col. 1253.
42 Hughes (1959, pp. 528–9); cf. Hart (1965, pp. 151–74).
43 Wootton (1963, p. 73).
44 See Hart (1968d, p. 152 and *passim*).
45 Goddard: Windle (1952) 2 Q.B. 826, pp. 833–4.
46 Hughes (1959).
47 Wootton (1963, p. 74).
48 Bedder v. D.P.P. (1954) 38 Cr. App. Rep. 133.
49 cf. Ives (1969) 3 All. E.R. 470, p. 475.
50 Marsack (1959); Howard (1961); Smith and Hogan (1973, pp. 243–4).
51 but contra. Raney (1942) Cr. App. Rep. 14. In this case the conviction for murder was quashed on appeal on the grounds that the accused was a one-legged man, and the judge had failed to point this fact out as a mitigating factor in his summing up. The jury had in fact been directed to consider only the response of a normal reasonable *two-legged man* to having a crutch kicked out from under him in assessing the accused's culpability!
52 Macniven (1944; in Morris, 1966, p. 408).
53 Brett (1970, p. 637).
54 see Smith and Hogan (1973, p. 239).
55 Powell (1957, p. 104).
56 Sheldon (1970); Gleuk (1956).

57 Montagu (1969, numerous references).
58 Walker (1965, pp. 62–3).
59 Franks (1957); Lykken (1961); Eysenck (1970, pp. 115, 119–20).
60 S. M. Smith *et al.* (1973).
61 see evidence of Eliot Slater and Basil Neal, Royal Commission on Capital Punishment, *Report* (1953); Hargrove (1960); Brett (1970); English (1970); Howard (1961); Marsack (1959); Samuels (1971).
62 Smith and Hogan (1973, p. 241).
63 Hargrove (1960, p. 209).
64 Aristotle, *Nichomacean Ethics* (bk 7, ch. 5).
65 cited Smith and Hogan (1973, p. 238).
66 Royal Commission on the Care and Control of the Feeble Minded, *Report* (1908, p. 151).
67 Royal Commission on Capital Punishment, *Report* (1922, pp. 53, 81).
68 Homicide Act (1957), Section 2 (i).
69 Byrne (1960) 2 Q.B.R., p. 396.
70 Byrne (1960) 2 Q.B.R., p. 403.
71 Byrne (1960) 2 Q.B.R., p. 403.
72 Committee on Mentally Abnormal Offenders, *Report* (Butler Report) (1975), 18.36 (p. 229).
73 cf. Butler Report (1975, 18.16, pp. 221–2).
74 Williams (1953a, p. 82).
75 Walker (1965, pp. 62–3).
76 cf. Geach (1971, pp. 5–7).
77 D. A. Black *et al.* (1974). Needless to say, his behaviour may conform to some *other* norms which do not prevail in his community. This raises different questions.
78 Ducasse (1969, pp. 63–4).
79 Wootton (1959); Butler Report (1975, p. 222).
80 Walker (1967; in Radzinowicz, 1971, p. 56).
81 de Tarde (1912, p. 84).
82 Wootton (1959, 1963).

CHAPTER XII   CRIME, DISEASE AND MALADJUSTMENT

1 cited Lombroso (1906) 1968 p. 386; Rees (1951, p. 6); Darrow (1934, p. 96).
2 Ausubel (1961; in Scheff, 1967, p. 260).
3 Ausubel (1961; in Scheff, 1967, p. 260).
4 Menninger (1968, p. 17).
5 Alexander and Selesnick (1966, ch. III).
6 Szasz (1960, 1961, 1963, 1971, 1974a, 1974b).
7 Breggin (1972, 1974).
8 Wootton (1959, 1963).
9 Flew (1973).
10 Szasz (1960; in Scheff, 1967, p. 244).
11 Hampshire (1950; in 1972, p. 88 and *passim*).

12 Bateson (1973).
13 Szasz (1960, 1961); Heather (1976).
14 von Krafft-Ebing (1965, p. 98).
15 Wootton (1959, p. 276); Flew (1973, p. 76); Butler Report (1975, p. 222).
16 Flew (1973, esp. p. 75 and *passim*).
17 Szasz (1974a, p. 100).
18 *The Guinness Book of Records* (9th edn., 1970, p. 27); cf. Soper (1939).
19 Public Health Act (1936), Section 120 (in Halsbury's *Laws of England* (3rd ed.), vol. 31, p. 86). Szasz points out that in the United States there are no provisions in the law authorising tuberculosis hospitals to hold and treat patients against their will (New York Public Health Law, para. 2223); cited Szasz (1974a, p. 104). Compare the Public Health Act (1936), Section 112. However, compulsory detention is dependent upon the severity of the disease. Cases such as typhoid and bubonic plague are likely to be treated more seriously than tuberculosis and have long been subject if necessary to compulsory detention orders (cf. Soper, 1939).
20 Benedict (1963).
21 Asimov (1965, pp. 46–7).
22 Ausubel (1961; in Scheff, 1967, p. 259).
23 See Barbara Wootton's criticism of the Mental Health Movement in Wootton (1959, ch. VII).
24 Wootton (1959, ch. VII).
25 Flew (1973, pp. 1–6); ref to Rees (1951); Menninger (1968).
26 Scheff (1967, p. 1; emphasis added).
27 Lord Denning. Bratty v. A-G for N. Ireland (1963), 386 at pp. 410–12.
28 Walker (1970, pp. 69–81).
29 Craik (1967).
30 Koestler (1967, see p. 64 and *passim*).
31 Laszlo (1972b, pp. 255–6).
32 Thibaut (1943); cited Wootton (1959, p. 220).
33 Ministry of Education Committee on Maladjusted Children *Report* (1955, p. 3).
34 cf. Hart (1968d, p. 183); Morris (1976, pp. 96–7).
35 A. Huxley (1958, pp. 34–5).
36 Allan (1964; in Radzinowicz and Wolfgang, 1971, p. 71).
37 Gerber and McAnany (1967).
38 Reddaway and Bloch (1977).
39 Silving (1966, p. 401; cited Gerber and McAnany in Radzinowicz and Wolfgang, 1971, p. 129).
40 Szasz (1974b).
41 cf. Ausubel (1961; in Scheff, 1967, p. 261).
42 Wootton (1959, p. 214 and *passim*).
43 Reitlinger (1971, p. 513).
44 Voltaire, *Oeuvres* iii, p. 381; cited Williams (1953b, pp. 223–4).

BIBLIOGRAPHY

Abelson, R. (1962–3), Review: A. I. Melden's *Free Action, Philosophy and Phenomenological Research*, XXIII, 616–17.

Acton, H. B. (ed.) (1969), *The Philosophy of Punishment* Macmillan, London.

Adenaes, F. A. (1966), 'The General Preventive Effects of Punishment', *University of Pennsylvania Law Review*, 114, 7 May, 949–83; in Radzinowicz and Wolfgang (1971), 74–104.

Adenaes, F. A. (1971), 'The Future of Criminal Law', *Criminal Law Review*, 615–29.

Aleksander, I. (1971), 'Artificial Intelligence and All That', *Wireless World*, October, 494–5.

Aleksander, I. (1973), 'Brains, Minds and Machines', *Electron Power*, no. 15, 499–502.

Aleksander, I. (1977), *The Human Machine*, Giorgi, St Saphorin.

Alexander, F. G. and Selesnick, S. T. (1966), *The History of Psychiatry*, Harper & Row, New York.

Alexander, S. (1920), *Space Time and Deity*, Macmillan, London.

Allan, F. A. (1964), 'Legal Values and the Rehabilitative Ideal', *The Borderland of Criminal Justice*, University of Chicago, 25–41; in Radzinowicz and Wolfgang (1971), 65–74.

Alston, W. (1967), 'Wants, Actions and Causal Explanations', in H. N. Castaneda, *Intentionality, Minds and Perception*, Wayne State University Press, Detroit, 301–41.

Angel, R. B. (1967), 'Explanation and Prediction', *Philosophy of Science*, 34, 276–82.

Angyal, A. (1941), *Foundations for a Science of Personality*, Harvard University Press, Cambridge, Mass.

Anscombe, G. E. M. (1957), *Intention*, Blackwell, Oxford.

Anscombe, G. E. M. (1958), 'On Brute Facts', *Analysis*, 18, no. 3, 69–72.

Anscombe, G. E. M. (1971), *Causation and Determinism*, Cambridge University Press.

Aristotle (1958), *Ethics* (trans. J. A. K. Thomson), Penguin, Harmondsworth.

Armstrong, D. M. (1968), *A Materialist Theory of the Mind*, Routledge & Kegan Paul, London.

Armstrong, D. M. (1970), 'The Nature of Mind', Inaugural Lecture of the Challis Professor of Philosophy at the University of Sydney (1965); in Borst (1970), 67–79.

Armstrong, K. G. (1969), 'The Retributivist Hits Back', *Mind*, LXX, no. 280 (1961, 471–90); in Acton (1969), 138–58.

Ashby, W. R. (1940), 'Adaptiveness and Equilibrium', *Journal of Mental Science*, 86, 476–82.

Ashby, W. R. (1947), 'The Nervous System as Physical Machine: With Special Reference to the Origin of Adaptive Behaviour', *Mind*, 56, no. 1, 44–59.

Ashby, W. R. (1952), *Design for a Brain*, Chapman & Hall, London.

Ashby, W. R. (1970), *An Introduction to Cybernetics* (1956), Chapman & Hall, London.

Asimov, I. (1965), *The Human Brain*, Signet, New York.

Aune, B. (1963), 'Abilities Modalities and Free-Will', *Philosophy and Phenomenological Research*, XXIII, 3, 397–413.

Aune, B. (1967), 'Can', *Encyclopaedia of Philosophy* (ed. P. Edwards), vol. 2, Collier Macmillan, London. 8–20.

Aurelius, M. (1960), *The Meditations* (1873) (trans. G. Lang), Doubleday, New York.

Austin, J. L. (1946), 'Other Minds', *Proceedings of the Aristotelian Society*, Supplement XX, 148–187; in Flew (1965), 342–80.

Austin, J. L. (1956), 'Ifs and Cans', *Proceedings of the British Academy*, XLII, 109–32; in Austin (1970), 205–32.

Austin, J. L. (1956–7), 'A Plea for Excuses', *Proceedings of the Aristotelian Society*, LVII, 1–29; in Austin (1970), 175–204.

Austin, J. L. (1970), *Philosophical Papers* (ed. Urmson, J. O. and Warnock, G. J.), Oxford University Press, London.

Ausubel, D. P. (1961), 'Personality Disorder is Disease', *American Psychologist*, 16, 69–74; in Scheff (1967), 254–66.

Ayer, A. J. (1940), *The Foundations of Empirical Knowledge*, Macmillan, London.

Ayer, A. J. (1972), *Probability and Evidence*, Macmillan, London.

Ayers, M. R. (1968), *The Refutation of Determinism*. Methuen, London.

Bacon, F. (1958), *The Advancement of Learning* (1605), Dent, London.

Baier, K. (1962), 'Smart on Sensations', *Australasian Journal of Philosophy*, XL; in Borst (1970), 95–106.

Bain, A. (1874), *Mind and Body*, Henry S. King, London.

Baker, R. (1971), 'The Search for Intelligent Machines', *Wireless World*, January, 266–9.

Bancroft, J. H., Jones, H. G., and Pullan, B.R. (1966), 'A Simple Transducer for Measuring Penile Erection with Comments on its Use in the Treatment of Sexual Disorders,' *Behavioural Research and Therapy*, 4, 239–41.

Bannister, D. and Fransella, F. (1971), *Inquiring Man: The Theory of Personal Constructs*, Penguin, Harmondsworth.

Barret, W. (1970), 'Determinism and Novelty' (1958)· in Hook (1970a), 46–54.

Barry, J. V. W. (1969), 'Judicial Sentencing or Treatment Tribunals', from *The Courts and Criminal Punishment*, Shearer, Wellington, NZ; in Radzinowicz and Wolfgang (1971), 660–4.

Bateson, G. (1967), 'Cybernetic Explanation', *American Behavioral Scientist*, 10:8, 29–32; in Bateson (1973), 375–86.

Bateson, G. (1973), *Steps to an Ecology of Mind*, Paladin, London.

Beck, W. S. (1961), *Modern Science and the Nature of Life*, Doubleday, New York.

Bell, E. T. (1962), *The Last Problem*, Gollancz, London.

Beloff, J. (1965), 'The Identity Hypothesis: A Critique', in J. R. Smythies (ed.), *Brain and Behaviour*, Routledge & Kegan Paul, London, 35–54.

Benedict, R. (1963), *Patterns of Culture* (1935), Routledge & Kegan Paul, London.

Bennet, E., Rosenzweig, M. and Diamond, M. (1969), 'Rat Brain: Effects of Environmental Enrichment on Wet and Dry Weights', *Science*, 63, 825–6.

Bergson, H. (1960), *Time and Free Will* (1889) (trans. F. L. Pogson), Harper, New York.

Bergson, H. (1965), *Creative Evolution* (trans. A. Mitchell), Macmillan, London.

Berlin, I. (1969), 'Historical Inevitability' (1953), in *Four Essays on Liberty*, Oxford University Press, London, 41–117.

von Bertalanffy, L. (1950), 'The Theory of Open Systems in Physics and Biology', *Science*, 3, 13 June, 23–9.

von Bertalanffy, L. (1962), 'General System Theory: A Critical Review', *General Systems Yearbook*, VII, 1–20.

von Bertalanffy, L. (1964), 'The Mind–Body Problem: A New View', *Psychosomatic Medicine*, XXIV, 29–45.

von Bertalanffy, L. (1971), *General System Theory* (1968), Penguin, Harmondsworth.

Bhaskar, R. (1975), *A Realist Theory of Science*, Leeds Books, Leeds.

Black, D. A., Blackburn, R., Blackler, C. D., Haward, L. R. C. and Summerfield, A. (1973), 'Memorandum of Evidence to the Butler Committee on the Law Relating to the Mentally Abnormal Offender', *Bulletin of the British Psychological Society*, 26, 331–42.

Black, D. A., Blackburn, R., Blackler, C. D., Haward, L. R. C. and Summerfield, A. (1974), 'Treatment of the Mentally Abnormal Offender', letter to *The Times*, 9 January.

Black, M. (1956), 'Why Cannot an Effect Precede its Cause?', *Analysis*, 16:3, 49–58.

Black, M. (1962), *Models and Metaphors*, Cornell University Press, Ithaca, NY.

Black, M. (1970), 'Making Something Happen' (1958); in Hook (1970a), 31–45.

Blakemore, C. B. (1967), 'Personality and Brain Damage', in H. J. Eysenck, *The Biological Basis of Behaviour*, Carter Thomas, Springfield, Ill., 319–39.

Blakemore, C. B. and Cooper, G. F. (1970), 'Development of the Brain Depends on the Visual Environment', *Nature*, 228, October, 447–78.

Blanshard, B. (1970), 'The Case for Determinism' (1958); in Hook (1970a), 19–30.

Bibliography

Boden, M. (1970), 'Intentionality and Physical Systems', *Philosophy of Science*, XXXVI, 200–14.

Bohm, D. (1952), 'A Suggested Interpretation of Quantum Theory in Terms of Hidden Variables', *Physical Review*, 85, 166, 180.

Bohm, D. (1957), *Causality and Chance in Modern Physics*, Routledge & Kegan Paul, London.

Bohr, N. (1958a), *Atomic Physics and Human Knowledge*, Inter Science, London.

Bohr, N. (1958b), 'Quantum Physics and Philosophy', in R. Kiblansky (ed.), *Philosophy in Mid-Century*, vol. 1, La Nouva Italia Editrice, Florence, 308–14.

de Bono, E. (1969), *The Mechanism of Mind*, Penguin, Harmondsworth.

Boring, E. G. (1933), *The Physical Dimension of Consciousness*, Appleton, New York.

Born, M. (1937), *Atomic Physics*, Black, London.

Born, M. (1953), 'The Interpretation of Quantum Mechanics', *British Journal for the Philosophy of Science*, 4, 95–106.

Borst, C. V. (ed.) (1970), *Mind Brain Identity Theory*, Macmillan, London.

Boyle, J. M., Grisez, G. and Tollefsen, O. (1972), 'Determinism, Freedom and Self-referential Arguments', *Review of Metaphysics*, XXVI:1, 3–37.

Braithwaite, R. B. (1953), *The Nature of Scientific Explanation*, Cambridge University Press.

Brandon, N. (1969), 'Free Will, Moral Responsibility and the Law', *Southern California Law Review*, 42, 264–91.

Brandt, R. (1969), 'Doubts about Identity Theory' (1959); in Hook (1969), 62–73.

Brandt, R. (1970), 'Determinism and the Justifiability of Moral Blame' in Hook (1970a), 149–54.

Breggin, P. R. (1972), 'The Return of Lobotomy and Psychosurgery', *U.S. Congressional Record*, 28 February, E1602–12.

Breggin, P. R. (1974), 'The Second Wave', *Mental Hygiene*, 57 (1), 10–13.

Bremer, F. (1954), 'The Neurophysiological Problem of Sleep', in Delafresnay (1954), 137–62; 'Discussion', 497.

Brentano, F. (1874), *Psychologie vom Empirischen Standpunkt*, Vienna, in Chisholm (1960), 39–61.

Bressler, D. and Bitterman, M. (1969), 'Learning in Fish with Transplanted Brain Tissue', *Science*, 163, 590–2.

Brett, P. (1970), 'The Physiology of Provocation', *Criminal Law Review*, 634–40.

Bridgeman, P. W. (1970a), 'Determinism in Modern Science' (1958), in Hook (1970a), 57–75.

Bridgeman, P. W. (1970b), 'Determinism and Punishment' (1958), in Hook (1970a), 155–6.

Brindling, G. S. (1970), 'Sensations Produced by Electric Stimulation of the Occipital Poles of the Cerebral Hemispheres and Their Use in Constructing Visual Prostheses', *Annals of the Royal College of Surgeons*, 47, no. 2, 106–8.

Broad, C. D. (1925), *Mind and its Place in Nature*, Kegan Paul, London.

Broad, C. D. (1970), 'Determinism Indeterminism and Libertarianism' (1952), in Dworkin (1970), 149–71.

Brown, C. C. and Sancen, R. T. (1968), *Electronic Instrumentation for the Behavioral Sciences*, Chas. Thomas, Springfield, Ill.

Brown, D. G. (1968), *Action*, University of Toronto Press.

Bruner, J. S. and Postman, L. (1949), 'On the Perception of Incongruity: A Paradigm', *Journal of Personality*, XVIII, 206–23.

Buck, R. C. (1956), 'The Logic of General Systems Theory', in H. Feigl and M. Scriven (eds), *Minnesota Studies in Philosophy of Science*, vol. 1, Minnesota University Press, Minneapolis, 223–38.

Buckley, W. (1967), *Sociology and Modern Systems Theory*, Prentice Hall, Englewood Cliffs, NJ.

Buckley, W. (ed.) (1968), *Modern Systems Research for the Behavioral Scientist*, Aldine, Chicago.

Bunge, M. (1959), *Causality: The Place of the Causal Principle in Modern Science*, Harvard University Press, Cambridge, Mass.

Bunge, M. (1967), *Scientific Research I*, Springer Verlag, New York.

Bunge, M. (ed.) (1968), *Quantum Physics and Reality*. Springer Verlag, New York.

Bunge, M. (1969), 'The Metaphysics, Epistemology and Methodology of Levels', in L. L. Whyte, A. G. Wilson and D. Wilson (eds), *Hierarchical Structures*, Elsevier, New York, 17–28.

Burkholder, L. (1974), 'The Determinist Principle as Synthetic and A-Priori', *Philosophia*, 4:1, 139–61.

Burtt, E. A. (1965), *In Search of Philosophic Understanding*, New American Library, New York.

Butler, J. (1969), *Fifteen Sermons* (1726), Bell, London.

Butterfield, H. (1949), *Origins of Modern Science 1300–1800*, Bell, London.

Caianiello, E. R. (1961), 'Outline of a Theory of Thought Processes and Thinking Machines', *Journal of Theoretical Biology*, 1, 204–35.

Campbell, C. A. (1938), 'In Defence of Free Will', Jackson, Glasgow; in Campbell (1967), 35–55.

Campbell, C. A. (1939–40), 'The Psychology of Effort of Will', *Proceedings of the Aristotelian Society*, 40, 50–69; in Campbell (1967), 56–77.

Campbell, C. A. (1951), 'Is Freewill a Pseudo Problem?', *Mind*, LX, 441–65; in Campbell (1967), 17–34.

Campbell, C. A. (1957), *On Selfhood and Godhood*, Allen & Unwin, London.

Campbell, C. A. (1967), *In Defence of Free Will*, Allen & Unwin, London.

Campbell, K. (1972), *Body and Mind*, Macmillan, London.

Campbell, N. R. (1920), 'The Structure of Theories', *Physics: The Elements*, Cambridge University Press (1920); in H. Feigl and M. Brodbeck (eds) (1953), *Readings in the Philosophy of Science*, Appleton Century Crofts, New York.

Cannon, W. B. (1927), 'The James–Lange Theory of Emotions: A Critical Examination and an Alternative Theory', *American Journal of Psychology*, 39, 106–24; in Pribram (1969), vol. 4, 433–51.

Cannon, W. B. (1932), *The Wisdom of the Body*, Norton, New York.

Carnap, R. (1960), 'Empiricism Semantics and Ontology', *Meaning and*

Necessity, Chicago University Press, 205–21.

Castberg, F. (1957), *Problems of Legal Philosophy*, Allen & Unwin, London.

Castell, A. (1965), *The Self in Philosophy*, Macmillan, New York.

Chappel, V. C. (ed.) (1962), *The Philosophy of Mind*, Prentice-Hall, Englewood Cliffs, NJ.

Chein, I. (1972), *The Science of Behaviour and the Image of Man*, Tavistock, London.

Cherry, C. (1971), *On Human Communication* (1962), MIT Press, Cambridge, Mass.

Chiaraviglio, L. (1968), 'Biology and Philosophy', in R. Kiblansky (ed.), *Contemporary Philosophy: Philosophy of Science*, La Nouva Italia Editrice, Florence, 376–86.

Child, A. (1965), *Interpretation: A General Theory*, University of California Press, Los Angeles.

Child, C. M. (1924), *Physiological Foundations of Behaviour*, Holt, New York.

Child, C. M. (1941), *Patterns and Problems of Development*, University of Chicago Press.

Chisholm, R. (1957), *Perceiving*, Cornell University Press, Ithaca, NY.

Chisholm, R. (ed.) (1960), *Realism and the Background of Phenomenology*, Free Press, Chicago.

Chisholm, R. (1964a), 'Human Freedom and the Self', Lindley Lecture, University of Kansas.

Chisholm, R. (1964b), 'The Descriptive Element in the Concept of Action', *Journal of Philosophy*, 61, 613–25.

Chisholm, R. (1966), *Theory of Knowledge*. Prentice-Hall, Englewood Cliffs, NJ.

Chisholm, R. (1967), 'Intentionality', in P. Edwards (ed.), *Encyclopaedia of Philosophy*, vol. 4, Collier Macmillan, London, 201–4.

Chisholm, R. (1976), 'The Agent as Cause', in M. Brand and D. Walton (eds), *Action Theory*, Rydel, Dortrecht, 199–211.

Chomsky, N. (1968),'Language and Mind', in Rothblatt (1968), 3–31.

Coburn, R. (1963), 'Shaffer on the Identity of Mental States and Brain Processes', *Journal of Philosophy*, LX, 89–92.

Coder, D. (1973), 'The Fundamental Error of Central State Materialism', *American Philosophical Quarterly*, 10, no. 4, 289–98.

Cohen, L. J. (1968), 'Criteria of Intentionality – II', *Proceedings of the Aristotelian Society*, Supplement XLII, 123–47.

Cohen, M. R. (1940), 'Moral Aspects of the Criminal Law', *Yale Law Journal*, 49, 6 April, 1009–26; in Radzinowicz and Wolfgang (1971), 27–42.

Collingwood, R. G. (1937–8), 'On the So Called Idea of Causation', *Proceedings of the Aristotelian Society*, XXXVIII, 85–112.

Collingwood, R. G. (1940), *An Essay on Metaphysics*, Clarendon, Oxford.

Conel, J. L. (1955), *The Post Natal Development of the Human Cerebral Cortex*, Harvard University Press, Cambridge, Mass.

Cornford, F. (1912), *From Religion to Philosophy: A Study in the Origins of Western Speculation*, Edward Arnold, London. (Harper, New York, 1957).

Cornman, J. (1962), 'The Identity of Mind and Body', *Journal of Philosophy*, 59, 486–92.

Cornman, J. (1964), 'Linguistic Frameworks and Metaphysical Questions', *Inquiry*, 7, 120–42.

Cornman, J. (1966), *Metaphysics, Reference and Language*, Yale University Press, New Haven, Conn.

Cornman, J. (1970), *Materialism and Sensations*, Yale University Press, London.

Coser, L. A. (1968), 'Sociology of Knowledge', in *Encyclopaedia of the Social Sciences*, vol. 8, Collier Macmillan, London, 428–34.

Cote, A. J. Jr (1967), *The Search for the Robots*, Basic Books, New York.

Cowan, J. D. (1965), 'The Problem of Organismic Reliability', in N. Wiener (ed.), *Cybernetics of the Nervous System, Progress in Brain Research*, vol. 17, Elsevier, London, 9–63.

Craig, W. (1953), 'On Axiomatisability Within a System', *Journal of Symbolic Logic*, XVIII, 30–2.

Craig, W. (1956), 'Replacement of Auxiliary Expressions', *Philosophical Review*, 65, 38–55.

Craik, K. (1967), *The Nature of Explanation* (1943), Cambridge University Press.

Crick, F. H. C. (1955), 'The Structure of the Hereditary Material', *The Physics and Chemistry of Life*, Scientific American, New York, 118–33.

Crossland, M. P. (ed.) (1971), *The Science of Matter*, Penguin, Harmondsworth.

Crosson, F. J. (1968), 'Information Theory and Phenomenology', in Crosson and Sayre (1968), 99–136.

Crosson, F. J. and Sayre, K. M. (eds) (1968), *Philosophy and Cybernetics*, Simon & Schuster, New York.

Dahlke, O. H. (1940), 'The Sociology of Knowledge', in E. H. Barnes, H. Becker and F. B. Becker (eds), *Contemporary Social Theory*, Appleton, New York, 64–89.

Dampier-Whetham, W. C. D. (1930), *A History of Science*, Cambridge University Press.

Danto, A. (1967), 'Persons', in P. Edwards (ed.) *Encyclopaedia of Philosophy*, vol. 6, Collier Macmillan, London, 110–14.

Danto, A. (1973), *Analytical Philosophy of Action*, Cambridge University Press.

Darrow, C. (1934), *Crime: Its Causes and Treatment*, Watts, London.

Davidson, D. (1963), 'Actions Reasons and Causes', *Journal of Philosophy*, 60, 685–700.

Davidson, D. (1970), 'Mental Events', in L. Forster and J. W. Swanson (eds), *Experience and Theory*, Duckworth, London, 79–101.

Davidson, D. (1971), 'Agency', in R. Binkley, R. Bronaagh, A. Marras (eds), *Agent Action and Reason*, University of Toronto Press, 3–25.

Davidson, D. (1973), 'Freedom to Act', in T. Honderich (ed.), *Essays in Freedom of Action*, Routledge & Kegan Paul, 137–56.

Davidson, D. (1974), 'Psychology as Philosophy', in S. C. Brown (ed.) *Philosophy of Psychology*, Macmillan, London; in Glover (1976), 101–10.

Davies, T. (1971), 'Pauline: The Mind of a Baby Stealer', *The Sunday Times*, 12 December.

Delafresnay, J. F. (ed.) (1954), *Brain Mechanisms and Consciousness*, Blackwell, Oxford.

Delgado, J. M. R. (1960), 'Intracerebral Radio Stimulation and Recording in Completely Free Patients', *Journal of Nervous and Mental Diseases*, 147:4; in Schwitzgabel (1973), 184–98.

Delgado, J. M. R. (1967), 'Aggression and Defense under Cerebral Radio Control', in C. D. Clements and D. B. Lindsley (eds), *Aggression and Defense, Neural Mechanisms and Social Patterns*, vol. V: *Brain Function*, University of California Press, Berkeley.

Delgado, J. M. R. (1969), *The Physical Control of the Mind: Towards a Psycho-civilised Society*, Harper & Row, New York.

Denning, L. J. (1953), *The Changing Law*, Stevens, London.

Descartes, R. (1966), *Essential Works of Descartes* (trans. L. Blair), Bantam, New York.

Descartes, R. (1969), *Philosophical Works*, 2 vols (trans E. S. Haldane and G. T. R. Ross, 1911), Cambridge University Press.

Deutsch, J. A. (1962), *The Structural Basis of Behaviour*, Cambridge University Press.

Deutsch, K. W. (1951), 'Mechanism Teleology and Mind', *Philosophy and Phenomenological Research*, XII, 185–223.

Devlin, Lord (1969), *The Enforcement of Morals*, Oxford University Press, London.

Dingman, W. and Sporn, M. B. (1964), 'Molecular Theories of Memory', *Science*, 144, 26–9.

Donaldson, P. E. K. (1970), 'Visual Prosthesis: An Implantable Electrical Aid for the Sightless', *Electronics and Power*, November, 439–40.

Dostoyevsky, F. (1864), *Notes from the Underground*. (Everyman edition, trans. C. J. Hogarth, Dent, London, 1957).

Downie, R. S. and Telfer, E. (1969), *Respect for Persons*, Allen & Unwin, London.

Dray, W. (1957), *Laws and Explanation in History*, Oxford University Press.

Ducasse, C. (1949), 'Explanation, Mechanism and Teleology', *Journal of Philosophy*, 23 (1926), in H. Feigl and W. Sellars (eds) *Readings in Philosophical Analysis*, Appleton, New York, 540–4.

Ducasse, C. (1968), *Truth, Knowledge and Causation*, Routledge & Kegan Paul, London.

Ducasse, C. (1969a), *Causation and the Types of Necessity* (1924), Dover, New York.

Ducasse, C. (1969b), 'In Defense of Dualism' (1959); in Hook (1969), 85–9.

Ducasse, C. (1970), 'Determinism, Freedom and Responsibility', (1958), in Hook (1970a), 160–9.

Duhem, P. (1954), *The Aim and Structure of Physical Theory* (1914), trans. P. Weiner, Princeton University Press.

Dummet, M. (1954), 'Can an Effect Precede its Cause?' *Proceedings of the Aristotelian Society*, Supplement XXVIII, 27–44.

Dworkin, G. (ed.) (1970), *Determinism Free Will and Moral Responsibility*, Prentice-Hall, Englewood Cliffs, NJ.

401

Bibliography

Eccles, Sir J. (1960), *The Neurophysiological Basis of Mind* (1953), Clarendon, Oxford.
Eccles, Sir J. (ed.), (1966), *Brain and Conscious Experience*, Springer Verlag, New York.
Eccles, Sir J. (1970), *Facing Reality*, English Universities Press, London.
Eddington, A. S. (1935), *New Pathways in Science* (1934), Cambridge University Press.
Edel, A. (1963), *Method in Ethical Theory*, Routledge & Kegan Paul, London.
Edwards, J. L. J. (1968), 'Social Defense and Control of the Dangerous Offender', *Current Legal Problems*, 21, 23–52.
Edwards, P. (1970), 'Hard and Soft Determinism' (1958); in Hook (1970a), 117–24.
Einstein, A. (1933), 'On the Methods of Theoretical Physics', The Spencer Lecture, Oxford, 10 June.
Einstein, A. (1950a), 'On the Generalised Theory of Gravitation', *Scientific American*, CLXXXII, 13–17.
Einstein, A. (1950b), 'Physics and Reality', *Out of My Later Years*, Thames & Hudson, London, ch. 12, 59–97.
Emery, F. E. (ed.) (1969), *Systems Thinking*, Penguin, Harmondsworth.
Emmet, D. (1966), *The Nature of Metaphysical Thinking* (1945), Macmillan, London.
Emmett, D. (1972), 'Is All Thinking Ideological?', unpublished paper read at Conference at Shap Wells, Cumberland, November 1972.
English, P. (1970), 'What Did Section 3 Do to the Law of Provocation?', *Criminal Law Review*, 249–67.
Epstein, F. L. (1973), 'The Metaphysics of Mind–Brain Identity Theories', *American Philosophical Quarterly*, 10, no. 42, April, 111–21.
Esposito, J. L. (1976), 'Systems, Holons and Persons', *International Philosophical Quarterly*, XVI (2), June, 219–36.
Eysenck, H. J. (1964), *Crime and Personality*, Routledge & Kegan Paul, London.
Eysenck, H. J. (1967), *The Biological Basis of Personality*, Charles Thomas, Springfield, Ill.
Farrel, B. (1950), 'Experience', *Mind*, LIX, 170–98.
Farrel, B. (1968), 'Some Reflections on the Nature of Consciousness', in Rothblatt (1968), 35–60.
Farrel, B. (1972), 'Thought and Time', *Philosophical Quarterly*, 22, no. 87, 140–8.
Feibelman, J. and Friend, J. W. (1969), 'The Structure and Function of Organisation', *Philosophical Review*, 54 (1945), 19–44; in Emery (1969), 30–55.
Fechner, G. T. (1860), *Elemente der Psychophysik*, vol. 1. von Breitkopsund Härtel, Leipzig. Passages translated in McDougal (1928, passim).
Feigl, H. (1949), 'Logical Empiricism' (1943), in H. Feigl and W. Sellars (eds), (1949), *Readings in Philosophical Analysis*, Appleton, New York, 3–26.
Feigl, H. (1967), *The Mental and the Physical* (1958), University of Minnesota Press, Minneapolis.

Feigl, H. (1969), 'Mind-Body Not a Pseudo Problem' (1960); in Hook (1969), 33–44.

Feigl, H. and Maxwell, G. (1961), 'Why Ordinary Language Needs Reforming', *Journal of Philosophy*, 58 (18), 488–98.

Fessard, A. E. (1954), 'Mechanisms of Nervous Integration and Consciousness', in Delafresnay (1954), 200–36.

Feyerabend, P. K. (1963a), 'Materialism and the Mind–Body Problem', *Review of Metaphysics*, XVII, 49–56; in Borst (1970), 142–56.

Feyerabend, P. K. (1963b), 'Mental Events and the Brain', *Journal of Philosophy*, x, 295–6; in Borst (1970), 140–1.

Feyerabend, P. K. (1965), 'Problems of Empiricism' in R. Colodney (ed.), *Beyond the Edge of Certainty*, Prentice-Hall, Englewood Cliffs, NJ, 145–260.

Fitzgerald, P. J. (1967), 'The Aims of the Penal System', *Criminal Law Review*, 621–30.

Fitzgerald, P. J. (1968), 'Criminal Responsibility and Freedom of Action', *Criminal Law Review*, 363–6.

Flew, A. (1949), 'Psycho-Analytic Explanation', *Analysis*, 10, 8–18.

Flew, A. (1954), 'Can an Effect Precede its Cause?' *Proceedings of the Aristotelian Society*, Supplement XXVIII, 45–62.

Flew, A. (ed.) (1956), *Essays in Conceptual Analysis*, Macmillan, London.

Flew, A. (ed.) (1965), *Logic and Language*, Doubleday, New York.

Flew, A. (1973), *Crime or Disease*, Macmillan, London.

Foot, P. (1957), 'Free Will as Involving Determinism', *Philosophical Review*, LXVI, 439–50.

Frankfort, H., Frankfort, H. A., Wilson, J. A., and Jacobsen, T. (1967), *Before Philosophy* (1946), Penguin, Harmondsworth.

Franklin, R. I. (1968), *Freewill and Determinism: A Study of Rival Conceptions of Man*, Routledge & Kegan Paul, London.

Franks, C. M. (1957), 'Personality Factors and the Rate of Conditioning', *British Journal of Psychology*, XLVIII, 119–26.

Frege, G. (1960), 'On Sense and Reference', in M. Black and P. T. Geach (eds), *Philosophical Writings*, Blackwell, Oxford, 56–78.

Funkenstein, D. H. (1957), *Mastery under Stress*, Harvard University Press, Cambridge, Mass.

Furth, R. (1969), 'The Role of Modelling in Theoretical Physics', in R. S. Cohen and M. Wartofsky (eds), *Boston Studies in the Philosophy of Science*, vol. V, Boston University Press.

Galileo, Galilei. (1953), *Dialogue on the Great World Systems*, trans. Georgio di Santinalla, Chicago University Press.

Garattini, S. and Sigg, E. B. (eds) (1969), *Aggressive Behaviour*, Excerpta Medica Fdn, Amsterdam.

Gardiner, H. (1976), *The Quest for Mind*, Quartet Books, London.

Gault, R. H. (1912), Introduction to G. de Tarde, *Penal Philosophy*, Heinemann, London, i–xxiii.

Gayer, J. (1972), 'Systems Theory: Ontological and Epistemological Object', *Scientia*, 107, 609–16.

Gazzaniga, M. (1970), *The Bisected Brain*, Appleton, New York.

Geach, P. T. (1956), 'Good and Evil', *Analysis*, 17, 33–42.

Geach, P. T. (1967), 'Identity', *Review of Metaphysics*, 21:1, 3–12.

Geach, P. T. (1971), *Mental Acts* (1957), Routledge & Kegan Paul, London.

Gellner, E. (1964), 'The Crisis in the Humanities and the Mainstream of Philosophy', in J. H. Plumb (ed.), *Crisis in the Humanities*, Penguin, Harmondsworth, 45–81.

Gellner, E. (1974) *Legitimation of Belief*, Cambridge University Press.

Gendin, S. (1973), 'Insanity and Criminal Responsibility', *American Philosophical Quarterly*, 10, no. 2, April, 99–110.

George, F. H. (1957), 'Logic and Behaviour', in *Science News* no. 45. Penguin, Harmondsworth, 45–60.

George, F. H. (1971), *Cybernetics*, English Universities Press, London.

Gerard, R. W. (1973), 'The Neurophysiology of Purposive Behaviour', in American Society for Cybernetics, *Purposive Systems*, Spartan, New York, 25–34.

Gerber, R. S. and McAnany, P. D. (1967), 'Punishment: Current Survey of Philosophy and Law', *St Louis Law Journal*, 11:4, Summer, 502–35; in Radzinowicz and Wolfgang (1971), 113–44.

Gibbons, T. C. (1963), *A Psychiatric Study of Borstal Lads*, Oxford University Press, London.

Ginet, C. (1962), 'Can the Will be Caused', *Philosophical Review*, LXXI, 49–55; in Dworkin (1970), 119–40.

Glass, B. (1965), *Science and Ethical Values*, Oxford University Press, London.

Gleuk, S. (1956), *Physique and Delinquency*, Harper & Row, NY.

Glover, J. (1970), *Responsibility*, Routledge & Kegan Paul, London.

Glover, J. (ed.) (1976), *The Philosophy of Mind*, Oxford University Press.

Goddard, Lord (1963), *The Observer*, 5 May.

Goldman, A. I. (1970), *A Theory of Human Action*, Prentice-Hall, Englewood Cliffs, NJ.

Gomez, A. O. (1966), 'The Brain-consciousness Problem in Contemporary Scientific Research', in Eccles (1966), 446–69.

Goudsmit, S. A. (1947), *ALSOS. The Failure in German Science*, Sigma, London; excerpt, 'The Gestapo in Science', in M. Gardiner (ed.), *Great Essays in Modern Science* (1957), Washington Square Press, New York, 339–57.

Grant, C. K. (1952), 'Free Will: A Reply to Professor Campbell', *Mind*, LXVI, 381–5.

Gray, W. (1972), 'Bertalanffian Principles as a Basis of Humanistic Psychiatry', in Laszlo (1972a), 123–33.

Gregory, R. (1970), *Eye and Brain*, Weidenfeld & Nicolson, London.

Grey-Walter, W. (1954), 'Theoretical Properties of Diffuse Projection Systems in Relation to Behaviour and Consciousness', in Delafresnay (1954), 345–73.

Grey-Walter, W. (1957), 'An Imitation of Life', in *Automatic Control*, (1955); *Scientific American* (eds), Bell, London, 123–31.

Grey-Walter, W. (1965), *The Living Brain* (1953), Penguin, Harmondsworth.

de Groot, D. (1966), 'Perception and Memory versus Thought: Some Old Ideas and Recent Findings', in B. Kleinmuntz (ed.), *Problem Solving*, John Wiley,

New York, 19–50.

Gruber, H. E., Fink, C. D. and Damm, V. (1957), 'Effects of Experience on Perception of Causality', *Journal of Experimental Psychology*, LIII, 89–93.

Grunbaum, A. (1952), 'Causality and the Science of Human Behaviour', *American Scientist*, 40, 665–76; in H. Feigl and M. Brodbeck (eds), *Minnesota Studies in Philosophy of Science*, vol. 1, Minnesota University Press, Minneapolis, 766–78.

Gustafson, D. (1973), 'A Critical Survey of the Reasons versus Causes Argument in Recent Philosophy of Action', *Metaphilosophy*, 4:4, 269–97.

Haas, W. (1972–3), 'Meaning and Grammar', *Proceedings of the Aristotelian Society*, LXXIII, 135–55.

Hademard, J. (1949), *The Psychology of Invention in the Mathematical Field*, Princeton University Press.

Haldane, J. B. S. (1927), *Possible Worlds*, Heinemann, London.

Hall, J. (1960), *General Principles of the Criminal Law*, 2nd edn, Bobbs-Merrill, Indianapolis; passages in Morris (1966), 425–35.

Hallowell, A. I. (1964), 'Ojibwa, Ontology Behaviour and World View', in S. Diamond (ed.) *Primitive Views of the World*, Columbia University Press, London, 49–82.

Hall-Williams, J. E. (1954), 'Trusting the Jury', *Criminal Law Review*, 434–9.

Hamlyn, D. W. (1953), 'Behaviour', *Philosophy*, XXVIII, 132–45; in Chappell (1962), 60–73.

Hamlyn, D. W. (1957), *The Psychology of Perception*, Kegan Paul, London.

Hampshire, S. (1950), Review article: G. Ryle's *The Concept of Mind*, *Mind*, LIX, 237–55; in Hampshire (1972), 87–113.

Hampshire, S. (1959), *Thought and Action*, Chatto & Windus, London.

Hampshire, S. (1965), *Freedom of the Individual*, Chatto & Windus, London.

Hampshire, S. (1972), 'Freedom of Mind' (1965), in *Freedom of Mind and Other Essays*, Oxford University Press, London, 2–20.

Hansel, C. E. M. (1966), *E.S.P. A Scientific Evaluation*, Scribner, New York.

Hanson, N. R. (1958), *Patterns of Discovery*, Cambridge University Press.

Hanson, N. R. (1963), 'Justifying Analytic Claims', *Analysis*, 23:5, 103–5.

Hare, R. M. (1970), *The Language of Morals* (1952), Oxford University Press, London.

Hare, R. M. (1972), *Freedom and Reason* (1963), Oxford University Press, London.

Hargrove, B. (1960), 'Revision of the Law Relating to Mental Health', *Current Legal Problems*, 13, 192–210.

Harlow, J. M. (1888), *Proceedings of the Massachusetts Medical Society*, vol. 2, 329; cited Wooldridge (1963), 146–8.

Harré, R. (1970), 'Powers', *British Journal for the Philosophy of Science*, 21, 81–101.

Harré, R. (1972), *The Principles of Scientific Thinking: Models and Theory*, Macmillan, London.

Harré, R. (1973), 'Surrogates for Necessity', *Mind*, LXXXII, 358–80.

Harré, R. and Madden, E. H. (1975), *Causal Powers*, Blackwell, Oxford.

Hart, H. L. A. (1965), 'The Ascription of Responsibility and Rights',

Proceedings of the Aristotelian Society, XLIX (1948–9), 171–94, in A. G. N. Flew (ed.) (1965), 151–74.

Hart, H. L. A. (1966), *Law Liberty and Morality*, Oxford University Press, London.

Hart, H. L. A. (1968a), 'Prolegomenon to the Principles of Punishment' (1959), in Hart (1968d), 1–27.

Hart, H. L. A. (1968b), 'Negligence Mens-Rea and Criminal Responsibility' (1961), in Hart (1968d), 136–57.

Hart, H. L. A. (1968c), 'Changing Conceptions of Responsibility' (1964), in Hart (1968d), 188–244.

Hart, H. L. A. (1968d), *Punishment and Responsibility*, Clarendon, Oxford.

Hart, H. L. A. (1970), 'Responsibility and Excuses' (1958), in Hook (1970a), 95–116.

Hart, H. L. A. and Honore, A. M. (1959), *Causation and the Law*, Oxford University Press.

Hart, H. M. (1958), 'The Aims of the Criminal Law', in *Law and Contemporary Legal Problems*, 23, 405.

Hartman, R. (1958–9), 'Value Theory as a formal system', *Kant Studien*, Band 50, Heft 3, 287–315.

Hartman, R. (1967), *The Structure of Value*, Feffer & Simons, London.

Harvey, W. (1963), *The Circulation of the Blood* (1649), trans. K. J. Franklin, Dent, London; in Crossland (1971), 63–5.

Hawkins, D. (1968), 'The Nature of Purpose' in *Purposive Systems*, American Society for Cybernetics, Spartan, NY, 163–79.

Healey, M. (1967), *Principles of Automatic Control*, English Universities Press, London.

Heather, N. (1976), *Radical Perspectives in Psychology*, Methuen, London.

Hebb, D. O. (1954), 'The Problem of Consciousness and Introspection', in Delafresnay (1954), 402–21.

Hebb, D. O. (1967) *The Organisation of Behaviour* (1949), John Wiley, New York.

Hecht, S., Schlur, S. and Pirenne, M. R. (1942), 'Energy Quanta and Vision', *Journal of General Physiology*, 25, 819–30.

Heisenberg, W. (1959), *Physics and Philosophy*, Allen & Unwin, London.

Heisenberg, W. (1966), 'Planck's Discovery and the Philosophical Problems of Quantum Physics' (1958), in *On Modern Physics* (trans M. Goodman and J. W. Binns), Collier, New York, 9–44.

Held, R. and Bossam, J. (1961), 'Neuronatal Deprivation and Adult Rearrangement', *Journal of Comparative and Physiological Psychology*, 54, no. 1, 33–7.

Held, R. and Hein, A. (1963), 'Movement-produced Stimulation on the Development of Visually Guided Behaviour', *Journal of Comparative and Physiological Psychology*, 56, no. 5, 872–6.

Hempel, C. (1942), 'The Function of General Laws in History', *Journal of Philosophy*, 39, 35–48.

Hempel, C. and Oppenheim, P. (1948), 'Studies in the Logic of Explanation', *Philosophy of Science*, 15, 135–75.

Hesse, M. B. (1953), 'Models in Physics', *British Journal for the Philosophy of Science*, 4, (15), 198–214.

Hesse, M. B. (1966), *Models and Analogies in Science*, University of Notre Dame.

Hesse, M. B. (1972), 'In Defense of Objectivity', *Proceedings of the British Academy*, LVII, Oxford University Press, London.

Hinton, J. M. (1967), 'Illusions and Identity', *Analysis*, 27, 65–76.

Hintz, H. W. (1970), 'Some Further Reflections on Moral Responsibility' (1958), in Hook (1970), 176–9.

Hirsh, H. and Spinelli, D. (1970), 'Visual Experience Modifies Distribution of Horizontal and Vertical Oriented Receptive Fields in Cats', *Science*, 168, 869–71.

Hobart, R. E. (1934), 'Free Will as Involving Determinism and Inconceivable Without It', *Mind*, XLIII, 169, 1–27.

Hobbes, T. (1841), *Edited Works* (ed. W. Molesworth), vol. V: *The Questions Concerning Liberty, Necessity and Chance*, Bohn, London.

Hoffman, R. (1967), 'Malcolm and Smart on Brain Processes', *Philosophy*, XLII, no. 160, 128–36.

Holmes, O. W. Jr (1881), *The Common Law*, Macmillan, London.

Holmes, O. W. Jr (1964), *The Holmes Einstein Letters* (ed. J. B. Peabody), Scribner, New York.

Honderich, T. (1970), 'A Conspectus of Determinism', *Proceedings of the Aristotelian Society*, Supplement, XLIV, 191–216.

Honderich, T. (1971), *Punishment: The Supposed Justifications* (1969), Penguin, Harmondsworth.

Honderich, T. (1973), 'One Determinism', in T. Honderich (ed.), *Essays on Freedom of Action*, Routledge & Kegan Paul, London, 187–215.

Honderich, T. (1977–8), 'Causes and Causal Conditions as Necessitating', *Proceedings of the Aristotelian Society*, LXXVIII, 63–86.

Hood, R. G. and Sparks, R. (1970), *Key Issues in Criminology*, Weidenfeld & Nicolson, London.

Hook, S. (ed.) (1969), *Dimensions of Mind* (1960), Collier, New York.

Hook, S. (ed.) (1970a), *Determinism and Freedom* (1958), Collier, New York.

Hook, S. (1970b), 'Necessity, Indeterminism and Sentimentalism' (1958), in Hook (1970a), 180–92.

Hooker, C. A. (1971), 'Empiricism, Perception and Conceptual Change', *Canadian Journal of Philosophy*, III (1), 59–74.

Hoskins, R. G. (1933), *The Tides of Life*, Kegan Paul, Trench & Trubner, London.

Hoskins, R. G. (1943), *Endocrinology*, Harvard University Press, Cambridge, Mass.

Hospers, J. (1950), 'Freewill and Psychoanalysis', *Philosophy and Phenomenological Research*, X, 313–30.

Hospers, J. (1970), 'What Means this Freedom?' (1958), in Hook (1970a), 126–42.

Howard, C. (1961), 'What Colour is the Reasonable Man?' *Criminal Law Review*, 41–8.

Hughes, G. (1959), 'The English Homicide Act of 1957', *Criminal Law, Criminology and Police Science*, 49, 528–9.

Huizinga, J. (1949), *Homo Ludens*, Kegan Paul, London.

Hume, D. (1962), *Treatise on Human Nature* (1738), vol. 1, Meridan, New York.

Hume, D. (1963a), Enquiry Concerning Human Understanding and Other Essays (2nd edn 1750), Washington Square Press, New York.

Hume, D. (1963b), 'On The Standard of Taste' (1757), in Hume (1963a), 246–66.

Hume, D. (1966a), *Treatise on Human Nature* (1738), vol. 2, Everyman, London.

Hume, D. (1966b), 'Dialogues Concerning Natural Religion' (1779), in R. Wollheim (ed.), *Hume on Religion*, Collins, London.

Hurd, D. L. and Kipling, J. J. (eds) (1964), *The Origins and Growth of Physical Science*, Penguin, Harmondsworth.

Huxley, A. (1958), *Brave New World Revisited*, Chatto & Windus, London.

Huxley, J. (1949), 'Soviet Genetics – The Real Issue', *Nature*, 63, June, 935–42, 974–82.

Huxley, T. (1898a), 'On the Hypothesis that Animals are Automata', in *Collected Essays*, vol. 1, Macmillan, London, 199–250.'

Huxley, T. (1898b) 'On the Physical Basis of Life: Methods and Results' (1868), in *Collected Essays*, vol. 1, Macmillan, London, 130–65.

Hyden, H. (1959), 'Biochemical Changes in Glial Cells and Nerve Cells at Varying Activities', *Proceedings of the 4th Annual Congress in Biochemistry*, vol. 3, Hoffman and Olsen (eds), Pergamon, London, 64–89.

International Centre for Theoretical Physics (1973), Proceedings of the Conference on Neural Networks, July 1972; in *International Journal of Neurosciences*, 6, no. 1.

James, W. (1958), *Varieties of Religious Experience* (1902), Mentor, New York.

James, W. (1961), *Psychology* (1892), Harper, New York (ed. G. Allport).

James, W. and Lange, G. V. (1922), *The Emotions*, Williams & Wilkins, London.

Jarvie, I. (1954), 'Frontal Wounds Causing Disinhibition', *Journal of Neurology, Neurosurgery and Psychiatry*, 17, 14–32.

Jeans, J. (1942), *Physics and Philosophy*, Cambridge University Press.

Jones, R. V. (1968), 'Irony as a Phenomenon in Natural Science and Human Affairs', *Chemistry and Industry*, 13 April, 470–7.

Jones, W. T. (1969–70), 'Philosophical Disagreements and World Views', *American Philosophical Association*, 43, 24–42.

Jones, W. T. (1972), 'World Views, their Nature and Function', *Current Anthropology*, 13, February, 79–109.

Jordan, N. (1968), 'Some Thinking about Systems', in *Themes in Speculative Psychology*, Tavistock, London, 44–65.

Joske, W. D. (1967), *Material Objects*, Macmillan, London.

Kanmer, P. (1973), 'A Cybernetic System Theoretic Approach to Rational Understanding and Explanation Especially of Scientific Revolutions with Radical Meaning Change', *Ratio*, XV, no. 2, December, 221–46.

Kant, I. (1953), *Prolegomena to Every Future Metaphysic*, (trans. P. E. Lucas), Manchester University Press.

Kant, I. (1965), *Critique of Pure Reason*, (trans. N. Kemp-Smith), Macmillan, Toronto.

Karczmar, A. G. and Eccles, J. C. (eds) (1972), *Brain and Human Behaviour*, Springer Verlag, New York.

Katz, J. J. and Fodor, J. (1963), 'The Structure of a Semantic Theory', *Language*, 39, no. 2, 170–210.

Kauffman, S. A. (1969), 'Metabolic Stability and Epigenesis in Randomly Constructed Genetic Nets', *Journal of Theoretical Biology*, 22, 437–67.

Kekule, F. A. (1865), *Bulletin of the Society of Chemistry*, 3, 98; cited in A. Findlay & T. Williams (eds) (1965), *A Hundred Years of Chemistry*, 3rd edn, Methuen, London, 39–40.

Keller, H. (1945), *The Story of My Life* (1932), Hodder & Stoughton, London.

Kemp-Smith, N. (1918), *Commentary on Kant's Critique of Pure Reason*, Macmillan, London.

Kim, J. (1972), 'Phenomenal Properties, Psychophysical Laws and Identity Theory', *Monist*, 2, 176–92.

Kleist, K. (1959), 'Die Lokalisation im Grosshirn und ihre Entwickelung', *Psychiatrie, Neurologie und Medizinische Psychologie*, 5 (6), 137; cited Luria, (1969), 40.

Kneale, W. (1961), *The Development of Logic*, Oxford University Press, London.

Kneale, W. (1966), *Probability and Induction* (1949), Oxford University Press, London.

Kneale, W. (1967), *The Responsibility of Criminals*, Clarendon, Oxford; in Acton (1969), 172–96.

Kneale, W. (1969), Review: D. M. Armstrong's *A Materialist Theory of the Mind*, in *Mind*, 78, 292–301.

Koestler, A. (1956), *Reflections on Hanging*, Gollancz, London.

Koestler, A. (1964), *The Act of Creation*, Hutchinson, London.

Koestler, A. (1967), *The Ghost in the Machine*, Hutchinson, London.

Koestler, A. and Smythies, J. R. (eds) (1969), *Beyond Reductionism*, Hutchinson, London.

Köhler, W. (1959), *Gestalt Psychology* (1947), Mentor, New York.

Kordig, C. R. (1971), 'The Theory Ladenness of Observation', *Review of Metaphysics*, 24, 448–84.

Körner, S. (1959), *Conceptual Thinking*, Dover, New York.

Körner, S. (1964), 'Science and Moral Responsibility', *Mind*, LXXIII, no. 290, 161–72.

Körner, S. (1967), 'Kant's conception of Freedom', *Proceedings of the British Academy*, 193–217.

Körner S. (1970), *Categorical Frameworks*, Blackwell, Oxford.

von Krafft-Ebing, R. (1965), *Psychopathia Sexualis* (tr. H. E. Wedeck), Putnam, New York.

Krech, D. and Crutchfield, R. (1948), *Theory and Problems of Social Psychology*, McGraw Hill, New York.

Kreisel, G. (1968), 'A Survey of Proof Theory', *Journal of Symbolic Logic*, 33, no. 3, 321–88.

Kremanskiy, V. I. (1960), 'Certain Peculiarities of Organisms as Systems from the Point of View of Physics, Cybernetics and Biology' (1958 in Russian), in *General Systems Yearbook*, 5, Society of General Systems Research, 221–30, and in Emery (1969), 125–46.

Kripke, S. A. (1971), 'Identity and Necessity', in M. Munitz (ed.), *Identity and Individuation*, New York University Press, 135–64.

Kripke, S. A. (1972), 'Naming and Necessity', in G. Harman and D. Davidson (eds), *Semantics of Natural Language*, Reidel, Dortrecht, 253–353; Addendum, 763–9.

Kubie, L. S. (1954a), 'Psychiatric and Psychoanalytic Considerations of the Problem of Consciousness', in Delafresney (1954), 444–69.

Kubie, L. S. (1954b), Discussion, in Delafresnay (1954), 502–3.

Kubie, L. S. (1968), 'The Nature of Psychological Change and its Relation to Cultural Change', in Rothblatt (1968), 135–48.

Kuhn, T. (1957), *The Copernican Revolution*, Harvard University Press, Cambridge, Mass.

Kuhn, T. (1970), *The Structure of Scientific Revolutions (1962)*, in *Encyclopaedia of Unity of Science*, II, no. 2, Chicago University Press (2nd edn 1970).

Kuno, M. (1964), 'Quantal Components of Excitatory Synaptic Potentials in Spinal Motor Neurones', *Journal of Physiology*, 175, 81–99.

Lajtha, A. (ed.) (1968–71), *Handbook of Neurochemistry* (3 vols), Plenum, New York.

Lakatos, I. (1968), 'Criticism and Methodology in Scientific Research Programmes', *Proceedings of the Aristotelian Society*, 69, 149–86.

Lakatos, I. and Musgrave, A. (1970), *Criticism and the Growth of Knowledge*, Cambridge University Press.

La Mettrie, J. O. (1747), *Man a Machine*; see Vartanian (1960).

La Mettrie, J. O. (1748), *Discours sur le Bonheur*; cited Lange (1925), vol. ii, 75.

Landé, A. (1968), 'Quantum Physics and Philosophy', in R. Kiblansky (ed.), *Contemporary Philosophy: Philosophy of Science*, La Nouva Italia Editrice, Florence, 286–97.

Landé, A. (1970), 'The Case for Indeterminism' (1958); in Hook (1970a), 83–9.

Landsberg, P. T. and Evans, D. A. (1970), 'Free Will in a Mechanistic Universe', *British Journal for the Philosophy of Science*, 21, 343–58.

Lange, F. H. (1925), *The History of Materialism*, 3rd edn (trans. E. C. Thomas), Kegan Paul, Trench & Trubner, London.

Langer, S. (1959), *Philosophy in a New Key* (1942), Mentor, New York.

Langford, G. (1971), *Human Action*, Macmillan, London.

de LaPlace, P. (1820), 'Theorie Analitique des Probabilités'; cited Suppes (1970), 37.

de LaPlace, P. (1951), *Philosophical Essay on Probabilities* (1814; trans F. N. Truscott and F. L. Emory, 1902), Dover, New York.

Lashley, K. W. (1958), 'The Brain and Human Behaviour', *Proceedings of the Association for Research into Nervous and Mental Diseases*, Williams & Wilkins, Baltimore, 1–18.

Laslett, P. (1950), *The Physical Basis of Mind*, Blackwell, Oxford.

Laszlo, E. (1969), *System Structure and Experience*, Gordon, New York.

Laszlo, E. (1972a), *The Relevance of General Systems Theory*, Braziller, New York.

Laszlo, E. (1972b), *An Introduction to Systems Philosophy*, Gordon & Breach, New York.

Laszlo, E. (1972c), 'The Case for Systems Philosophy', *Metaphilosophy*, 3, no. 2, 123–41.

Law Commission (1967), *Imputed Criminal Intent*, HMSO, London.

Lehrer, K. (1966), 'An Empirical Disproof of Determinism' *Freedom and Determinism*, Random House, New York; in Dworkin (1970), 172–95.

Leibnitz, G. (1968), 'Discourse on Metaphysics' and 'Monadology', in *Basic Writings* (trans. G. R. Montgomery), Open Court, La Salle, Ill.

Leibovic, K. W. (1972), *Nervous System Theory*, Academic Press, London.

Lenneberg, E. (1967), *Biological Foundations of Language*, John Wiley, London.

Lévi-Strauss, C. (1972), 'Social Structure', in *Structural Anthropology*, Penguin, Harmondsworth, 277–323.

Lewes, G. H. (1877), *The Physical Basis of Mind*, Trubner, London.

Lewis, C. I. (1960), *A Survey of Symbolic Logic*, Dover, New York.

Lewis, C. S. (1953), 'The Humanitarian Theory of Punishment', *Res Judicatae*, 6, 224–38.

Lighthill, Sir J. (1973), *Artificial Intelligence*, Department of Education and Science Report, April 1973.

Lilley, J. C. (1974), *The Human Biocomputer*, Sphere, London.

Locke, D. (1972), 'Can a Materialist See What Isn't There?' *Philosophical Quarterly*, 22, 55–6.

Locke, J. (1968), *An Essay Concerning Human Understanding* (1690), Patterson-Smith, Montclaire, N.J.

Lombroso, C. (1968), *Crime, Its Causes and Remedies* (1909), Patterson-Smith, Montclaire, N.J.

Lorenz, K. (1962a), 'Kant's Doctrine of the A-Priori in the Light of Contemporary Biology' (1941), in *General Systems Yearbook*, 7, 23–35.

Lorenz, K. (1962b), 'Gestalt Perception as Fundamental to Scientific Knowledge' (1959), in *General Systems Yearbook*, 7, 37–56.

Losciutio, L. O. and Hartley, E. L. (1963), 'Religious Affiliation and Open Mindedness in Binocular Resolution', *Perceptual and Motor Skills*, 17, 427–30.

Lowe, J. T. (1954), 'Murder and the Reasonable Man', *Criminal Law Review*, 289–98; 374–82; 453–65.

Lucas, J. R. (1970), *Freedom of the Will*, Clarendon, Oxford.

Lucretius, (1969), *On the Nature of Things* (trans. M. F. Smith), Sphere, London.

Luria, A. R. (1969), 'Human Brain and Psychological Processes' (1966), in Pribram (1969), vol. 1, 37–53.

Luria, A. R. (1973), *The Working Brain*, Penguin, Harmondsworth.

Lykken, D. T. (1961), 'A Study of Anxiety in the Sociopathic Personality', in T.

411

R. Sarbin (ed.), *Studies in Behavioural Pathology*, Holt Rinehart & Winston, New York, 149–54.

McCulloch, W. S. (1965), *Embodiments of Mind*, MIT Press, Cambridge, Mass.

McCulloch, W. S. and Pitts, W. (1943), 'A Logical Calculus of the Ideas Immanent in Nervous Activity', *Bulletin of Mathematical Biophysics*, 5, 115–33.

McCulloch, W. S. and Pitts, W. (1947), 'How We Know Universals: The Perception of Auditory and Visual Form', *Bulletin of Mathematical Biophysics*, 9, 127–47.

Macdonald, J. E. (1955), 'The Concept of Responsibility', *Journal of Mental Science*, 704–17.

McDougal, D. A. M. (1973), 'Descriptive and Revisionary Metaphysics', *Philosophy and Phenomenological Research*, XXIV (2), 209–23.

McDougal, W. (1928), *Body and Mind* (1911), 7th edn, Methuen, London.

McDougal, W. (1929), *Modern Materialism*, Methuen, London.

McGuigan, F. J. (ed.) (1966), *Thinking: Studies of Covert Language Processes*, Appleton Century Crofts, New York.

Mach, E. (1959), *The Analysis of Sensations* (1897) (Trans C. M. Williams, and S. Waterlow), Dover, New York.

McIlwain, H. (1972), *Biochemistry and the Central Nervous System*, London, Churchill.

Macintyre, A. (1959), 'Hume on Is and Ought', *Philosophical Review*, LXVIII, 451–68.

MacKay, D. M. (1956), 'Towards an Information Flow Model of Human Behaviour', *British Journal of Psychology*, 47, 30–43.

MacKay, D. M. (1957), 'Brain and Will', *The Listener*, 9 May; in Vesey (1964), 392–402.

MacKay, D. M. (1960), 'The Logical Indeterminacy of Free Choice', *Mind*, LXIX, 31–40.

MacKay, D. M. (1966), 'Cerebral Organization and Conscious Control of Action'; in Eccles (1966), 422–44.

MacKay, D. M. (1967), *Freedom of Action in a Mechanistic Universe*, Cambridge University Press.

MacKay, D. M. (1969a) 'A Mind's Eye View of the Brain' (1965); in Pribram (1969), vol. 4, 478–93.

MacKay, D. M. (1969b), *Information, Mechanism and Meaning*, MIT Press, London.

MacKay, D. M. (1970), communication; cited Gazzaniga (1970), p. 144. Mackie, J. L. (1973), *Truth Probability and Paradox*, Oxford University Press, London.

Mackie, J. L. (1974), *The Cement of the Universe*, Oxford University Press, London.

MacNiven, A. (1944), 'Psychosis and Criminal Responsibility', in L. Radzinowicz and J. W. C. Turner (eds), *Mental Abnormality and Crime*, Macmillan, London; in Morris (1966), 396–412.

McWhirter, N. and McWhirter, R. (eds) (1970), *Guinness Book of Records* 9th edn, Bantam, New York.

Madden, E. H. (1969), 'A Third View of Causality', *Review of Metaphysics*, XXIII, 67–84.

Madden, E. H. and Harré, R. (1973), 'In Defense of Natural Agents', *Philosophical Quarterly*, 23–91, 117–32.

Maine, H. J. S. (1887), *Ancient Law* (1861) 11th edn, John Murray, London.

Mair, L. P. (1934), *An African People in the Twentieth Century*, Routledge, London.

Malcolm, N. (1964), 'Scientific Materialism and Identity Theory', *Dialogue*, III (2), 115–25; in Borst (1970), 171–80.

Malcolm, N. (1965), 'Rejoinder to Mr. Sosa', *Dialogue*, III (4), 424–5; in Borst (1970), 183–4.

Mannheim, K. (1952), *On Interpretations of Weltanschauung* (1923), Oxford University Press, New York.

Margenau, H. and Van Fraasen, B. (1968), 'Causality', in R. Kiblansky (ed.), *Contemporary Philosophy: Philosophy of Science*, La Nouva Italia Editrice, Florence, 319–28.

Margolis, J. (1971), 'Difficulties for Mind–Body Identity Theories', in M. K. Munitz (ed.), *Identity and Individuation*, New York University Press, 213–31.

Marhenke, P. (1952), 'The Criterion of Significance', in L. Linksy (ed.), *Semantics and the Philosophy of Language*, University of Illinois Press, Urbana, Ill., 139–59.

Mark, U. H. and Ervin, F. R. (1970), *Violence and the Brain*, Harper & Row, London.

Marks, R. W. (1967), 'Mind, Nature and Cybernetics', in R. Marks (ed.), *Great Ideas in Modern Science*, Bantam, London, 228–63.

Marsack, C. C. (1959), 'Provocation and Trials of Murder', *Current Legal Problems*, 697–704.

Marx, K. (1913), *A Contribution to the Critique of Political Economy* (1859), Kerr, Chicago.

Matson, W. I. (1956), 'On the Irrelevance of Free Will to Moral Responsibility and the Vacuity of the Latter', *Mind*, LXV, 489–97.

Matson, W. I. (1966), 'Why Isn't the Mind–Body Problem Ancient?', in P. K. Feyerabend and G. Maxwell (eds), *Mind Matter and Method*, Minnesota University Press, Minneapolis, 92–102.

Matson, W. I. (1972), 'How Things Are What They Are', *The Monist*, 56, no. 2, 234–49.

Maxwell, G. (1962), 'The Ontological Status of Theoretical Entities', in *Minnesota Studies in Philosophy of Science*, III, Minnesota University Press, Minneapolis, 3–37.

Mead, G. H. (1934), *Mind Self and Society*, Chicago University Press.

Medawar, P. (1969), Review: *The Act of Creation*, by Arthur Koestler, *New Statesman* (19 June 1964); in *The Art of the Soluble*, Penguin, Harmondsworth, 95–108.

Medawar, P. (1969), *Induction and Intuition in Scientific Thought*, Methuen, London.

Mei, Tsu-Lin (1961), 'Subject and Predicate, a Grammatical Preliminary', *Philosophical Review*, LXX, 153–75.

Melden, A. I. (1961), *Free Action*, Routledge & Kegan Paul, London.

Melzack, R. and Thompson, W. (1956), 'Effects of Early Experience on Social Behaviour', *Canadian Journal of Psychology*, 10, 82–90.

Menninger, K. (1968), *The Crime of Punishment*, Viking, New York.

Meyerson, E. (1964), *Identity and Reality* (1930), Allen & Unwin, London.

Michotte, A. (1963), *The Perception of Causality* (trans. E. R. Miles), Methuen, London.

Miles, E. R. (1963), 'Michotte's Experiments and the Views of Hume', in Michotte (1963), 410–15.

Mill, J. S. (1884), *A System of Logic* (1843), Longman, London.

Miller, G. A. (1969), *The Psychology of Communication*, Penguin, Baltimore.

Miller, G. A., Gallanter, E. and Pribram, K. R. (1960), *Plans and the Structure of Behavior*, Holt, New York.

Miller, J. G. (1955), 'Towards a General Theory for the Behavioral Sciences', *The American Psychologist*, 10, 513–31.

Miller, J. G. (1965), 'Living Systems', *Behavioural Science*, 10, 193–237, 337–79; 380–411.

Miller, J. G. (1971), 'Living Systems', *Currents in Modern Biology*, 4, 55–256.

Miller, S. L. (1953), 'A Production of Amino Acids under Possible Primitive Earth Conditions', *Science*, 117 (3046), 528–9.

Milligan, D. E. (1974), 'Reasons as Explanations', *Mind*, LXXIII, 180–93.

Mogal, J. E. (1949), 'Causality Determinism and Probability', *Philosophy*, 24, 310–17.

Monod, J. (1974), *Chance and Necessity* (1970), Fontana, London.

Monro, H. (1973), 'Nonsense Nonsense', *Analysis*, 33, April, 167.

Montagu, A. (1969), 'Chromosomes and Crime' in *Readings in Psychology Today*, C. R. M. Del Mar, 370–6.

Moore, G. E. (1968), *Principia Ethica* (1903), Cambridge University Press.

Moore, G. E. (1962), *Some Main Problems of Philosophy* (1911), Collier, New York.

Moore, G. E. (1966), *Ethics* (1912), Clarendon, Oxford.

Morris, H. (ed.) (1966), *Freedom and Responsibility*, Stanford University Press.

Morris, T. (1976), *Deviance and Control*, Hutchinson, London.

Morton, J. D. (1962), *The Function of Criminal Law*, Butterworths, Toronto.

Moruzzi, G., Fessard, A. and Jasper, H. (eds) (1963), *Brain Mechanisms: Progress in Brain Research*, vol. 1, Elsevier, London.

Mottram, V. H. (1960), *The Physical Basis of Personality*, Penguin, Harmondsworth.

Mountcastle, V. B. (1966), 'The Neural Replication of Sensory Events in the Somatic System', in Eccles (1966), 85–109.

Mucciolo, L. F. (1974), 'The Identity Theory and Criteria for the Mental', *Philosophy and Phenomenological Research*, XXXV, 167–80.

Munitz, M. (1970), 'The Relativity of Determinism' (1958); in Hook (1970a), 76–82.

Munitz, M. (ed.) (1971), *Identity and Individuation*, New York University Press.

Nagel, E. (1960), 'Determinism in History', *Philosophy and Phenomenological Research*, XX, 3, 291–317; in Dworkin (1970), 49–81.

Nagel, E. (1961), *The Structure of Science*, Routledge & Kegan Paul, London.

Nagel, E. and Newman, J. (1959), *Gödel's Proof*, Routledge & Kegan Paul, London.

Nagel, T. (1965), 'Physicalism', *Philosophical Review*, LXXIV, 339–56; in Borst (1970), 214–30.

Nathan, P. (1969), *The Nervous System*, Penguin, Harmondsworth.

von Neumann, J. (1955), *Mathematical Foundations of Quantum Physics*, Princeton University Press.

von Neumann, J. (1957), *The Computer and the Brain*, Yale University Press, New Haven, Conn.

von Neumann, J., Goldstein, H. H. and Burks, R. A. W. (1962), 'Preliminary Discussion of the Logical Design of an Electronic Computing Instrument', US Army Ordinance Report, 28 June 1946; in *Datamation*, Thompson, Los Angeles, September–October 1962.

Newnham, R. (1971), *About Chinese*, Penguin, Harmondsworth.

Northrop, F. S. C. (1948), 'The Neurological and Behaviouristic Psychological Basis of the Ordering of Society by Means of Ideas', *Science*, 107, 23 April, 411–17.

Northrop, F. S. C. (1970), 'Causation, Determinism and the Good' (1958); in Hook (1970a), 201–11.

Nowell-Smith, P. (1956), *Ethics*, Penguin, Harmondsworth.

Nowell-Smith, P. (1960), 'Ifs and Cans', *Theoria*, XXVI, 85–101.

Ockham, W. (1964), *Philosophical Writings* (ed. P. Boehner), Bobbs-Merrill, New York.

Ofstad, H. (1961), *The Freedom of Decision*, Allen & Unwin, London.

Ofstad, H. (1967a), 'Libertarianism and the Belief in Transempirical Entities: L. J. Russell on Causation and Agency', in *Philosophical Essays in Honour of Gunnar Aspelin*, Lund, Stockholm.

Ofstad, H. (1967b), 'Recent Work on the Free Will Problem', *American Philosophical Quarterly*, 4:3, 179–207.

Ogden, F. and Richards, I. A. (1960), *The Meaning of Meaning*, (1923), Routledge & Kegan Paul, London.

Okakura-Kakuzo, K. (1919), *The Book of Tea*, T. N. Foulis, Edinburgh.

Olds, J. (1956), 'Pleasure Centres in the Brain', *Scientific American*, October, 105–16.

Olds, J. (1960), 'Differentiation of Reward Systems in the Brain by Self-stimulation Techniques', in R. R. Ramey and D. S. O'Docherty, (eds) *Electrical Studies in the Unanesthetised Brain*, Harper & Row, New York, 17–51.

Olds, J. (1967), 'Emotional Centres in the Brain', *Science Journal*, 3, 87; in *The Human Brain* (1972), Paladin, London, 103–18.

Onians, R. B. (1951), *The Origins of European Thought*, Cambridge University Press.

O'Shaughnessy, B. (1963), 'Observation and the Will', *Journal of Philosophy*, LX, no. 14, 367–92.

Pask, G. (1968), *An Approach to Cybernetics*, Hutchinson, London.

Patton, G. W. (1973), *A Textbook of Jurisprudence*, 4th edn, Clarendon, Oxford.

Pavlov, I. P. (1966a), 'The First Sure Steps Along the Path of a New Investigation' (1904 Nobel Prize-winning address); in M. Kaplan (ed.), *The Essential Works of Pavlov*, Bantam, New York, 42–57.

Pavlov, I. P. (1966b), 'Scientific Study of the So-Called Psychical Processes in Higher Mammals' (1906 Huxley Memorial Lecture); in M. Kaplan (ed.), *The Essential Works of Pavlov*, Bantam, New York, 75–91.

Peetz, D. W. (1968), 'Falsification in Science', *Proceedings of the Aristotelian Society*, LXIX, 17–31.

Peirce, C. S. (1933–5), *Collected Papers* (ed. C. Hartshorn and P. Weiss), Harvard University Press, Cambridge, Mass.: vol. 1 1933; vol. 5 1934; vol. 6 1935.

Peirce, C. S. (1970), 'The Doctrine of Necessity Examined' (1892); in Dworkin (1970), 33–48.

Penfield, W. (1950), 'The Cerebral Cortex and the Mind of Man', in Laslett (1950), 56–64.

Penfield, W. (1954a), 'Studies in the Cerebral Cortex of Man', in Delafresnay (1954), 284–309.

Penfield, W. (1954b) Discussion, in Delafresnay (1954), 492.

Penfield, W. (1966), Discussion, in Eccles (1966), 254.

Penfield, W. (1967), 'The Permanent Record of the Stream of Consciousness', in T. K. Landauer (ed.), *Readings in Physiological Psychology*, McGraw-Hill, London, 351–76.

Penfield, W. and Roberts, L. (1959), *Speech and Brain Mechanisms*, Princeton University Press.

Pepper, S. C. (1942), *World Hypotheses*, University of California Press, Berkeley.

Pepper, S. C. (1958), *Sources of Value*, University of California Press, Berkeley.

Pepper, S. C. (1966), *Concept and Quality*, Open Court, La Salle, Illinois.

Pepper, S. C. (1969), 'A Neural-Identity Theory of Mind' (1960), in Hook (1969), 45–61.

Pepper, S. C. (1970a), 'Survival Value', in E. Laszlo and J. B. Wilbur (eds), *Human Values and Natural Science*, Gordon & Breach, New York, 107–14.

Pepper, S. C. (1970b), 'Autobiography of an Aesthetics', *Journal of Aesthetics and Art Criticism*, Spring, 275–86.

Pepper, S. C. (1972), 'Systems Philosophy as a World Hypothesis', *Philosophy and Phenomenological Research*, XXXIII, 548–53.

Peters, R. S. (1958), *The Concept of Motivation*, Routledge & Kegan Paul, London.

Peters, R. S. (1966), *Ethics and Education*, Allen & Unwin, London.

Peters, R. S. (1973), *Authority Responsibility and Education*, 3rd edn, Allen & Unwin, London.

Phipson, S. L. (1970), *Phipson on Evidence*, 11th edn (ed. J. H. Buzzard, R. D. Amlot and S. Mitchell), Sweet & Maxwell, London.

Piaget, J. (1930), *The Child's Conception of Causality* (trans. M. Gabain), Kegan Paul, London.

Piaget, J. (1955), *The Child's Construction of Reality* (trans. M. Cook), Routledge & Kegan Paul, London.

Pierce, J. R. (1961), *Symbols, Signals and Noise*, Harper, New York.

Pirenne, M. H. (1967), *Vision and the Eye*, Chapman & Hall, London.

Place, U. T. (1956), 'Is Consciousness a Brain Process?', *British Journal of Psychology*, 47, 44–50; in Borst (1970), 42–51.

Place, U. T. (1960), 'Materialism as a Scientific Hypothesis', *Philosophical Review*, LXIX, 101–4; in Borst (1970), 83–6.

Planck, M. (1934), 'Causality in Nature', in J. G. Crowther (ed.), *Science Today*, Eyre & Spottiswood, London, 345–68.

Planck, M. (1936), *The Philosophy of Physics*, Allen & Unwin, London.

Planck, M. (1950), *Scientific Autobiography and Other Papers*, trans. F. Gaynor, Williams & Norgate, London.

Plato, (1954), *Phaedo* (trans. H. Tredennick), Penguin, Harmondsworth.

Plato, (1971), *Laws* (trans. T. Saunders), Penguin, Harmondsworth.

Platt, J. R. (1962), 'How a Random Array of Cells Can Learn to Tell Whether a Straight Line is Straight', in H. von Foerster and G. W. Zopf (eds), *Principles of Self-Organising Systems*, Pergamon, New York, 315–21.

Platt, J. R. (1968), 'The Two Faces of Perception', in Rothblatt (1968), 63–116.

Pledge, M. T. (1959), *Science Since 1500* (1939), Harper, New York.

Poincaré, H. (1952), 'Mathematical Creation', from *The Foundations of Science* (1913) (trans. B. Halstead, 1946), in B. Ghiselin (ed.), *The Creative Process*, University of California Press, Berkeley, 33–42.

Poincaré, H. (1929), *Science and Method*, T. Nelson, London.

Polanyi, M. (1958), *Personal Knowledge*, Routledge & Kegan Paul, London.

Polten, E. P. (1973), *Critique of Psycho-Physical Identity Theory*, Mouton, The Hague.

Popkin, R. (1953), 'Joseph Glanville: Precursor of Hume', *Journal of the History of Ideas*, 14, 292–303.

Popper, K. (1950), 'Indeterminism in Quantum Physics and in Classical Physics', *British Journal for the Philosophy of Science*, 1, 117–33; 173–95.

Popper, K. (1959), *The Logic of Scientific Discovery*, Hutchinson, London.

Popper, K. (1971), *Objective Knowledge*, Oxford University Press, London.

Popper, K and Eccles, J. C. (1977), *The Self and Its Brain*, Springer, London.

Postman, L., Bruner, J. S. and McGuinness, E. (1948), 'Personal Values as Selective Factors in Perception', *Journal of Abnormal Psychology*, 43, 142–54.

Powell, R. (1957), 'The Unreasonableness of the Reasonable Man', *Current Legal Problems*, 10, 104–26.

Powers, W. T., Clark, R. K. and McFarland, R. I. (1960), 'A General Feedback Theory of Human Behaviour', *Perception and Motor Skills*, II, 71–88.

Pribram, K. H. (1969a), 'The New Neurology: Memory, Novelty, Thought and Choice' (1963), in Pribram (1969c), vol. 3, 54–64.

Pribram, K. H. (1969b), 'Proposal for a Structural Pragmatism: Some Neurophysiological Considerations of Problems in Philosophy' (1965), in Pribram, (1969c), vol. 1, 11–19.

Pribram, K. H. (ed.) (1969c), *Brain and Behaviour*, 4 vols, Penguin, Harmondsworth.

Price, G. R. (1955), 'Science and the Supernatural', *Science*, 122, 359–67.

417

Prince, M. (1906), *The Dissociation of Personality (Sally Beauchamp)*, Longmans, London.

Prior, A. N. (1949), *Logic and the Basis of Ethics*, Oxford University Press, London.

Putnam, H. (1967), 'The Mental Life of Some Machines', in H. N Castaneda (ed.), *Intentionality, Minds and Perception*, Wayne State University Press, Detroit, 177–213.

Putnam, H. (1969), 'Minds and Machines' (1960), in Hook (1969), 138–64.

Putnam, H. and Oppenheim, P. (1958), 'Unity of Science as a Working Hypothesis', in *Minnesota Studies in Philosophy of Science*, vol. II, Minnesota University Press, London, 3–36.

Quine, W. V. O. (1963), 'Two Dogmas of Empiricism', in *From a Logical Point of View*, Harper & Row, London, 20–46.

Quine, W. V. O. (1968), *Ways of Paradox*, Random House, New York.

Raab, F. (1955), 'Free Will and the Ambiguity of "Could" ', *Philosophical Review*, LXIV, 60–77.

Radcliffe, Lord, (1961), *The Law and its Compass*, Faber, London.

Radin, P. (1957), *Primitive Man as Philosopher*, Dover, New York.

Radzinowicz, L. (1966), *Ideology and Crime*, Columbia University Press, New York.

Radzinowicz, L. and Wolfgang, M. E. (eds) (1971), *Crime and Justice*, vol 2, *The Criminal in the Arms of the Law*, Basic Books, London.

Ramsay, I. T. (1964), *Religion and Science*, SPCK, London.

Ramsey, P. (1957), Editor's Introduction, *Freedom of the Will* (Jonathan Edwards), Yale University Press, London, 1–128.

Randi, J. (1975), *The Magic of Uri Geller*, Ballantine, New York.

Rapoport, A. (1962), 'An Essay on Mind', in *General Systems Yearbook*, vol 7, 85–101.

Rapoport, A. (1972), 'The Search for Simplicity', in Laszlo (1972a), 15–30.

Rapoport, A. (1974), *Conflict in the Man-Made Environment*, Penguin, London.

Rawls, J. (1955), 'Two Concepts of Rules', *Philosophical Review*, LXIV, 3–32.

Reddaway, P. and Bloch, S. (1977), *Russia's Political Hospitals*, Gollancz, London.

Rees, J. R. (1949), 'Mental Health and the Offender', seventh Clarke Hall Lecture, London.

Rees, J. R. (1951), 'The Health of the Mind (1929), 3rd edn Faber & Faber, London.

Reichenbach, H. (1951), 'On Observing and Perceiving', *Philosophical Studies*, II, 92–3; cited Chisholm (1957), 180–1.

Reichenbach, H. (1966), *Elements of Symbolic Logic*, Macmillan, London.

Reid, R. W. (1971), *Tongues of Conscience*, Panther, London.

Reid, T. (1819), *Essays on the Powers of the Human Mind*, 3 vols, Bell & Bradfute, Edinburgh.

Reid, T. (1895), *Essays on the Active Power of Man*, in W. Hamilton (ed.), *Philosophical Works*, vol. 2, 8th edn, Thin, Edinburgh.

Reid, T. (1970), 'Some Arguments for Free Will' (1815), in Dworkin (1970), 85–97.

Bibliography

Reitlinger, G. (1971), *The Final Solution* (1953), Sphere, London.
de Reuck, A. V. S. and Porter, R. (1968), *The Mentally Abnormal Offender*, Little Brown, Boston.
Riesen, A. H. (1947), 'The Development of Visual Perception in Man and Chimpanzee', *Science*, 106, 107–8.
Riesen, A. H. (1958), 'Plasticity of Behaviour: Psychological Aspects', in H. F. Harlow and C. N. Woosley (eds), *The Biological and Biochemical Basis of Behaviour*, University of Wisconsin Press, Madison, 425–50.
Rioch, D. M. (1954), 'Psychopathological and Neuropathological Aspects of Consciousness', in Delafresnay (1954), 470–8.
Rorty, R. (1965), 'Mind–Brain Identity, Privacy and Categories', *Review of Metaphysics*, 19, 24–54; in Borst (1970), 187–213.
Rorty, R. (1970), 'In Defense of Eliminative Materialism', *Review of Metaphysics*, 24, 112–21.
Rose, S. (1976), *The Conscious Brain*, Penguin, Harmondsworth.
Rosenbleuth, A. (1970), *Body and Mind: A Philosophy of Science*, MIT Press, Cambridge, Mass.
Rosenbleuth, A. and Weiner, N. (1950), 'Purposive and Non-purposive Behaviour', *Philosophy of Science*, 17, 318–26.
Rosenbleuth, A., Weiner, N. and Bigelow, J. (1943), 'Behaviour Purpose and Teleology', *Philosophy of Science*, 10, 18–24.
Rothblatt, B., (ed.) (1968), *Changing Perspectives on Man*, Chicago University Press.
Ruddick, W. (1971), 'Physical Equations and Identity', in Munitz (1971), 233–50.
Russell, B. (1948), *Human Knowledge, its Scope and Limits*, Allen & Unwin, London.
Russell, B. (1953a), 'On the Notion of Cause' (1912), in *Mysticism and Logic*, Penguin, Harmondsworth, 171–96.
Russell, B. (1953b), 'The Ultimate Constituents of Matter' (1915), in *Mysticism and Logic*, Penguin, Harmondsworth, 120–38.
Russell, B. (1957), *Why I Am Not a Christian*, Allen & Unwin, London.
Russell, B. (1962), *The Problems of Philosophy* (1912), Oxford University Press, New York.
Russell, B. (1960), 'On the Notion of Cause with Application to the Free Will Problem', in *Our Knowledge of the External World* (1929), Mentor, New York, ch. 8.
Russell, B. (1967), *An Inquiry into Meaning and Truth* (1940), Penguin, Harmondsworth.
Russell, L. J. (1935–6), 'Ought Implies Can', *Proceedings of the Aristotelian Society*, XXXVI, 151–86.
Russell, W. R. (1959), *Brain Mechanisms and Memory*, Clarendon, Oxford.
Ryle, G. (1938), 'Categories', *Proceedings of the Aristotelian Society*, XXXVIII, 189–206; in Flew (1965), 281–98.
Ryle, G. (1966), *The Concept of Mind*, (1949), Penguin, Harmondsworth.
Ryle, G. (1950), 'Comments on the Physical Basis of Mind', in Laslett (1950), 75–9.

Ryle, G. (1954), *Dilemmas*, Cambridge University Press.

Samuels, A. (1971), 'Excuseable Loss of Self Control in Homicide', *Modern Law Review*, 34, 163–7.

Sapir, E. (1933), 'Language', in *Encyclopaedia of the Social Sciences*, Macmillan, New York, 155–68.

Sartre, J. P. (1948), *Existentialism and Humanism*, Methuen, London.

Sartre, J. P. (1963), *Saint Genet: Actor and Martyr* (trans. B. Frechtman), W. H. Allen, London.

Saunders, T. (1973), 'Plato on Killing in Anger', *Philosophical Quarterly*, 23, 350–6.

de Saussure, F. (1959), *Course in General Linguistics* (1914), (ed. C. Bolly and A. Sechehaye, trans. W. Baskin), Philosophical Library, New York.

Sawyer, W. A. (1970), *The Search for Pattern*, Penguin, Harmondsworth.

Sayre, K. M. (1968), 'Philosophy and Cybernetics', in Crosson and Sayre (1968), 3–33.

Sayre, K. M. (1976), *Cybernetics and the Philosophy of Mind*, Routledge & Kegan Paul, London.

Schaeffer, F. A. (1973), *Back to Freedom and Dignity*, Hodder & Stoughton, London.

Scheff, T. J. (ed.) (1967), *Mental Illness and Social Process*, Harper & Row, London.

Scheffler, I. (1967), *Science and Subjectivity*, Bobbs-Merrill, Indianapolis.

Schilpp, P. A. (ed.) (1942), *The Philosophy of G. E. Moore*, Open Court, Evanston, Ill.

Schlick, M. (1939), *Problems of Ethics*, Dover, New York.

Schlick, M. (1949), 'Causality in Everyday Life and In Recent Science', in H. Feigl and W. Sellars (eds), *Readings in Philosophical Analysis*, Appleton Century Crofts, New York, 515–33.

Schon, D. (1967), *Invention and the Evolution of Ideas* (1963), Tavistock, London.

Schon, D. (1973), *Beyond the Stable State* (1971), Penguin, Harmondsworth.

Schopenhauer, A. (1960), *Essay on the Freedom of the Will* (1841), (trans. K. Kolenda), Bobbs-Merrill, New York.

Schrödinger, E. (1967), *What is Life?* (1944), Cambridge University Press.

Schwitzgabel, R. K. (1969), 'A Behavioural Supervision System with Wrist Carried Transceiver', US Patent no. 3,478,344, 11 November 1969.

Schwitzgabel, R. K. and R. L. (eds) (1973), *Psychotechnology: Electronic Control of Mind and Behaviour*, Holt, Reinhart & Winston, London.

Schwitzgabel, R. K. (1974), *Changing Human Behaviour*, McGraw Hill, London.

Sciama, D. (1970), 'Observations' (1958), in Hook (1970a), 222–3.

Science Journal (1967), 'The Human Brain', 3, 5 May; also Paladin, London, 1972.

Science Journal (1968), 'Machines Like Men', 4, 10 October.

Scientific American (eds) (1957), *Automatic Control*, Bell, London.

Scott, P. D. (1970), 'Punishment or Treatment: Prison or Hospital?' *British Medical Journal*, 2, 167–9.

420

Scriven, M. (1958), 'Definition, Explanation and Theories', in M. Scriven, H. Feigl and G. Maxwell (eds), *Minnesota Studies in Philosophy of Science*, vol. II, University of Minnesota Press, Minneapolis, 99–195.

Scriven, M. (1969), 'The Compleat Robot: A Prolegomenon to Androidology', in Hook (1969), 113–33.

Scruton, R. (1970–1), 'Intensional and Intentional Objects', *Proceedings of the Aristotelian Society*, LXXI, 187–207.

Searle, J. (1964), 'How to Derive Ought from Is', *Philosophical Review*, 73, 43–58.

Sechzer, J. A. 'Prolonged Learning in Split-Brain Cats', *Science*, 169, 889.

Seddon, G. (1972), 'Logical Possibility', *Mind*, LXXXI, no. 324, October, 481–94.

Sellars, W. (1956), 'Empiricism and the Philosophy of Mind', in H. Feigl and M. Scriven (eds), *Minnesota Studies in Philosophy of Science*, vol. 1, Minnesota University Press, Minneapolis, 253–329.

Sellars, W. (1958), 'Intentionality and the Mental'. Appendix: in H. Feigl and G. Maxwell (eds), *Minnesota Studies in Philosophy of Science*, vol. II, Minnesota University Press, Minneapolis, 507–39.

Sellars, W. (1963a), 'Philosophy and the Scientific Image of Man', in *Science Perception and Reality*, Routledge & Kegan Paul, London, 1–40.

Sellars, W. (1963b), 'The Language of Theories', in Sellars (1963a), 102–226.

Sellars, W. (1965), 'The Identity Approach to the Mind–Body Problem', *Review of Metaphysics*, 18, 430–51.

Sellars, W. (1968), *Science and Metaphysics*, Routledge & Kegan Paul, London.

Sellars, W. (1969), 'Metaphysics and the Concept of a Person', in K. Lambert (ed.), *The Logical Way of Doing Things*, Yale University Press, New Haven, Conn.

Sellars, W. (1971), 'Science, Sense, Impressions and Sensa', *Review of Metaphysics*, 25, 391–447.

von Senden, M. (1960), *Space and Sight* (trans. P. Heath), Methuen, London.

Sereny, G. (1974), *The Case of Mary Bell*, Arrow, London.

Shaffer, J. (1961), 'Could Mental Events be Brain Processes', *Journal of Philosophy*, VIII, 813–22.

Shannon, C. and Weaver, W. (1949), *The Mathematical Theory of Communication*, University of Illinois Press, Urbana.

Sheldon, W. H. (1970), *Varieties of Delinquent Youth*, (1949), Collier Macmillan, London.

Sher, G. (1973), 'Causal Explanations and the Vocabulary of Action', *Mind*, LXXXII, 22–30.

Sher, J. M. (ed.) (1962), *Towards a Definition of Mind*, Free Press, New York.

Sherrington, Sir C. S. (1955), *Man on his Nature* (1940), Penguin, Harmondsworth.

Shimony, A. (1947), 'An Ontological Examination of Causation', *Review of Metaphysics*, 1 (1), 52–68.

Shoemaker, S. (1963), *Self Knowledge and Self Identity*, Cornell University Press, Ithaca, New York.

Shotter, J. (1975), *Images of Man in Psychological Research*, Methuen, London.

421

Silverman, H. (1969), 'Determinism, Chance, Responsibility and the Psychologist's Role as an Expert Witness', *American Psychologist*, 22 (1), 5–9.

Silving, H. (1966), 'A Plea for a New Philosophy of Criminal Justice'. *Revista Juridica de la Universidad de Puerto Rico*, 35; cited Gerber and McAnany (1971), 129.

Skinner, B. F. (1953), *Science and Human Behaviour*, Macmillan, London.

Skinner, B. F. (1973), *Beyond Freedom and Dignity*, Penguin, Harmondsworth.

Slater, E. (1950), 'Consciousness', in Laslett (1950), 56–64.

Sluckin, W. (1954), *Minds and Machines*, Pelican, Harmondsworth.

Smart, J. J. C. (1951), 'Theory Construction', *Philosophy and Phenomenological Research*; in Flew (1965), 446–67.

Smart, J. J. C. (1959), 'Sensations and Brain Processes', *Philosophical Review*, LXVIII, 141–56; in Borst (1970), 52–66.

Smart, J. J. C. (1961a), 'Further Remarks on Sensations and Brain Processes', *Philosophical Review*, LXX, 406–7; in Borst (1970), 93–4.

Smart, J. J. C. (1961b), 'Free-will Praise and Blame', *Mind*, LXX, 291–306; in Dworkin (1970), 196–213.

Smart, J. J. C. (1962), 'Brain Processes and Incorrigibility', *Australasian Journal of Philosophy*, XL; in Borst (1970), 107–9.

Smart, J. J. C. (1963a), *Philosophy and Scientific Realism*, Routledge & Kegan Paul, London.

Smart, J. J. C. (1963b), 'Materialism', *Journal of Philosophy*, LX, 651–62; in Borst (1970), 159–70.

Smart, J. J. C. (1972), 'Further Thoughts on the Identity Theory', *The Monist*, 56, no. 2, April, 149–62.

Smith, J. C. and Hogan, B. (1973), *Criminal Law*, 3rd edn, Butterworth, London.

Smith, M. B., Bruner, J. S. and White, R. W. (1967), *Opinions and Personality* (1956), John Wiley, New York.

Smith, S. M., Brown, H. O., Tolman, J. E. P. and Goodman, L. S. (1947), 'The Lack of Cerebral Effects of U-Tubocurarene', *Anaesthesiology*, 8, 1–14.

Smith, S. M., Hongisberger, L. and Smith, C. A. (1973), 'E.E.G. and Personality Factors in Baby Batterers', *British Medical Journal*, 2, July, 20–2.

Smythies, J. R. (ed.) (1965), *Brain and Mind*, Routledge & Kegan Paul, London.

Sommerhoff, G. (1969), 'The Abstract Characteristics of Living Systems', in Emery (1969), 147–202.

Sommerhoff, G. (1974), *Logic of the Living Brain*, John Wiley, London.

Soper, G. A. (1939), 'The Curious Case of Typhoid Mary', *Bulletin of the New York Academy of Medicine*, 15, 638.

Sparkes, J. J. (1972), 'Pattern Recognition and Scientific Progress', *Mind*, LXXXI, no. 321, 29–41.

Spencer, H. (1937), *First Principles* (1862), Watts, London.

Sperry, W. R. (1966), 'Brain Bisection and Mechanisms of Consciousness', in Eccles (1966), 298–313.

Sperry, W. R. (1970), 'An Objective Approach to Subjective Experience', *Psychological Review*, 77, no. 6, 585–90.

Spinoza, B. (1951), *Ethics* (trans. R. H. L. Elwes), Dover, New York.

Sprague, E. (1969), 'The Mind–Brain Problem' (1960), in Hook (1969), 71–3.

Sprenger, J. and Kramer, H. (1971), *Malleus Maleficarum* (1490) (trans. M. Summers, 1928) Arrow, London.

Stark, L. (1968), *Neurological Control Mechanisms: Studies in Bioengineering*, Plenum, New York.

Stark, W. (1967), 'Sociology of Knowledge', in P. Edwards (ed.), *Encyclopaedia of Philosophy*, vol. 7, Collier Macmillan, London, 475–8.

Stebbing, L. S. (1958), *Philosophy and the Physicists* (1938), Dover, New York.

Stephen, Sir J. F. (1883), *A History of the Criminal Law of England*, 3 vols, Macmillan, London.

Stephenson, J. T. (1960), 'Sensations and Brain Processes', *Philosophical Review*, LXIX, 505–10; in Borst (1970), 87–92.

Stern, G. (1965), *Meaning and Change of Meaning* (1931), Indiana University Press, Bloomington.

Stern, L. (1967), *The Life and Opinions of Tristram Shandy, 1759–67*, Penguin, Harmondsworth.

Stout, G. F. (1935), 'Mechanical and Teleological Causation', *Proceedings of the Aristotelian Society*, Supplement, XIV, 46–65.

Strang, C. (1961), 'On the Perception of Heat', *Proceedings of the Aristotelian Society*, 61, 239–52.

Strawson, P. F. (1958), 'Persons', in H. Feigl, M. Scriven, G. Maxwell (eds), *Minnesota Studies in Philosophy of Science*, vol. II; in Chappell (1962), 127–46.

Strawson, P. F. (1959), *Individuals*, Methuen, London.

Strawson, P. F. (1962), 'Freedom and Resentment', *Proceedings of the British Academy*, 9 May, 187–221.

Stritch, S. J. (1956), 'Diffuse Degeneration of the Cerebral White Matter in Severe Dementia Following Head Injury', *Journal of Neurology, Neurosurgery and Psychiatry*, 19, 163–85.

Suits, B. (1973), 'The Elements of Sport', in R. G. Osterhout (ed.), *The Philosophy of Sport*, Thomas, Springfield, Ill., 48–64.

Suppes, P. (1970), *A Probablistic Theory of Causality*, North Holland, Amsterdam.

Swinbourne, R. G. (1970), 'Physical Determinism', in *Knowledge and Necessity*, R.I.P. Lectures, vol. III, Macmillan, London, 155–68.

Szasz, T. (1960), 'The Myth of Mental Illness', *American Psychologist*, 15 February, 113–18; in Scheff (1967), 242–54; Szasz (1974a), 12–24.

Szasz, T. (1961), *The Myth of Mental Illness*, Harper & Row, New York.

Szasz, T. (1963), *Law, Liberty and Psychiatry*, Macmillan, New York.

Szasz, T. (1971), *The Manufacture of Madness*, Routledge & Kegan Paul, London.

Szasz, T. (1974a), *Ideology and Insanity* (1970), Penguin, Harmondsworth.

Szasz, T. (1974b), Letter: *The Listener*, 24 July.

de Tarde, G. (1912), *Penal Philosophy*, Heinemann, London.

Taylor, C. (1964), *The Explanation of Behaviour*, Routledge & Kegan Paul, London.

Bibliography

Taylor, C. (1967), 'Mind–Body Identity a Side Issue?', *Philosophical Review*, LXXVI, 201–13; in Borst (1970), 231–41.

Taylor, C. (1971), 'Interpretation and the Sciences of Man', *Review of Metaphysics*, XXV, 3–51.

Taylor, C. (1972), 'Conditions for a Mechanistic Theory of Behaviour', in A. G. Karczmar and J. C. Eccles (eds), *Brain and Human Behaviour*, Springer Verlag, New York, 449–65.

Taylor, D. (1970), *Explanation and Meaning*, Cambridge University Press.

Taylor, J. G. (1971a), *The Shape of Minds to Come*, Michael Joseph, London.

Taylor, J. G. (1971b), 'The Shadow of the Mind', *New Scientist*, 51, no. 771, 30 September, 735–7.

Taylor, J. G. (1972a), 'The Physical Problem of Mind', (paper) read at meeting of the Philosophical Society, Newcastle upon Tyne Polytechnic, 27 November 1972.

Taylor, J. G. (1972b), 'Spontaneous Behaviour in Neural Networks', *Journal of Theoretical Biology*, 36, 513–28.

Taylor, R. (1950a), 'Comments on a Mechanistic Conception of Purposefulness', *Philosophy of Science*, 17, 310–17.

Taylor, R. (1950b), 'Purposeful and Non-purposeful Behaviour: A Rejoinder', *Philosophy of Science*, 17, 327–32.

Taylor, R. (1958), 'Determinism and the Theory of Agency' in Hook (1970a), 224–30.

Taylor, R. (1960), 'I Can', *Philosophical Review*, LXIX, 78–89.

Taylor, R. (1966), *Action and Purpose*, Prentice-Hall, Engelwood Cliffs, NJ.

Ter-Har, D. (1958), *Introduction to the Physics of Many-Body Systems*, Interscience, London.

Thalberg, I. (1976), 'How Does Agent Causality Work?', in M. Brand and D. Walton (eds), *Action Theory*, Reidel, Dortrecht, 213–18.

Thibaut, H. W. (1943), 'The Concept of Normality in Clinical Psychology', *Psychological Review*, 50, no. 1, May, 338–44.

Thigpen, C. H. and Cleckley, H. (1954), 'A Case of Multiple Personality', *Journal of Abnormal and Social Psychology*, 49 (supplement), 135–51.

Tinbergen, N. (1951), *The Study of Instinct*, Oxford University Press, London.

Tinbergen, N. (1957), 'On Anti-predator Responses in Certain Birds – A Reply', *Journal of Comparative and Physiological Psychology*, 50, 412–14.

Tolstoy, L. (1968), Epilogue: pt II, *War and Peace* (1869) (trans. Anne Dunnigan), New American Library, New York, 1412–55.

Toulmin, S. (1948), 'The Logical Status of Psycho-analysis', *Analysis*, 9, 23–9.

Toulmin, S. (1970), 'Reasons and Causes', in R. Borger and F. Cioffi (eds), *Explanation in the Behavioural Sciences*, Cambridge University Press, 1–26.

Toulmin, S. (1972), 'The Mentality of Man's Brain', in A. G. Karczmar and J. C. Eccles (eds), *Brain and Human Behaviour*, Springer Verlag, New York, 449–65.

Trigg, R. (1973), *Reason and Commitment*, Cambridge University Press.

Tuckett, I. L. L. (1932), *The Evidence for the Supernatural*, Watts, London.

Ullman, S. (1954), 'The Prism of Language', *The Listener*, LII, 22 July.

Ulrich, R., Stachnick, T. S. and Mabry, J. (eds) (1966), *Control of Human*

Behaviour, Scott Foresman, Glenview, Ill.

Ungar, G., Galvan, L. and Clark, R. H. (1968), 'Chemical Transfer of Learned Fear', *Nature*, 217, no. 5135, 30 March, 1259–61.

Urban, W. M. (1939), *Language and Reality*, Allen & Unwin, London.

Urmson, J. O. (1952), 'Motives and Causes', *Proceedings of the Aristotelian Society*, Supplement, XXVI, 179–94.

Urmson, J. O. (1968), 'Criteria of Intentionality – I', *Proceedings of the Aristotelian Society*, Supplement, XLII, 107–22.

Vartanian, A. (1960), *La Mettrie's L'Homme Machine*, Princeton University Press.

Venables, P. H. and Martin, I. (1967), *A Manual of Psycho-Physiological Methods*, John Wiley, New York.

Vesey, G. N. A. (ed.) (1964), *Body and Mind*, Allen & Unwin, London.

Vesey, G. N. A. (1966), *The Embodied Mind*, Allen & Unwin, London.

Vogt, E. Z. (1960), 'On the Concept of Structure and Process in CulturalAnthropology', *American Anthropologist*, 62 (1), 18–33.

Vygotsky, L. S. (1960), *Development of the Higher Mental Functions* (1960; Russian); cited Luria (1973), 246–7.

Waismann, F. (1952), 'Analytic–Synthetic V', *Analysis*, XIII, 1 October, 1–14.

Waismann, F. (1965), 'Language Strata', in Flew (1965), 226–47.

Walker, N. (1965), *Crime and Punishment in Britain*, Edinburgh University Press.

Walker, N. (1967), 'The Aims of Punishment', evidence before the *Royal Commission of Inquiry into the Penal System*, 1–13; in Radzinowicz and Wolgang (1971), 48–65.

Walker, N. (1970), *Crime and Punishment in Britain*, Edinburgh University Press.

Wallis, R. (1968), *Time: Fourth Dimension of the Mind* (trans. B. B. and D. B. Montgomery) Harcourt, Brace & World, New York.

Warnock, G. J. (1953), *Berkeley*, Penguin, Harmondsworth.

Warnock, G. J. (1965), 'Every Event has a Cause', in Flew (1965), 312–30.

Warr, P. B. (ed.) (1970), *Thought and Personality*, Penguin, Harmondsworth.

Watson, J. B. (1930), *Behaviourism*, 2nd ed, Chicago University Press.

Watts, A. W. (1962), *Zen Buddhism*, Penguin, Harmondsworth.

Weaver, W. (1949), 'Recent Contributions to the Mathematical Theory of Communication', in Shannon and Weaver (1949), 95–117.

Weiss, P. (ed.) (1971), *Hierarchically Organised Systems in Theory and Practice*, Haffner, New York.

Whewell, W. (1847), *The Philosophy of the Inductive Sciences*, vol. 1, J. W. Parker, London.

White, A. R. (1962), 'Explaining Human Behaviour', inaugural lecture, University of Hull.

White, A. R. (1972), 'Mind-Brain Analogies', *Canadian Journal of Philosophy*, 4, no. 4, June, 457–72.

Whiteley, C. H. (1968), *'Mental Causes'*, in the Human Agent, Royal Institute of Philosophy/Macmillan, London, 98–114.

Whiteley, C. H. (1973), *The Mind in Action*, Oxford University Press, London.

425

Whorf, B. L. (1956), *Language, Thought and Reality* (ed. J. B. Carroll), John Wiley, New York.

Whyte, L. L. (ed.) (1968), *Aspects of Form* (1951), 2nd edn, Lund Humphries, London.

Whyte, L. L., Wilson, A. G. and Wilson D. (eds) (1969), *Hierarchical Structures*, Elsevier, New York.

Wiener, N. (1961), *Cybernetics* (1948), 2nd edn, MIT Press, Cambridge, Mass.

Wiener, N. (1969), *The Human Use of Human Beings*, Sphere, London.

Wiener, N. and Schade, J. P. (1965), *Cybernetics of the Nervous System, Progress in Brain Research*, 17, Elsevier, London.

Wilkerson, T. E. (1974), *Minds, Brains and People*, Oxford University Press, London.

Williams, B. (1973), *Morality*, Penguin, Harmondsworth.

Williams, G. R. (1953a), *Criminal Law: The General Part*, Stevens, London.

Williams, G. R. (1953b) 'The Defense of Necessity', *Current Legal Problems*, 6, 216–35.

Wilson, H. van R. (1970), 'On Causation' (1958), in Hook (1970a), 237–43.

Wilson, J. (1972), *Philosophy and Educational Research*, National Foundation for Educational Research, Slough.

Wisdom, J. (1963), *Problems of Mind and Matter* (1934), Cambridge University Press.

Wisdom, J. O. (1972), 'Scientific Theory: Empirical Content Embedded Ontology and Weltanschauung', *Philosophy and Phenomenological Research*, XXIII (1) 62–77.

Wittgenstein, L. (1971), *Tractatus Logico Philosophicus* (1922) (trans. D. F. Pears and B. F. McGuiness), Routledge & Kegan Paul, London.

Wittgenstein, L. (1972), *Philosophical Investigations*, (1953) (trans. G. E. M. Anscombe), Blackwell, London.

Wittgenstein, L. (1958), *Blue and Brown Books*, Blackwell, London.

Woodfield, A. (1976), *Teleology*, Cambridge University Press.

Wooldridge, D. E. (1963), *The Machinery of the Brain*, McGraw Hill, New York.

Wootton, B. (1959), *Social Science and Social Pathology*, Allen & Unwin, London.

Wootton, B. (1963), *Crime and the Criminal Law*, Stevens, London.

von Wright, G. H. (1970), *Explanation and Understanding*, Routledge & Kegan Paul, London.

Wright, L. (1976), *Teleological Explanations*, University of California Press, London.

Wynn Reeves, J. (1958), *Body and Mind in Western Thought*, Penguin, Harmondsworth.

Yolton, J. (1973), 'Action: Metaphysics and Modality', *American Philosophical Quarterly*, 10, no. 2, 71–85.

Young, D. Z. (1952), *Doubt and Certainty in Science*, Oxford University Press, London.

Young, R. (1973a), 'Two-domainism and Human Freedom', *Metaphilosophy*, 4:1, 23–46.

Young, R. (1973b), 'A Sound Self-referential Argument?', *Review of Metaphysics*, XXVII, 1, 112–19.
Young, R. (1974), 'Compatabilism and Freedom', *Mind*, LXXXIII, 329, 19–42.
Zemach, E. (1973), 'The Nature of Consciousness', *Dialectica*, 27, 43–65.
Zerbst, E. (1969), 'Use of Electric Pressoreceptor Analogue in Baropacing of Hypertension in High Blood Pressure', *Proceedings of the Third International Congress of Biophysics*, Cambridge, Mass.

SUPPLEMENTARY BIBLIOGRAPHIES

(i) *Official Records and Reports*

Homicide Act (1957)
Ministry of Education Committee on Maladjusted Children (Chairman J. E. A. Underwood), *Report* (1955) (II.270197.3).
Parliamentary Debates: House of Commons *Hansard*, vol. 560 (1956) (Mr A. Greenwood, 15 November, col. 1163–4; R. Manningham Buller, 15 November, col. 1253).
Parliamentary Debates: House of Lords *Hansard* (1965) (Coggan, Archbishop of York, 26 October, col. 536).
Royal Commission on Care and Control of the Feeble Minded (Chairman Lord Radnor), *Report* (1908), Cd no. 4202.
Royal Commission on Capital Punishment (Chairman Lord Aitken), *Report* (1922) Cmd no. 2005.
Royal Commission on Capital Punishment (Chairman Sir E. Gowers), *Report* (1953) Cmd no. 8932.
Royal Commission on Mentally Abnormal Offenders (Chairman, Lord Butler), *Report* (1975) Cmnd no. 6244.

Cases

Bedder v. D.P.P. (1954), 38 Cr. App. Rep. 133 H.L.
Bratty v. A-G. for Northern Ireland (1963), A.C. 386
Byrne (1960), 2 Q.B.R. 396
Charlson (1955), 1 All. E.R. 8 59
Creighton (1909), 14 Can. Crim. Cas. 349
D.P.P. v. Smith (1961), A.C. 290
Dennison v. State (1966), 49 Misc. 2d. 533, 267 N.Y. State 2d. 290.
Duffy (1949), 1 All. E.R. 932 n. C.C.A.
Ford (1969), 1 W. Law Repts. 1703.
Ives (1969), 3 All. E.R. 470
Kemp (1957), 1 Q.B. 399
Kemp (1964), 2 Q.B. 341
Kopsch (1925), 19 Cr. App. Rep. 50, C.A.A.
Lesbini (1914), 3 K.B. 1116
Lupien (1969), 1 Can. Crim. Cas. (Times) 32
McCarthy (1954), 2 Q.B. 105

Raney (1942), Cr. App. Rep. 14, C.C.A.
Simpson (1957), Crim. L.R. 1957, 815
Rivette (1950), Crim. App. Rep. 87, C.C.A.
Welsh (1869), 11 Cox C.C. 336
William Gray, The, 29 Fed. Cas. 1300, no. 17,694
Windle (1952), 2 Q.B. 826

INDEX

Action: basic, 210; causal account of, 218 f, 251; explanation of, 200 f; incoherence of orthodox view, 206 f; language of, 215, 217, 238; as omission, 212, 217, 236, 310; spurious coherence of orthodox account, 216 f
Action at a distance, 47
Adverbial elimination, 71
Adverbial sensing, 92 f, 115; and criteria for identity, 124
Aitken Commission, 321
Aleksander, I., 87, 92
Anaxagoras, 61, 200
Analogies of identity, 80, 81, 107, 112 f
Analogy principle (crimes), 349
Analytic-synthetic distinction, 35, 111, 182 f
Animate-inanimate dichotomy, 50, 51
Animism, 28
Anscombe, G. E. M., 98
Aristotle, 70, 163, 267, 280, 281, 321
Armstrong, D. M., 69 f, 80, 102
Artificial intelligence, 86 f
Aurelius, M., 238
Austin, J. L., 21, 99, 254
Automata, 225 f

Bacon, F., 18
Becquerel, A. H., 117

Behaviour: of finite automata, 225 f; goal directed, 28, 32, 58, 229 f; rational determinants of, 28, 34, 131 f, 140 f, 162, 200 f, 204 f, 206 f, 211, 213, 216, 222 f, 234, 235 f, 332
Behaviourism, 54, 288; and the meaning of mental terms, 69
Bertalanffy, L. von, 8, 83, 233
Biddel, J., 312
Bismark, O. F. von, 95
Boring, E. G., 127
Brain: bisection (commissurotomy), 57, 96 f; empirical data, 56 f, 320; experimental models, 59; and external aids to organisation, 153; research techniques, 56; theoretical models, 32, 57, 85 f, 89 f, 225 f
Breggin, P., 331
Brett, P., 309
British Psychological Society, 9, 295, 300
Bunge, M., 9, 189
Butler Commission, 295, 300
Butler, J., 49
Butler, S., 305, 331

Campbell, C. A., 250
Cartesian dualism, 27, 45
Causal: conditions, 184 f; connection,

429

434